TRADE AND AID

THE JOHNS HOPKINS UNIVERSITY STUDIES
IN HISTORICAL AND POLITICAL SCIENCE

One Hundredth Series (1982)

1. Trade and Aid: Eisenhower's Foreign Economic Policy, 1953–1961
     By Burton I. Kaufman

Burton I. Kaufman is professor of history at Kansas State University. He is the author of *Efficiency and Expansion: Foreign Trade Organization in the Wilson Administration* and *The Oil Cartel Crisis: A Documentary Study of Antitrust Activity in the Cold War Era.*

TRADE AND AID

Eisenhower's Foreign Economic Policy 1953–1961

Burton I. Kaufman

THE JOHNS HOPKINS UNIVERSITY PRESS
Baltimore and London

Copyright © 1982 by The Johns Hopkins University Press
All rights reserved
Printed in the United States of America

The Johns Hopkins University Press, Baltimore, Maryland 21218
The Johns Hopkins Press Ltd., London

Library of Congress Cataloging in Publication Data
Kaufman, Burton Ira.
  Trade and aid.

  Bibliography: pp. 253–67.
  Includes index.
  1. United States—Foreign economic relations.
2. Eisenhower, Dwight D. (Dwight David), 1890–1969.
I. Title.
HF1455.K282   337.73   81–15594
ISBN 0–8018–2623–3   AACR2

For Diane, Heather, and Scott

Contents

Acknowledgments

There are a number of people whose help in this project I wish to acknowledge. Most important are the archivists at the Eisenhower Library, particularly David Haight, whose courtesy and help over a number of years are greatly appreciated. In addition, I want to thank my colleagues at Kansas State University, particularly Joe Hawes, Jake Kipp, Al Hamscher, Don Mrozek, and Don Nieman, for reading the manuscript and making invaluable comments both on style and content. Department seminar and coffee-room dialogues on sundry related and unrelated matters were refreshing and incisive. May the tradition continue. I want also to express my deep appreciation to my friends Bob Griffith of the University of Massachusetts and Bob Zieger of Wayne State University for reading the manuscript in its entirety and for forcing me to make a number of substantive changes. Finally, I wish to thank the National Endowment for the Humanities for the grant that made the writing of this manuscript possible, and the Bureau of Grants and Research at Kansas State University for its financial support over the years.

This book is dedicated to my wife, Diane, and to my two children, Heather and Scott, for tolerating my absences—and my presence—during the preparation of this book.

List of Abbreviations

AAA	Agricultural Adjustment Act
AFB	American Farm Bureau
AID	Act for International Development
BOB	Bureau of the Budget
CCC	Commodity Credit Corporation
CEA	Council of Economic Advisers
CED	Committee on Economic Development
CFEP	Council on Foreign Economic Policy
CIA	Central Intelligence Agency
DLF	Development Loan Fund
DPA	Defense Production Act
ECA	Economic Cooperation Administration
ECOSOC	United Nations' Economic and Social Council
EEC	European Economic Community
EFTA	European Free Trade Area
EPU	European Payments Union
Eximbank	Export-Import Bank
FAO	Foreign Agricultural Organization
FOA	Foreign Operations Administration
FTC	Federal Trade Commission
GATT	General Agreement on Tariffs and Trade
IADB	Inter-American Development Bank
IBRD	International Bank for Reconstruction and Development
ICA	International Cooperation Administration
IDA	International Development Association (Authority)
IDAB	International Development Advisory Board
IFC	International Finance Corporation
IMF	International Monetary Fund
ITO	International Trade Organization
MEEC	Middle East Emergency Committee
NAC	National Advisory Council for International Monetary and Financial Affairs

NATO	North Atlantic Treaty Organization
NFTC	National Foreign Trade Council
NSC	National Security Council
ODM	Office of Defense Mobilization
OECD	Organisation for Economic Co-operation and Development
OEEC	Organization for European Economic Cooperation
OTC	Organization for Trade Cooperation
P.L. 480	Public Law 480
SEATO	Southeast Asia Treaty Organization
SUNFED	Special United Nations Fund for Economic Development
TCA	Technical Cooperation Administration
UNCTAD	United Nations Conference on Trade and Development

TRADE AND AID

1. Introduction

SINCE THE COLLAPSE of the American dollar in 1971 and the oil embargo of 1973–74, international attention has focused increasingly on world economic and monetary problems—on the instability of the international financial structure, the world energy crisis, and the plight of the Third World, particularly the impoverished nations of sub-Saharan Africa and parts of South Asia. An apocalyptic literature has appeared predicting dire consequences unless a solution to the world's economic problems is found soon. A special commission headed by former Chancellor Willy Brandt of West Germany warns of mass starvation and international chaos in the absence of a major redistribution of wealth from the Northern Hemisphere to the Southern. A study prepared for the Carter administration projects the exhaustion of much of the world's natural resources and a bleak standard of living even for the Western industrial powers by the year 2000.[1]

The Quest for a New Economic Order

In the United States the present pessimism about the international economy is in sharp contrast to American optimism immediately after World War II. Foreign economic policy after the war was addressed primarily to the task of building an economic order that would avoid the mistakes that had contributed to the onslaught of war. Most policy makers advocated a departure from the passive role the United States had followed after World War I to one of aid in the development of a prosperous world that would assure peace. Such a world would be predicated on the principles of multilateral cooperation, trade liberalization, nondiscrimination, and exchange and monetary stability.[2] Toward these ends, the United States, in concert with its allies and other industrial nations, built an economic structure that included the International Bank for Reconstruction and Development (the IBRD or World Bank), the International Monetary Fund (IMF), and the General Agreement on Tariffs and Trade (GATT).

Yet by the early 1950s much of this initial postwar optimism had been shattered. The goals of peace and prosperity proved elusive as the United States

1

concentrated its resources on the reconstruction of Europe and the containment of communism. The building blocks of the new economic order were found wanting. In the first place, the GATT stood as a weak substitute for a more powerful International Trade Organization (ITO), which the United States had intended as an administrative structure for promoting and regulating trade on a multilateral basis. The Department of State hailed the ITO (whose charter it had largely written) as the greatest step ever taken in behalf of free trade.[3] But because of growing disenchantment over the prospects for peace and prosperity and a reluctance to turn over the administration of the nation's tariff laws to an international body, Congress refused to ratify the ITO charter.

Instead, the GATT, which was to have served as an interim trade agreement pending the approval of the ITO, was forced to assume many of ITO's organizational responsibilities. Lacking even a firm legal basis, since it was never approved by Congress, the GATT suffered also from an inadequate secretariat and budget and, in general, did not have the machinery to undertake many of the more ambitious projects intended for the ITO, such as sponsoring across-the-board tariff cuts and dealing with regional trade groups. Rather, it concerned itself mainly with formulating rules for the conduct of trade and with dismantling tariffs on an item-by-item basis.

Significantly, the GATT, worked out in Geneva in 1947, largely ignored issues that concerned the predominantly agricultural and commodity-exporting countries of the Third World, such as the negotiation of commodity agreements and the removal of restrictions on agricultural imports. Indeed, the cuts made under GATT auspices were almost exclusively on industrial goods, and article 11 of the GATT specifically allowed quantitative restrictions on agricultural products protected by price-support programs.[4]

Much the same organizational weakness and neglect of Third World problems was also evident in the operations of the World Bank and IMF. Established at Bretton Woods, New Hampshire, in 1944 as twin institutions of a new international monetary system, the Bank and Fund were never intended to be particularly useful to underdeveloped nations. The IBRD was to serve as a reconstruction rather than a development bank, and the Fund's primary purpose was to stabilize exchange rates, mainly by setting par values and supporting them with short-term balance-of-payments loans. In neither case was much thought given to the needs and requirements of Third World nations.[5]

Nor in subsequent years did the Bank and Fund prove especially effective as instruments of a new economic order. The problems of reconstruction and the degree of international financial instability after the war were far greater than the architects of the Bretton Woods system had anticipated. Unable to meet Europe's reconstruction needs with its own limited resources, and seeking to win the confidence of the American investor in order to float its bonds on the American capital market, the Bank followed conservative lending policies. It made a few reconstruction loans, but after the inauguration of the Marshall Plan in 1948, it purposely subordinated its lending activities to the new aid program. Similarly, the IMF, faced with a staggering imbalance of trade and a severe dollar shortage, husbanded its resources and acquiesced in the growing number of exchange restrictions that took place as nations sought to protect their exchange values from the pressures of the free market.[6]

Besides these institutional weaknesses there were other problems with the world system the United States sought to establish after the war. In the first place, the liberalization of world trade was opposed by forces against opening more American markets to foreign imports. As the *Congressional Digest* reported in 1951, the reciprocal trade program, first begun in Franklin Roosevelt's administration, underwent its most exhaustive reexamination in seventeen years. In 1943, Congress had added to the program an "escape clause" permitting the United States to withdraw from a reciprocal trade agreement if it was found that "unforeseen developments" had hurt domestic industry. Five years later, the Republicans, who had always voted against the trade agreements program, inserted a "peril-point clause" requiring that the Tariff Commission establish a limit or "peril point" at which a rate cut would be considered a threat to domestic industry. The president could not negotiate a trade agreement lower than the peril point without explaining his action to Congress in writing. In 1949 the newly Democratic controlled Congress threw the peril-point amendment out and extended the reciprocal trade program for another two years. The program was renewed for another two years in 1951, but this time the opposition was strong enough to reinstate the escape clause and peril-point provisions.[7]

In addition to this mounting opposition against liberalized trade, the early 1950s saw the reemergence of the dollar gap in world trade whereby a shortage in the world's dollar holdings made payment for essential imports from the United States difficult. By 1950 the Marshall Plan had relieved much of Europe's dollar shortage and moved the world closer to the full exchange convertibility of world currencies anticipated at Bretton Woods. But a rearmament program in Europe checked further progress in reducing the dollar gap and led some economic experts to prophesy that the shortage would become a permanent fixture of the world economy.[8]

Finally, American foreign aid, intended as a temporary expedient to assist in the economic reconstruction of a war-ravished world, took on a more permanent, military orientation, especially after the outbreak of the Korean War in 1950. With the Mutual Security Act of 1951 Congress abolished the Economic Cooperation Administration of 1948 (ECA), which had administered the nation's foreign-aid program, and established the Mutual Security Agency to perform ECA functions until they expired on June 30, 1952. Acting on the presumption that the international situation required a more heavily military foreign-aid orientation, Congress made ECA provisions available only for mutual defense purposes; this was interpreted as defense support for countries having military assistance programs. In 1952 the House and Senate extended ECA functions until June 30, 1954.[9]

Thus, by 1952, as America geared up for another presidential election, the postwar expectation of a world characterized by peace and prosperity and based on liberal economic principles seemed far from realization. To be sure, some modest progress toward these goals had been made. At the very least the Bretton Woods system and the GATT provided an institutional framework for further progress toward the establishment of a new world economic order. Moreover, these institutions were not entirely ineffectual. In 1947, 1949, and again in 1950–51 the contracting members of the GATT successfully negotiated tariff reductions on a broad range of items. As the Department of State reported following the 1949 negotiations at Annecy, France, the ten nations that acceded to the GATT at Annecy, along with the twenty-three original contracting parties, carried on nearly eighty percent of the world's trade, and the tariff concessions made earlier at Geneva and at Annecy accounted for more than two thirds of the import trade of the participating countries and more than one half of the world's import trade. Furthermore, the agreement provided for a permanent council to operate between meetings and for an international forum to discuss and work out the rules of international trade.[10]

Other institutions made similar progress. By 1952 the IBRD had established itself as a reliable and prudent lending institution whose bonds, guaranteed by borrowing governments and its paid-in capital, were a sound investment. This would be extremely important when the Bank began to float its securities in order to make development loans to Third World countries. Similarly, the IMF, although largely moribund, developed a staff of trained technical experts, many of whom later became leading financial officials in underdeveloped countries.[11] The Export-Import Bank (Eximbank), established by the U.S. in 1934 to make short-term loans to American exporters, continued to aid international economic cooperation and development. Although intended as an arm of the government to expand foreign markets for American goods, Eximbank assumed a number of other functions, including making a limited number of long-term loans for development purposes. Over the years its lending authorization was increased from $200 million to $4.5 billion.[12] Finally, of course, the Marshall Plan was instrumental in the reconstruction of Europe, which by 1952 was on the way to economic recovery and perhaps to instituting currency convertibility. Because of this success, there was widespread talk in the United States of eliminating economic aid entirely.

The Gray and Rockefeller Reports

Certain assumptions about the prospects of peace and prosperity underlined U.S. foreign policy as it developed prior to 1952, particularly its foreign-aid programs. Though unsupported at the time, they became particularly important in subsequent years. Government leaders and policy makers took it for granted, for example, that American assistance would nurture democratic forms of government abroad, thereby preventing the expansion of world communism. Two reports—one by Gordon Gray and his deputy Edward S. Mason, and the other by Nelson Rockefeller, head of the International Development Advisory Board—assimilated this view. Both reports clearly delineated the issues involved in the question of public versus private investment in Third World nations—a question that would be at the heart of the debate over foreign economic policy during the Eisenhower administration. In a 1950 report to the president on foreign economic policy, special presidential assistant Gray and deputy Mason thus outlined the need for the administration's foreign economic program to preserve "stable democratic" societies that would provide for their own defense and raise their standards of living. The common interests of both the United States and these countries was "to meet the immediate necessities presented by Soviet aggressive designs."[13] In almost the same language, Rockefeller's 1951 report argued that America's defense to a large extent depended upon strengthening the economies of the underdeveloped regions. For example, an increased flow of strategic raw materials into America would result from economic development abroad. But a rise in standards of living abroad was equally important in trying to forestall Soviet aggression and subversion. Furthermore, the report warned that economic policy toward the underdeveloped areas should be regarded as only part of broader policy objectives; policy "must be both global, embracing every part of the world, and total, with political, psychological, economic, and military considerations integrated into the whole."[14]

Significantly, the Gray and Rockefeller reports differed greatly on how to achieve these economic (and political) objectives. After analyzing the similar problems of Western Europe and Japan, the Gray Report for the first time focused attention on the special problems of the world's underdeveloped areas. It acknowledged that private investment was the "most desirable" means of providing capital to underdeveloped countries. Yet it emphasized that American overseas investment since World War II had not been very extensive, had been heavily concentrated in industrialized countries, and had left untouched the basic problems of the underdeveloped areas. The report thus recommended a "heavy reliance" on a program of public loans in order to bring about economic growth abroad. In general, it was thought that these loans should flow through the World Bank and Eximbank, but where development projects were urgently needed to further U.S. objectives and could not be financed by loans, a program of foreign grants should apply. More specifically, the Gray Report called for a threefold increase in grants for technical assistance and advised that the government's foreign economic program be reorganized into a single administrative agency. It left the size of the loan program undefined, recommending only that it should be smaller than that used to stimulate European recovery.[15]

The Rockefeller Report supported the Gray Report's contention that some public-works projects did not meet the ordinary standards of bankability and thus required public loans. But it proposed that the United States turn over the responsibility for making these loans to a new, multilateral International Development Authority that would operate under management contracts with the World Bank. In contrast to the Gray Report, it paid attention to the role of private investment in development abroad, maintaining that an investment of $2 billion, spread over four or five years, could increase the flow of raw materials critical to American and European industry by $1 billion per year. It also noted that this rise in production could "best be carried out under private auspices" (i.e., by American and foreign firms). Yet on the subject of how private investment could be shifted away from Latin America and Canada, where it had long been concentrated, to the strategically more important areas of Asia and the Middle East, the report said little. However, it did make five recommendations designed to raise the amount of American and indigenous private investment in the underdeveloped countries: (1) to help American firms, overseas income should be exempted from U.S. income taxes; (2) a fund of $100 million should be set up to insure American investors against the risk of currency inconvertibility (the report expressed the hope that such a device would revive the now-insignificant market for foreign securities in the United States); (3) more bilateral tax and commercial treaties should be negotiated; (4) an assistant administrator in a new Overseas Economic Administration should be charged with the sole task of promoting the role of private enterprise in foreign economic development; and (5) to meet the needs of indigenous private enterprise, a new International Finance Corporation should be created. Affiliated with the World Bank, the IFC would use its capital ($400 million) to make equity investments with private investors as well as loans not secured by country guarantees as required in World Bank loans.[16]

Despite the emphasis placed on the underdeveloped regions by the Gray and Rockefeller reports, when Eisenhower became president in 1953 economic planning continued to consist mainly of making the existing Western economy work and paid little attention to the needs of underdeveloped or developing nations. For example, there were no long-term development programs to assist Third World countries. Foreign aid was largely for military purposes or served a military function. Communist threats to particular countries cropped up in most of the discussions on aid to the Near East and South Asia. And while some government officials stressed the importance of strengthening the Western Hemisphere, not much thought was given to a new Latin American aid program. Except for the technical assistance provided through the Point Four Program, the United States gave areas like Latin America, the Near East, Asia, and Africa relatively little economic help.[17]

Thesis and Themes of This Book

During Eisenhower's administration (1953–61), however, America's attitude and policies toward the Third World changed fundamentally. Under

Eisenhower's leadership, the United States became more attentive to the problems of Third World countries and assumed greater responsibility for meeting their economic needs. Indeed, the economic development of the Third World became one of the administration's highest priorities. The principal purpose of this book is to trace this shift in U.S. foreign economic policy. In addition, the book has three themes: (1) the transition from a foreign economic program based on the concept of "trade not aid" when Eisenhower took office, to one predicated on the principle of "trade *and* aid" (the emphasis clearly being on the flow of public capital abroad) by the time he left the White House in 1961; (2) the leadership qualities of the United States' thirty-fourth president; and (3) the questionable success of President Eisenhower's economic programs.

The first of these themes relates directly to the assumptions behind the administration's change of policy toward the Third World. When Eisenhower took office, he was committed, like most other U.S. government leaders, to a foreign economic program of eliminating foreign aid and relying instead on liberalized world trade and the encouragement of private foreign investment to assure world economic growth and prosperity. Except for the provision of military assistance to stop the spread of communism, Eisenhower's program focused on Europe rather than the Third World. But the pressing problems of the Third World—its economic development, the rising tide of nationalism, the inadequacy of trade and private investment as a solution to its economic problems, and Soviet economic efforts among underdeveloped countries— caused Eisenhower to modify his thinking. Beginning in 1954, he increasingly emphasized economic aid to Third World countries as the basis of his foreign economic policy.

The second theme of the book is an evaluation of Eisenhower's leadership qualities. The common image of Eisenhower as a bumbling, stumbling, fumbling, and generally ineffectual president who preferred a game of golf to the duties of his office has in recent years undergone major revision. The latest scholarship suggests an "activist president" who preferred to operate quietly behind the scenes, but who was fully informed and completely in charge of his own administration. Proponents of this view reject especially the depiction of Eisenhower as an essentially inarticulate and incoherent leader who was controlled and manipulated by his cabinet, particularly the tough-minded, deeply intellectual, and self-confident Secretary of State John Foster Dulles. Instead, recent writers stress Eisenhower's intellectual capacity, his political astuteness, and his command of policy, particularly in the area of foreign policy.[18]

This study agrees with much of the reassessment of the Eisenhower presidency. More specifically, it concurs in the view that Eisenhower was a political leader of considerable talents with a keen, and often penetrating, intellect. Eisenhower was in control of his own foreign policy; certainly in economic matters Secretary of State Dulles followed the president's lead. Eisenhower cultivated close relations with congressional leaders of both political parties and made effective use of grass-roots organizations to gain public support for controversial legislation such as the administration's 1958 foreign-aid and trade programs. He demonstrated the quality and character of his intellect as well as cogency and forcefulness in his arguments in defense of administration policy. Finally, Eisenhower remained flexible as president and had the capacity to alter his views in response to changing world conditions.

Yet this study also suggests that the case in support of Eisenhower has been overstated and that a more balanced assessment is required. In the first place, there were frequent inconsistencies in the administration's foreign economic program, especially in its foreign trade policy. For example, throughout his administration, Eisenhower maintained a liberal trade policy based on an open and free exchange of goods in world markets and a reduction or elimination of tariffs and other barriers to international commerce. Yet this policy seems inconsistent with his realization that, by themselves, trade and private investment would not assure adequate economic growth and that some form of public assistance was needed for Third World countries. This conflict between free trade and government intervention is evident in the government's protectionist foreign agricultural policy, in the concessions the president made to protectionist forces in Congress, and in the White House's position on foreign antitrust matters. The administration on several occasions waived the antitrust laws to permit normally illegal business combinations to engage in international trade. It also refused to agree to a United Nations covenant that would have made many such restrictive trade practices illegal.

In part, the administration's inconsistent trade policy can be attributed to Eisenhower's reluctance to confront the growing protectionist sentiment in Congress. And this reluctance points to another limitation of the Eisenhower presidency. Although revisionist writers have correctly observed that Eisenhower was an active president who often worked inconspicuously but decisively to gain approval of administration programs, they have neglected his own views on the limits of presidential power, views that sometimes impaired his effectiveness in dealing with Congress. As one of the president's former speechwriters, Emmet John Hughes, noted in 1963, Eisenhower believed he had to have the support of Congress on major national issues. He also remained persuaded that to gain congressional backing for his programs, he had to employ conciliation and education rather than threats and intimidation. Finally, he was convinced that it was necessary to work through the existing party organization in the Senate and House; in any case, he believed that the separation of branches of government required that the White House not trespass too far onto the congressional domain.[19] Certainly most of these concerns influenced the administration's efforts between 1953 and 1955 to win a three-year extension of reciprocal trade legislation and additional presidential authority to cut tariff rates. Eisenhower was able to get his legislation approved by Congress, but not without making major concessions to protectionist forces.

As contemporaries often charged, Eisenhower could also be politically lazy. Revisionist writers have strongly disputed this charge, but there seems to be no other way to explain the hastiness with which he often retreated on trade and tariff matters. For example, in 1955 the White House failed to win congressional approval for U.S. membership in the Organization for Trade Cooperation (OTC). Although this organization was meant to be a substitute for the ill-fated ITO and the president at first threatened to use the full weight of his office to get it approved by Congress, he gave up the struggle with hardly a whimper for apparently no other reason than that he was unwilling to make the necessary fight.

Another weakness of the Eisenhower presidency was Eisenhower's strident anticommunism. For the most part, revisionist writers have skirted this issue. Either they emphasize the president's antimilitarism by pointing out that, unlike his successors, he avoided military engagements abroad; or they stress his moderation as compared to Secretary of State Dulles, to whom they attribute responsibility for doctrines of massive retaliation and brinkmanship.[20] In addition to being inconsistent in holding the president responsible for the conduct of foreign policy, on the one hand, and blaming Dulles for the administration's hard-line anticommunist policies, on the other, these revisionists ignore Eisenhower's own virulent anticommunism.[21] Indeed, this book argues that the thawing of Cold War attitudes that was supposed to have come about following the 1955 Geneva Summit Conference between Eisenhower and Premier Nikita Khrushchev of the Soviet Union was largely illusory. Moreover, it contends that Eisenhower's determination to contain the spread of communism in Third World countries circumscribed much of the dialogue on foreign economic policy and distorted the purposes and objectives of much of the foreign-aid program.

The president's concern with the Communist menace led to a dangerously expanded and ill-defined concept of national security that was also apparent in the formulation of foreign economic policy. The administration justified the entire program of economic assistance to Third World nations, whether on a short- or long-term basis, as serving the national security because it was expected to contain the spread of communism. Thus the concept of national security, which prior to Eisenhower's administration had been defined largely in conventional political and military terms, took on an increasingly economic dimension as well. For example, it was for the purpose of national security that several of the nation's major oil companies were allowed to contravene the nation's antitrust laws in the 1950s; the oil companies were given antitrust immunity in order to assure a continued supply of oil to Western Europe and to serve other related political objectives in the Middle East.

Broadening the concept of national security and considering national security from an economic as well as a political and military standpoint were certainly legitimate administration policies. But the practice of approaching world economic problems and changing world conditions primarily with a view to containing the Communist menace or of using private concerns to carry out major national policy was fraught with serious foreign and domestic implications that the White House largely ignored.

The third theme of the book is an assessment of the overall effectiveness of the administration's trade and aid programs. The inconsistencies and contradictions in the trade program not only limited the contribution of U.S. trade to world economic development and international cooperation (objectives Eisenhower always hoped trade would promote), but they also raised doubts about the United States' role as a world economic leader. As for Eisenhower's foreign-aid program, the administration made claims for economic assistance much along the lines of the Gray and Rockefeller reports, claims that were later shown to be unfounded. In formulating his aid program, Eisenhower was heavily influenced by the ideas of a number of economic experts, particularly Walt Rostow and Max Millikan of M.I.T.'s Center for International Studies. These pioneers in the field of economic growth assumed that foreign aid would lead to economic development and that economic growth would prevent the spread of communism by promoting political growth along democratic and capitalist lines. As other economists have more recently suggested, the Millikan-Rostow model failed to emphasize the effect of social programs and internal government reforms on economic and political development abroad. The relation between aid and development along economic and political lines was tenuous at best, and policy experts ignored the possibility of incompatible goals in foreign assistance. As a result, the administration failed to bring about significant economic and political changes or to realize its other objectives abroad. By almost every measure, Third World countries were worse off economically when Eisenhower left office than they had been when he took office eight years earlier. Furthermore, there is little indication that Third World governments were politically more stable or democratic or even that they were more friendly to the United States.

The rest of this book deals at length with the three themes just presented. Chapter 2 traces the broad outlines of Eisenhower's foreign economic policy of "trade not aid" as it had developed by the summer of 1954. Chapter 3 describes the shift in policy toward greater public assistance for Third World nations as a result of the rising tide of nationalism in Asia and other Third World regions and the French debacle in Indochina. Chapter 4 details the role of Soviet economic efforts abroad in furthering America's own interest in promoting Third World economic development. Chapter 5 outlines some of the inconsistencies in the Eisenhower administration's trade program, particularly in regard to foreign antitrust policy and the foreign operations of the oil industry. By 1956, the White House's entire foreign economic program was strewn with contradictions, and because serious questions were being raised in Washington about the purposes of foreign aid, Congress ordered the most intensive examination of the foreign-aid program since the founding of the

Marshall Plan. Chapter 6 describes this foreign-aid inquiry and its results, including a decision by the administration to establish a Development Loan Fund for Third World countries. Despite the foreign-aid inquiry, by 1957 the White House had clearly moved away from its earlier policy of "trade not aid" to one of "trade and aid." Chapters 7 and 8 describe the major battles in Congress over these trade-and-aid programs during the second session of the Eighty-fifth Congress (1957–58). Chapter 9 traces the White House's effort to broaden the framework of foreign aid by relying more heavily on multilateral and regional efforts at promoting economic growth abroad. One reason for this shift was America's growing balance-of-payments problem. Chapter 10 outlines the administration's efforts to deal with this problem, which by 1959 had become its most pressing economic concern. Chapter 11 describes Eisenhower's final struggle with Congress over foreign aid, and Chapter 12 presents the conclusions of this study—that while the Eisenhower administration was the first to respond to the economic needs of Third World nations through the use of public resources, it failed to achieve the type of economic (and political) world order the president sought.

2. Trade Not Aid
1953–1954

WHEN DWIGHT D. EISENHOWER assumed the presidency in January 1953, he was a leading advocate of international cooperation who believed that the United States had the major responsibility for bringing about a peaceful and prosperous world. As the military commander who had directed the liberation and postwar defense of Europe, he was also a staunch proponent of a strong Atlantic alliance. On the domestic front, he was a fiscal conservative who was deeply troubled by the growth in the size of the federal government. His international orientation and commitment to the principles of peace and prosperity, his belief in the Atlantic alliance, and his fiscal conservatism would determine his position on matters of foreign economic policy. As a fiscal conservative, he firmly believed that growth in Europe and the rest of the world could be achieved with a minimum of public assistance. Instead of foreign aid, such as that provided by the Mutual Security Program, he advocated a policy of expanded foreign trade and private investment abroad, which he believed would assure a flourishing world economy. Indeed, when he took office, he made the concept of "trade not aid" the basis of his world economic program.

The Trade-Not-Aid Program

Eisenhower's views on international cooperation and collective security had developed from his experience as a war hero, former president of Columbia University, and the supreme commander of the North Atlantic Treaty Organization (NATO). In his best-selling *Crusade in Europe* (1948), he had pointed out that more than military preparedness was needed to combat the Soviet menace that threatened the Western world. It was first necessary to eliminate the social and economic evils that bred international discord. "Wherever popular discontent is found or group oppression or mass poverty or the hunger of children," he wrote, "there Communism may stage an offensive that arms cannot counter. Discontent can be fanned into revolution, and revolution into social chaos." At the same time, he stressed the need to subordinate national sovereignty to a broader concept of world participation. "The democracies must learn that the world is now too small for the rigid concepts of national sovereignty that developed in a time when nations were self-sufficient for their own well-being. None of them today can stand alone."[1]

At Columbia and then as commander of the NATO forces in Europe, Eisenhower elaborated on these themes and became a leading proponent of European economic and political unity. He also addressed the problem of the United States' dependency on the rest of the world for raw materials and other imports essential to its economy. Differing most strongly with the traditional wing of the Republican party on these international issues, he decided to oppose its candidate, Senator Robert Taft of Ohio, for the party's 1952 presidential nomination. Just before leaving for Europe to resume his NATO duties in 1951, he met with Taft to discuss the European alliance. Dismayed by Taft's talk of limiting the number of American divisions in NATO and by the isolationist mood he sensed was growing in Congress, Eisenhower concluded that Taft's advocacy of such a "fortress America" foreign policy indicated an ignorance of world affairs. He later claimed that had Taft indicated any commitment to collective security, he would have withdrawn his own name from consideration.[2]

Once he decided to run for president, the former general sought to shape the Republican platform to reflect his internationalist views. His candidacy was promoted by the internationalist wing of the Republican party, a group of lawyers, businessmen, and politicians who, like Eisenhower, believed that Taft was an isolationist and who therefore wanted a candidate who was committed to the principle of collective security with Western Europe.[3] Eisenhower, a hardened Cold Warrior, was convinced that Moscow was engaged in a political and military conspiracy aimed at world-wide Communist domination. Nevertheless, he rejected some of the more strident proposals for unilateral military containment being made in Republican circles. Only through collective security and political and economic cooperation among the Western powers and other friendly and nonaligned countries, he believed, could the West keep the Kremlin from achieving its goal of world conquest. Writing to John Foster Dulles, the principal Republican spokesman on foreign policy, who by this time had become his foreign-policy adviser and was already known for his belligerent stand with respect to the Soviet Union, Eisenhower outlined what he expected of the Republican platform. He made it clear that he wanted the platform to be one "of positive, forward looking action and leadership in the promotion of collective security." The minimal requirements of any foreign policy had to be the United States' right to trade freely—and without Soviet interference—with those areas from which it obtained its raw materials. Collective security was essential if the nations of the free world were to develop their own "economic and political and spiritual strength." Exclusive reliance upon the threat of retaliation was not a sufficient response to the Soviet challenge.[4]

Following a bitter struggle, Eisenhower secured the nomination and won acceptance of a platform endorsing the principle of collective security and repudiating isolationism. He attempted to mollify the right wing of the party by adopting his own militant stand toward the Soviet Union, but his commitment to the principles of international cooperation and collective security remained strong throughout the campaign, and after his election in November 1952, they were incorporated into his inaugural address and his first State of the Union message to Congress.[5] In both speeches he emphasized the need to increase the channels of international trade and to eliminate most forms of foreign assistance. As president, Eisenhower was not entirely opposed to foreign aid. One reason he had run for the presidency was the issue of providing economic and military assistance abroad, and soon after taking office, he told his close friend General Alfred Gruenther that to cut foreign aid in any large way would be "very penny-wise and pound foolish." At a conference with congressional leaders a few months later, he stressed the importance of the mutual security program to U.S. security and indicated that a reduction in foreign assistance would probably cause an increase in the defense budget.[6]

As his remarks to both Gruenther and the congressional leaders indicated, however, Eisenhower was thinking largely in terms of providing assistance for military rather than economic purposes. The president was well aware that the delineation between these categories of aid could not always be made; for example, that defense support was a form of economic assistance to countries with whom the United States had military agreements and who could not or would not otherwise meet their military obligations. Nevertheless, the president remained persuaded that by promoting the expansion of world trade and the development of American business abroad, most forms of U.S. economic assistance could be eliminated.[7]

Eisenhower's desire to cut foreign aid also reflected his fiscal conservatism. As the Republican nominee, Eisenhower had made the growth of big government and big spending one of the major issues of the campaign. During the campaign he had written: "Next to war perhaps the greatest threat to our security arises from statism and its attendant bureaucracy. To overthrow this tendency is one of the principal aims of my candidacy."[8] As president, one of his first decisions was to trim funds from the $80 billion fiscal 1954 budget proposed by the Truman administration. His appointment of such fiscal conservatives as the Detroit banker Joseph Dodge to head the Bureau of the Budget, and the president of M. A. Hanna and Co., George M. Humphrey, as treasury secretary thus indicated the direction his administration was to take.[9] Eisenhower firmly believed that the basis of a strong nation was a sound economy and that the basis of a sound economy was a balanced budget. By sharply cutting back on foreign aid and substituting an expanded program of foreign trade and private investment abroad, the president hoped to ensure a sound domestic economy and world economic growth at the same time.[10]

Essential to increased trade and economic prosperity, however, was the elimination of all obstacles to the mutual and free exchange of goods, capital, and services. For the United States this meant liberalization of tariff regulations as well as the removal of such procedural obstacles to profitable commerce as cumbersome customs regulations. But America's friends and trading partners also had obligations. First, they would have to liberalize their own tariff and trade regulations. Second, they needed to work toward the establishment of currency convertibility so that international trade and investment could flow more readily; this would require stringent financial and other economic controls on their part. Finally, the underdeveloped countries in particular would have to promote a climate conducive to private investment as well as foster the development of domestic private enterprise.[11]

In his inaugural address, Eisenhower spelled out the problems facing the United States and the opportunities awaiting the country in the realm of international exchange and economic interdependency.[12] Two weeks later, in his State of the Union message, he outlined his foreign economic program. Most important of his proposals was the request that Congress revise the nation's customs regulations and extend the Reciprocal Trade Agreements Act, on which American tariffs had been based since 1934. He also called for government encouragement of private American investment abroad; for making offshore or foreign purchases of defense articles that were not in competition with American products; and for increasing America's purchase of raw materials abroad. Speaking to America's allies, he expressed the hope that they would take the initiative in broadening their markets, freeing the currents of international trade, and stabilizing their currencies. Action along these lines, the president concluded, would "invite help" from the United States.[13]

Most controversial were Eisenhower's tariff proposals. Since 1934 U.S. tariffs had been based on the Reciprocal Trade Agreements Act of that year, which itself was an amendment to the Smoot-Hawley Tariff of 1930. This legislation granted the president a three-year period in which to negotiate reciprocal trade agreements with other countries, agreements that could lower American tariffs by as much as 50 percent. The measure, which had last been renewed in 1951, also gave the president authority to cut existing rates by an additional 50 percent.[14] In his State of the Union message, Eisenhower urged that the Trade Agreements Act be extended for another three years and that he be authorized to make additional tariff cuts. In a long entry in his personal diary we find his case for freer trade. He had been impressed daily "by the short-sightedness bordering upon tragic stupidity of many who fancy themselves to be the greatest believers in and supporters of capitalism (or a free competitive economy) but who blindly support measures and conditions that cannot fail in the long run to destroy any free economic system."[15]

The Communist leader Lenin, the president continued, had noted a number of contradictions internal to capitalism that were certain to bring about a revolution of the proletariat. These were the capitalist-labor contradiction, the inevitable conflict among capitalists themselves as they struggled for the sources of raw materials and other means of production, and the inherent conflict between the advanced, industrialized nations of the world and the dependent masses of backward peoples. Eisenhower dismissed Lenin's analysis as plausible only to extremists, but he noted that Lenin had failed to mention one contradiction in the capitalist system—the inability of men to forgo immediate gain for a long-term good. That, he believed, was the choice facing the United States with regard to tariff legislation. "No longer is it in the interest of America to keep imports down and exports up just to preserve the financial soundness of our whole system," he wrote. "Unless the free world espouses and sustains, under the leadership of America, a system of world trade that will allow backward people to make a decent living—even if only a minimal one measured by American standards—then in the long run we must fall prey to the Communist attack."[16]

The Tariff Issue

When Eisenhower assumed the presidency, there was already strong support in Congress and elsewhere for tightening, rather than liberalizing, the nation's tariff structure. In fact, by July 1953 the tariff had become the central issue in foreign economic policy and a divisive political question as well. In February, the Public Advisory Board for Mutual Security, established at the end of Truman's term of office, had delivered to the president a report on trade and tariff policy in which it called for a simplified, consolidated, and moderately reduced tariff structure.[17] A month later a British delegation led by Foreign Secretary Anthony Eden and Chancellor of the Exchequer Richard Butler came to Washington to discuss Prime Minister Winston Churchill's plan for restoring the pound sterling to full convertibility and bring about an Anglo-American partnership similar to that which had existed in World War II. The plan that Eden and Butler presented to the United States called for dollar-sterling cooperation (including dollar support for the pound) and the liberalization of American tariffs in order to open American markets to British imports.[18]

The White House rejected this "key currency" approach to world currency convertibility. Not only was the administration—and Congress—opposed to the additional financing called for in the British plan, but Eisenhower also opposed Churchill's scheme for an Anglo-American partnership as an alternative to broader European cooperation and integration. The White House did recognize that sterling convertibility was essential to an open world economy, however, and so it sought to bring about the full convertibility of sterling and other currencies through a gradual strengthening of the British and other free-world economies. An essential part of this program was the restoration of world trade, including the opening of American markets to British and other foreign imports. As Eisenhower remarked to Treasury Secretary George

Humphrey, "Most of my advisers believe that general world prosperity—which means also general peace and security—based upon equitable and mutually profitable trade is the sine qua non to currency convertibility."[19]

Not everyone agreed with the president's position. To that substantial segment of the Republican party which had long been committed to protectionism, freer trade through lower tariffs was a Democratic-inspired program that challenged the nation's economic interests by fostering increased foreign competition. Representatives of many small and medium-sized business interests, who felt particularly threatened by foreign imports, shared similar views.[20] Together these groups exerted considerable pressure on Eisenhower. Hesitant to involve himself too deeply in the legislative process because of his strongly held views on the separation of governmental powers, the president also was not anxious to begin his new administration by challenging much of his party's congressional leadership.[21] Moreover, he felt it would be wise to delay action on major tariff legislation until a commission, such as had been suggested to him by the former director of the Marshall Plan, Paul Hoffman, could be established to review the nation's entire foreign economic program. Forwarding a copy of Hoffman's proposal to Secretary of State Dulles, Eisenhower commented that his administration "[would] not even be in the saddle before the legislative hoppers [would] be filled by bills—each sponsored by some pressure group and each seeking to establish some new kind of obstacle to throw into the path of international trade." But the moment a study group such as that suggested by Hoffman was appointed, "there would be an automatic brake upon speedy enactment of unwise laws."[22]

Because of this opposition, the president decided to ask Congress for only a one-year extension of the Reciprocal Trade Agreements Act and to drop his request for additional rate-cutting powers. He also promised not to negotiate new major trade deals during that year and to maintain the legislation's "peril point" and "escape clause" provisions, which protectionist-minded congressmen had earlier inserted into the legislation. Meanwhile, the administration would concentrate on creating an administrative structure to develop and coordinate a comprehensive economic program. It would also undertake a study of the nation's entire foreign economic policy. On the basis of this study the president would make his recommendations to Congress on tariffs and other related matters. In May 1953, Congress easily approved the one-year extension of the trade agreements program—in the House by a vote of 363 to 34, in the Senate by voice vote.[23]

The Randall Commission

Eisenhower's plan to establish new administrative machinery for formulating and carrying out foreign economic policy was part of an overall program aimed at restructuring the federal bureaucracy. With a goal of greater efficiency, the president shaped various reorganizational schemes into executive orders or submitted his plans to Congress for approval. He was deeply concerned about the process of decision making and sought to set up his administration in such a way that minor issues could be resolved, and major issues fully explored, by members of the administration before proposals reached his desk for final action. As Eisenhower made clear, he kept himself well informed on developments within the administration and made all the important decisions, but he believed effective leadership required delegation of authority and extensive preparatory staff work.[24]

Accordingly, one of the first issues his cabinet took up was his proposal to have the National Advisory Council on International Monetary and Financial Affairs (NAC) strengthened and expanded. The NAC coordinated the policies of the Eximbank with the World Bank and advised the administration on international financial and monetary matters. The president wanted the NAC to include a working staff that would become the central organization for developing foreign economic policy.

In addition, a special group that included the president's brother, Milton, was formed to consider recommendations for reorganizing U.S. foreign-aid agencies in an effort to make the mutual security program more efficient and effective. In June 1953, Eisenhower sent to Congress a message based on the group's reorganization plan whereby the Mutual Security Agency would be abolished and its functions transferred to a new Foreign Operations Administration (FOA). The FOA would receive from the Department of State authority to administer AID and American participation in various United Nations programs, including those involving technical assistance. The president indicated that he expected the director of the FOA to look to the secretary of state for foreign-policy guidance.[25]

The administration also went ahead with its plans for a review of U.S. foreign economic policy. From the first it intended the study to support the concept of liberalized trade in lieu of expanded aid. White House officials discussed at some length the composition of the body that was to make the study. At first they considered establishing a study group composed of representatives from each executive department and agency concerned with foreign economic policy. But in order to draw widespread support for the study group's conclusions and to assure easier passage of the tariff extension legislation in Congress, the administration decided to establish a bipartisan special commission like the second Hoover Commission, which Congress had recently established to study executive organization. Representatives would be drawn from Congress and the public. The president made this decision despite the fact that protectionist-minded Republican leaders, including Senator Taft, Senator Eugene Millikin of Colorado, and Representative Charles Halleck of Indiana, warned that any House and Senate Democrats appointed to the commission would be free-traders.[26] As finally determined by the White House, the study group, known as the Commission on Foreign Economic Policy, was to be composed of ten congressmen (five each from the House and Senate) and seven public members, the latter chosen by the president. On May 2 Eisenhower asked Congress to establish the study commission, and the House and Senate approved the commission as part of the legislation extending the Reciprocal Trade Agreements Act for one year.[27]

The first order of business after congressional approval was the naming of commission members. Those whom Congress selected included both supporters and opponents of liberalized trade, but three members were among the most ardent advocates of protectionism—Senator Millikin of Colorado and Representatives Daniel Reed of New York and Richard Simpson of Pennsylvania. As his appointees, President Eisenhower picked a group composed for the most part of free-traders, although one member, Cola Parker, was a known protectionist. To head the commission, Eisenhower named Clarence Randall, chairman of the board of Inland Steel.[28] A strong advocate of liberalized trade, Randall had served as a steel consultant to the Marshall Plan in 1948 and, since 1952, as a member of the Department of Commerce's Business Advisory Council. His book, *A Creed for Free Enterprise*, published in 1952, had gone into three hardcover editions and a 150,000-copy paperback edition. Randall's position on free trade was clear. "Obviously whoever receives must give in exchange," Randall wrote in 1952, and then described why it was necessary to relieve the American taxpayer of foreign aid by opening American markets to European goods.[29]

Eisenhower made clear the importance he attached to the commission from the time it was organized in the summer of 1953. Anticipating that it would come out in favor of liberalized trade as the paramount objective of the nation's foreign economic policy, the president made known his intention to make the commission's report the basis of his foreign economic program. Policy questions having to do with foreign economic matters would purposely be delayed until the commission reported its findings.[30]

Although the legislation establishing the Randall Commission required that it transmit its report no later than March 1954, Randall was determined to deliver a report to the president and Congress by January. A number of administration officials and Randall himself believed that by March it would be too late for Congress to pass any legislation based on the commission's recommendations. In an election year, Congress would be reluctant to act so late on controversial matters like the tariff and would probably delay hearings until at least 1955. This could have serious consequences abroad. Lincoln Gordon, chief of a special mutual security mission to England, told Gabriel Hauge that a delay in the commission's findings would increase the political pressures in England to organize a self-sufficient non-dollar world that might even include expanded trade with the Soviet Union and China.[31]

In October 1953, Randall outlined the commission's course. It would hold hearings in two stages: first, closed hearings of former government officials involved in foreign economic policy, and then public hearings for citizens and organizations outside government. No hearings would be held except those for which the commission issued invitations, and at no point would the commission permit appearances on behalf of particular industries or products. To limit testimony, Randall would ask for written statements and recommendations from over fifteen hundred organizations and individuals, including federal agencies concerned with foreign economic policy, and these would take the place of oral testimony. These statements would then be condensed for commission use into a five-hundred-page report prepared by the commission's staff under the direction of Alfred C. Neal of the Federal Reserve Bank of Boston. "To meet our deadline," Randall cautioned commission members, "our time must be strictly rationed."[32] At the same time, Randall divided the commission's inquiry into a number of sections, assigning each public member to them in such a way as to commit the members to positions that were least palatable to them. For example, David McDonald, head of the United Steel Workers, was assigned responsibility for the section on foreign competition and labor standards, while the protectionist Cola Parker was given the section on tariffs.[33]

Randall ruled the commission with an iron hand. He selected and severely limited the number of witnesses for the public hearings held in the United States and Europe in October and November 1953, and also tightly controlled the hearings. He permitted only twenty minutes of testimony for each witness, abruptly cut off commission questioning, enveloped the commission's deliberations in secrecy, and generally rode roughshod over commission members. Many members of the commission, particularly those from Congress, objected to the dictatorial manner in which Randall conducted the group's business.[34]

Both supporters and opponents of liberalized trade testified before the commission, but the majority of witnesses favored free trade. A number of witnesses also called for a more precise clarification of foreign economic policy. Lawrence Wilkinson of Continental Can Company proposed establishing some kind of continuing advisory body to deal with foreign economic policy. Eugene Black of the World Bank recommended serious consideration of the proposal put forth in the Rockefeller Report of 1951 for the establishment of an International Finance Corporation to promote private investment abroad. Boris Shishkin of the American Federation of Labor noted the need for increased foreign investment to raise the standard of living abroad. Milton Eisenhower urged that more attention be given to Latin America's economic needs, and Meyer Kestenbaum of the Committee for Economic Development called for abolition of the Buy American Act (which required government procurement agencies to give preference to domestic suppliers) and for the elimination of import quotas on agricultural products.[35]

As the commission held its hearings and conducted its deliberations, the rift between its free-trade and protectionist members became a matter of public record. Randall followed a policy of silence with respect to commission matters, but in Congress and in leaks to the press, Representatives Reed and Simpson railed against liberalized trade. Furthermore, they indicated that they expected support for their position from the four other Republican congressmen on the commission. As *Business Week* suggested, that left Randall with two options: to seek a compromise between the protectionists and free-traders, which would mean little or no trade liberalization; or to push for a free-trade recommendation that would pass the commission by a one- or two-vote majority.[36]

Randall tried unsuccessfully to follow a course that contained elements of both alternatives. Beginning at the end of November and continuing until Christmas, the commission met three times a week to deliberate policy recommendations. In an effort to win near-unanimous support for a report favoring liberalized trade—including the backing of Senator Millikin, who remained silent about his position during the commission's proceedings—Randall prodded the free-traders into agreeing to a number of concessions to the protectionists. These included retention of the escape clause and peril-point provisions of the Trade Agreements Act and additional limitations on the president's bargaining power with respect to tariffs.[37] But when the final report was drafted in January, the protectionists, including Millikin, dissented from its trade provisions. In a statement appended to the report, Millikin warned that the report "would be subject to further study and hearings by the appropriate Committees in Congress and those who work in these fields in other departments of the Government." Representatives Reed and Simpson also published a separate minority report. As a result, while Randall was able to deliver a report that was acceptable to the majority of the commission in time for congressional action in 1954, the report contained numerous differences of opinion on almost all issues, its trade recommendations were seriously limited, and it lacked the support of the protectionists which Randall had sought.[38]

The report itself was built around the various economic policies that had been designed to alleviate the world's dollar shortage. It paid special attention to the termination of the emergency aid policies that had marked the postwar period, and it strongly recommended an early end to economic aid on a grant basis. Technical assistance (both bilateral and through the United Nations) should be continued, but should not become a "big money" program. In assisting foreign economic development, the government should rely primarily on private investment. Since postwar investment had been disappointing, the government should do everything possible to encourage conditions favorable to investment in foreign countries. The commission recommended several revisions in the Revenue Code to encourage a higher rate of private investment abroad. It also noted the uncertainty about the application of the nation's antitrust laws to American business abroad and recommended that the antitrust laws be rewritten in a manner that would clearly acknowledge the right of each country to regulate trade within its own borders.[39]

In the crucial trade policy field, the commission endorsed freer, but not free, trade. The Tariff Commission should frame proposals for the simplification of commodity definitions and rate structures and the Treasury should study customs administration. The General Agreement on Tariffs and Trade should be renegotiated in the interest of confining GATT to sponsoring multilateral trade negotiations, recommending broad trade policies for consideration by individual members, and providing a forum for consultation regarding trade disputes. The Buy American Act should be amended in such a way as to give foreign countries a better chance to bid successfully on government contracts. The Reciprocal Trade Agreements Act should be renewed for not less than three years, and thereafter for an unspecified longer period. The president's authority to reduce tariffs should be limited to 5 percent of the present rates in each of the first three years, or 50 percent of the 1945 rates in the case of goods not being imported in 1954. The peril point and escape clause provisions should be retained. The commission rejected a proposal by David McDonald that the government aid companies, workers, and communities in adjusting to increased imports. It called the problem of displaced workers "but one phase of a much broader problem." However, it did propose that tariff negotiators for the United States not make reductions on goods manufactured by workers receiving wages "well below accepted standards in the exporting country."[40]

Speaking to issues it considered less critical, the Commission expressed the hope that the conflict between U.S. domestic farm price supports and agricultural exports could be reduced by substituting flexible supports for rigid ones. To dampen the impact of fluctuations in raw-material prices, the commission recommended economic diversification of single-commodity economies rather than international commodity agreements.[41]

With respect to Communist countries, the commission took a hard line. It endorsed an absolute ban on U.S. and allied exports to Communist China and North Korea as well as on exports to the Soviet Union's European satellites that "might contribute to its military strength." But it favored "more trade in peaceful goods between Western Europe and the Soviet bloc."[42]

Finally, the commission described currency convertibility as a factor essential to world economic growth. It noted, however, that progress had to be gradual, with considerable help being provided by a more active utilization of the International Monetary Fund's holdings of gold and hard currencies. Of two schools of thought concerning the restoration of currency convertibility, the commission remarked, one regarded the restoration of convertibility as mainly a matter of curbing inflation abroad. By this reasoning, only appropriate monetary, fiscal, and exchange-rate policies were required. The other school believed that the problems associated with currency convertibility were essentially structural in nature and involved such matters as the loss of Europe's overseas investments, the breakdown of the triangular pattern of world trade, and the growing predominance of the United States in the world economy. Because of these structural developments, advocates of this view approached convertibility more cautiously. The commission adhered to this point of view.[43]

The Randall Commission report offered few conceptual innovations in foreign economic policy. As a group of economists meeting in Princeton, New

Jersey, noted, by building its report around the dollar gap problem, the commission neglected the broader issue of the proper relationship of foreign economic policy to foreign policy in general. Nor did the commission deal with the possible impact of an American depression on the rest of the world or with U.S. policy with regard to the pressing matters of European integration and the languishing Japanese economy. Finally, although the commission had been warned by one of its advisers, Eugene Staley of the Stanford Research Institute, not to neglect the world's underdeveloped countries in its report,[44] the commission said scarcely anything about specific Third World problems. In the words of the Princeton economists, the commission lacked any basic philosophy and had not produced "a document from which the nation could derive inspiration or on which it could rest for any length of time."[45]

Several of the commission's recommendations, especially those on tariff cuts and trade extension, also fell far short of what many free-traders, including some on the commission, wanted, such as elimination of the peril point and escape clause provisions of the Reciprocal Trade Agreements Act. Furthermore, in a number of areas the commission was either hazy about what it meant, unclear about its objectives, or simply unaware of the full implications of its proposals. For example, in the field of technical assistance, the commission attempted to distinguish sharply between providing technical assistance and offering capital assistance. But as several economists at the Princeton conference pointed out, technical assistance without capital aid would be artificial and probably wasteful. Likewise, the commission's recommendations concerning convertibility implied the need for total free trade on the part of countries moving toward convertibility, whereas convertibility could coexist with domestic restraints on imports.[46]

Within the Eisenhower administration there was general agreement on most of the commission's recommendations, partial agreement on others, and widespread disagreement on a few. In the latter category were the commission's recommendations concerning the Buy American Act and foreign aid. Only the FOA backed the commission's proposal on Buy American completely. Other agencies objected to it for reasons ranging from support of the current level of trade preference to favoring the act's outright repeal. With respect to the commission's proposals on foreign aid, the Treasury Department alone supported its recommendations. Other agencies expressed the belief that while economic aid should be held to a minimum and eliminated as quickly as possible, its use as a tool of foreign policy should not be excluded entirely.[47]

On the important issue of extending the Trade Agreements Act, all agencies agreed to an extension for three years—as a minimum. The Department of Commerce objected to increasing the president's rate reduction authority. It maintained that American manufacturers could not compete successfully with the low wage scales in some foreign industries and that the United States already had one of the lowest tariff rates in the world. On the other hand, the Department of Labor questioned whether any percentage limitation was necessary or appropriate in view of the existence of the peril point and escape clause provisions. It also questioned the desirability of continuing the peril point provision, although it did not propose that it be abandoned.[48]

Despite the limitations of the Randall Commission report and the doubts expressed about some of its recommendations within the administration, President Eisenhower made the report the basis of his own foreign economic program. He asked Randall to serve as a special consultant to the White House to coordinate the development of the administration's foreign economic policy. He also sought the advice of executive agencies as to how to win support for the commission's proposals. In response, commission staff member Alfred Neal outlined to Presidential Adviser Gabriel Hauge a program that he and Randall had put together. The program centered on four major issues: aid termination, encouragement of private investment abroad, currency convertibility, and trade liberalization. On the first three of these there was commission consensus, Neal remarked, and he anticipated congressional support as well. But the key to achievement of these objectives was passage of the tariff and trade recommendations. "The 'trade not aid' slogan reflects a part of this argument," Neal stated. But inasmuch as the slogan was "somewhat shopworn, though nevertheless still true," other arguments in behalf of free trade had to be emphasized. What he was suggesting, Neal concluded, was (1) that the commission's report would be well received in Congress if its program was presented properly and (2) that its trade recommendations would be adopted as part of that program.[49]

Neal could not have been more wrong. The commission report provoked a national debate on foreign economic policy. In a well-organized campaign, the nationwide Committee of Industry, Agriculture, and Labor on Import-Export Policy, attacked the commission's tariff proposals as a threat to the national interest. Formed in 1953 by O. R. Strackbein, a former organizer for the American Federation of Labor and trade commissioner with the Department of Commerce, the Strackbein Committee drew most of its support from minor labor organizations and from trade associations whose members were affected by foreign imports. But the committee also had the backing of the United Mine Workers, the National Coal Association, and the Manufacturing Chemists Association. A rash of speeches, apparently prepared by Strackbein and his followers, were delivered in Congress against the Randall Report. On the other side of the debate, the Committee for a National Trade Policy, a liberal trade group headed by John Coleman of the Burroughs Corporation, attempted to stem the protectionist tide in Congress. Organized in 1953 with White House encouragement, it became a major source of propaganda on behalf of freer trade and it rallied behind the Randall Commission program.[50]

On March 30, in a special message to Congress prepared for him by Randall, Eisenhower asked for approval of most of the Randall Commission's recommendations. Senator Millikin warned Eisenhower that the message would increase tensions and divisions within the Republican party and across the nation. But the president argued that the issues were too important to be decided by partisan politics and that he was giving his general approval to the program advanced by the Randall Commission.[51] In his address, which stressed the dollar gap existing between the United States and its trading partners, the president commented: "Our aim must not be to fill the dollar gap, but rather to help close it. Our best interest dictates that the dollar gap be closed by raising the level of trade and investment." He then endorsed the Randall program, calling for the reduction of tariffs over three years, a clearer definition of the functions of the GATT, exemption from the Buy American Act of countries that treated American bidders on an equal basis with their own nationals, passage of legislation to encourage foreign investment, and a review of the nation's antitrust laws as they applied to the conduct of American business abroad. Finally, Eisenhower recommended that, consistent with the national interest, economic aid on a grant basis be terminated as soon as possible.[52] He reiterated these policies in a speech before the U.S. Chamber of Commerce in April, remarking then that the United States could not forever be an "Atlas" supporting the rest of the world through grants and loans.[53]

In the end, however, the president again settled for a one-year extension of the Reciprocal Trade Agreements Act. In the first place, the country was in the midst of a recession caused in part by a drop in retail sales early in 1953 and by the prospect of a reduction in military sales. Second, biennial elections were only a few months away. Under these circumstances it was hardly the time to ask for congressional approval of an increasingly unpopular measure opposed by powerful interest groups. Furthermore, Congress faced a surfeit of legislation, including foreign-aid bills and labor, tax, and social security measures. Thus, the time needed for full hearings on the president's recommendations was lacking. Finally, the Republican party was split on tariff legislation, and the House Ways and Means Committee, through which any tariff legislation had to pass, was chaired by Daniel Reed, who had dissented from the Randall Commission report.[54]

Faced with these obstacles to his foreign economic program and worried particularly about a protectionist struggle within his own party during an election year, Eisenhower went public. In May, he revealed the contents of a letter he had written to Chicago businessman Charles Percy, a letter he had cleared with Reed two weeks earlier. In it he told Percy that he was dropping his proposal for a three-year extension of the Trade Agreements Act and for gradual tariff reductions. Instead, he would ask the House and Senate for only a second one-year extension, providing that full hearings would be held later on the more extensive tariff proposals he had outlined in his message to Congress in March.[55]

Once Reed's support had been won, the House passed the one-year extension the president had requested. In the Senate, Albert Gore of Tennessee, a Democrat and free-trader, tried to embarrass the administration by offering an amendment to the House-passed bill, substituting for it the original three-year proposal. Senate Republicans were able to defeat the Gore amendment, but by only seven votes. In the words of Democratic Senator J. William Fulbright of Arkansas, the Republicans had killed "trade not aid" through procrastination, hesitation, and doubt. Fulbright's remarks were hyperbolic, but for the moment, at least, the centerpiece of Eisenhower's foreign economic program had been shelved.[56]

Foreign Agricultural Policy

Even as Eisenhower struggled on one level for freer trade, the administration maintained its own protectionist policies on agricultural imports. It also subsidized the shipment abroad of America's agricultural products under the guise of foreign aid. In this respect, the White House's policy was at odds with the Randall Commission report. Although the commission had recognized the domestic constraints on foreign agricultural policy, it had also remarked that "dynamic foreign economic policy as it relates to agriculture cannot be built out of a maze of restrictive devices such as inflexible price-support programs."[57] The administration maintained that there was no contradiction between its agricultural foreign policy, on the one hand, and its advocacy of liberalized world commerce, on the other. It simply regarded agricultural commodities as being in a class by themselves and its protectionist and interventionist policy as being justified by the nation's domestic price support programs and the huge surpluses they produced. But even though other countries, hard pressed by the United States, bowed to the American position, this could not hide the real inconsistency that existed in Eisenhower's trade program.

As the White House noted, when Eisenhower became president in 1953, the United States was already committed to a program of agricultural price supports coupled with the purchase and storage of agricultural commodities. A system of protection had also developed to prevent imports from adding to the nation's already huge agricultural surpluses. Section 22 of the Agricultural Adjustment Act of 1933 (AAA) directed the president, following a Tariff Commission investigation, to impose fees or quotas on any import that interfered with any program administered under AAA. The Trade Agreements Extension legislation of 1951 and 1953 introduced special procedures for dealing with emergency conditions involving perishable products. Section 104 of the Defense Production Act of 1950 (DPA) placed import controls on a number of specific agricultural commodities, including butter, cheese, flaxseed, nonfat dry milk, and various types of peanuts and rice. In addition, U.S. agriculture was protected by the escape clause provision of the Reciprocal Trade Agreements Act.[58] The difficulty with this legislation was that it led to complaints and retaliatory measures against American agricultural exports by such countries as Canada, New Zealand, Denmark, and the Netherlands. Foreign countries objected especially to section 104 of the DPA, with its provision for licensing specific commodities.[59]

The position of the U.S. agricultural community on import restrictions—a position represented by the major farm organizations—was murky to say the least. Farmers were hurt by retaliation against American agricultural exports, and as a general principle such groups as the American Farm Bureau, the National Farmers' Union, and the National Grange supported the concept of freer trade. But they also believed in safeguards against the importing of agricultural commodities for which the United States provided price supports. While they thus strongly opposed the licensing of specific commodities as provided by the DPA, they supported section 22 of the AAA, with its provision for fees or quotas on imported commodities covered by the legislation.

Of the farm groups, the most influential in the Eisenhower administration was the American Farm Bureau (AFB), from which most of the top echelon of the Agriculture Department was drawn.[60] As the legislative director of the AFB, John C. Lynn, explained his organization's position on import restrictions to Secretary of Agriculture Ezra Taft Benson, section 104 of the DPA was "proving harmful to foreign trade, particularly the export market for agricultural products." In the bureau's view, section 22 of the AAA was adequate to provide agriculture the protection it needed. Besides, section 104 was about to expire in June and the Farm Bureau feared that unless the Tariff Commission took action under section 22 to place restrictions on commodities formerly covered by section 104, these commodities would flood the American market.[61]

Secretary Benson concurred in the Farm Bureau's position. In April, he asked the president to instruct the Tariff Commission to begin proceedings on specified commodities covered by the DPA to see if they threatened programs administered under the AAA. At the same time, he issued a statement expressing his belief that protectionism should not be applied as arbitrarily as it had been under the provisions of the DPA. He preferred the procedures of section 22, however less convenient and more cumbersome they might be.[62] In July the DPA licenses were abandoned, as required by law, and a system of quotas and fees was substituted under section 22 of the AAA. The severity of restrictions on agricultural imports was thus lessened somewhat, but for all practical purposes the domestic market remained separate from the world market.[63]

At the same time that the administration protected the domestic market from foreign imports, however, it sought to penetrate foreign markets by agreeing to promote the export of America's agricultural surpluses. Because these surpluses were costing the government $1 million a day, the legislation won strong congressional support. Similar programs had been attempted since 1896, when the Foreign Marketing Section of the Department of Agriculture shipped perishable surplus commodities abroad in an effort to develop foreign markets.[64] More recently, under an amendment to the Mutual Security Act of 1953, the United States agreed to accept inconvertible funds from developing countries in exchange for food products. But Congress was considering a more ambitious proposal that contained most of the provisions of earlier programs. Testifying before the Senate Committee on Agriculture and Forestry, Senator Hubert Humphrey of Minnesota proposed an extensive surplus-disposal program that included sales for local currencies, donations of food abroad, sales at concessionary prices, and trade of commodities for stockpile purposes. The Senate approved a bill incorporating most of Humphrey's suggestions in July, but before the House could consider the legislation, Congress adjourned, and the bill was held over for the next session.[65]

At first the administration was reluctant to support this legislation. Although it had decided that one way to relieve the nation's agricultural surpluses was to support the earlier amendment to the mutual security program accepting inconvertible funds for food products, the Agriculture Department had expressed reservations about the new Senate proposal. On the one hand, if the amendment proved effective, it would move as much as $1 billion of surplus food into foreign markets. On the other hand, Agriculture Department experts doubted whether so large a quantity of goods could be moved without harming commercial markets by displacing normal sales and knocking down the prices farmers received abroad.[66] Similarly, Secretary Benson commented that the Mutual Security Act provided sufficient "opportunity, on a trial basis, to see whether we can effectively sell our agricultural surpluses for foreign currencies. . . . If we find this feasible, we will give broader support to programs of this kind."[67]

Seeing an opportunity to get rid of some of the burden of surpluses while aiding needy countries, the president, however, decided to back the measure. In his annual budget message to Congress in January 1954, he asked for authorization to use up to $1 billion in farm surpluses over a three-year period.[68] Although the Senate had already passed the surplus-disposal legislation, witnesses were called to testify on the measure as part of the hearings the Senate and House conducted on the administration's overall farm program. Several senators expressed opposition to any plan to dispose of $1 billion in goods in outright grants. But the administration defended the measure as necessary to get rid of some of the $5.5 billion in surplus commodities then held by the Commodity Credit Corporation. The American Farm Bureau Federation also endorsed the legislation, as did the National Cotton Council and numerous relief organizations. In June, the House approved its own version of the bill and then, in conference committee, accepted a number of Senate amendments, the most important of which reduced the total value of commodities that could be used in overseas sales for foreign currencies from $1 billion to $700 million. In July, Eisenhower signed the bill into law, remarking that it would "lay the basis for permanent expansion of our export of agricultural products, with lasting benefits to ourselves and peoples in other lands."[69]

The legislation, known as Public Law 480 (P.L. 480), consisted of three major titles. Title I provided for the sale of U.S. agricultural products to friendly foreign governments for local currencies. These products were to be used for a number of purposes, including the promotion of economic development abroad and the development of new markets for America's farm products. At least 10 percent of the local currencies generated by P.L. 480 were subject to congressional appropriations. Title II provided for donations of food for famine relief or emergencies. Title III authorized food donations for emergencies within the United States and allowed for donations to nonprofit organizations abroad or in the United States. The barter program, also under title III and under other legislation, enabled the United States to exchange surplus agricultural commodities for strategic and other materials that were less expensive to store and less subject to deterioration than farm products.[70]

Once P.L. 480 became law, the administration made the disposal of food surpluses abroad a major part of its foreign-aid program. This annoyed not only other exporters of farm products but many Third World nations, which regarded P.L. 480 for what it was—a surplus-disposal program rather than a program aimed primarily at providing economic aid. These nations realized that some local currencies generated by P.L. 480 would be used for development purposes, but they also knew that Washington still intended to rely on trade and private investment to meet the needs of the underdeveloped world.

The Export-Import Bank Fight

Indeed, the administration believed that trade and private investment could and should carry the burden of development abroad. The Mutual Security Act of 1953 had continued economic aid to Europe and the Far East and had given the president authority to make aid available for the economic development of the Near East, Africa, India, and Pakistan. The bulk of the funds in the act were for military aid or had a military purpose, such as bolstering the economies of countries receiving military assistance (i.e., primarily Korea, Formosa, and other Far Eastern countries). Eisenhower challenged neither the scope nor the intent of these measures. Tariffs and investments, not development aid, were his solution to the Third World's economic problems.[71]

Eisenhower's relative lack of interest in providing development aid abroad was reflected in the generally passive and largely ineffectual role he played in the attempt by Treasury Secretary George Humphrey to reorganize the Export-Import Bank (Eximbank) in order to bring the bank under Treasury control and to tighten its purse strings. Although the question of using public funds to promote economic growth abroad was involved in Humphrey's efforts, and his reorganization plan pitted the Treasury Department against the Department of State, the president's response to Humphrey's scheme was to support Treasury against State and then to back off entirely when the reorganization plan, implemented in April 1953, became the subject of congressional investigation.[72] The result was a compromise. The Eximbank's old organizational structure was restored and its loan funds actually increased, but the Treasury Department's authority over the bank was largely retained.

Treasury Secretary Humphrey was disturbed that since its establishment in 1934 the Eximbank had wandered from its original purpose of making short-term loans to promote American exports and had become involved in long-term development lending. He was determined to give his department authority over the bank's activities in order to return it to its original function. An Ohio industrialist who had supported Robert Taft for the presidency in 1952, Humphrey quickly became one of Eisenhower's closest and most trusted advisers. Friendly and gregarious like the president, he was extremely bright and conversant about most major policy matters.[73] On fiscal matters he was even more conservative than the president. Unlike Eisenhower, he was against using tax incentives and what he called "other artificial stimulants" (like investment guarantees) to promote foreign investments. Instead, he believed the United States should use its influence to obtain favorable treatment for American investors, including the establishment of convertibility, political stability, and freedom from unreasonable discrimination.[74] He was also persuaded that long-term development lending should be left entirely to the World Bank rather than sometimes given to the Eximbank to handle. "The government must question both its right and its financial ability to continue to use taxpayer's money to finance investments abroad on a large scale in the development of competitive enterprises," he remarked to the president. It seemed to him, he added in a letter to FOA director Harold Stassen, that the Eximbank should not make any further political loans. "They are really not justifiable under the existing law, which requires that the loans have reasonable prospects of repayment."[75]

In his effort to limit Eximbank lending, Humphrey encountered considerable opposition from Secretary of State John Foster Dulles. Normally Dulles did not become involved in matters of foreign economic policy. Concerned with the more purely political problems of international relations and deeply involved in the diplomacy of foreign policy, Dulles tended throughout most of his seven years as secretary of state to follow the lead of others within the administration, and particularly the president, on foreign economic issues. But on the question of Eximbank lending he chose to take a strong stand.[76] Although historians have quite correctly regarded the secretary as a moralist and as a rigid foe of the Soviet Union whose view of world affairs was distorted by his almost obsessive determination to contain Communist expansion, they have neglected his broad-mindedness on many issues and his tactical flexibility. They have also ignored the fact that, more than most members of the administration, the secretary of state sensed the compelling force of nationalism in much of the underdeveloped world and understood the economic dimension of Third World protests against Western political hegemony. For these reasons Dulles considered it disastrous for the United States to cut back on Eximbank lending to underdeveloped countries. Instead, he sought to use the bank to speed long-term economic growth abroad by expediting foreign trade and investment.[77]

But while Eisenhower had great respect for Dulles and relied heavily on his counsel, on the issue of the Eximbank the president sided with Humphrey. Over Dulles's opposition and that of the State Department, Humphrey persuaded the president in April 1953 to propose to Congress the reorganization of the Eximbank in such a way as to place it almost entirely under Treasury direction. According to this plan, announced on April 30, the bank's bipartisan board of directors would be replaced by a single managing director. Thus the State Department, which had selected one member of the bank's board of directors, would lose its voice in Eximbank policy, and the bank itself would lose its representation on the NAC.[78] When Congress approved the reorganization plan, Eisenhower named General Glen E. Edgerton to manage the bank. *Business Week* described Edgerton as "[having] varied experience around the world in everything but international banking." A conservative and a retired Army engineer, Edgerton could be expected to follow closely the dictates of the Treasury Department. Indeed, long-term development loans quickly dried up, dropping from $275 million in 1952 to $40 million for all of 1953.[79]

This precipitous cutting of loans proved to be too much even for supporters of the reorganization plan, however, many of whom regarded Eximbank lending as a legitimate means of helping America's friends abroad even as it promoted the foreign sale of American goods. The chairman of the Senate Banking and Currency Committee, Homer Capehart of Indiana, was particularly incensed by the cutback in Eximbank lending. Once one of the most conservative members of the Senate, Capehart had changed many of his views since becoming chairman of the Banking and Currency Committee in 1953.[80] As a result of a trip his committee had made to Latin America in 1953, he had become persuaded of the need to cooperate more closely with other nations of the Western hemisphere on political and economic issues. More specifically, he believed that the Eximbank and the World Bank should provide more short- and long-term credits to Latin America, and he organized a citizens' advisory group of one hundred to press the case in behalf of expanded Eximbank lending activities. "It looks to me," Treasury Secretary Humphrey told Eisenhower with respect to the work of the Capehart committee, "as though it was being pretty well packed by those who want to use Government money. Unlike the International Bank, the funds of the Export-Import Bank come right out of the Treasury's cash."[81] In January, the Senate Banking and Currency Committee opened hearings on the Eximbank and the World Bank, the first such congressional inquiry since the Eximbank's establishment twenty years earlier. The majority of the testimony before the committee concerned the functions of the two banks in providing international trade. Even Capehart criticized the Eximbank for making more loans to foreign governments than to private enterprise. But the majority of witnesses urged that the Eximbank be allowed to make development loans.[82]

By March, Eisenhower found it necessary to reverse his earlier position on the Eximbank. The immediate problem facing the president was the forth-coming Inter-American Conference in Caracas, Venezuela. During his first year in office he had largely ignored relations with Latin American countries, thereby continuing a pattern established by his predecessor. Soon after taking office, he had sent his brother, Milton, on a fact-finding mission to the region, and at a cabinet meeting the next summer he had commented on the generally unsatisfactory nature of U.S. policy toward Latin America, a policy that had resulted from Washington's preoccupation with Europe and Asia.[83] But for a number of reasons, including the belief that the problems of Latin America were largely due to declining commodity exports and that its most pressing financial needs could be met by the private sector in cooperation with the Eximbank and the World Bank, the White House had done little to assist Latin America or to otherwise improve relations with the region.[84]

The freezing of long-term lending by the Eximbank was particularly hard on Latin America (where lending dropped from $147 million in 1952 to just $7.6 million in 1953) and it only exacerbated the region's relations with the United States. Anticipating a hostile reception at Caracas and the likelihood of radical demands for economic relief and being anxious to gain support for collective action against the reportedly Communist government of Guatemala, Secretary of State Dulles convinced the president to allow him to announce at Caracas that the Eximbank would resume long-term lending.[85]

Three months later a compromise over the future status of the Eximbank was worked out at a White House meeting. At the meeting, attended by the chairmen and ranking minority members of the House and Senate Banking and Currency committees, the administration agreed to a measure, sponsored by Senator Capehart, that would reestablish a board of directors for the bank and return the bank to its seat on the NAC. The White House also agreed to support legislation that would increase the bank's lending authority by $500 million to a total of $5 billion. In return, however, the bank would be expected to confine its lending for the most part to short-term loans and leave most long-term lending to the World Bank. In its report on the meeting, the *New York Times* noted that Treasury Secretary Humphrey had succeeded in keeping from the Eximbank the long-term function its backers wanted it to have. In fact, despite the White House compromise, the bank was already making and would continue to make long-term loans for development purposes. Over the years these would become rather substantial. In this respect the State Department had won its point with the president and the Treasury Department. But as the *New York Times* also noted, nothing at the White House meeting indicated that the bank would have more say in formulating its own policy than before. Humphrey's evident satisfaction with the outcome of the meeting indicated that as chairman of the NAC he intended to maintain his dominant role in formulating Eximbank policy.[86]

Conclusion

Throughout the struggle over the Eximbank, President Eisenhower remained discreetly silent. He agreed to allow Dulles to announce in Caracas the resumption of long-term lending by the bank, and the final compromise worked out at the White House would not have been reached without his approval. But his actual role in bringing about the compromise or in the earlier behind-the-scenes struggle between the State and Treasury departments over Eximbank lending policy remains unclear. What does seem clear is his opposition to the use of public capital and his intention to rely on the private sector to promote economic growth abroad. By the summer of 1954, in fact, the broad outlines of the president's foreign economic policy had become apparent. The slogan "trade not aid" best described it. Foreign economic policy would rest on the secure foundations of lower tariffs and private investments abroad. These, and not public capital, would meet the world's economic needs and assure world economic prosperity. It was easy to overlook the inconsistencies apparent even within the administration's own trade program.

Already, however, there were critics, some within and some close to the administration, who were calling for substantial changes in the nation's foreign economic policy, especially as it concerned underdeveloped countries. These critics became more insistent as events in the Third World undermined earlier U.S. assumptions and forced the nation to direct its attention increasingly to Third World regions.

3. The Transition 1954–1955

IN ITS FIRST eighteen months the Eisenhower administration formulated a foreign economic policy predicated on the concept of "trade not aid." During the next year it tried to carry out that program. To handle foreign economic matters for the White House, Clarence Randall remained as a special consultant to the president. In November 1953 Randall outlined his foreign economic policy proposals for the following year; they were based, he said, on extensive deliberations and a wide consensus within the administration. Similar to proposals contained in President Eisenhower's special message to Congress the previous March, Randall's program became the basis for the president's legislative recommendations to Congress in January 1954. The program once again called for a three-year extension of the Trade Agreements Act and a corresponding rate reduction authority for the president. In addition, it included recommendations on renegotiation of the General Agreement on Tariffs and Trade (GATT), tax incentives to encourage American investment abroad, clarification of the Buy American Act, and alignment of the nation's foreign agricultural and economic programs. Randall also introduced two proposals that had not been among the president's earlier recommendations. One was for the establishment of a new International Finance Corporation to provide capital for private enterprises investing abroad, and the other was for the creation of an organization to develop and coordinate foreign economic policy.[1]

Considering the White House's commitment to trade liberalization as presented in the Randall Report and the president's message to Congress in January 1954, the administration's record on trade and tariff matters left much to be desired. The president took several actions that contradicted his policy of freer commerce. In addition, the administration failed to win congressional approval for U.S. membership in a new international organization to administer GATT, and it only partly succeeded in tying the Japanese economy more closely to that of the West. The White House did win from Congress a three-year extension of the Reciprocal Trade Agreements Act along with additional presidential authority to cut tariff rates, but even in this case it had to make concessions to protectionist forces which vitiated much of the intent of the legislation.

Thus, even as Eisenhower made his proposals to Congress on trade and other foreign economic matters, the White House began to reexamine some of the assumptions on which it had based these policies. Events in the Third World, particularly the defeat of the French in Indochina, forced the administration to reevaluate its program of trade-not-aid. On the one hand, events in Southeast Asia compelled the White House to pay more attention to the development needs of Third World nations. On the other hand, it was becoming increasingly clear that existing policies were inadequate to meet the most essential requirements of any development program. As a result, the White House took its first steps to expand the role of public capital in promoting economic growth abroad.

Promotion of Foreign Trade and Establishment of the CFEP

In his legislative recommendations to Congress in January 1955, Eisenhower remarked that his foreign economic program was designed to increase foreign trade and investment opportunities for American business even as it stimulated world economic growth and contained the spread of communism.[2] In the twelve months from the summer of 1954 to the summer of 1955 the administration stepped up considerably its promotion of foreign trade. For example, the Eximbank increased its annual credit authorizations from $250 million in fiscal 1954 to $460 million for fiscal 1955 and $665 million for fiscal 1956 and extended new lines of credit to exporters of certain types of capital equipment in order to meet foreign competition.[3] Likewise, the Department of Agriculture expanded its Foreign Agricultural Service by increasing the number of commodity specialists it stationed abroad. Furthermore, in September 1954 President Eisenhower issued a statement on agricultural foreign trade in which he made it clear that although the United States did not intend to depress world commodity prices by flooding foreign markets with America's surpluses, neither did it intend to limit its exports until other nations had disposed of their products. The United States would sell abroad at competitive prices while trying to increase world consumption.[4] For these purposes Eisenhower established the Interagency Committee on Agricultural Surplus Disposal, appointing as its head Clarence Francis of the Agriculture Department.[5]

Scarcely less important to the White House than the expansion of U.S. trade abroad was the need to coordinate the administration of America's foreign economic policy and improve the policy-making process. Since becoming president, Eisenhower had been intrigued by questions of administrative organization and policy development. Soon after his inauguration he had proposed making the National Advisory Council on International Monetary and Financial Problems (NAC) the central organization for formulating and administering foreign economic programs, but this idea was dropped with the establishment of the Foreign Operations Administration (FOA). Eisenhower anticipated that the FOA would centralize foreign assistance and related economic responsibilities until he could recommend legislative changes in the entire operation and structure of foreign policy. He expected to offer these proposals early in 1955.[6]

Establishment of the FOA failed to resolve the problems of coordination and decision making, however. As Nelson Rockefeller of the President's Advisory Committee on Government Organization told Eisenhower in July 1954, important areas requiring coordination had become apparent even as the FOA began its operations.[7] In at least one instance the FOA itself became involved in a dispute with the Department of Commerce over their respective responsibilities in promoting foreign trade and investment opportunities abroad.[8] Similarly, UN Ambassador Henry Cabot Lodge, Jr., quarreled with the Department of Agriculture about whether the United Nations should exercise greater control over its Food and Agriculture Organization (FAO); Lodge favored more control and Secretary Benson argued for maintaining the existing, largely independent relationship.[9]

This internal bickering and lack of coordination conflicted with Eisenhower's insistence upon operational efficiency. The president demanded of his subordinates a well-organized administrative structure able to resolve disputes through general consensus and to leave him with only the important policy decisions. In this respect he disagreed emphatically with Treasury Secretary Humphrey's contention that it was impossible to avoid the daily problems of foreign economic policy through organizational changes. Instead, he stressed the importance of an agency that would insure some digestion of ideas prior to the presentation of problems to the president.[10] Thus, when Rockefeller proposed to Eisenhower that his group undertake with the Bureau of the Budget a study of the organizational needs for developing and coordinating foreign economic policy, the president immediately approved the proposal.[11] To direct the study the president named Joseph Dodge, a Detroit banker and former head of the Bureau of the Budget. According to Eisenhower's chief-of-staff, Sherman Adams, the president admired Dodge for his post–World War II work in reorganizing the German banking system as adviser to the military government in Berlin and then in developing an economic program for Japan as economic consultant to General Douglas MacArthur. Known for his keen analytical mind and conservative fiscal and monetary views, Dodge exemplified the type of publically oriented business leader Eisenhower was seeking for his administration. As appealing to the president as any of Dodge's other qualities was his reputation for efficiency and good management.[12]

Dodge undertook his investigation of U.S. foreign economic policy in the summer and fall of 1954, delivering a preliminary report to Rockefeller at the end of October and a final report to the president the next month. In his reports Dodge stressed the need for a White House staff organization with direct access to the president on foreign economic policy. The head of the organization should be an individual who had no other duties and who would not engage in working details but would leave that to a carefully selected staff. This individual should be independent of the agencies involved in foreign economic policy and should serve exclusively as a coordinating representative of the president.[13]

Others within the administration, particularly Eisenhower's economic adviser, Gabriel Hauge, shared these views. Hauge told Sherman Adams that the organization proposed by Dodge, a Council on Foreign Economic Policy, should be independent even of the National Security Council. "The basis for my view," Hauge commented, "is that I think foreign economic policy has a base much broader than the military or security aspects."[14]

Eisenhower accepted the recommendations of these advisers. At the end of 1954 he issued an order establishing as an executive agency the Council on Foreign Economic Policy (CFEP) to coordinate and develop foreign economic policy. The CFEP was to be composed of the director of the FOA and the secretaries of state, treasury, commerce, and agriculture, or their principal deputies, and of White House staff members. Eisenhower named Dodge to head the council and to serve as a special assistant to the president. Hauge predicted that establishment of the agency might well prove to be one of Eisenhower's most important steps in the whole area of organizing government business.[15]

Trade and Tariff Program

As important as these measures to expand foreign commerce and coordinate foreign economic policy were to the administration, however, they were subordinate to the president's larger program of promoting world trade and investment opportunities. Only by freeing the reins of international commerce and exchange, he believed, was world economic growth and prosperity possible. Only by allowing trade and commerce to move unencumbered by tariff barriers, import quotas, or other restrictive devices could international trade be used effectively as an instrument of world peace. As part of this policy the United States had to lower its own trade barriers and to place the Trade Agreements Act on an extended three-year basis. At the same time, it needed to encourage the movement of American private investment abroad through tax and other business incentives. By contributing to world economic development, the liberalization of trade and the flow of American capital abroad would serve the immediate and long-term interests of the United States and its friends and allies abroad.[16] Yet in a number of instances the administration confronted obstacles to free trade, and its record in response to these obstructions was disappointing to many free-trade advocates. Normally it championed the cause of liberalized world commerce, but at times it approved or tolerated protective measures. Moreover, it was not entirely successful even in the steps it took to expand the flow of international trade.

Immediately facing the administration in the summer of 1954 were decisions in two cases before the Tariff Commission, one involving the import of watches, and the other, that of lead and zinc. Citing the escape clause of the tariff law, the commission recommended raising the tariff in both cases. Key to its decisions were the arguments by the two industries that considerations of national defense warranted restrictions. The watchmakers (as distinguished from importers of Swiss watch movements, who merely assembled the complete watches in the United States) claimed that because of foreign competition they were losing employees whose skills were essential in time of war. The lead and zinc producers, who enjoyed greater influence in Congress because production of these metals was spread across several states, claimed that Americans were losing jobs and that the nation was becoming dangerously dependent on foreign sources of these critical raw materials.[17]

At the beginning of June the Senate Armed Services Preparedness Subcommittee began four days of hearings to determine how essential the watch industry was to the national defense. Numerous witnesses, including the Director of the Office of Defense Mobilization, Arthur S. Flemming, Assistant Secretary of Defense Thomas P. Pike, and Assistant Secretary of Commerce Lothair Teetor, testified that the industry was vital to national security. Representing the American Watch Association, a group of importers of Swiss watch movements, former Senator Millard E. Tydings of Maryland disagreed, maintaining that domestic watchmakers were simply trying to eliminate import competition. But the Preparedness Subcommittee issued a report reaffirming the Tariff Commission's recommendations. After reading the subcommittee's report and assessing the findings of the Tariff Commission, the president, who had earlier expressed the belief that the skills required by the watch industry were essential to the national defense, announced that he was raising tariffs by as much as 50 percent on certain types of imported watch movements.[18]

The case involving lead and zinc producers was more complicated because it affected influential interest groups in the United States and bore even more directly on defense considerations. Lead and zinc were part of a national stockpile program designed in part to assure ample supplies of essential raw materials in wartime and in part to absorb surplus production by ailing industries.[19] Despite the stockpile program, however, the prices for lead and zinc had fallen considerably since the end of the Korean War (although they were again rising). Domestic producers, who had powerful support in the Republican party and in Congress, sought relief through tariffs on foreign imports from Canada, Australia, Mexico, and the whole of South America. In recommending extension of the Trade Agreements Act for one year in 1954, the House Ways and Means Committee had even considered a provision for quotas or import taxes on lead, zinc, and petroleum products.[20]

The political pressures to raise tariffs were brought to bear on Eisenhower by his own party, especially by congressmen from mineral-producing states, who warned that failure to mandate adequate protection from foreign imports under the escape clause of the Trade Agreements Act would jeopardize the administration's chances of winning extension of that legislation.[21] But the president was also worried about the effects of a tariff hike on Mexico. "If we erect stronger barriers against trade with Mexico," he remarked in August, "I know that the possibility of her turning communist would mount rapidly. At the moment we do not fear Mexico, but let her once form an alliance with Moscow and it takes no great imagination to see what would happen."[22] Weighing the alternatives, Eisenhower finally decided not to raise tariffs in the lead and zinc case, but to rely instead on a program of voluntary export restrictions by other countries that had been recommended to him by the Department of State and that was one of several alternatives offered by the Department of Commerce.[23]

In both the watch and lead and zinc cases, Eisenhower based his actions on defense considerations. On numerous occasions, however, he emphasized that his purpose remained one of liberalizing world trade.[24] In line with this policy, he rejected in September a Tariff Commission recommendation to increase the import duty on foreign hand-blown glass.[25] In November he told members attending the ninth annual session of GATT that in the next session of Congress his administration would push vigorously for adoption of the Randall Commission's trade liberalization policy recommendations.[26]

Neither the president's statements nor his subsequent actions could alter the fact, however, that his decisions in the watch and lead and zinc cases had deeply offended free-trade advocates. Harry S. Radcliffe of the National Council of American Exporters called Eisenhower's action on watches "a major setback in the movement toward the reduction of trade barriers." *Business Week* warned that European countries, now reducing discrimination against dollar goods and pushing toward currency convertibility, might tend to slow up, fearful of a drift toward higher tariffs in the United States. The watch decision might also lead to increased European trade with the Soviet Union, which could now argue that the United States' trade policy could not be trusted.[27]

As *Business Week* indicated, Eisenhower's action in the watch case disturbed America's European trading partners. Another decision by the administration, this time to bring Japan into GATT as a full contracting party, also caused many of these countries considerable trouble. Here, however, the positions of the parties were reversed. Whereas the United States championed the cause of freer trade by attempting to broaden the membership of GATT, many of its European allies, along with members of the British Commonwealth, sought to restrict the flow of world trade by refusing to accord Japan the full privileges of membership in the international trading community. The United States did succeed in making Japan a contracting party to GATT, but as subsequent events showed, this proved to be a Pyrrhic victory that was embarrassing to GATT and that did not accomplish much in tying the Japanese economy more closely to that of the West.

The administration's position on admitting Japan to GATT was part of the White House's policy of strengthening the Japanese economy by expanding that country's opportunities to develop foreign markets in the West and in Asia. It was also aimed at keeping Japan from drawing economically closer to Communist China. The administration regarded an economically strong Japan tied to the West as essential to U.S. interests in the Pacific. Secretary of State Dulles stated that the economic security of Japan was vital to the military security of the United States. Similarly, Eisenhower remarked that Japan was "the key to the future political complexion" of much of the Far East and that the policies the United States adopted regarding Japanese trade might "well dictate whether these areas remain[ed] in the free world or [fell] within the Communist orbit." France's loss of Indochina increased the strategic necessity of bolstering the shaky Japanese economy, which had not yet recovered from the sharp recession it had experienced since the end of the Korean War.[28]

As a result of an intense, seven-month diplomatic effort by the United States, Japan gained admission to GATT in August 1955. It also gained tariff concessions on items that accounted for about 40 percent of its export trade in 1953.[29] But fourteen of the thirty-three contracting parties of the GATT, including a number of European and British Commonwealth countries, refused to apply the GATT in their relations with the new member. This was allowed under article 35 of GATT, the escape clause that permitted member nations to protect themselves against unfair and unusual competition.[30] What the European and British Commonwealth countries especially feared was Japanese competition in textile goods. Most trade experts acknowledged that because Japanese wage rates were so much lower than those of other industrial nations, it would be years before they approached what even the most ardent free-traders regarded as a reasonable basis for fair competition. Even in the United States, pressure mounted from the women's blouse industry to apply restrictions on Japanese imports of blouses, despite the fact that Japan had already restricted its exports of blouses and a few other items to the United States in an effort to avoid flooding the market and arousing protectionist sentiment.[31]

Washington and Tokyo applied considerable pressure to end the trade discrimination against Japan. Speaking to the tenth session of GATT in Geneva in October 1955, the head of the American delegation, Ambassador James Bonbright, informed the other delegates that it was "a matter of serious concern to the United States" that so many members continued to deny Japan its normal privileges under GATT.[32] Japan's ambassador to Switzerland warned that nondiscrimination by the West was essential if Japan was not to establish trade ties with Communist countries. The Japanese delegation also threatened to retaliate by raising their own tariffs against countries utilizing the escape clause.[33] At one point, member nations considered a plan to remove textiles from the GATT system of rules. But delegates to the Geneva meeting quickly realized that textiles were too important a segment of world trade to be taken out of the system, which had already been weakened by the special protective measures authorized for virtually all agricultural products. Similarly, the delegates discarded a proposal to permit bilateral agreements on textiles, although some interest in the idea was shown even by Japan.[34]

The delegates at Geneva failed to resolve the question of discrimination against Japan under article 35 of GATT. Despite U.S. and Japanese efforts to that effect, they agreed merely to take up the problem at intersessional meetings and at the next annual session of GATT. Not until the mid-1960s did Japan establish formal GATT relations with all the major contracting parties. In the meantime the very structure of GATT was seriously undermined. As the *New York Times* editorialized, the application of the escape clause in such a wholesale fashion against one country "destroy[ed] the whole concept of GATT and the purpose for which it was formed." In addition, the administration failed to free the flow of international commerce or to align the Japanese economy more closely with that of the West.[35]

Although the Eisenhower administration was more successful at home in winning an extension of the Trade Agreements Act, approval of the measure represented considerably less than the "victory" the president claimed. In fact, protectionist forces in Congress began to circumscribe the trade agreements program by means of crippling amendments rather than by attacking the program directly. When Eisenhower outlined his tariff program for 1955 in his January message to Congress, he asked for a three-year extension of the reciprocal trade program (scheduled to expire at the end of June) together with authority to reduce tariffs by 5 percent each year for three years. He emphasized that the program was a gradual and reciprocal one. Radical or sudden tariff reductions could be counterproductive, he remarked, but a moderate program "[could] add immeasurably to the security and well-being of the United States and the rest of the free world." As a supplement to the president's message, the White House also sent to Capitol Hill a list of items slated for tariff concessions in the negotiations with Japan that were about to begin in Geneva.[36]

Nevertheless, a lengthy and bitter struggle followed over the proposed legislation. House Speaker Joseph Martin of Massachusetts warned the president of the heavy opposition he could expect from Congress, although he predicted the measure would pass.[37] Hearings on the bill began before the House Ways and Means Committee at the end of January. Veteran House members later said that opponents of reciprocal trade mounted the biggest pressure campaign that they could recall. Opponents included southern textile interests, independent oil producers and coal operators, wool growers, and bicycle makers, all of whom were afraid of what imports would do their businesses.

Protectionist members of the Ways and Means Committee attacked the list of trade concessions being negotiated with Japan. Republican Representatives Richard M. Simpson of Pennsylvania and Thomas A. Jenkins of Ohio asked why such items as hand-blown glass tableware had been included in the list when three of the five members of the Tariff Commission had already decided that present imports of this product were threatening serious injury to domestic industry.[38]

Eisenhower enjoyed remarkable success with his program in the House, although as it turned out, the administration's bill cleared the House by a single vote. The bill that the Ways and Means Committee reported to the full House contained virtually everything the president had requested, including the three-year extension of the Trade Agreements Act and presidential authority to lower tariffs by 15 percent over a three-year period. A series of restrictive amendments calling for greater protection against imports of residual oil, chemicals, electric equipment, and other goods was voted down in committee. The only restriction the committee added to the bill was a clause that made mandatory, rather than permissive, a section calling for suspension of trade concessions if a country discriminated against American imports. By one vote the House then adopted a closed ruling prohibiting amendments to the committee report and in effect quashed the nearly successful efforts of protectionist forces to make significant changes in the legislation. Having barely survived a major setback, supporters of the administration's program then approved extension of the Trade Agreements Act and sent it to the Senate after only two days of floor debate.[39]

In the Senate, however, the going proved much rougher, and Eisenhower, who had earlier stated that his tariff program was too important to be subjected to political exigency,[40] had to agree to a number of concessions. Even as the Finance Committee began hearings on the trade legislation, Democratic Majority Leader Lyndon Johnson of Texas warned the president that his trade bill was "in deep trouble" in the Senate. Democratic Senator Joseph O'Mahoney of Wyoming confirmed Johnson's analysis when in testimony before the committee he urged adoption of an amendment that would require congressional approval of each trade agreement. Similarly, Republican Senator Styles Bridges of New Hampshire and Democratic Senator John O. Pastore of Rhode Island told the committee they would make the recommendations on the Tariff Commission binding on the president except in cases involving the national defense. Opposition to the trade bill coalesced behind a series of amendments that were intended to protect domestic industry by broadening the scope of required and permissive action under the national security, peril point, and escape clause provisions of the trade legislation. These amendments, which the Finance Committee attached to the measure after three weeks of hearings, strengthened the escape clause in such a way that relief could be considered for a product that was adversely affected by foreign competition even if the rest of the industry was thriving. Another amendment stipulated that the Tariff Commission had to regard imports as the reason for an industry's economic troubles even if they were a contributory cause rather than the primary reason for its woes. Finally, the president was given authority, which he did not request, to fix quotas on imports if he felt they were injuring domestic industries vital to the national defense.[41]

Acknowledging the bipartisan strength of the opposition to the House-passed bill and believing that he could not get more from Congress, Eisenhower decided to accept the Senate Finance Committee's amendments. Senator Albert Gore, a Democrat from Tennessee, announced that he and a group of senators would try to overturn these amendments if the president would "stand by his position" as outlined earlier to Congress. But on May 4, Press Secretary James C. Hagerty announced that the bill the committee had approved was "satisfactory to the administration" and "preserve[d] the principle of reciprocal trade which the President had so ardently advocated in the past two years."[42] With the administration's backing, the Senate then passed the trade extension legislation after rejecting a number of other amendments aimed at giving additional protection to domestic industry, including a proposal to put quotas on oil imports. In conference committee the House agreed to most of the changes added to the bill, making only slight alterations in some of the language used by the Senate and adding a requirement that industries suffering from import competition must produce their goods in "commercial quantities" in order to qualify for relief under the measure's escape clause and peril point provisions. In June the House and Senate agreed to the conference report.[43]

President Eisenhower called the extension legislation "a tremendous victory," noting that its enactment represented "an important milestone in the development of our country's foreign economic policy."[44] In reality the legislation encouraged the forces of protectionism in the United States and was a keen disappointment to most advocates of freer trade. Senator Gore refused even to take part in the Senate's three-day debate on the bill, while Democrats Estes Kefauver of Tennessee and J. William Fulbright of Arkansas called the measure "a watered-down version of a modest piece of legislation."[45]

Closely tied to the struggle for liberalized trade was the attempt by the administration to win congressional approval for U.S. membership in an international organization to administer GATT, the Organization for Trade Cooperation (OTC). Members of the GATT had met in Geneva for over four months to revise GATT's regulations, and at this meeting they had agreed to the protocol admitting Japan into full membership. But not everyone within the Eisenhower administration was pleased with the revisions. Loring Macy of the Department of Commerce, who had attended the meeting, complained that acknowledgment by other nations of America's right to restrict imports of agricultural products and subsidize their export considerably weakened the United States' chances of getting a stronger and simpler GATT.[46] Generally, though, the Geneva revisions were favorable to the United States and other industrial countries and included a tightening of the rules by which Third World countries could impose discriminatory import duties. Countries that were threatened with a loss of monetary reserves or that had balance-of-payment problems or that sought to protect an infant industry were permitted import quotas. This, of course, meant primarily the Third World nations. But stiffer review and consultation procedures were laid down for these countries to follow when imposing quotas.[47]

Besides making changes in GATT's trade rules, the delegates to the Geneva meeting also proposed to establish the OTC to administer the organization's agreements, facilitate trade negotiations, and deal with trade disputes and complaints. As agreed upon at Geneva, the OTC was to consist of a secretariat, an executive committee of seventeen members, and an assembly representing all governments that adhered to GATT. Because of weighted voting procedures, the OTC could not be established until the United States agreed to join the organization.[48]

In a special message to Congress in April 1955, President Eisenhower urged approval of U.S. membership in the OTC. He maintained that by joining the OTC the United States would be able to work more effectively for world trade liberalization as well as for the convertibility of currencies, the expansion of markets for American products, and the development of conditions conducive to the international flow of investment capital. "Failure to assume membership in the Organization for Trade Cooperation," the president warned, "would be interpreted throughout the free world as a lack of genuine interest on the part of this country in the effort to expand trade."[49]

Despite the president's warning, protectionists in Congress succeeded in deferring consideration of the OTC until 1956. Eisenhower's comments notwithstanding, many congressmen feared that the OTC would become a supranational agency like the ill-fated ITO of the 1940s. They also objected to the GATT system as a whole, which, like other agreements negotiated under the Reciprocal Trade Agreements Act, had never been approved by Congress. Indeed, some of these legislators attempted to bring GATT within the jurisdiction of Congress. The White House beat back this effort to curtail its control over trade and tariffs; the final bill merely declared that enactment of the legislation would not indicate approval or disapproval of GATT by Congress. But the administration decided that the opposition to OTC membership was too strong, and consequently it did not even bring the bill to the House floor for debate. Once again the administration disappointed advocates of freer trade with its lackluster support of a measure that it itself had claimed was essential to the cause of liberalized world commerce.[50]

Further Setbacks for Liberalized Trade

The final setbacks for the proponents of freer trade came in the summer of 1955. First the president accepted a Tariff Commission recommendation to raise tariffs on imported bicycles (mainly from England) by 50 percent. Then, in a Buy American action, the Defense Department rejected a British bid on heavy generating equipment in favor of a substantially higher American bid. Proponents of freer trade—even those within the administration—strongly opposed both actions. "We feel that the imposition of higher tariffs on the imports of bicycles will cause serious injury to American farmers," Secretary of Agriculture Benson told Eisenhower before he made his decision in the bicycle case. Similarly, Ambassador Winthrop Aldrich advised Secretary of State Dulles from London of the adverse effect the bicycle case was having in England. "Bicycles are . . . a crucial test of the whole idea of 'trade not aid.' [The] Entire British business community, and of course the Government, are watching this case with intense concern."[51]

Administration officials also expressed strong disagreement over the Defense Department's use of the Buy American Act. Intended to give domestic bidders an advantage over foreign competitors in government procurement, this legislation, originally passed during the Great Depression, clearly contradicted the principles of free trade. The Randall Commission had even proposed to give the president authority, under certain conditions, to exempt foreign bidders from its provisions.[52] Although Eisenhower agreed that the differential granted to American bidders over foreign bidders (about 25 percent) was too high, he did not favor eliminating the differential entirely. Instead, in December 1954 he issued an order that lowered the preference to 6 percent of the delivered foreign price or 10 percent of the price at port of entry. By this order domestic bidders were also given higher preference if their production facilities were located in areas with high unemployment rates. Many free-traders, including those within the administration, found this order unsatisfactory and were further disturbed by the fact that the British bid on generating equipment which the Defense Department had rejected was actually under the 6–10 percent differential established by the president.[53]

The administration's response to its critics was lame and unconvincing. In defending his decision in the bicycle case, Eisenhower said he had no other legal choice since the Tariff Commission had found sufficient evidence to warrant higher tariffs. The Defense Department maintained that the Buy American award was dictated by considerations of unemployment. Moreover, the White House stressed that the bicycle case and the Buy American action were special cases. "Policy is a fundamental guide to action and is not a categorical rule," Joseph Dodge told a Paris audience.[54] But as *Business Week* reported from Europe after the Pentagon made its decision on the British generating equipment, the "sincerity of President Eisenhower's trade policy is again being challenged in virtually every world trade center." "Whatever the merits of the case," it noted with regard to the bicycle decision, "U.S. trade relations are hurt. . . . Washington's decision [on generating equipment and bicycles] will be seized upon by European protectionists."[55] Together with the president's earlier decisions in the watch and lead and zinc cases, the amendments added by Congress to the Trade Agreements Act and accepted by the president, the failure by Congress to consider the OTC, and the administration's indifferent efforts in behalf of that organization, these most recent actions by the administration portended for some a new protectionism in the United States.[56]

Establishment of the International Finance Corporation

Trade liberalization was only one part of the administration's program for expanding world commerce. Almost as important, in its view, was the need to encourage the flow of U.S. private investment abroad, particularly to the world's underdeveloped countries. As Eisenhower had explained to Congress in January 1953, an increase in American private investment overseas, especially to Third World countries, would contribute much to international trade. It would allow underdeveloped nations to acquire the capital they so urgently needed for sound economic growth and higher living standards. "This would do much to offset the false but alluring promises of the Communists."[57]

The administration debated just how much the government should do to promote private investment abroad. The FOA was anxious to play a major role in encouraging the flow of American capital overseas, but the Department of Commerce was hesitant. Although the Commerce Department later established an Office for Foreign Investment which reported directly to the assistant secretary for international affairs, that official, Marshall M. Smith, thought the FOA was acting precipitously. It was stimulating a flow regardless of need or justification and without regard to the long-term implications of its policy.[58]

Most administration leaders believed, though, that without some major incentives from the public sector, private investors would hesitate to move into Third World areas, except in extractive industries. Even Joseph Dodge, one of the most conservative members of the administration, believed that the government had to stimulate American business to invest abroad. Private dollars would not simply move out at the request of Washington or some other government; businessmen had to be attracted by the likelihood of profit.[59]

To encourage American investment abroad, President Eisenhower made a number of recommendations to Congress, including extension of a 1942 provision (applicable to firms in South America) to reduce taxes on business income from foreign subsidiaries or branches to 14 percent below the rate on domestic corporate income.[60] The president also called for a deferral of taxes on income from foreign branches until repatriated in the United States and for exploring the idea of giving credits for foreign tax concessions made to overseas investors. Even more important, Eisenhower recommended American participation in an International Finance Corporation (IFC), which, it was proposed, would be affiliated with the World Bank.[61] The International

Advisory Board (the Rockefeller Committee) had made a similar proposal as early as 1951 as part of a series of recommendations to stimulate private investment abroad. According to the board, the IFC would use its $400 million in capital to make loans in local foreign currencies to private investors without government guaranty and to make equity investments in participation with private investors. The World Bank had also been interested in the IFC concept, having in fact, first proposed the idea to the Rockefeller Committee as a way of promoting a partnership between public and private investment. The United Nations' Economic and Social Council (ECOSOC) had invited the World Bank to consider whether an IFC could make significant contributions to economic development beyond those that could be made by existing organizations.[62]

At first the United States strongly opposed the IFC concept. Government leaders from the Treasury Department, the Federal Reserve Board, and the Eximbank especially objected to the concept of equity ownership of private enterprise by an intergovernmental organization. Officials of these financial agencies were also constrained by budgetary considerations since the bulk of the initial capital would come from the United States, and they were sensitive to business opposition to the proposal on the grounds that the IFC would encroach upon a field that should be reserved for private enterprise.[63] But as one high-level official of the World Bank later commented, the Bank kept in close contact with Washington about establishing an IFC affiliate.[64]

Bank President Eugene Black played a particularly crucial role in gaining U.S. support for the IFC. Black, who became president in 1949, had been brought into the Bank in 1947 as executive director for the United States by his predecessor, John McCloy. A former vice-president of the Chase Manhattan National Bank, Black was greatly concerned about the needs of the Third World and was anxious to expand the Bank's role in promoting economic development abroad, but he was limited by the Bank's requirement of government guarantees on its loans. He, too, favored the establishment of the IFC as an alternative to the Bank's normal lending channels.

To win U.S. backing for the IFC, Black altered the proposal first made by the Rockefeller Committee so as to keep the institution from making equity investments. Treasury Secretary Humphrey later announced that the United States had switched its position only on condition that the IFC not invest in stocks or other securities that would give it a voice in management. Instead, the IFC would be authorized to buy convertible income debentures, which it would sell when the enterprise became profitable. The purchasers could then convert the debentures into capital stock. Black also suggested lowering the capital of the IFC from the proposed $400 million to $100 million.[65]

Also decisive in changing the administration's position on the IFC was the White House's realization that, for reasons to be made clear shortly, it was simply not doing enough to promote economic development in the Third World. The United States was being hard pressed at the United Nations with a variety of demands from Third World countries, including a proposal for establishment of a development authority to make public grants. Likewise, the Soviet Union was trying to lure the underdeveloped nations with attractive trade proposals. Furthermore, the State Department felt strongly that the government had at least to make a gesture to Latin American nations, which were certain to promote economic development schemes at the Inter-American Conference of Finance Ministers in Rio de Janeiro in November.[66] By supporting the establishment of the IFC, the White House hoped to maintain its position in the Third World against Soviet penetration and, at the same time, to stave off more radical development proposals. Establishment of the IFC also comported with the administration's emphasis on working through the private sector to meet the capital needs of the underdeveloped countries. A group of experts assembled by the White House concluded that the problem of capital formation in Third World countries was "of critical importance" to the United States and that to the extent the IFC offered a solution to that problem, it merited the administration's serious consideration.[67]

In November 1954, therefore, Secretary Humphrey announced in Rio that the NAC had decided to seek congressional approval for U.S. membership in an IFC capitalized at $100 million. In May, Eisenhower sent a special message to Congress formally asking that it approve American participation in the IFC along with other measures to promote trade, including extension of the Trade Agreements Act, which Congress had not yet passed. Some opposition continued against the proposal. The influential National Foreign Trade Council (NFTC) stated that American participation in an IFC was "wrong in principle and dangerous in practice." Representative Wright Patman of Texas predicted the IFC would get a "cold shoulder" in Congress.[68] But accepting Secretary Humphrey's argument that the IFC was an experiment in government promotion of private enterprise abroad, the House and Senate passed the IFC legislation with little debate. Senator Fulbright expressed a widespread Capitol Hill sentiment when he remarked that establishment of the IFC would cut foreign-aid costs and create more demand for American products abroad. In approving U.S. membership in the IFC, Congress also authorized $35 million as the nation's subscription to the corporation's fund. By the end of 1955 the IFC was established as an affiliate of the World Bank with the United States as its principal member.[69]

In seeking U.S. participation in the IFC the White House clearly intended to rely on the private sector to promote economic development abroad. In this respect, its request for American membership in the new financial institution was consistent with its overall foreign economic program as defined by the concept of "trade not aid." In at least two other respects, however, its proposal marked a significant departure from previous policy. First, it represented the White House's recognition that the United States would have to do more to meet the economic growth needs of Third World nations. Second, it constituted a modest acknowledgment by the administration that government would have to become more active in assuring the basic requirements of economic growth.

Trade-Not-Aid Reconsidered

By the spring of 1955, in fact, the administration had begun to rethink its entire policy of relying almost exclusively on expanded trade through lower tariffs and on private investment to promote economic development abroad. The White House continued to stress the importance of world commerce and private capital in bringing about world-wide economic prosperity. But by the spring, a number of persons, including some close to Eisenhower, were urging the administration to make foreign economic policy more responsive to the special needs of the underdeveloped world. They were concerned about the recent loss of Indochina by the French. They were afraid that other Third World nations, particularly in the Far East, might fall within the Communist orbit unless these nations were propped up economically. They especially feared the rising tide of nationalism that was sweeping Asia and other Third World regions. Pointing to Communist gains in Indochina and raising the specter of Communist expansion in the rest of Asia, they called for increased economic aid to the world's most economically hard-pressed areas. Under pressure at home and abroad, the Eisenhower administration responded by taking the first steps toward increasing the flow of public capital sent abroad for development purposes.

Undoubtedly the most persistent champion of a new foreign economic policy was C. D. Jackson, a former special assistant to Eisenhower and now a vice-president of *Time* magazine. Reported to have been on Senator Joseph McCarthy's list of "dangerous liberals" within the administration, Jackson had resigned his position in March 1954, frustrated over the administration's handling of Soviet policy following the death of Joseph Stalin.[70] In lengthy correspondence with the president and leading White House officials, Jackson called for a "new world economic policy" by the administration. As early as August 1954 the former special assistant urged Eisenhower to make a speech outlining a bold new—but undefined—foreign economic program. "I am convinced," he told the president, "that both this country and the rest of the world need a big, imaginative, and dramatic foreign policy proposition from you now. It is the kind of big, bold approach that is typically American, and that American people want."[71]

Eisenhower responded unfavorably to Jackson's proposal for a speech, saying it would "take some doing" to make a talk "appear as a new bold and broad approach" and pointing out that any new proposals were liable to be viewed by cynics as "bigger and better give-aways."[72] But Jackson persisted with his proposal throughout the rest of the summer and fall. In November he sent Joseph Dodge a copy of a report which Professors Walt Rostow and

Max Millikan of M.I.T.'s Center for International Studies had written at Jackson's request and which outlined a number of recommendations for economic assistance.[73] This report is of considerable interest because it greatly influenced Jackson and, through him, received wide distribution within the administration. It also contained many of the ideas Millikan and Rostow later developed in a highly influential book and in a study prepared at the request of a special Senate committee investigating the U.S. foreign-aid program. Rostow, who met Eisenhower only once during his administration but served as an occasional consultant on such matters as the preparations for the Geneva Summit Conference of 1955 and the Lebanon-Jordan crisis of 1958, is particularly important. Not only was he a pioneer in the field of economic development theory, but he was also a transition figure, later serving as special assistant for national security affairs under Presidents Kennedy and Johnson. Many of his ideas on such matters as the pace of economic change abroad and the problem of indirect Communist aggression, which he first developed during the Eisenhower administration, influenced his recommendations in the 1960s, particularly as they involved Southeast Asia.[74]

In their report, which Jackson forwarded to Dodge, Rostow and Millikan called for a massive loan fund to aid the world's needy countries. The United States, they remarked, had fallen into a policy of relying too heavily on military and other "negative" policies. This had cost the country the confidence of underdeveloped nations, which looked to the Communist world as the model of economic progress. If the United States wished to maintain its own rate of economic growth and its free way of life, the industrialized trading nations, especially Germany and Japan, would have to find expanding markets not now in sight and the underdeveloped countries would have to be persuaded that the Western way of life offered an environment superior to that of the Communist world for economic growth. For these and other reasons, Rostow and Millikan proposed a $20 billion international loan fund for underdeveloped countries to which the United States would contribute $10 billion over a five-year period. (In a separate letter Rostow expressed his belief that most of this money should go to Asia, which, he remarked, was at the stage of economic development where assistance would be most productive.) They also sought increases in the United States' and United Nations' technical assistance programs and measures to liberalize world trade.[75]

In transmitting a copy of the Rostow and Millikan report to Dodge, Jackson stressed the importance he and his superiors attached to developing a new foreign economic program. "I think you should also know," he told Dodge, "that the Time Inc. publications feel very strongly about the need for a U.S. world Economic Policy, which must be more than just a warm-over of the hardy perennials which become a bore in this country and an irritation abroad." Jackson's letter was followed a few weeks later by a major story in *Time* magazine on the "new economic front" the United States was reported to be staking out in the Cold War.[76]

It is difficult to determine just what bearing Jackson's proposal for a new world economic program had on administration planning. Despite the extensive correspondence he undertook on behalf of his plan, Jackson never defined precisely what he had in mind other than the international loan fund recommended by Rostow and Millikan and grants-in-aid of about $360 million a year. Yet as *Time* reported, by the end of 1954 the administration had begun a major review of its foreign policy in which meeting the economic needs of Third World countries assumed great importance. While it seems certain that the Jackson proposal, along with the Rostow and Millikan report, were not by themselves responsible for this policy review, they did play an important role in bringing it about.[77]

Within the administration Secretary of State Dulles was particularly close to Jackson. The *Time* executive even claimed that his concept of a new world economic policy originated in a conversation he had had with the secretary of state in April.[78] Dulles was clearly not satisfied with the direction of U.S. foreign economic policy. He had already clashed with Treasury Secretary Humphrey over the lending policy of the Eximbank, and he was displeased with the president's decision in the Swiss watch case. According to Jackson, the secretary of state had complained to him about the watch decision and blamed Humphrey for what appeared to be an administration swing toward greater protectionism.[79] Dulles was not prepared to assume the lead in pushing the policy being promoted by Jackson. He told his friend that he found it "just not practical . . . to be a crusader for some particular program." At the same time, he also told Jackson that he was "100 percent" behind his type of investment scheme and remarked that it would be difficult to stop communism in much of the world if the United States could not "in some way duplicate the intensive Communist effort to raise productive standards."[80]

Although unwilling to fight very hard in behalf of Jackson's proposal, the secretary of state persuaded Eisenhower to establish a special interdepartmental committee to study the scheme. In two reports the committee concluded that the proposal was "essentially a wrap-up of existing programs" which contained nothing "really new in the sense of the atoms-for-peace proposal of last year." But the committee also remarked that a "bold, far reaching initiative in foreign economic policy should be undertaken." As to what that initiative should be, the committee remained as unclear as Jackson. The committee merely asserted that foreign economic policy should be based on the United States' short- and long-term interests and should contain the elements already outlined by the president. These included trade, public and private investment, convertibility, technical assistance programs overseas, stockpiling, and surplus disposal.[81]

At least one person in the administration, Harold Stassen, Director of the FOA, had something more precise in mind. A member of the Republican party's liberal wing, the former Minnesota governor had been brought into the administration in part because of his large following of young party progressives. In charge of the foreign-aid program, Stassen possessed considerable breadth of view on world affairs, but his self-indulgence and independence of action alienated most cabinet members and other administration officials.[82] In the fall of 1954 he was fighting to keep his agency from being abolished the following June as provided by the Mutual Security Act of 1954. Most of Eisenhower's advisers, including Dodge, Hauge, Randall, and Secretary Humphrey, favored terminating the FOA and transferring most of its functions to the Department of State. They felt personal animus toward Stassen, but more than that, they believed that the secretary of state's authority to provide policy guidelines had been weakened by the placing of foreign economic activities in an agency outside the State Department. In addition, many of them felt that the FOA had failed in its purpose of supervising and coordinating the nation's foreign-assistance programs.[83]

Although he had great personal respect for Stassen and was anxious to find him another government position, President Eisenhower, following the advice of most of his closest aids, decided not to save the FOA.[84] Instead, he chose to divide its functions between the Departments of State and Defense. To carry out the FOA's responsibilities within the State Department, the president established the International Cooperation Administration (ICA) as a semiautonomous agency with a relationship to the Department of State similar to that of the Federal Bureau of Investigation to the Justice Department.[85] As head of the ICA Eisenhower named former Congressman John B. Hollister, a law partner of the late Senator Robert Taft, who at the time of his appointment was serving as executive director of the Hoover Commission. The general feeling among government leaders was that Hollister would be much more conservative than Stassen in administering the foreign-aid program and more willing to adhere to policy guidelines laid down by the White House. Certainly he was less likely to undertake such efforts as developing state-owned industries abroad, as Stassen had done.[86]

Realizing the likelihood that the FOA would be abolished in June, Stassen strove to gain a new lease on life for his agency by proposing a broad program of development aid through grants to be administered by the FOA.[87] This proposal was not entirely self-serving. As early as 1950 he had proposed a "Marshall Plan for Asia,"[88] and in the aftermath of the French debacle in Indochina he believed a massive infusion of grant aid (as opposed to the loan fund recommended by Rostow and Millikan) was necessary to save the rest of Asia from falling to the Communists. In October 1954, Stassen spoke in Ottawa, Canada, at a meeting of members of the Colombo Plan, a mutual self-help organization for Asian members of the British Commonwealth which had been formed in 1950 and which the United States had joined the following year. He pledged increased economic aid to the non-Communist countries of Asia. He also expressed the expectation that the Colombo Plan would provide the basis for a regional economic organization to handle aid on a multilateral basis, much as the Organization for European Economic Cooperation

(OEEC) had handled the Marshall Plan. The organization would integrate investment and development, encourage freer regional trade, and provide a link between Japan's industrial economy and the producers of raw materials in South and Southeast Asia.[89]

Stassen's speech to the Colombo Plan conference stirred considerable controversy within the administration. The outline of the plan he presented at Ottawa had been approved by the National Security Council (NSC), and the State Department was by now also sympathetic to increasing economic assistance to Asia. But in his speech the FOA director left the impression that the United States would undertake a massive program for Asia like the one he had first proposed in 1950—that is, a program modeled after the Marshall Plan for Europe. In fact, Premier Shigeru Yoshida of Japan called for a $4 billion a year program for Asia patterned after the Marshall Plan to save it from falling entirely under Communist control. But no one within the State Department anticipated a program of that dimension. Opposition to any new program of economic aid also surfaced within the Treasury Department, which wanted to phase out economic assistance, and among such White House advisers as Clarence Randall, who maintained that such a program actually imperiled world economic recovery and would antagonize Congress unnecessarily.[90]

President Eisenhower remained outside the controversy as long as he could. But in December he, too, reached the conclusion that if Asia were not to fall entirely under Communist control, the United States would have to develop a new economic aid program for that continent. Months of discussion within the administration had convinced the president that the government would have to provide some public assistance. At a news conference he thus confirmed reports that in addition to normal mutual security grants, he would recommend to Congress the establishment of a special economic fund for Asia.[91] The only issues to be resolved were how large this fund was to be and who would control it. On these questions the president sided with those within the administration who wanted a frugal program run by the State Department rather than with Stassen. According to one news report, in a meeting with Eisenhower, Treasury Secretary Humphrey told the president that Congress would never approve a large foreign-aid package. The secretary was reportedly reassured that any special program for Asia would be in terms of millions and not hundreds of millions or even billions of dollars.[92]

The next month Secretary of State Dulles announced that while Asia would get more economic aid, the program would not be anything like the Marshall Plan. Unlike Europe, which had an industrial plant that could be rebuilt with American dollars, the industrial plant in Asia had to be built from scratch and needed trained men to run it. This would require a much longer process of planning and programming and less initial funding. To determine the actual level of spending for Asia, the NSC established a committee on Asian economic policy headed by Undersecretary of State Herbert Hoover, Jr. In January the committee decided upon $205 million for the special Asian economic fund, a sum that was, of course, far less than either Stassen or Asian leaders had hoped for.[93]

In February the FOA outlined the rationale for the Asian fund in its instructions for preparing the next year's mutual security requests. The fund "would not be . . . primarily . . . a catch-all or general contingency fund for the Far East," the FOA stated, "but rather [would serve] as one of the tools through which a rational approach to the economic development of the free nations in the area could be stimulated and furthered." The fund would also contribute to the planning and carrying out of a sound and comprehensive long-range plan for economic development. "[It] would be aimed at dealing constructively with the economic problems that threaten the political, social and economic stability [of Asia] and which are creating the kind of conditions which lend themselves to successful political and economic aggression and subversion on the part of the Communists."[94] To publicize the fund, Stassen made a month-long trip to Asia at the end of February and, along with Secretary Dulles, attended the final session of the 1955 Southeast Asia Treaty Organization (SEATO) conference in Thailand. From his trip he concluded that while the odds were at least even that the policy and programs established by the NSC could be implemented, their success was by no means certain. But the alternative to Western participation in Asian economic development was "an Asian wildfire with Communists included and white men excluded."[95]

On April 20 Eisenhower sent his annual foreign-aid requests to Congress. In his message the president asked for an appropriation of $200 million for the establishment of a President's Fund for Asian Economic Development. Although he sought only a one-year appropriation, he requested authority to expend the money over a period of years. The immediate threat to world security and stability was now Asia, Eisenhower noted, and he indicated he would use most of the funds requested of Congress in that region. It was his belief that most of the responsibility for economic development in Asia rested with the Asians themselves. Foreign capital and foreign aid could only stimulate the development process. Recognizing this, he added, the United States nonetheless had "the capacity, the desire, the concern to take the lead in friendly help for free Asia."[96]

Congressional debate over the 1955 mutual security bill followed an already well-established pattern. In July, Congress authorized a $3.29 billion foreign-aid measure that was only $245 million less than what the president had asked for and included the $200 million for the special Asian economic fund Eisenhower had requested. As a result of Democratic victories in the 1954 off-year elections, key congressional committees had been organized by the Democrats rather than by Eisenhower's opponents within the right wing of the GOP. These committees included the House Foreign Affairs Committee, now chaired by James P. Richards of South Carolina, and the Senate Foreign Relations Committee, headed by Walter F. George of Georgia. Both men were respected internationalists who worked closely with the president to defeat efforts to restrict economic assistance, including the cutting or elimination of the Asian fund.[97]

In a process already familiar to Eisenhower, however, the foreign-aid measure fared less well in the final appropriations vote. Restive over annual foreign-aid requests and piqued by the administration's use of uncommitted foreign-aid funds in the final moments of fiscal 1955, the House and Senate cut the White House's mutual security proposals by over $560 million. Although the biggest cut was in military assistance, the reductions also pared $100 million from the Asian fund, leaving only $100 million for fiscal 1956. The President's Fund for Asian Economic Development, Republican Senator William E. Jenner of Indiana had remarked during the appropriations debate, was "designed to fit the will-o'-the-wisp nonsense that . . . American spending in poor areas of the world will prevent Communists from getting in. This idea is so completely fallacious that it has been used again and again by the Communists to help us spend our way to bankruptcy."[98]

Even within the administration, opposition to special economic aid for Asia remained strong. In a lengthy report and memorandum on Asia and other underdeveloped areas, Joseph Dodge analyzed what he regarded as the fundamental problems related to economic progress in Asia. There was in the government a general lack of understanding of the obstacles to economic development in South and Southeast Asia and of the fundamental differences between encouraging economic progress in the region and reconstructing Europe. In his view the real problem was overcoming the obstacles to private investment in the region. The accumulation of savings for capital purposes was not being generated or encouraged in Asia. There was little or no investment market and hardly any security for foreign capital. Socialism and expropriation, limitations on the export of earnings, and government monopoly and control of markets and foreign exchange loomed as very real dangers. "Progress grows from within," Dodge commented. "[It] cannot be imposed from without, cannot be imported like a finished industrial product, or supplied merely by massive injections of dollars."[99]

Dodge's arguments against increased economic assistance abroad and the fact that he was supported by others within the administration, including Clarence Randall and Secretary Humphrey, suggested how committed the administration remained to promoting world economic progress through the private sector. But Eisenhower's endorsement of a special Asian fund also made it clear that the White House was prepared to increase foreign aid in order to promote development in Third World areas deemed crucial to the United States. Indeed, even Dodge recognized that in some instances the United States would have to do more to foster development abroad. Under his direction the CFEP issued a memorandum recommending the establishment of a U.S. International Development Fund. According to the memorandum, the fund would "fill a gap in present loan and assistance programs that seriously limit their [own] effectiveness in getting the development process underway in the Free World." Its basic objective would be political as well as economic: to keep the underdeveloped countries from falling to the Communists. In administering the fund, therefore, emphasis would "often be upon securing the greatest possible political impact, and not necessarily upon securing the greatest possible economic impact."[100]

The questions that would increasingly face the administration, then, were not whether to promote development abroad through increased public assistance, but for what purpose and in what form. With respect to the first question, the administration would have to weigh the relative importance of the short-term political objectives stressed by the CFEP against the nation's longer-term economic and political goals. It would not always be clear which goals had higher priority within the administration and among advocates of expanded foreign economic aid. As to the second question, there were essentially two options, grants or loans. Most U.S. economic aid took the form of grants. The mutual security program authorized four categories of grant assistance: (1) defense support for nations that need to expand their defense facilities beyond their normal levels; (2) development assistance; (3) technical cooperation; and (4) "other programs," a loose category that included a number of UN funds and the Asian development fund. Of these categories, defense support was by far the largest, accounting in the Mutual Security Act of 1955 for over $1 billion versus only $182 million for development assistance, $172 million for technical cooperation, and $459 million for "other programs."[101] In addition, the Eximbank made loans for development purposes. Finally, the United States relied heavily on the World Bank to finance economic development abroad, and the IFC had been established to promote private investment overseas through nonequity loans to private enterprise.

All these agencies were hard lenders, however; they followed, or in the case of the IFC it was intended that they follow, strict commercial banking practices in matters such as the rates of interest they charged and the periods they allowed for repayment.[102] In contrast to "hard loans," "soft loans" involved concessions by the lender, such as a longer repayment period than was customary in commercial banking circles, lower interest rates than normal, repayment in inconvertible funds, or any combination of these easier terms. The Mutual Security Act of 1954 mandated the use of loans and allowed for repayment on soft terms. It required that $200 million of the total authorization be made available only as loans repayable in U.S. or foreign currencies or by transfer of materials needed for stockpiling. It also required that 30 percent of development assistance to Bolivia, India, the Near East, and Africa consist of loans repayable in soft currencies. Although the 1955 act eliminated the 30 percent provision, it stipulated that at least 50 percent of the special Asian fund be granted on a soft-loan basis.[103]

As the Eisenhower administration moved increasingly to promote development abroad through public assistance, it adopted the strategy of relying on soft lending. There were several reasons why it decided to pursue this policy. First, soft lending was in keeping with the president's commitment to curtail grant aid as much as possible. Second, soft lending was more acceptable to Congress than grants, which bore the burden of being a "give-away" program. Those to whom loans were made were expected to repay them, albeit on concessionary terms. Having the obligation to repay, recipients were likely to be more prudent in their use of funds than nations that had no obligations—or at least so Congress reasoned. In contrast, hard loans imposed repayment obligations upon recipients which most countries in need of development assistance would be reluctant to accept, in part because they would not be easily able to meet these obligations without curtailing their development programs. Thus, soft loans appeared to the administration to be a compromise between increasingly unacceptable grant aid and hard loans. Soft loans would make possible a real transfer of resources from the United States to underdeveloped countries in a manner that they could handle and that Congress was more likely to tolerate.

For this reason the CFEP recommended as early as March 1955 that the administration use more soft loans. "While there are many problems to be resolved in connection with this type of transaction," the committee pointed out, "it seems reasonable to assume that a proposal to expand the lending approach and reduce the grant approach would strike a responsive chord in the Congress and with the public." The CFEP even proposed that a Foreign Development Loan Corporation be established as a second window of the Eximbank, much as the IFC was to be a second window of the World Bank. The loan corporation would finance projects that not only benefited foreign nations but "further[ed] the foreign policy objectives of the United States."[104] In 1957 the administration established the Development Loan Fund much along the lines first recommended by the CFEP in 1955.

Conclusion

From the summer of 1954 to the summer of 1955 the Eisenhower administration began to consider alternatives to world economic development other than its stated policy of "trade not aid." In this sense, the year was a transition period for the administration. Trade-not-aid remained its preferred approach to world economic problems, but the White House recognized that in light of the threat posed by Communist expansion, this program by itself was insufficient to deal with the pressing problems of Third World economic development. Toward the end of 1955 the problem of economic development appeared even more urgent as the Soviet bloc began what the White House termed an "economic offensive" in the world's underdeveloped regions.

4. The Soviet Economic Challenge 1955–1956

PRIOR TO THE MID-1950s the United States had perceived the Soviet threat to the West as largely a military one, and thus, much of its mutual security assistance had been military in nature. For fiscal 1951, for example, Congress had appropriated $5.2 billion for military aid and $2.1 billion for economic and "other" assistance. For fiscal 1952 the figures were $5.3 billion and $2.0 billion; for 1953, $4.1 billion and $1.9 billion; and for 1954, $3.2 billion and $1.5 billion. Only for fiscal 1955, when the size of the military assistance program dropped to $1.3 billion (largely because the forward programming of military assistance was reduced) did the appropriation for economic and "other" assistance exceed that for military aid. Even then the figure for "other" assistance, $1.5 billion, was about the same as for the previous year. Except for a few economic development programs, purely economic aid had been virtually eliminated by fiscal 1955. Of these development programs, aid to India in support of its five-year plan of economic development was the largest.[1]

Since the United States' embarkation on a major foreign-aid program in 1948, the program's emphasis had shifted from economic assistance to Europe to military assistance to Europe and then to military assistance to Asia. The perception of the Soviet threat as fundamentally a military one was evident in the Senate Foreign Relations Committee's report on the mutual security program for 1955. "The magnitude of the Soviet threat has in no wise diminished in the last year," the committee noted. "Indeed, it has, if anything, increased. The Soviets continue to build airfields in Eastern Europe; they continue to increase the strength of the military forces available to them."[2]

As the United States began to pay more attention to the development needs of Third World countries, however, beginning sometime around 1955 the administration and Congress began to view the Soviet challenge to the West as being economic and political. This change in perception did not come about by mere chance. Prior to 1953 the Soviet Union had displayed little interest in developing trade or other economic ties with Third World nations. Because its foreign policy was based on the concept of a bipolar world and was oriented toward Europe, it had failed to exploit the growing sense of nationalism already evident in Southern Asia and the Middle East. Soviet professions of support for newly developing nations rang empty as local Communist parties remained alienated from mass movements abroad.[3]

The death of Joseph Stalin in 1953 led to a change in Soviet policy. The new leadership—first of Georgi M. Malenkov, then of Nikolai Bulganin and Nikita Khrushchev, and finally of Khrushchev alone—adopted a global strategy that sought to expand Soviet influence in Third World and neutralist nations. A policy based on bipolarity was modified to one predicated on "zones of peace," which justified the Soviet appeal to neutralist nations on the grounds of their importance and the ability of "socialist" forces to gain power through parliamentary means. This policy was formally enunciated in 1956 at the Twentieth Congress of the Soviet Communist party. Meanwhile, Soviet leaders courted Third World nations by visiting such countries as India and Burma, where they made lavish promises of economic assistance. Soviet delegates to the United Nations also attempted to align themselves with underdeveloped and neutral nations by supporting expanded programs of UN economic aid.[4]

Soviet economic and diplomatic efforts in Third World countries were also part of a fundamental shift in Soviet policy toward relaxing some of the Cold War tensions of the previous ten years and reaching a political accommodation with the West. Instead of stressing the inevitability of military confrontation with the West, the emphasis in Moscow became one of peaceful economic cooperation and competition. As part of this new policy, the Soviets sought to expand the channels of East-West trade even as they competed with the West among the world's neutral and nonaligned nations. This policy of "peaceful coexistence" resulted in the Austrian peace treaty of 1955 and, in July of that year, in a summit conference of the Western powers and the Soviet Union in Geneva.[5]

The response by the United States to the Soviet peace initiative was a mixture of cautious optimism and unrelenting suspicion and distrust. Returning from Geneva, Eisenhower talked of a new spirit of conciliation and cooperation that had developed between the Soviet Union and the Western powers.[6] This "spirit of Geneva" left many Americans persuaded that the end of the Cold War was at hand. In terms of the nation's foreign economic policy, it encouraged the movement for relaxation of controls on East-West trade. Under pressure from Europe, Eisenhower was already proposing to lift some of these restrictions. The new spirit of cooperation engendered at Geneva added momentum to his efforts. Yet Congress not only rejected these efforts at peaceful coexistence; it also accused the administration of trying to subvert the intention of the legislation regulating East-West trade by allowing strategic goods to reach the Soviet Union through third countries. Moreover, the president and his advisers remained deeply distrustful of Moscow and regarded the shift in Soviet policy as only a change in tactics, with the Soviet purpose still being world domination.

The United States was especially concerned about the Soviets' economic efforts in the Third World. It perceived Moscow's courtship of Third World countries as a Soviet "economic offensive" that threatened to tie the world's underdeveloped areas closely to the Communist bloc. The continued growth of nationalism in such areas as Southern Asia and the Middle East and this "economic offensive" underscored for the Eisenhower administration the urgency of increasing the United States' own program of economic assistance to needy nations. Given the spread of neutralism and nonalignment among Third World countries, the Soviet offensive also raised fundamental questions in the White House and in Congress about the purpose and effectiveness of the nation's mutual security legislation and led to the most exhaustive studies of the foreign-aid program since adoption of the Marshall Plan in 1948.

East-West Trade

When Eisenhower assumed office in 1953, economic ties between the West and Communist bloc nations were closely regulated. The Mutual Defense Assistance Control Act of 1951 (the Battle Act) controlled exports of strategic materials that posed a threat to the United States. It also provided for the termination of aid to friendly nations that violated controls on such trade. The Battle Act embargo list, established unilaterally by the United States, was one of several lists used to regulate Western exports to Communist countries. The Department of Commerce controlled American exports to these nations under authority of the Export Control Act of 1947, which provided for regulation of exports for reasons of short supply, foreign policy, and national security. According to this legislation, exporters had to secure licenses from the Commerce Department before they could ship goods out of the United States. The principal means of regulating trade with the Soviet bloc, however, was an agreement between the United States and fourteen other nations, including most of the NATO powers, Japan, and West Germany. Goods embargoed by this group were similar to, although not the same as, those on the Battle Act and Commerce Department lists.[7]

After the Korean War, however, the countries of Western Europe began to pressure Washington to relax restrictions on East-West trade, and particularly on trade with the Soviet bloc. Regarding expanded commerce as crucial to Europe's continued economic recovery from World War II and as a substitute for further U.S. aid, Washington agreed to soften its trade controls. In 1954 it revised all three of its control lists. The effect was to reduce the number of embargoed items and to tighten controls on the remainder. Announcing changes in the Battle Act lists, FOA director Harold Stassen pointed out that the changes applied only to the Soviet Union and its European satellites. The much more restrictive UN embargo on trade with Communist China that had been instituted during the Korean War remained in effect.[8]

During the next year pressure grew in the United States among farm and business groups to relax East-West trade even more, and the "spirit of Geneva" that resulted from the July 1955 summit meeting strengthened this movement. The president of the Iowa Farm Bureau Federation wrote Secretary

Benson in August that farm sentiment he had surveyed was "universally favorable" to expanding trade with the Soviet Union. Undersecretary of Agriculture True D. Morse told Herbert Hoover, Jr., that it would be "short-sighted policy" not to trade with Eastern Europe, and that commerce in "soft goods" with the Soviet Union would diminish the Soviets' capacity to purchase the "hard goods" that added to their war-making potential. Trade in soft goods, Morse added, would also lead Soviet citizens to demand more consumer goods at the expense of war-related industries.[9]

President Eisenhower strongly supported these efforts to increase economic ties with Eastern Europe. True, when questioned at the beginning of 1955 as to whether he approved of a statement by Secretary of Defense Charles Wilson favoring nonstrategic trade with the Communist bloc, he said he did not.[10] But the administration remained divided on the issue of East-West trade. In a paper prepared for the CFEP, George Nebolsine, a staff member, argued that strategic controls remained necessary and were a useful part of the collective security framework.[11] Joseph Dodge opposed any relaxation of controls on trade with the Soviet bloc and, while in Europe, spoke out against official trade talks between the Soviet Union and West Germany. Even if the Soviets' apparently peaceful intentions could be taken at face value, the CFEP chairman noted, any resources supplied to the Soviet Union by the West would free Soviet resources for use by China, whose peaceful intentions were not assured. "We should not be willing," Dodge added, "to move soon to relieve an acknowledged adversary of his economic problems."[12]

Others within the administration, including the president, took a different view. As Eisenhower's former speechwriter, Emmet Hughes, later noted, the president generally supported economic contact with Communist-controlled countries as part of his policy of widening the channels of trade and commerce throughout the world. Eisenhower thus remarked at a news conference that so long as the United States was not helping the war-making powers of other nations, it would study the question of East-West trade objectively "and not just go by preconception."[13] The favorable diplomatic climate generated by the Geneva Summit Conference in July inclined the president even more to relax controls with the Soviet bloc countries. In a statement issued at Geneva, Eisenhower noted that one of the meeting's purposes was to "create conditions which will encourage nations to increase the exchange of peaceful goods throughout the world."[14] Although nothing concrete developed as a result of the summit, at a meeting of foreign ministers in October the United States joined with England and France in offering to remove barriers to Soviet trade, travel, and cultural exchange. Two days later the Commerce Department announced that it would relax controls on exports to the Soviet Union and its satellites on January 1 by issuing general, instead of individual, licenses for nonembargoed goods. Agriculture Secretary Benson even hinted in Washington that the United States might be ready to sell government-owned farm surpluses to the Soviets at cut-rate prices.[15]

At the beginning of 1956, however, England asked the United States to loosen controls on trade with Communist China as well. Prime Minister Anthony Eden presented President Eisenhower with a list of items for decontrol during his visit to the United States at the end of January. The British view was that ultimately the same control list should apply to China as applied to other Communist countries. Eden proposed that some items be decontrolled immediately, but indicated that he was willing to wait on other items if the United States would consider putting China on the same basis as other Communist bloc countries.[16] Eisenhower was not yet prepared to modify the United States' embargo on trade with China, and he and Eden reached an understanding on the continuation of these controls, but the president did agree that a study should be made of the commodities subject to those controls. On this basis he directed the CFEP to review the list of items on the British decontrol list, and a joint British-American press release to this effect was issued.[17]

This announcement by the White House caused a wave of criticism throughout the United States, and in Congress it added to an already growing movement against any relaxation of controls on East-West trade. The chairman of the Senate's Permanent Investigations Subcommittee, John McClellan of Arkansas, reported that his subcommittee had received "very disturbing" information on the extent of strategic commerce with the Soviet bloc since the relaxation of controls in 1954 and announced that the subcommittee would begin hearings in February on trade with the Soviet Union and its satellites.[18] At the hearings a number of serious allegations were made against the White House. Senator Stuart Symington, Democrat of Missouri, for example, said that some machine tools taken off the control list could actually handle up to 90 percent of the work load of a plant producing goods for use in war. John H. Williams, a Defense Department machine tool specialist, remarked that the United States had agreed to relax restrictions on the sale to the Soviet Union of machine tools "whose use for peacetime purposes would be the exception." He added that these sales amounted to allowing Moscow to "overtake" the United States in arms production.[19]

At a news conference President Eisenhower attempted to defend his administration against the charges that relaxation of the 1954 embargo list had been a mistake by pointing out the importance of East-West trade to the nation's European allies.[20] Testifying before the McClellan Committee, former FOA director Stassen remarked that pressure from the Western allies had reached a point in 1954 where "it was no longer possible to hold the higher levels of control." Stassen also denied that relaxation of controls had harmed the West. But this argument was brought into serious question when, on the grounds of national security and executive privilege, the administration refused to transmit documents sought by the subcommittee or to testify in public about the United States' role in reshaping East-West trade policies.[21] By the end of February, sentiment in Congress was running so strong against the White House that Joseph Dodge, who had the major responsibility for reviewing the British request to ease controls with China, advised the administration to proceed cautiously before responding to the British. He reminded State Department and White House officials that hasty or ill-conceived action by the administration could destroy the chances of getting its foreign-aid program through Congress.[22]

Eisenhower continued to favor some relaxation of controls with the Communist bloc. He told Bernard Baruch that a few types of machinery that the Soviet Union wanted as patterns and models should be kept on the embargo list. Otherwise he was persuaded that the effort to dam up "the natural currents of trade," particularly between such areas as Japan and Communist China, would fail.[23] But faced with a hostile, even rebellious, Congress and a divided administration, Eisenhower agreed not to take any additional steps to expand East-West trade.[24] Ten days later, Commerce Secretary Sinclair Weeks warned against giving Moscow any technical knowledge through trade and soon thereafter rejected an application by Dresser Industries of Dallas, Texas, to swap technical data on rock drill bits for rights to manufacture a new Soviet turbodrill. The Commerce Department also shelved plans to free a long list of goods for export to Soviet bloc countries.[25]

In July the McClellan Committee filed its report on East-West trade. The committee accused the administration of violating "the spirit if not the letter" of the Battle Act, which called for termination of aid to countries that knowingly shipped goods to Communist countries. It also accused the White House of permitting the sale of strategic materials to the Soviet Union and its satellites. It recommended that the Battle Act be either repealed entirely or strengthened in order to assure adherence to its purpose of regulating trade in strategic items.[26] Commenting on the committee's report, Sinclair Weeks quoted from a *New York Times* article which stated that the Senate had ignored the essential issues involved in East-West trade.[27] In truth, Congress had effectively forced the administration to retreat from its efforts to expand the channels of commerce with the Soviet bloc, which might have contributed to the spirit of conciliation that came out of the Geneva conference of July.

The Soviet Economic Offensive

Whereas the White House had been at odds with the hard line adopted by Congress on the issue of East-West trade, it followed its own hard line with respect to Soviet economic efforts in Third World countries. Instead of viewing Moscow's economic activities in the Third World as peaceful competition with the West, it regarded the Soviet effort as a dangerous ploy whose implications for the West were almost as serious as military aggression. In this respect, the much-heralded "spirit of Geneva" proved largely illusory.

The Soviet Union actually began its economic efforts among underdeveloped countries in July 1953, when it announced at the sixteenth session of ECOSOC that it was contributing four million rubles to the UN's Expanded

Program of Technical Assistance. The next year Moscow expressed to India its willingness to aid that country in constructing a huge steel mill. Even though its previous economic relations with that country had been confined to trade, it sent a survey team to India to conduct a feasibility study and select a site for the mill. In February 1955 it signed a contract to construct at Bhilai a mill that would have an annual capacity of 1 million tons of ingot steel.[28]

Soviet economic efforts in the Third World took three forms—technical assistance, expanded trade, and the extension of credits. By August 1956 the Soviet bloc had technicians working in at least fourteen countries in Asia and the Middle East. It also had contracted with many of these countries to train their nationals as technicians in the Soviet Union—among them, over 700 Indian steel workers, engineers, and technicians. Meanwhile, Soviet bloc trade agreements with non-Communist countries increased from 113 at the end of 1953 to 203 by the third quarter of 1956. In 1953 one third of these agreements were with underdeveloped countries; by late 1956 more than half were with these nations. Practically all new Soviet bloc agreements signed in 1956 were with Third World countries. Total turnover in the Soviet bloc's trade with underdeveloped nations increased from approximately $850 million in 1954 to $1.44 billion in 1956, or by about 70 percent.[29]

The most striking aspect of the Soviets' new foreign economic policy, however, was the extension of foreign credits. Unlike the United States, the Soviet Union almost never made foreign grants. Moreover, compared to the U.S. foreign-aid program, including both grants and loans, the Soviet effort was minuscule. Since 1945, U.S. loans had totaled $9.5 billion, and grants, $47.5 billion, while only $1.4 billion in credits had been extended or committed by the Soviet bloc. In addition, Soviet credits were limited to a few countries— Egypt, Syria, India, Afghanistan, Indonesia, and Yugoslavia—and the purpose of these loans varied considerably. Credits were extended for such projects as steel mills, sugar processing plants, cement plants, textile mills, fertilizer plants, and atomic research facilities, and approximately $300–$400 million was loaned to Egypt, Syria, and Afghanistan to purchase arms.[30] Thus, the increase in economic credits to Third World nations beginning in 1954 represented a major departure for the Soviet bloc. Moreover, the program grew rapidly after 1954. During the first eight months of 1956 alone, Soviet bloc countries extended $600 million in credits and were negotiating other loans estimated to have a value of $200 million.[31]

Recipient and other Third World nations were generally impressed by this Soviet effort. Seeking support for their economic development programs, they welcomed Soviet aid. India took aid wherever it could find it. Afghanistan and Indonesia accepted assistance not only for development purposes but also to strengthen their military positions in regional disputes. Anxious to industrialize quickly, Third World nations admired the rapidity with which the Soviet Union had industrialized, and, for the most part, they responded positively to the Soviet emphasis on centralized planning. Often distrustful of the West and fearful of threats to their independence, many of them preferred long-term loans at low interest rates (usually 2.0 or 2.5 percent, and repayable over forty years) to the obligations implicit in grant assistance. Furthermore, neutralist nations objected to the United States' growing emphasis on military pacts (SEATO and the Baghdad Pact of 1955) and were quick to play off the Soviet Union against the West in anticipation of obtaining more aid from Washington. Finally, Third World nations regarded expanded trade with the Soviet Union as an opportunity to barter surplus commodities such as Egyptian cotton or Burmese rice for needed industrial goods.[32]

Soviet economic activity in Third World regions affected the United States' relations with those areas in a number of ways. For example, Burma asked Washington to end its aid program and withdraw its mission from Burma (although subsequent bad economic and political dealings with the Soviet bloc led the government to reopen negotiations with the United States). Similarly, Indonesia objected to the terms of a P.L. 480 loan and used more favorable Soviet terms as a bargaining tool with American negotiators.[33] The major impact of the Soviet foreign economic program, however, was in the Middle East, where the Soviets were able to exploit the long-festering Arab-Israeli problem, the Anglo-Egyptian dispute over the Suez Canal, and widespread anticolonial sentiment to strengthen their position in the region. As part of its program to gain political influence in the Middle East, Moscow sold large quantities of arms to Egypt and Syria and made substantial purchases of Egyptian cotton.[34]

The American Response

Washington responded with considerable alarm to these efforts at economic diplomacy by the Soviet Union. The administration's first reaction to the Soviet initiative came as early as December 1954, when in a legislative leadership meeting at the White House, FOA director Stassen warned that the Soviet Union was using trade and technical assistance as instruments of foreign policy. Six months later Stassen again referred to Soviet economic activity abroad, this time expressing the need to prevent Soviet domination of India's economy. On this ground alone he justified the emphasis being given to Asia in the mutual security program for 1955, including the special Asian economic fund. Above all, he said, a patient, persistent, tireless effort was necessary to offset the Communist move in Asia.[35] Secretary of State Dulles made similar comments at the end of June. Pointing out that a sizeable portion of the mutual security program was in the form of soft loans, the secretary commented that the loss of India's vast population to communism would have a great and serious impact throughout Asia. The United States was not awarding gifts for policies it liked, he remarked with reference to India's program of nationalization. It was simply trying to prevent India from moving toward communism.[36]

Passage of the final mutual security legislation for 1955, with its $100 million cut in the special Asian economic fund, only added to the concern of those who saw mounting evidence of Soviet economic penetration throughout the world. C. D. Jackson renewed his efforts on behalf of a new world economic policy. Czechoslovakia had concluded a spectacular arms sale to Egypt, he told Nelson Rockefeller, and it was common knowledge that Syria, Saudi Arabia, Lebanon, and Afghanistan were considering similar offers. A Soviet treaty of friendship had just been signed with Yemen, and Libya was being promised Soviet support in its bid for a seat at the UN. The Hungarians were shipping locomotives and freight cars to Egypt. Czech trucks were being sent to Jordan, Czech tractors to the Sudan. "The moment of decision is upon us in a great big way on world economic policy," Jackson remarked to Rockefeller. "So long as the Soviets had a monopoly on covert subversion and threats of military aggression, and we had a monopoly on Santa Claus, some kind of seesaw game could be played." But now the Soviets were "muscling in on Santa Claus," which placed the United States in a dangerous position.[37]

No one was more concerned about the Soviet economic threat than the president himself. Notwithstanding the moderating effect of the Geneva summit conference on White House perceptions of the Soviet leadership and Eisenhower's eagerness to expand economic and cultural contact with the Soviet Union and other Communist countries, the president remained deeply distrustful of Moscow's intentions. In a letter written just a few months before he went to Geneva, Eisenhower bitterly assailed the Soviet Union and China and left no doubt about his belief that their ultimate aim was world conquest. To his friend Lewis Douglas he described a life-and-death struggle of ideologies. Freedom was pitted against dictatorship, communism against capitalism, concepts of human dignity against the materialistic dialectic. The Communists had announced their commitment to world revolution. They were contemptuous of the concepts of honor, decency, and integrity, on which international law and order was based. It was clear "that if the Communists achieve[d] their world aims, there [would] be no American history as we know it."[38]

Nothing that occurred at Geneva led Eisenhower to alter these basic views. Indeed, the failure of the summit to settle any concrete Cold War issues, together with expanded Soviet economic activity abroad, persuaded the president that the United States could not afford to slacken its efforts to contain the Communist threat. In December he even commented about the "irony" of Moscow's having chosen economic grounds for competition with the United States. Although the United States' economy was stronger than that of the Soviet Union, Eisenhower noted that a dictatorship such as Moscow's could overcome this inherent disadvantage by choosing its own grounds on which to compete. In January he told Douglas that it "was idle to suppose" that the Soviet Union had "any friendly interest in the countries that she proposes to help"; Moscow's purpose was to damage the United States' relationship with those countries and then to use its "economic penetration to accomplish political domination."[39]

At the end of January, Eisenhower met with Dodge and Secretary Dulles to discuss Soviet Cold War economic activities. Dodge thought the administration was overreacting to the Soviet economic threat in the Third World. As he later commented to Herbert Hoover, Jr., there was "too much of [a] tendency [at the White House] to make the Russians twelve feet high and way ahead of [the United States] in everything." The CFEP chairman questioned, for example, Moscow's ability to expand its economic initiatives abroad considering its pressing domestic needs and its relatively low gross national product.[40] One reason that he opposed lifting controls on trade with the Soviet Union was his belief that this would relieve Moscow of an obstacle to economic activity abroad. Nevertheless, Dodge concurred with the others at the meeting on the need to centralize information and distribute a biweekly report on the "Soviet economic offensive," as it was now called. The Central Intelligence Agency (CIA) was given responsibility for preparing the biweekly reports as well as for preparing a summary of current Soviet activities. Meanwhile, acting independently, the ICA prepared its own study of Soviet bloc economic efforts in the Near East, Africa, and Asia.[41]

In March, the White House organized a private citizens' group and a government policy agency composed of representatives from the Departments of State, Treasury, Commerce, Defense, and Agriculture and from the ICA to consider the United States' response to the Soviet offensive abroad.[42] That same month Eisenhower made the Soviet economic offensive the theme of his message to Congress on the mutual security program for 1957. The Soviets had replaced military aggression with new economic maneuvers, the president told Congress. These included bilateral trade agreements on arms and capital goods as well as technical assistance. If he could believe that Moscow had abandoned its "sinister objectives" to help achieve freedom and independence for other nations, he would welcome the new Soviet program. But this was not the case. The Soviets were selling arms and seeking to exploit ancient animosities. "We must therefore assume that Soviet expansionism has merely taken on a somewhat different guise and that its fundamental objective is still to disrupt and in the end to dominate the free nations."[43]

Although Eisenhower remarked that he did not intend to allow the Soviet offensive to influence his mutual security requests, his aid recommendations did reflect this concern. Most important was his request for a flexible aid program that would allow him to make long-term aid commitments of up to ten years' duration, but that would limit those commitments to $100 million in any one year. Long-term commitments, he explained, would enable non-Communist nations to mobilize their resources and plan an intelligent development program. In addition, Eisenhower asked for a second $100 million for the President's Emergency Fund (established in 1955) and for authority to use part of these funds for such purposes as the president determined vital to national security. Pointing to the need to solicit the friendship of nations in the Middle East and Africa, Eisenhower also called for a special $100 million fund for these areas. Finally, the president requested release of the $100 million for the Asian fund that had been authorized but not appropriated in 1955.[44] The total mutual security request of $4.67 billion for fiscal 1957 was almost $1.4 billion higher than that authorized by Congress the previous year and nearly $2 billion more than the aid funds actually appropriated for fiscal 1956. But as the president had commented earlier at a news conference, the Soviet economic offensive was forcing the United States to review its foreign economic policy.[45]

The 1956 Struggle over Mutual Security

In planning its mutual security requests for fiscal 1957, the White House misread the temper of Congress. It expected some objections to its requests, particularly for aid to neutralist nations like India. But for the most part the White House believed that the House and Senate would approve its foreign-aid package.[46] It was surprised, therefore, at the widespread opposition to the program in Congress, which included not only die-hard Republican opponents of foreign aid like Senator William Knowland of California but Democratic internationalists like Senators Walter George and Richard Russell of Georgia and Mike Mansfield of Montana. Even Dodge was taken aback by Congress's reaction to Eisenhower's foreign-aid requests. "This is inherent in our established government process but is self-defeating against the arbitrary and opportunistic actions and decisions which can be quickly made and implemented by the Soviet leadership," he remarked.[47]

During the next several months the administration sought to mobilize congressional support for its mutual security program. In hearings that began before the House Foreign Affairs Committee in March and before the Senate Foreign Relations Committee in April, administration witnesses stressed the need for adequate funds to counter the Soviet economic offensive. John B. Hollister of the ICA told the Foreign Affairs Committee that the proposed program was "a balanced effort to meet the Communist challenge for world domination." Similarly, Secretary of State Dulles testified before the Senate Foreign Relations Committee that "new Communist tactics [made] it more than ever imperative that the U.S. should continue the economic phase of [its] Mutual Security Program . . . with greater flexibility and . . . greater assurance of continuity than ever before."[48] In private meetings with legislative leaders President Eisenhower made much the same argument. He also commented on the danger to the United States of turning its back on neutralist nations. Of course, he remarked, he would like to see these countries friendlier to the United States. But the United States had to rely on persuasion; it had no chance to persuade anyone if it isolated itself.[49]

Despite administration appeals and intervention, Congress appropriated only $3.8 billion for the mutual security program for fiscal 1957, $1 billion less than the administration had requested. The House, which considered the bill first, cut it by $1.1 billion. The Senate then restored the authorization to within $361 million of the president's recommendation, and in conference committee a compromise was reached about midway between the House and Senate figures. But in the appropriations process that followed, additional cuts were made after the House and Senate Committees on Appropriations recommended, and the two chambers approved, reductions of $1.4 billion and $800 million respectively. Again, the final appropriation was a compromise between these two figures. As part of its cuts, Congress eliminated the Asian Economic Development Fund established in 1955 and failed to include the president's newly requested funds for the Middle East and Africa. It also required that 80 percent of the development assistance funds contained in the measure be extended to individual nations as loans, not grants (the exception being funds to finance the sale of farm surpluses). Finally, it barred the use of new funds for military aid to Yugoslavia except to maintain equipment that had already been sent to that country.[50]

The administration's setback in Congress was due in part to long-standing, but growing, congressional opposition to foreign aid. Although Republican "nationalists" had long been anxious to reduce America's global commitments, the opposition began to attract more Democrats as the mutual security program took on the appearance of permanence. Many of those who opposed the mutual security program regarded the apparent success of the Soviet economic offensive as a reason to limit, not expand, foreign aid. As one House member from Wisconsin commented, "If we are so foolish as to enter into a competitive economic aid race with the Communists, we will come out second best. We know they can offer a sales program that promises the moon or everything that the people of Asia desire."[51]

Other congressmen objected to giving foreign aid to "neutralist" nations like India and Yugoslavia. India was only one of a relatively few countries that had received development assistance from the United States prior to the establishment of the special Asian fund in 1955. In 1953 Congress appropriated $75 million in development aid for India and Pakistan, and in 1954 it gave $60.5 million to India alone. The next year Congress authorized $70 million for India, although that figure was cut by $10 million in the final appropriations bill. As for Yugoslavia, that country and Spain received most of the $70 million in defense support appropriated for Europe in 1954 and the $85.5 million provided in 1955.[52] The administration justified economic assistance to India as a means of strengthening the forces of democracy in Asia and supported aid to Yugoslavia because of the military and psychological benefits it derived from Yugoslavia's break with the Soviet Union.[53] Moreover, many proponents of foreign aid, both in and out of government, regarded India as the principal test of the theories behind development aid.[54] But India's neutral and nonaligned foreign policy and its program of national economic planning and centralized control alienated many congressmen. House and Senate members protested even more strongly against granting aid to a Communist country like Yugoslavia, which was supporting the neutralization of Germany and the admission of Communist China to the UN and was negotiating a military assistance agreement with the Soviet Union.[55]

During the debate over the 1955 mutual security program, Eisenhower clashed with Senate minority leader William Knowland of California over aid to Yugoslavia and India. Eisenhower and Dulles argued that Yugoslavia was a showcase of the suffering experienced by Communist satellites and afforded the best leverage for encouraging independence among the other satellite nations. In response, Knowland warned of the adverse effect any favoritism shown toward Yugoslavia and India would have on America's allies. He insisted on some form of inspection of the equipment provided Yugoslavia, and with respect to India, remarked that it would be bad if the impression were established around the world that the United States rewarded neutralism.[56] In 1956 Knowland again made clear to the president his opposition to aid for Yugoslavia, which by now had also signed a military aid agreement with the Soviet Union.[57] Knowland's rigid conservatism, implacable anticommunism, and lack of support for such key administration programs as foreign aid often angered Eisenhower and made the president's own conservative views on domestic and foreign matters seem all the more moderate. Yet the fact that others in Congress shared the minority leader's position accounted for passage of the amendment forbidding military aid to Yugoslavia and explained much of the opposition to the entire foreign-aid program.

But the response by Congress to the president's 1957 mutual security legislation was not as negative as it might appear. In the first place, as several congressmen later pointed out, the House and Senate did appropriate $1 billion more for fiscal 1957 than they had for 1956. In this respect, the Soviet economic offensive cut both ways in Congress. Used by some to oppose increased foreign aid, it was referred to by many others as justification for such aid. "The Soviet strategy has been changing again, and so must ours," one New Jersey House member thus remarked. "We cannot be guilty of 'too little and too late,' for the fate of humanity is at stake."[58]

In the second place, most congressmen directed their opposition not to the entire foreign-aid program but specifically to its military assistance sections. In fact, Congress cut nonmilitary assistance by only $73 million, as compared to the $982 million cut from Eisenhower's military requests. It also increased the president's discretionary spending limit from $50 million to $150 million and authorized a second $100 million for the President's Emergency Fund. In addition, although it denied the president the authority to make long-term aid commitments, it included in the legislation a statement pledging that the

United States would continue foreign aid as long as there was danger to the peace and security of the United States and aid was needed.[59]

Even the defeat of the economic fund for Asia and the special fund for the Middle East and Africa was not a complete rejection of the president's bid for special aid to these areas. The two funds were merged into the development assistance section of the mutual security program. The total amount of money authorized remained $100 million less than the combined White House request (i.e., $143 million for development assistance, $100 million for the Asian fund, and $100 million for the Middle East and African fund). But Congress allowed the administration to carry over to 1957 the unobligated portion of the Asian fund for 1956, which was estimated at another $90 million.[60]

What many congressmen protested most about the mutual security legislation was not the principle of foreign aid per se but rather the program's lack of any guiding concept other than the negative one of stopping the spread of communism, and thus its continued emphasis on military rather than economic assistance. Representative Lawrence Smith, a nationalist Republican from Wisconsin, spoke out against the strong military orientation of the foreign-aid bill, which, he said, was "fatal to the establishment of a sound relationship with other nations in the world."[61] Similarly, Senator Theodore Green, an internationalist Democrat from Rhode Island, said he had decided to support the bill "only after a good deal of soul-searching." Although the Soviet Union had changed its tactics since the previous July, Green continued, "there is little evidence that the Administration has shown the flexibility . . . to meet these fresh challenges."[62] Thus, while Congress made substantial cuts in military assistance appropriations, it also stated the sense of Congress that in preparing the following year's foreign-aid program, the president ought to take fully into account the desirability of using foreign aid to promote the economic development of Third World countries.[63]

Plans to Study the Foreign-Aid Program

The debate over the mutual security program revealed a widespread feeling in Washington, however, that the entire program needed to be reexamined in order to clarify its relationship to the national interest. Even congressional supporters of foreign aid recognized that a study was needed to meet critics' objections to the program and to assuage their own doubts about the program's purposes.[64] The administration also decided that a review of the foreign-aid program was necessary. In April, Senator George informed Eisenhower that he was considering establishing a special study committee, and Secretary Dulles told the president that the House Foreign Affairs Committee would probably want to do the same. The president, who believed that the executive branch should participate in any such study, told Senator George that the administration and the House also were considering establishing committees to study foreign aid, and that he hoped these efforts could be combined.[65] George agreed with Eisenhower, and at a White House meeting in May, legislative leaders decided to introduce a bill to establish a bipartisan committee whose members would be appointed by the president and subject to Senate confirmation.[66]

In separate actions, however, the Senate defeated a proposal to establish a Hoover-type commission (half-public, half-private) and then approved a resolution sponsored by Senator Mansfield calling for "exhaustive studies" of foreign aid by a special Senate committee. In reporting favorably on the resolution, the Foreign Relations Committee explained that "it believe[d] that a thoroughgoing legislative study of foreign aid, independent of the executive branch, [was] necessary for an accurate evaluation of foreign aid at this time." As approved by the Senate, the special committee was to be composed of members of the Foreign Relations Committee and the chairmen and ranking minority members of the Appropriations and Armed Services committees. It was to make its report by January 31, 1957. Acting independently, the House Foreign Affairs Committee announced that it, too, would conduct a study of the mutual security program.[67]

Rebuffed by Congress in its effort to organize a combined executive-congressional review panel, the administration appointed its own citizens' committee. As Edward Galbreath of the White House staff explained, the committee would not be an investigative body, such as that being set up by the Senate. Instead, it would be concerned with assisting in the formulation of future foreign-aid programs. It might begin its task by examining world conditions that threatened the nation's foreign policy. "An important element of this background," Galbreath noted, "would be a firm understanding of the Soviet economic offensive that is being waged around the world."[68] In August, Eisenhower asked the chairman of the Chase-Manhattan Bank and former president of the World Bank, John McCloy, to head the panel. When McCloy declined the offer, the president turned to the retired president of the United States Steel Corporation, Benjamin F. Fairless, who accepted the appointment. Others then named to the panel were United Mine Workers' President John L. Lewis; the former head of the CIA, General Walter Bedell Smith; the chairman of the *New York Herald-Tribune*, Whitelaw Reid; President Colgate W. Darden, Jr., of the University of Virginia; the board chairman of Procter and Gamble, Richard R. Deupress; and Board Chairman Jesse W. Tapp of the Bank of America.[69]

Conclusion

The Fairless Committee was formed because of growing disenchantment with the mutual security program, particularly in Congress. The same reason was behind the Senate's establishment of a special committee on foreign aid and the decision by the House Foreign Affairs Committee to make its own investigation. At issue was the basic question of whether the concept of "mutual security" was still appropriate in a world increasingly populated by neutrals, whose major concerns were economic and social, not military. In a paper prepared for use by the Fairless Committee, the CFEP stated the problem clearly. "It becomes increasingly questionable," it noted, "whether the concept of 'mutual security' which seemed so appropriate for Western Europe several years ago is appropriate in 1956." Earlier the major concern in the world had been Soviet military aggression. This was no longer the case, and many countries on the borders of the Soviet bloc now preferred to remain neutral. They would welcome assistance from the United States provided they did not have to take sides to qualify. If they could receive assistance while remaining neutral, "the program would be more palatable psychologically." And since the program would be geared to peace rather than to war, it could not be a target of Soviet propaganda.[70]

The Soviet economic offensive in the Third World was by no means solely responsible for the United States' reexamination of its foreign-aid program, but it played an important role in bringing that reexamination about. First, the apparent success of the Soviets' new policy made clear the prevalence of neutralism and nonalignment throughout the world and the limited success the United States would have in winning friends and allies in these regions. Second, the success of the Soviet offensive underscored again the urgent need for the United States to be more responsive to Third World economic needs. When asked at a news conference whether the United States was losing the Cold War, Eisenhower responded that the "free world" was stronger in 1956 than it had been when he took office in 1953, but he added that Soviet strategy had changed. "They have changed into more, apparently, of an economic propaganda plan rather than depending upon force and the threat of force," he said. This would require "intelligent, fast work on our side to put our own case better before the world and to operate better." As the administration and Congress reviewed the nation's foreign-aid program, they remained fully cognizant of the Soviet economic challenge abroad.[71]

5. Trade, Antitrust, and Oil Policy

1955–1957

EVEN AS THE Eisenhower administration responded to the Soviet economic challenge by making economic assistance abroad a high priority and by undertaking a major review of the nation's foreign-aid programs, the White House continued to emphasize the importance of opening up channels of world commerce. Despite its concessions to protectionist forces in Congress, the administration regarded the three-year extension of the Trade Agreements Act in 1955 as one of its most significant accomplishments. As an indication of continued commitment to free trade, the president renewed his effort in 1956 to gain congressional approval for U.S. membership in the OTC. Eisenhower even threatened political retaliation against those who did not support the administration on this issue.

Yet the administration's overall record in the area of liberalized world commerce remained inconsistent and disappointing to many free-trade advocates. In a number of trade-related cases involving foreign agricultural policy, foreign antitrust policy, the foreign operations of the oil industry, and oil imports, the administration made decisions that contravened the principles of free trade. The administration's actions were dictated in part by domestic constraints and in part by national security considerations, but when viewed alongside previous concessions to protectionist forces and the president's earlier decisions in the watch, lead and zinc, and bicycle tariff cases, this drift away from liberalized trade raised new concerns about Eisenhower's leadership and his commitment to free trade.

The Renewed Struggle over OTC

Even the president's efforts on behalf of U.S. membership in the OTC lacked firm commitment. Following hearings on foreign economic policy in November 1955, a subcommittee of the Joint Committee on the Economic Report recommended that the United States join the OTC.[1] In his 1956 State of the Union and Budget messages and in his annual Economic Report, the president again called for U.S. participation in the proposed trade body.[2] In hearings before the House Ways and Means Committee, cabinet officials and numerous witnesses representing such diverse groups as the New York Bar Association, the League of Women Voters, the National Grange, the AFL-CIO, Chrysler Corporation, and Gulf Oil also spoke in behalf of the OTC. But the opposition was equally as strong. Dan Jones of the Independent Petroleum Association testified that membership in the OTC would mean "a dangerous delegation of [congressional] authority over trade and other matters to an international body." Sidney C. Moody of the Synthetic Organic Chemical Manufacturers Association remarked that import quotas, outlawed by GATT, might "be the only really effective long-term means of curbing serious injury in some areas of our domestic production." Democratic Representative Cleveland M. Bailey of West Virginia claimed that if the United States joined the OTC, the House Ways and Means Committee would no longer have jurisdiction in tariff and trade legislation.[3]

As it turned out, the House Ways and Means Committee recommended authorizing U.S. membership in the OTC. But the protectionist forces in the House lined up solidly against the proposal. And although Eisenhower had threatened political action against those who did not support OTC membership, he failed to carry through with his threat. Opponents—mostly Republicans, but also a number of Democrats from textile-producing and mining states affected by foreign imports—maintained that approval of the committee's recommendations would commit the United States to further tariff reductions. Moreover, since Congress had never had an opportunity to approve or disapprove GATT, enactment of the bill providing for American membership in the OTC would constitute approval of the trade agreement as well.[4] In meetings with legislative leaders from both parties, Eisenhower made clear how strongly he felt about the OTC legislation. At one such meeting he stated that if the measure was not passed by this Congress and he was reelected in November, he would return to the next Congress with the same proposal.[5] At a conference with Minority Leader Joseph Martin of Massachusetts he warned that many Republicans would be asking for his political endorsement in the fall, and he told Martin that as always he stood for principles and important measures and that one of the measures he insisted on was American membership in the OTC. "I think that Mr. Martin got the point," the president later recorded in his diary.[6]

Despite Eisenhower's threat and a report from the State Department that it had successfully negotiated tariff reductions with twenty-one nations at Geneva, House Majority Leader John W. McCormack of Massachusetts concluded the next month that it would be useless to bring the OTC measure before the full House because it would be defeated. McCormack remarked that polls showed about a two-to-one margin of Republicans and some Democrats against the bill.[7] Given the news of this opposition in the House, the president simply dropped the matter of American membership in the OTC from his list of legislative priorities for the current session of Congress. There is no indication that he ever brought the matter up again at White House meetings with legislative leaders. Nor did he mention it in any of his public statements until near the end of the year, when he released a letter to Thomas J. Watson, Jr., Chairman of the U.S. Council of the International Chamber of Commerce, in which he said he intended to renew his request for membership in the OTC to the incoming Congress.[8] It is not clear whether Eisenhower feared that pushing a proposal as unpopular as the OTC measure would harm the rest of his legislative program, or believed that any effort on his part would be futile, or simply felt that the executive branch should not become too deeply involved in the business of Congress.[9] But it is clear that his lack of presidential leadership contributed to the failure of the OTC measure to make its way through Congress.

Agricultural Trade Policy

Many congressmen who opposed U.S. participation in the OTC feared that the organization might dictate trade terms to the United States. The White House maintained that the trade body was important precisely because it offered an opportunity for an international exchange of views on trade matters.[10] However, there was one subject on which the administration refused to allow international discussion—namely, agricultural trade policy. As part of its farm policy in 1956, the White House expanded its agricultural export program. The administration also reviewed long-standing policy with respect to U.S. participation in international commodity agreements. But as it made clear in renewing U.S. membership in an International Wheat Agreement, it would not permit any international deliberation—even if authorized by the agreement—on internal U.S. farm programs.

By the end of 1955 considerable doubts were being expressed about the effectiveness of any program in expanding the sale of American farm products abroad. Widespread concern also existed about the foreign repercussions of a farm surplus disposal program. Even the Francis Committee, established by President Eisenhower in 1954 to formulate surplus-disposal policy, shared some of these views. The chairman of that committee, Clarence Francis, reported to the CFEP that it was unlikely the problem of surplus agricultural products could be resolved in any substantial way by increased exports. He indicated that increases in exports would probably be small relative to the total surplus disposal problem. They would also involve complicated transactions, thereby creating serious additional problems in international relations, and they would require some form of subsidy. Finally, although previous agricultural export programs might have succeeded in keeping down agricultural surpluses, they displaced some dollar sales and involved an estimated $860 million in grants and other dollar costs.[11]

Nevertheless, the administration remained committed to promoting agricultural sales abroad. On November 8 the CFEP approved a recommendation by the Francis Committee to develop programs for agricultural surpluses in order to increase consumptions and accelerate economic development in low-income, low-consumption areas. It requested that the ICA implement this policy since any failure or delay in setting up implementation programs could increase the pressures for less desirable types of programs and thereby create greater international complications.[12]

The following January, President Eisenhower sent Congress a nine-point program for dealing with what he described as the "critical farm problems" confronting the United States. "The mountainous surpluses" caused primarily by wartime incentives too-long continued were the main problem, Eisenhower said. But there were other problems as well. "Both at home and abroad markets have been lost. Foreign farm production has been increased. American exports have declined. Foreign products have been attracted to our shores." As part of his nine points, therefore, Eisenhower asked Congress to step up disposal of surplus commodities, including repeal of a ban under the P.L. 480 program on selling government-owned surpluses to Communist countries. He also suggested seeking expanded opportunities for bartering surpluses.[13]

Considerings its opposition to East-West trade, it was not surprising that Congress failed to lift the ban on P.L. 480 sales to the Soviet bloc. During consideration of a bill to increase the P.L. 480 program, Congress also struck from the legislation a clause permitting the administration to barter surpluses with Communist satellite nations. But at the end of July the House and Senate easily doubled the limit on government-financed sales of farm surpluses under P.L. 480 from $1.5 billion to $3 billion. Questions remained as to what to do with the foreign currencies generated by these sales, and many administration officials continued to express strong reservations about the P.L. 480 program. But the action taken by Congress had the obvious approval of the president and was consistent with his policy of exporting part of the nation's farm problem abroad.[14]

The International Wheat Agreement

Precisely because the United States sought to dispose of its agricultural surpluses overseas while protecting itself from foreign imports, the administration remained defensive about its agricultural trade policy and attempted to isolate it from outside criticism. This was most evident in 1956, when the White House took up the question of renewing U.S. membership in the International Wheat Agreement.

Brought into force in 1949 and then revised for the first time in 1953, the International Wheat Agreement established minimum and maximum prices for wheat sold on world markets. It was one of two commodity agreements to which the United States adhered, the other being a sugar agreement. Historically, the United States had opposed such restrictive trade arrangements. The Randall Commission had been against the Wheat Agreement, arguing that it contributed "little to the solution of wheat problems," and in 1954, during GATT negotiations, the United States had prevented adoption of a proposal that would have allowed commodity agreements under the auspices of the proposed OTC. That same year the United States also opposed the creation of a special UN Commission on International Commodity Trade under the United Nations Economic and Social Council (ECOSOC) and announced that it would not participate as a member.[15]

As its membership in the wheat and sugar agreements indicated, however, the United States' position was not entirely consistent, and increasing pressure was being brought to bear on the administration to adopt a more flexible policy. Not only was the United States participating in international agreements covering wheat and sugar, but it had taken part in an international commission established in Rio de Janeiro in 1954 to study the coffee problem. International commodity agreements had also been proposed or were being formulated for tea, tin, wool, cotton, and rubber. These arrangements took a number of forms, such as surplus-disposal agreements, restrictive export-quota agreements, or international buffer-stock arrangements. The leading proponents of the agreements were the primary producers of the commodities—mostly countries in the Third World—and they argued that the agreements were needed to bring about price stability and an orderly sharing of world markets.[16]

Within the Eisenhower administration the Department of Commerce and the Treasury Department urged that the United States take a public stand against all such arrangements. Commerce and Treasury officials contended that the agreements were ineffective, introduced undesirable economic rigidities and restraints, and led to substantial outlays of federal funds. Although it, too, was generally opposed to commodity agreements, the State Department argued for a more flexible policy that would better serve the nation's interests, a policy of dealing with such agreements on a case-by-case basis. By remaining flexible, Washington would avoid the criticism that it was unsympathetic to the problems of other countries. There might even be cases where America's interests would be served by participating in such an agreement—for instance, where the political stake in the stabilization of a foreign economy was especially great. The State Department also argued that in those instances in which national programs to support prices and state trading were expected to continue, international agreements might not add appreciably to restraints on trade or government controls. Its views were generally shared by the ICA and Department of Agriculture.[17]

At a meeting in February 1956 the CFEP attempted to bridge the gap that existed within the administration over commodity agreements. The council released a policy statement to the effect that the United States would generally oppose such agreements, but would consider exceptions when participation in those arrangements was shown to be clearly in the national interest.[18] In effect, the CFEP supported existing policy and thereby satisfied the Commerce and

Treasury departments. Certainly nothing in its policy statement gave advocates of commodity agreements cause to expect the United States to be more receptive to these agreements than it had been in the past. But by also including the element of flexibility that the State Department had urged, the CFEP left open the possibility that under very special circumstances the United States might participate in one or more of these plans to stabilize world markets and prices.

At the same meeting, the CFEP also took up the question of U.S. participation in a revised International Wheat Agreement. Although several administration officials opposed participation, the CFEP approved continued American membership in the agreement provided it did not become an international forum for discussion of the nation's domestic agricultural policy. The CFEP stipulated that before the United States would agree to any provision allowing the Wheat Council (the agreement's functioning body) to become a forum for discussion of the world wheat situation, that provision would have to be referred to the CFEP for its consideration.[19] On May 4, Secretary of Agriculture Benson advised Secretary of State Dulles that the newly concluded International Wheat Agreement was in harmony with the nation's agricultural policies and should therefore be ratified. Upon later inquiry from the CFEP, however, Benson conceded that one provision of the agreement enabled the Wheat Council to become the platform for international discussion of the world wheat situation.[20]

Almost immediately, CFEP Chairman Dodge wrote Undersecretary of State Hoover advising against signing the agreement until that provision had been eliminated. According to Dodge, the new provision in the agreement allowed other nations and intergovernmental organizations to discuss America's agricultural policy. "In other words," he noted, "every possible forum of international discussion is included and members of the Soviet bloc are not barred from participation." By this time, however, it was too late for the United States to make any substantive changes in the agreement. Four months of negotiations had preceded completion of the pact, and almost forty countries had already signed it. Moreover, as Secretary Benson told Dodge, although the agreement authorized the Wheat Council to study and exchange information on the world wheat situation, member nations still retained control over their own internal agricultural and price policies.[21] The White House therefore signed the pact in May without making any changes. But in June, in transmitting the agreement to the Senate for ratification, Secretary of State Dulles stressed the same point that Benson had made in May. Acknowledging the new provision that authorized the Wheat Council to study the world wheat situation, Dulles stated that it was "the intention of the executive branch not to participate in discussions of the internal wheat policies of importing and exporting countries." There was in the pact, he also noted, an expressed reservation "of liberty of action with regard to internal policies." On this basis the Senate ratified the Wheat Agreement in July 1956.[22]

Thus, discussion of American agricultural policy continued to be excluded from international forums, and the administration continued to limit foreign imports and to promote agricultural exports. The White House acted irrespective of world opinion and even of the consequences that such a policy might have in terms of encouraging the very agricultural production that had caused the nation's farm problems in the first place. But for the most part the administration enjoyed the support of most farm organizations, particularly that of the powerful American Farm Bureau Federation.

Foreign Antitrust Policy

Another issue raised by consideration of international commodity agreements was how the United States could reconcile such agreements with the nation's antitrust laws, which were based on the principles of free trade.[23] As it turned out, the principles of free trade were reaffirmed by the Eisenhower administration, but the laws themselves were often ignored. Questions of antitrust and free trade were subordinated to what the White House regarded as the more pressing issues of national security and defense.

The problem of antitrust in foreign commerce really developed during and after World War II, although it had surfaced sporadically since 1918, when Congress passed the Webb-Pomerene Act, which exempted business combinations engaged in export trade from the provisions of the antitrust laws. Revelations of product and territorial agreements between American and Axis firms during the war led the Justice Department to adopt a vigorous antitrust policy.[24] Justice officials contended that these agreements had restricted domestic production and contributed to the nation's lack of preparedness for war. Along these same lines, the Federal Trade Commission's investigations of eight major industries between 1946 and 1949 left little doubt that businessmen within these industries had violated the Sherman and Clayton antitrust laws by restricting foreign commerce.[25] At the same time, the rapid development of American business overseas after World War II posed a host of legal questions concerning such matters as foreign subsidiaries, foreign and foreign-related joint ventures, patents and technology, and trademarks in foreign trade.[26]

For the most part the courts followed the same "rule of reason" in foreign antitrust cases that they adhered to in domestic cases; they based their decisions on the degree of public harm caused by commercial restraints. But in a series of important cases involving international cartels and other restrictive business practices, the courts tended to apply the antitrust laws to foreign commerce more vigorously. In a number of decisions they made foreign trade more competitive by narrowing the range of permissible business activity. In the landmark Timken decision of 1951 the courts ruled that even in arrangements between a parent company and a foreign affiliate the restraint of foreign and domestic commerce violated the antitrust statutes.[27]

The Truman administration and Congress generally concurred with the courts' interpretations of the antitrust laws, especially as they related to international cartels. President Truman called for an end to all restrictions on free trade, including not only tariffs and other trade barriers but cartels and other forms of combination. In the fall of 1951 his administration sponsored a successful ECOSOC resolution to establish an intergovernmental committee to make recommendations to ECOSOC on the prevention and control of restrictive business practices.[28] In the Benton amendment to the Mutual Security Act of 1951, Congress asked the Economic Cooperation Administration (which administered the Marshall Plan) to intensify its antitrust activity in foreign countries. The next year Congress appropriated funds to carry out the provisions of this amendment, and in 1953 it approved the Thye amendment to the act, declaring that it was the policy of the United States "to encourage the efforts of other free nations to increase the flow of international trade, to foster private initiative and competition, [and] to discourage monopolistic practices."[29]

Yet even during the Truman administration the United States often violated its own antitrust principles. The Webb-Pomerene Act, with its exemption from the antitrust statute of combinations engaged in foreign commerce, remained law, although it came under increasing public and judicial scrutiny. More important, in response to the Korean War, Congress passed the Defense Production Act of 1950 (DPA). This sweeping piece of legislation gave the president various requisition and allocation powers for defense purposes and provided for government loans and guarantees to expand the nation's productive capacity and permit the purchase of strategic raw materials. The DPA also authorized the president, after consultation with the attorney general and the chairman of the FTC, to exempt from the antitrust laws "those [enterprises] entering into voluntary agreements and programs to achieve the objectives of the act."[30]

Under the provisions of the DPA, Truman permitted the establishment of a number of voluntary agreements, including one to meet European oil shortages resulting from a world-wide boycott of Iranian oil. The boycott followed Iran's nationalization of the holdings of British Petroleum in 1951 and was part of a much larger crisis involving the Shah of Iran's loss of power to Prime Minister Mohammed Mossadegh of the leftist National Front Movement. Truman supported this voluntary oil agreement despite the fact that the United States had brought criminal proceedings against the world's seven largest oil corporations, charging them with maintaining a huge international cartel over Mideast oil in violation of the United States' antitrust laws. The president acted over the objections of the Justice Department and the FTC, which maintained that the agreement constituted a waiver of the antitrust laws as applied to the foreign cartel arrangements of the oil majors. Over the objections of the Justice Department, the president also substituted lesser civil litigation for the criminal proceedings pending against the oil companies.

Truman acted for national security reasons: to resume the flow of Iranian oil to Europe, to gain an American presence in Iran, and to resolve the Iranian crisis in order to prevent the Communists from gaining control of the Teheran government. But by responding as he did, Truman set a precedent for the Eisenhower administration, which would subordinate antitrust considerations to the foreign-policy priorities growing out of the Cold War.[31]

The antitrust question was first taken up during the Eisenhower administration by the Randall Commission and the Justice Department. The commission's recommendations with respect to the antitrust laws dealt mainly with the restrictive business practices of foreign nations. The commission recognized the right of each country to regulate trade within its own borders, but it warned that foreign laws and business practices that encouraged restrictions in prices, production, or market arrangements would "limit the willingness of United States businessmen to invest abroad."[32] The next year, a committee that had been established in 1953 by Attorney General Herbert Brownell, Jr., to study the antitrust laws delivered its final report, part of which reviewed the major court decisions affecting foreign commerce. The committee came out in support of existing judicial interpretations of the antitrust statutes. In fact, by advocating the application of the rule of reason to foreign and domestic commerce, it recommended that the Sherman Antitrust Act apply only to those trade conspiracies that "are intended to, and actually do, result in substantial anticompetitive effects on our foreign commerce." As a number of critics of the report pointed out, such a policy would actually weaken enforcement of the antitrust laws by introducing the element of intent in weighing the evidence of an antitrust conspiracy. Some persons, including committee members, also criticized the report's recommendation that the Webb-Pomerene Act be retained.[33]

In 1955, lengthy Senate and House hearings were held on antitrust problems, including foreign trade practices. The hearings were called largely in response to the growth of the merger movement in the United States, publication of the attorney general's report, and businessmen's complaints about the alleged uncertainty created by the antitrust laws. During the hearings the attorney general's report came under heavy fire from some Democrats because of its pro-business biases. Representative Wright Patman called the report "contaminated" because many members of the committee that had prepared it were lawyers representing large corporations, some of which had been or were then under antitrust investigation. In the Senate, Estes Kefauver referred to the report as "an intellectual exercise performed in a vacuum without knowing or trying to find out the ever growing trend toward monopoly." Other witnesses made similar comments. Insofar as foreign trade was concerned, however, the House and Senate hearings proved nebulous. Among the matters discussed were the future of the Webb-Pomerene Act, the supposed ambiguity of the antitrust laws, and, related to that, the need for greater clarity in the laws in order to promote private investment abroad. But the two committees holding these hearings made no formal recommendations to Congress with respect to any of these matters.[34]

While Congress was probing the antitrust question, the National Security Council (NSC) directed the CFEP to begin its own review of the effects of the antitrust statutes on foreign commerce and investment. By this time the White House was receiving a growing number of protests from the business community, which complained that the ambiguities of the anti-trust laws were discouraging private investment abroad and making it difficult for businessmen already operating overseas to know when they might be in violation of the law. Businessmen also contended that it was sometimes necessary to conduct business in accordance with foreign laws even when they conflicted with American statutes.[35] The special task force established by the CFEP conducted a ten-month study, delivering a preliminary report in November and a final draft the following January. In the course of its review the task force, which was made up of a number of the nation's most prominent lawyers, law professors, and economists, asked probing questions that revealed serious inconsistencies between the nation's foreign business practices and its stated commitment to free trade. In addition to noting the antitrust implications of commodity agreements, the task force asked how the administration could square the Webb-Pomerene Act with its opposition to foreign combinations. It also raised questions about the extent to which the Department of Agriculture's export subsidy program and the government's encouragement of private investment undermined free trade.[36]

The CFEP concluded, however, that the United States had been enforcing the antitrust laws in a way that was consistent with the principles of free trade and should continue in that vein. Its only significant recommendation for change concerned the need, through executive action and the institution of informal advisory procedures, to clarify existing antitrust statutes as they applied to such business practices as foreign marketing arrangements, joint ownership of foreign subsidiaries by competing firms, participation in restrictive business arrangements abroad, and the awarding of exclusive foreign distributorships.[37] Except for this recommendation, the report lacked much substance. What was missing was an attempt to reconcile conflicting views within government such as those between the State and Justice departments over the scope and priorities of the antitrust laws. No effort was made, for example, to deal with such basic questions as the limits of antitrust jurisdiction over the overseas activities of American firms, the nature and limit of the proposed clarifications, or the criteria to be used in the informal advisory procedures recommended in the report.[38]

This last issue involved another dispute within the administration, that between the Justice Department, on the one hand, and the Department of Commerce and the CFEP, on the other, over the White House's commitment to free trade and its encouragement of private investment abroad. The greater clarity sought by the CFEP in the enforcement of the antitrust laws could be interpreted as a general loosening of the application of these statutes to foreign commerce. In fact, much of the clamor for clarification appears to have involved complaints against restrictions *properly* enforced under the antitrust statutes. As Robert Macy of the Bureau of the Budget said of the CFEP's report, "A good deal of the analysis in this report indicates [that] at least some of the authors in some degree accept the vocal business view, and that the 'clarification' proposed really means loosening or shrinkage of the impact of the anti-trust rules on U.S. overseas business operations."[39]

The truth of Macy's observations became evident in the CFEP's response to a Commerce Department report, "Bearing of Antitrust on Foreign Distributorships and Private Investments." On the basis of a 1952 survey of American businessmen, the Department of Commerce concluded that the present antitrust laws, aggravated by uncertainty as to what was permissible, were operating as an important deterrent to the flow of American capital and technology abroad. The CFEP's task force accepted the Commerce Department's findings and included them in its draft proposal for changes in the antitrust laws. But the Justice Department, in this case supported by the State Department, refused to provide an administrative procedure for granting advance antitrust clearance to businessmen wishing to operate abroad. The Justice Department was also unwilling to issue official statements of antitrust policy or provide consultative facilities for the business community as recommended by the Commerce Department and the CFEP task force. In fact, the Justice Department was so dissatisfied with the general tone of the CFEP's draft report that it had the work of the task force postponed and eventually canceled.[40]

For the most part, President Eisenhower remained silent throughout the administration's debate over application of the antitrust laws to foreign trade. He spoke only infrequently on the subject of antitrust, and then only in the most general terms. In 1953 he approved the attorney general's plan to study the antitrust question, saying that it would "provide an important instrument to prepare the way for modernizing and strengthening our laws to preserve American free enterprise against monopoly and unfair practices." In 1954 he remarked that government had to "remain alert to the social dangers of monopoly and must continue vigorous enforcement of the antitrust laws."[41] The only indication of Eisenhower's interest in the application of the antitrust laws to foreign commerce, however, was a meeting he had on the subject in 1954 with Attorney General Brownell. From the brief and unclear summary of their conversation that is contained in the Eisenhower Papers, it appears that the president recommended the following: If the antitrust laws were found to be inimical to business operations abroad, some form of remedial legislation should be proposed in the next session of Congress. To the extent that he considered the matter at all, therefore, it seems that Eisenhower believed enforcement of the antitrust laws should not interfere with programs and policies deemed important or essential to the national interest, such as the promotion of trade and investment overseas.[42]

Antitrust and Foreign Oil Operations

Certainly this was the policy the White House followed with respect to the foreign operations of the oil industry. The president had inherited from the previous administration the cartel case against the major oil companies operating in the Mideast. The administration also had to deal with other oil-related matters, such as the cutoff of Western oil supplies as a result of the closing of the Suez Canal in 1956 and the problem of increased dependence on foreign oil throughout the 1950s. In all three matters the administration pursued policies that were damaging to antitrust enforcement but defended them in the name of national security and the national interest.

In the oil cartel case, President Truman had dropped the criminal proceedings against the multinational oil giants in favor of civil litigation just before Eisenhower took office. Truman had acted over the objections of the Justice Department, which warned of the dangers of relying on private business interests to carry out national policy. But the department had been enjoined from pursuing criminal proceedings by considerations of national security. The Justice Department fared no better under the new administration. Soon after it filed its civil suit, it became apparent that foreign policy, not antitrust considerations, would determine the final outcome of the oil cartel case. The department was ordered to confine its action to those firms headquartered and doing their primary business in the United States, a definition that thereby excluded as defendants British Petroleum and Royal Dutch Shell. The decision to limit the case to American firms was made at the highest levels of government and under great pressure from the Department of State, which was concerned about the foreign-policy implications of a broader antitrust suit. A NSC memorandum stating "that the enforcement of the antitrust laws of the United States against the western oil companies operating in the Near East [was] to be deemed secondary to the national interest," was approved by President Eisenhower, who thus made clear his support of this approach to the suit.[43]

In fact, Eisenhower's major concern in the oil case was a favorable settlement of the oil impasse in Iran. Accepting as his own Truman's plan to establish an American presence in Iran, Eisenhower appointed Herbert Hoover, Jr., as his personal emissary to the major American oil firms, British Petroleum, and the Teheran government in an effort to establish an international consortium to work the Iranian oil fields.[44] The oil majors, which had abundant supplies elsewhere, were by no means eager to enter into an Iranian consortium. They advised the administration that they would do so only in the interest of national security—that is, to protect U.S. interests against Communist expansion in Middle East—and only if they were provided antitrust immunity in the production of Iranian oil. "We, of course, desire to cooperate in every way with the National Security Council," Chairman of the Board of Texaco J. S. Leach wrote the Department of State. "However . . . we feel that we should not become finally obligated under any agreement or understanding in pursuance of such a plan, until they have been first reexamined and approved by the Attorney General."[45] The White House accepted these terms. The Department of Justice granted to the newly formed Iranian oil consortium (consisting of British Petroleum, Royal Dutch Shell, the five American majors, and a number of smaller independents) antitrust immunity in the exploration and refining of Iranian oil. Shortly thereafter, oil began to flow from Iran to Western Europe. The threat of Communist expansion into Iran appeared contained as the pro-Western Shah of Iran, who had been restored to power with the help of the CIA, began to receive the oil revenues that would maintain his political hold over the country for the next twenty-five years.[46]

In terms of foreign antitrust policy, however, the cost of settling the Iranian oil crisis was high. First, although they had been given a small (5 percent) share of the consortium as a result of Justice Department efforts, independent producers had for the most part been excluded from the Iranian oil fields. The seven major oil companies already operating in the Mideast were able to extend their control into Iran and determine the supply and cost of its oil. Second, Eisenhower's decision to permit the formation of the Iranian consortium undercut much of the Justice Department's case against the majors in the Mideast. Although Attorney General Brownell gave only a qualified opinion on the legality of the consortium and reserved the right to prosecute the case, his opinion had an obvious, detrimental effect on those parts of the suit involving the joint exploration, production, and refining of oil. The government found it difficult to prosecute the very actions that it had just encouraged and sanctioned on the grounds of national interest. The officials within the Justice Department's Antitrust Division who were responsible for bringing the case to trial were fully aware of the difficult position in which the Iranian settlement had placed them. Although on the record they were still seeking redress in these areas as well as in the marketing and price-fixing of oil, they actually narrowed the suit to the last two points only.[47]

The case itself moved through the courts slowly; it would not be finally settled until 1968, when the government obtained limited consent decrees from three of the five defendants, which left the basic scaffolding of the cartel arrangements among the oil majors intact. The decrees obtained were limited to price-fixing and marketing arrangements only. They permitted the continuation of joint syndicates for the foreign exploration, production, transportation, and refining of oil.[48] Thus, settlement of the Iranian crisis was achieved at the expense of the government's prosecution of the oil cartel case. In addition, the settlement was reached only because the multinational oil giants were persuaded by the Eisenhower administration to enter Iran in return for a grant of antitrust immunity.[49]

The Suez Oil Crisis of 1956–1957

The president adopted much the same approach in relying on the multinational oil corporations to carry out national policy during the Suez oil crisis of 1956–57. The immunity granted the oil majors in 1956 was more limited than that of 1954 and led to an extensive congressional investigation of foreign petroleum and the antitrust laws. But once again the administration's policy enabled the multinationals to maintain their hold over Mideast oil, and once again there were no compensating factors in the form of additional antitrust legislation or significant changes in government policy toward the multinational corporations.

Growing out of the Arab-Israeli war of 1956, the Suez oil crisis came about because of a sharp drop in Mideast oil shipments to Europe following the closing of the Suez Canal and the cutting of the Iraqi pipeline to the eastern Mediterranean. How serious a crisis actually existed remains unclear, but the oil companies claimed that Europe was faced with imminent disaster during the winter and spring of 1956–57, while congressional investigators contended that Europe had adequate stocks and alternative sources to meet its essential needs reasonably well. Similar differences developed over the degree of help the oil industry actually rendered Europe.[50] Despite these conflicting claims, the administration assumed that the crisis was major and sought to handle it by having the major oil companies redirect as much as possible of the world's oil supplies outside the Mideast to Europe. To this end it sponsored the oil lift program of 1956–57, in which a committee of oil companies known as the Middle East Emergency Committee (MEEC) was given antitrust immunity (under a voluntary agreement made a few months earlier) in controlling the transportation of oil throughout the world. Originally composed of fifteen members, MEEC included the five American majors, four of their subsidiaries, and three other companies, each with assets of over $1 billion. In forming the committee, the White House assumed that the principal problem facing Europe was insufficient transportation to handle what it otherwise believed was an ample world oil supply. Administration officials expected MEEC to solve this problem by redistributing tanker schedules so as to assure the most efficient delivery of oil to world markets.[51]

In later hearings and in a final majority report, the Senate Judiciary Committee questioned several government practices involved in the oil lift program and made a number of serious charges against MEEC. The committee even challenged MEEC's legality under the 1955 DPA amendments, which limited voluntary agreements to those involving military items. Senator Estes Kefauver was particularly astute in his examination of administration witnesses, forcing Assistant Secretary of the Interior Felix Wormser into the embarrassing admission that while the government had granted MEEC antitrust immunity in the transportation of oil, it regarded as contrary to the antitrust laws any effort on its part to force members of MEEC jointly to regulate gasoline prices.[52] Oil company witnesses and several senators— including Everett Dirksen of Illinois in a lengthy minority report—attempted to refute the charges against MEEC. In response to the claim that MEEC had been established illegally, for example, Dirksen argued that since the voluntary agreement under which it had been organized was a modified version of the earlier oil agreement of 1953, it was exempt from the 1955 DPA provisions that applied to new agreements. In accordance with other 1955 provisions, the modified agreement provided for strict regulation and supervision of MEEC, including prior government approval before MEEC could even begin to function. According to Dirksen, all these antitrust safeguards had been met.[53]

Majority members of the Judiciary Committee contested these and other claims made by Dirksen and the oil companies, such as the need to form MEEC in the first place. But no one disputed the point, which Dirksen repeated, that MEEC had been organized at the request of the government to meet a world emergency. Furthermore, although the majority of the committee criticized the administration for relying on private industry to carry out governmental policy and accused the oil companies of illicit practices under the guise of antitrust immunity (e.g., forcing up the price of gasoline), it made few recommendations for changes in the antitrust laws. To the contrary, while calling for stricter enforcement of the DPA provisions concerning antitrust immunity, the committee noted that these provisions should be retained. As the committee explained, "Interested Government agencies [had] reiterated their belief in the necessity for maintaining the emergency functions of [the DPA in] preparing possible future plans of action," and it saw no reason to disagree. Consequently the antitrust provisions of the DPA remained unchanged even after the Judiciary Committee investigation.[54]

Oil Import Restrictions

The question of antitrust enforcement was also at issue in the White House's efforts after 1955 to impose voluntary restrictions on the import of foreign oil. As in the case of the oil lift program and the oil cartel suit, the administration chose to ignore the antitrust implications of its policy as it wrestled with what it regarded as more pressing matters of national security.

During the Truman administration the United States had for the first time since the early 1920s imported more oil than it exported. By the time Eisenhower took office in 1953, oil imports had increased to the point where the Texas Railroad Commission, which regulated the Texas oil industry, had practically shut down oil production in the state because of the oil glut. Imports of foreign oil continued to climb steadily after 1953. Whereas domestic production of oil increased 29 percent between 1951 and 1956, imports of crude jumped by 135 percent. During the same period the percentage ratio of foreign to domestic oil rose from 6.6 percent to 12.0 percent. Most important, the percentage of imported crude as part of the nation's total supplies climbed from 6 percent in 1951 to more than 10 percent by 1956.[55] Given the perils and complexity of securing a steady flow of commodities world-wide, Eisenhower became all the more convinced that America's growing dependence on foreign oil threatened its national security. In 1954 the president established the Cabinet Committee on Energy Supplies and Resources to review the nation's energy needs and policies, especially with respect to oil. In its report to the president the following February, the committee concluded that for reasons of national defense, the ratio of foreign imports of oil to domestic production should be the same as existed in 1954 (about 8.7 percent). Otherwise, there would be inadequate incentives for exploration and discovery of new domestic sources of energy.[56]

In the Senate the movement to limit oil imports gained sufficient strength to force Eisenhower to agree to a program of voluntary import quotas. Price Daniel of Texas argued for a mandatory limitation on oil imports of 10 percent of domestic demand. Matthew M. Neely of West Virginia, a coal-producing state that also felt the impact of oil imports, sought to attach the 10 percent limitation to the Trade Agreements Extension Act then under consideration, but the administration strongly opposed this mandatory quota. "We are trying to liberalize trade," Eisenhower argued. "I would very much deplore seeing us going backward and establishing quotas that were at least fixed by law." According to the State Department, there was little evidence that either the domestic crude oil or the coal industry had suffered much from imports. The State Department also maintained that low fuel costs were an important factor in ensuring industrial prosperity. Nevertheless, the administration recognized the strength of the protectionist forces in Congress and agreed to a compromise (worked out in the Senate Finance Committee) whereby the Director of the Office of Defense Mobilization (ODM) would notify the president if any article was being imported into the United States in quantities that he believed threatened the national security. If the president found this to be the case, he was authorized to adjust the level of imports accordingly. What was meant by "a threat to national security" was never precisely stated.[57]

As a result of protectionist pressure, then, the question of oil import restrictions was left to the president, and his decision was to be based upon considerations of national security. The antitrust implications of a program of voluntary or mandatory quotas was obvious even to administration officials. While in the oil cartel case the Justice Department was attempting to prosecute the major importers of oil, in part for cooperating in a noncompetitive fashion to restrict imports, the ODM was trying to get the importers to reduce their oil imports to a fixed percentage. Speaking before the House Ways and Means Committee, Secretary of State Dulles described the dilemma facing the administration: "In practice quotas are extremely difficult to administer and they impose upon those who are subjected to quotas almost a cartel system, and an allocation of the market."[58]

In 1957, after imports increased to 12.6 percent of domestic crude production and to 11 percent of total production (domestic and imported crude), the director of the ODM, Gordon Gray, reported to Eisenhower that he believed oil imports threatened national security. The president responded by invoking the national security amendment to the Trade Agreements Extension Act and established the President's Special Committee to Investigate Crude Oil Imports. The committee recommended, and the president approved, a program for assigning voluntary quotas to importing companies based on a figure 10 percent below their average imports for 1954 and 1955; a special provision was made for new importers, whose quotas would be based on their July 1957 schedules. This action was taken in response to a Justice Department request "that any plan for the limitation of oil imports include equal opportunities for new as well as established importers."[59]

The opportunity set aside for newcomers notwithstanding, the government's voluntary import program did just what the Justice Department was trying to prevent; it allowed the major oil companies to regulate imports of foreign oil and maintain the existing market price structure. The problem was accurately described by the Senate Judiciary Committee when it noted that the recommendations of the President's Cabinet Committee had "definite anti-competitive implications and tend[ed] to preserve the market position of the international oil companies." A flat percentage cutback by the majors, the committee added, perpetuated the market shares which the Justice Department charged in its cartel suit against the importers were arrived at by illegal agreements for dividing up world markets.[60]

The establishment of voluntary oil quotas did not resolve the oil import problem, and in 1959 the White House imposed mandatory quotas.[61] Once again the Eisenhower administration sacrificed antitrust enforcement and the principles of free trade to what it regarded as the more pressing issue of national security. Considering the rapid growth of demand for oil during and after the 1950s and the fact that because of the nature of oil technology and markets, the refining and distribution of petroleum since the 1880s has been dominated by a small number of larger firms, it is possible to argue that the United States had no other choice; that it had to work through the majors both with respect to the Iranian oil impasse and the oil lift program. That Eisenhower believed this to be the case is understandable, considering the fact that the majors were the only firms in the 1950s with established facilities for refining and distributing Mideast oil. Eisenhower regarded as vital the continued flow of Mideast oil to Western Europe and Japan, and in 1957 he even raised the possibility of war against the oil-producing countries in the Mideast in case of an oil embargo. In a letter to the president, Dillon Anderson, a friend and adviser, wrote of the growing danger of relying too heavily on foreign oil, but shrugged off as an "unacceptable alternative" resorting to force to prevent an embargo. Responding to Anderson, Eisenhower commented that in a crisis which threatened to cut off Mideast oil to the Western world, "we would *have* to use force [Eisenhower's italics]." An adequate supply of oil to Western Europe, he added, "ranks almost equal in priority with an adequate supply for ourselves." For reasons of "self-preservation" the West had to retain access to Mideast oil.[62]

As for the oil import quota program, it might be conveniently argued that it contributed to the energy crisis of the 1970s and 1980s by helping to deplete the nation's oil reserves at a time when foreign oil was both cheap and plentiful. But the issue facing the administration in the 1950s was not one of undersupply; rather, it was one of an oversupply that appeared to threaten the domestic oil industry. The White House thus believed that the nation's security was endangered by increased dependence on foreign sources of petroleum.[63] It is on the basis of considerations such as these that the president's import quota program must be evaluated. Certainly it is erroneous to suggest, as some critics have, that in attempting to restrict oil imports the White House was acting at the behest of the oil industry and without much regard for the national interest. Indeed, just the opposite was true.

The fact remains, however, that in all its policies on foreign oil, the administration let itself be guided by a concept of national security that ignored other basic questions of national interest, such as the serious implications of relying on private concerns to carry out major national policy. In the process, the White House undermined enforcement of the nation's antitrust laws in the realm of foreign trade, even though this trend was resisted from within the administration, most notably by the Justice Department.

The UN Proposal on Restrictive Business Practices

The Eisenhower administration also undermined UN efforts to establish an international code to curb restrictive business practices, even though the United States had initiated the effort in the first place. As a result of a successful American resolution in 1951, an intergovernmental committee had been established to make recommendations to the ECOSOC on the prevention and control of such practices. But when the UN finally considered the draft proposal in 1955, the United States refused to ratify it, claiming that it was unsatisfactory in a number of respects. Although there was validity to the U.S. position, there were serious flaws in it as well. By refusing to approve the proposal, the administration provided new cause for free-traders to question its commitment to liberalized world commerce and raised doubts about its loyalty to the concept of international cooperation in resolving world economic problems.

The report of the UN committee, completed in March 1953, proposed making business practices in foreign trade the subject of an international convention. An investigatory and regulatory tribunal would make recommendations on government complaints of restrictive practices as defined by the convention. Although the recommendations would have no sanction except the informal one of publicity, governments adhering to the convention would be obligated to implement the remedial measures recommended by the tribunal. Restrictive practices specifically required by governments were to be excluded from investigation. Moreover, remedial measures recommended by the tribunal would have to be in accordance with the laws and procedures of the accused nations.[64]

The UN committee's report was opposed in the United States by a broad cross section of the business and legal communities, including the National Foreign Trade Council, the National Association of Manufacturers, the U.S. Chamber of Commerce, and the American Bar Association. These groups objected to the lack of a well-developed body of antitrust law in most nations and an international definition of "restrictive business practices." They also opposed the exclusion from the tribunal of investigations of restrictive business practices sanctioned by foreign governments and an alleged lack of proper judicial procedures for carrying out tribunal investigations. Finally, they protested against the limitations placed on the tribunal in taking remedial action against the laws and procedures of accused nations. All this, they maintained, was bound to create discrimination against American business in the international enforcement of restrictive business practices.[65]

The Eisenhower administration took the same position on the UN report. Although the United States had recommended the study in the first place, when the committee submitted its report in March 1955, the administration vigorously opposed it. There were just too many differences between the antitrust laws and procedures of the United States and those of other governments. Also, there was no clear international agreement as to what constituted a violation of free trade. Without the support of the United States, there was no chance that the proposal would ever be implemented. Thus, instead of going forward with plans to establish an international convention on restrictive trade practices, ECOSOC adopted an innocuous U.S. recommendation that the council place its present emphasis on further development of national programs of antitrust.[66]

The White House was not entirely wrong in its position on the UN report. As Acting Deputy Undersecretary of State Thorsten K. Kalijarvi reminded the Senate Judiciary Committee, "While encouraging progress has been made in the adoption of foreign laws on the subject [of antitrust], these developments have not reached the stage at which the recommendations of the proposed international body could be carried out effectively at the national level."[67] But Sigmund Timberg, a former member of the Justice Department's Antitrust Division who had served as secretary to the committee that prepared the report, pointed out a number of discrepancies and inconsistencies in the White House's position and clarified several points about the UN recommendations that had concerned many congressmen and government officials. Testifying before the Judiciary Committee, he noted that restrictive business practices were not only defined in the report but were specifically listed as exclusion from markets or dividing markets, price-fixing, price discrimination, limitations on production, and specific types of patent, trademark, and copyright prohibitions. As for the exclusion of practices specifically required by governments, mandatory cartels—as opposed to permissive cartels, which were not excluded—were the exception rather than the rule, so the exemption would probably prove to be a limited one.[68]

Timberg acknowledged the gap between the United States and other countries in the area of antitrust practices, but he also raised questions about America's own regulatory and noncompetitive practices in the areas of shipping, air travel and transportation, marine insurance, and telecommunications. Similarly, he referred to the export combinations permitted under the Webb-Pomerene Act, the antitrust exemptions allowed under the DPA, and the government's involvement in agriculture and the importation of strategic raw materials. Finally, he pointed to the substantial progress that had been made in antitrust legislation and enforcement throughout Europe: "We should . . . avoid too smug notions of this country as dwelling on a high plateau of competitive perfection while the rest of the world resides in the sunless valleys of restrictionism and cartelization."[69]

More important than the merits of the White House's objections to the UN report, however, was the fact that in rejecting the report the administration appeared also to reject international cooperation in favor of unilateralism and to take a stand contrary to its avowed purpose of freeing the channels of world commerce. As Timberg also remarked to the Judiciary Committee, "The United States' position in rejecting the report will, in my judgment, have an adverse effect on the achieving of the foreign economic policy objectives expressed in the Thye amendment [to the Mutual Security Act] and still currently voiced by the State Department."[70]

Conclusion

In 1958 Raymond Vernon, a noted economist and advocate of free trade, attacked the Eisenhower administration for what he regarded as the drift of the administration away from liberalized world commerce. Vernon wrote of a "crisis" in trade policy which he attributed in large measure to the lack of presidential leadership. Vernon was especially concerned about the effects on the United States of the newly formed European Common Market, but he traced the origins of the trade crisis to the administration's failure to go beyond the mild trade recommendations contained in the Randall Commission report of 1954. He criticized Eisenhower's opposition in 1955 to the UN draft proposal on restrictive trade practices. Vernon accused the United States of arresting and reversing its earlier efforts to deal with the harmful effects of international cartels and said that the nation had "slipped from a position of clear leadership in international trade matters to one of moderate participation or passive observation."[71]

In describing the trade crisis facing the United States in 1958, Vernon was probably too harsh on President Eisenhower. As Vernon acknowledged, the president was faced with rapidly growing protectionist sentiment in the United States, which made it difficult for him even to get congressional approval for American membership in the OTC.[72] Nevertheless, the general thrust of Vernon's criticism remains valid. The president displayed little leadership in the matter of the OTC, and his interest in foreign antitrust enforcement was negligible. Indeed, in such trade-related matters as foreign antitrust enforcement, foreign agricultural policy, and the foreign operations of the nation's major oil companies, the White House pursued policies that can only be described as contradictory and illiberal.

6. The Foreign-Aid Inquiry and Establishment of the Development Loan Fund 1957

BY THE END OF 1956 the Eisenhower administration's foreign economic program was strewn with contradictions. Exceptions to its initial rule of "trade not aid" and violations of its proclaimed goal of trade liberalization had accumulated to the point where the administration seemed to lack an effective and coherent program at all. In this respect the White House had reached an impasse in the development of its foreign economic policy. Not only were serious questions being raised about its trade and tariff policies, but doubts expressed about the purposes of the mutual security program had led the White House and both branches of Congress to initiate independent studies of the foreign-aid program. In addition, the International Development Advisory Board (IDAB), an executive body established by Congress in 1950 as the chief public advisory group for the nation's economic assistance program, had decided to undertake a fourth independent review.

These inquiries into the foreign-aid program differed on a number of important issues, such as the amount of economic assistance that should be extended abroad and the relative roles of trade, aid, and private investment in promoting foreign economic growth. They also revealed conflicting—and sometimes internally inconsistent—assumptions about the short- and long-term problems facing the United States in Third World countries. The studies generally agreed, however, that the foreign-aid program lacked clear and well-defined goals, a shortcoming that had led to widespread operational problems and had undermined the effectiveness of foreign aid as an instrument of national policy. Furthermore, the consensus was that the character of the Cold War since the end of the Korean conflict required a redefinition and reconstitution of the nation's foreign-aid policies. The reports pointed particularly to the altered circumstances of the military threat to the United States and its allies, the changing strategy of the Soviet Union in underdeveloped areas, and the altered attitude and aspirations of the underdeveloped countries themselves. Finally, the reports concurred in the view that while foreign aid served an essential national purpose, it should respond more to the development needs of Third World nations. Aid should complement, not be a substitute for, private investment abroad. Aid should also be in the form of soft loans rather than grants. In sum, the United States needed to reconsider old programs and devise new approaches to foreign economic development.

The White House had already begun to move in this direction. But aware of continued Soviet economic activity in the Third World and of demands by Third World countries for the establishment of a Special United Nations Fund for Economic Development, the administration sent new proposals to Congress. In 1957, as part of his mutual security requests for 1958, President Eisenhower asked the House and Senate to establish a Development Loan Fund that would make public loans for development purposes to Third World countries, loans that would be repayable in local currencies. Eisenhower also sought new authority to make aid commitments that extended over a number of years.

These requests generated a major conflict in Congress and caused another setback for the president. As one commentator later remarked, the foreign-aid debate of 1957 "was the occasion for a resounding collision between a greatly intensified crusade to redirect and reinvigorate the [foreign-aid] program, particularly in support of long-range development, and an equally determined campaign to bear down on the brakes."[1] Once again Congress cut the president's aid requests sharply and rejected most of his proposals for extended lending authority. Nevertheless, the mutual security legislation for 1958 was significant. By approving a much battered version of the president's proposal for creation of a Development Loan Fund, Congress established an organizational framework through which public capital in the form of soft loans could thenceforth be made available to underdeveloped countries.

The Foreign-Aid Studies

Of the studies on foreign aid undertaken by the administration and Congress, that by the Senate was the most extensive. The Senate empowered its special committee to make "full use . . . of the experience, knowledge, and advice of private organizations, schools, institutions, and individuals," and accordingly, the committee authorized various private institutions to undertake research and analysis. It also arranged for a number of individuals to survey foreign-aid programs in different geographical regions.[2] The projects and surveys commissioned by the special committee touched on all aspects of foreign aid, including questions of personnel and administration, the use of private contractors, the agricultural disposal program, the Soviet economic offensive, and the foreign-aid activities of other non-Communist countries. Several projects also attempted an overall evaluation of the foreign-aid program.[3] Of these, the most comprehensive and influential was the study that the Center for International Studies at M.I.T. undertook on the objectives of foreign aid. Prepared under the direction of Max F. Millikan, the inquiry elaborated on many of the concepts and ideas that Millikan and Walt Rostow had already transmitted to the administration through C. D. Jackson. A different version of the same study, which Millikan and Rostow had already drafted and which had been considered by the National Security Council in the spring of 1956, was published separately.[4]

In their report for the Senate, Millikan and Rostow emphasized the changing circumstances of the Cold War. They maintained that the altered nature of Cold War conflict necessitated a reorientation of the nation's foreign economic programs away from military and defense support and toward a program of economic development that would foster self-sustaining growth in the world's underdeveloped countries. The growth of Soviet nuclear power, had undermined the confidence of America's allies—even that of the NATO countries—in traditional military alliances supported by American money. At the same time, the shift in Soviet strategy from overt military aggression to more subtle forms of expansion that emphasized political, psychological, and economic means had diminished the need for further U.S. military efforts and had made the Soviet Union appear more attractive in Third World regions.[5]

Development aid to Third World nations was clearly in the United States' interest, Millikan and Rostow wrote. A comprehensive and sustained program of economic assistance over a twenty- or thirty-year period would create "a preponderance of stable, effective, and democratic societies"—the best hope for a favorable settlement to the Cold War. Moreover, the international interests of successful democratic societies were more likely to coincide with those of the United States. Therefore, Millikan and Rostow argued, the nation's economic aid program should be politically neutral, development aid planning should be carried out separately from military and other aid planning, and the nation's long-term interests should outweigh short-run tactical considerations.[6]

In analyzing the objectives of U.S. foreign economic assistance, Millikan and Rostow noted carefully the likely short- and long-term effects of foreign aid. They also pointed to the difficulty of predicting the political consequences of economic growth. An aid program that was intended to promote economic growth had to focus entirely on that single purpose if it were to be successful. Economic inducements were unlikely to gain allies for the United States or win acceptance of its foreign-policy objectives. Indeed, at certain low levels of income, improved living standards brought about by foreign aid could lead to political and social unrest and make a society more susceptible to demagogic appeals of a nationalist or Communist nature.[7]

Yet the premise of Millikan and Rostow's study was precisely the political consequences of U.S. aid, the democratic, effective, and stable world order that economic growth was intended to produce. In this respect, the context of their analysis remained the Cold War struggle with the Soviet Union, which development along the lines they proposed was supposed to end favorably for the United States. Moreover, although they emphasized the long- rather than short-term benefits of economic assistance, they did not adhere rigorously to this position. "Economic aid can have a constructive effect on political behavior from its inception," they noted. "By making it possible for a poor country to make progress with its internal problems, aid can sharply alter its leaders' conception and evaluation of the choices they confront."[8]

More important, Millikan and Rostow made assumptions about the causal relationship between development aid and economic development, on the one hand, and between economic development and its political consequences, on the other, that were without foundation. Likewise, they failed to realize that the goals of anticommunism, stability, and democracy were not necessarily compatible. Absent from their analysis was any sense of a social, cultural, or political dimension to economic (or political) development abroad.[9] For example, they did not discuss social programs or internal reforms of government that might facilitate achieving them. In stressing economic growth almost exclusively, they ignored such fundamental questions as the distribution of growth, how it was to be achieved, at whose expense, or its impact on the definition of social justice. They seemed to assume that the Western experience of economic and political development could easily be transplanted abroad. Their model of development was India, Pakistan, or perhaps Burma. They ignored countries in the Middle East and Latin America where political corruption was rampant and the government's commitment to economic and political development along the lines they set forth was dubious.

Nevertheless, most of the other studies commissioned by the Senate's special committee on foreign aid agreed with the recommendations and conclusions of the Millikan-Rostow Report.[10] Also in general harmony with the Millikan-Rostow study was the report on foreign aid by the House Foreign Affairs Committee, although the House committee's emphasis was more clearly on the political imperatives of economic assistance. Maintaining that institutional and human elements were greater obstacles to development than the lack of capital, the committee actually called for a reduction, rather than an increase, in foreign aid. It also reiterated the importance of promoting private investment abroad, but stressing the success of the Soviet economic offensive abroad, supported a program of expanded development aid on a long-term, soft-loan basis to counter the Soviet initiative.[11]

The IDAB, headed by Eric Johnston of the Motion Picture Association of America, presented its report to the president in March 1957. The board pointed to "the considerable doubts and confusion at home and abroad about United States foreign assistance" and noted moral reasons as well as reasons of national interest for helping Third World nations develop along "moderate" lines. It called for the establishment of an International Development Fund to operate through the ICA. The fund would place the nation's development program on a flexible, long-term basis. Although it advised that the fund ordinarily make loans on a soft-term basis, the IDAB acknowledged that there were cases where grant aid would be preferable. The board did not attempt to estimate the size of the fund; it merely stated that the initial appropriations for it "should be sufficient for a substantial increase in capital investment and technical assistance."[12]

Of all the studies on foreign aid, that by the Fairless Committee, also presented to the president in March, was the most conservative. To a much greater extent than the other reports, the Fairless study emphasized the primary role that trade and investment should play in bringing about development abroad. Guaranties, loans to private investors (with the sharing of losses), and joint investment of private and public capital should be tried in selected areas. The wider use of private firms by host governments on a contract basis also was desirable. Finally, the Fairless committee submitted that grants to provide capital for development purposes should be severely limited, and that in awarding foreign assistance "a higher priority should be given to those countries which have joined in the collective security system."[13]

As President Eugene Black of the World Bank later commented, the Fairless Committee failed to consider the purposes of foreign aid or to recognize the different development needs of various countries and regions, and it leaned far too heavily on the justification of all aid on strategic grounds.[14] But like the other studies of the foreign-aid program, even the Fairless Report called for continued foreign economic aid, and it urged that the aid be concentrated in a long-term economic development program. To this end, it recommended the separation of military and nonmilitary forms of assistance and the submission of the latter to Congress under the label "economic assistance." It also proposed that the military and economic assistance programs be presented to Congress for approval every two years instead of annually, and urged greater flexibility in program expenditures. "Economic development is—in the long run—as important to the collective security of the Free World as the military measures we have taken," the committee concluded.[15]

By the time President Eisenhower received the IDAB and Fairless Committee reports in March, then, the administration and Congress had completed the most searching review of the U.S. foreign-aid program since the adoption of the Marshall Plan. Stressing the long-term objectives of foreign aid, the authors of the most sophisticated of the studies—Millikan and Rostow—framed their proposals within the political context of the Cold War struggle between East and West. Furthermore, most of the reports reflected an economic determinism that equated economic assistance with economic development and, ultimately, with political stability and the evolution of democratic societies in Third World regions. Nevertheless, there was general agreement about the need for a foreign-aid program that would respond more effectively to the Third World's economic needs. To that end, all the reports called for the expansion of development aid primarily in the form of soft loans.

U.S. Opposition to SUNFED

The Eisenhower administration agreed with these general conclusions. A year earlier the president had sought authority to make commitments of up to ten years' duration to assist less developed countries in their long-term development programs. During the hearings on the mutual security legislation for 1957, White House officials had emphasized the need for adequate long-term funding to counter the Soviet economic offensive abroad. However, Congress had rejected the president's request for such aid commitments. It had also abolished the Asian economic fund and had refused to include in the foreign-aid program for 1957 a requested new fund for the Middle East and Africa.

Toward the end of 1956, the White House renewed its efforts in behalf of long-term economic aid. By this time the administration was under considerable pressure at the United Nations to support the creation of a Special United Nations Fund for Economic Development (SUNFED). Although the underdeveloped nations at the UN had pushed for the establishment of SUNFED for a number of years, the United States had opposed these efforts, wanting instead to keep economic aid costs down, to control the use of its own funds, and to emphasize private investment over public capital movements. It had endorsed the establishment of the IFC as an alternative to a special UN fund. As late as the spring of 1956, the administration had turned down a request by UN Ambassador Henry Cabot Lodge, Jr., that the United States support the creation of SUNFED; Lodge had hoped to embarrass the Soviet Union, whose own support for SUNFED was equivocal.[16]

Faced with growing support for SUNFED, even among a number of the industrialized nations, and still hoping to undercut the Soviet Union's position in Third World nations, Lodge renewed his efforts in behalf of SUNFED at the end of 1956. By this time the Soviet Union had invaded Hungary, and President Eisenhower had persuaded England to accept a cease-fire in the Suez crisis. Because of these international developments, Ambassador Lodge believed that the United States enjoyed new favor among Third World nations and that the time was propitious to consolidate these gains by supporting the establishment of SUNFED. Because of previous suspicions and prejudices, many Third World countries would find the extension of foreign aid through SUNFED more acceptable than bilateral assistance. American support for SUNFED would embarrass the Soviet Union and produce a great propaganda victory for the United States.[17]

The White House remained unpersuaded, however. Treasury Secretary Humphrey led the opposition against SUNFED. Because of the financial position of most other countries, he argued, the United States would have to contribute most of the capital for the fund. Given the country's international exchange position, he believed it should seek ways of reducing, not increasing, its contributions abroad. "I agree that it is desirable to try to beat Russia to the punch in things that are sound and right," Humphrey told Lodge, "but just to beat them to the punch as an end in itself, regardless of the desirability of the program, is something that we should avoid."[18] Although Secretary Dulles was more willing to consider what Lodge had to say, he, too, believed that the United States should wait until the review of the foreign-aid program (then under way) was completed before embarking on new programs. As an interim measure, he instructed the American delegation to the UN to survey other nations for support of a multilateral aid plan.[19]

Thus the United States continued to oppose the establishment of SUNFED. But the pressure of Third World countries at the UN for increased long-term development funding made it seem all the more urgent that the United States expand its own aid program. At the same time, the White House had to contend with the worsening Western position and the growing Soviet presence in the Middle East following the Suez crisis and the Arab-Israeli war. Responding to the Mideast situation, Eisenhower told Congress in January 1957 that he intended to ask for $200 million in discretionary economic and military assistance for the Middle East.[20] In his inaugural and State of the Union messages the president also stressed the importance of making economic aid available to less developed countries throughout the world.[21]

The DLF Alternative

In fact, by the beginning of February, the White House was already making plans to ask Congress for a revolving loan fund that would enable it to provide development assistance to these nations. On February 7, the policy-planning staff of the State Department issued a memorandum calling for the establishment of a development loan fund capitalized at $2 billion. "In the past the U.S. has given economic aid primarily to achieve short-run political objectives," the memorandum stated. "This use of aid may still be necessary on occasion but *our dominant aim should henceforth be to foster economic growth* [State Department italics], for this will best advance our basic objective." The policy-planning staff also called for separating the administration of development assistance from defense support and from programs designed to meet political emergencies.[22]

In March, the administration's response to the reports on foreign aid by the Fairless Committee and the IDAB indicated just how committed most of the administration had become to providing development assistance on a long-term, continuing basis. Both reports were carefully scrutinized by the CFEP, which solicited the views of other departments and offices after it received the reports. Government agencies criticized a number of the Fairless Committee's recommendations to limit or make difficult the extension of foreign aid, among them the committee's proposals that loans by the United States that were repayable in inconvertible funds be terminated and that grant assistance be given only in exceptional cases. Most government agencies also criticized the committee's recommendations that capital grants for development purposes be severely limited and that in foreign-assistance programs higher priority be given to those countries that joined in the collective security system. The State Department and the Council of Economic Advisers (CEA) objected to these recommendations most strongly, but other agencies also expressed dissent. Treasury Secretary Humphrey continued to oppose programs that he felt would strengthen the power of the state at the expense of individual freedom.[23] With the exception of the Treasury Department, however, a consensus developed within the administration that the Fairless Committee's proposals were too restrictive and conflicted with the White House's program of promoting economic growth overseas.[24]

The administration's response to the report by the IDAB was much more favorable. In contrast to the cool reception it gave many of the Fairless Committee's recommendations, the State Department strongly supported most of the proposals on economic assistance made by the IDAB. Noting that the board called for a new emphasis on long-term economic development as a major objective of foreign policy, the State Department contended that its report "complemented" the proposals of the Fairless Committee in two important ways: (1) it set forth a fuller statement of the United States' interest in promoting foreign economic development; and (2) it proposed a specific organizational structure that would give development aid the continuity and flexibility recommended in the Fairless report and in the studies prepared as part of the Senate's study of foreign aid. Specifically, the department supported the recommendation to create an International Development Fund as a way "of establishing a mechanism which would put the U.S. program for foreign economic development on a flexible and long-term basis."[25]

Similarly, the State Department favored separating the military from the economic aspects of the foreign-aid program, as recommended by the IDAB (and also by the Fairless Committee), and it endorsed the IDAB's proposal to allow the administrator of the development fund substantial flexibility in setting the conditions and terms of the loans the fund made. Indeed, the department believed that the fund's coverage should be broader than that recommended by the IDAB; its resources should be made available to all underdeveloped countries not under Communist control. The only crucial reservation the State Department expressed about the IDAB's proposals concerned the size of the fund. Whereas the IDAB called for a "substantial increase" in capital investment and technical-assistance programs, which the fund was to administer, the State Department did not believe that this would be "feasible or realistic" in the fund's first year of operation. Over a longer period of time, however, increased appropriations might well become necessary.[26]

Other government agencies also expressed support for the establishment of a development fund as recommended by the IDAB. Of those agencies that commented on the IDAB report, in fact, only the Department of Commerce indicated any opposition to the fund. On practical and ideological grounds the Commerce Department argued against placing foreign aid on what appeared to be a permanent basis, and it stressed the need for fiscal restraint. In contrast, the Department of Agriculture remarked that the fund should function as the major instrument of foreign economic policy. The ICA pointed out that any arrangement that permitted more time to plan and develop useful projects was highly desirable.[27]

The Decision to Support the DLF

President Eisenhower, who anticipated a difficult struggle with Congress over the mutual security program for 1958, doubted that the House and Senate would agree to the establishment of a development loan fund as recommended by the IDAB. Even though the House Foreign Affairs Committee had proposed that economic aid be placed on a long-term loan basis, the president thought that the chances of getting the fund through Congress "were approximately nil." He also expressed reservations, mostly administrative in nature, about separating economic aid for development purposes from economic aid for defense support.[28] Nevertheless, during the administration's review of the Fairless Committee report, Eisenhower found himself "more in accord" with the comments of the Department of State and the CEA than with those of any other agency. At a White House meeting in March, he also supported Secretary Dulles on the merits of establishing a lending agency to handle the major part of economic aid. Thus the president decided to undertake a major campaign in behalf of the mutual security program for 1958 and to make the creation of a loan fund a top priority.[29]

Eisenhower's decision to press ahead with a program of long-term development aid placed him squarely at odds with his close friend Treasury Secretary Humphrey and undercut much of the influence that Humphrey still enjoyed with the president. In a rambling letter to Paul Hoffman, the treasury secretary attacked Hoffman's recommendation for a modestly expanded program of technical assistance administered through the UN. Maintaining that Hoffman's proposal and many of the United States' own aid programs encouraged statism at the expense of private enterprise, Humphrey recounted examples of how during his own career individual initiative had contributed to America's growth. Upon receiving a copy of the letter from the treasury secretary, Eisenhower responded that Humphrey was out of touch with reality. Concepts of "personal rights" and "personal freedom" such as those set forth by Humphrey, he argued, had little meaning for Third World countries that were reaching the saturation point in population. It was essential to America's own interests to realize "that the spirit of nationalism, coupled with a deep hunger for some betterment in physical conditions and living standards, creates a critical situation in the under-developed areas of the world."[30]

On April 8, Secretary Dulles presented the administration's proposal for a $750 million aid fund to the Senate's special committee on foreign aid, which was still conducting hearings on the aid program. Dulles told the committee that military and economic aid should be separated. Defense support should be limited to that part of the economic burden of military defense which foreign countries themselves could not handle, and the military portion of foreign aid, including defense support, should be authorized on an annual basis as part of the Defense Department's budget. All economic development aid, including that which went to countries involved in military agreements with the United States, should be considered together, and more emphasis should be placed on long-term development assistance. True, such aid would constitute only a small part of any country's development program, but it could prove instrumental in breaking foreign-exchange bottlenecks and in stimulating more effective development programs.[31]

In the weeks following Dulles's appearance before the Senate's special committee, the administration undertook a well-orchestrated campaign to win public and congressional support for the loan fund as well as for the other foreign-aid proposals that Eisenhower planned to present to Congress in May. Working closely with C. D. Jackson, who continued to press his own proposal for a new world economic policy,[32] Dulles and the newly appointed undersecretary of state, Christian Herter, organized a private citizens' group, headed by the chairman and president of Owens-Corning Fiberglass Corporation, Harold Boeschenstein, to promote the mutual security program. The White House also drew up a list of key organizations that might be persuaded to support the program, including such respected groups as the Committee for Economic Development, the Business Advisory Council of the Department of Commerce, and the American Assembly. Finally, Jackson convinced Eisenhower to make a major radio and television address stressing the importance of foreign aid to the preservation of world peace.[33]

The president announced that he intended to give the highest priority to getting his foreign-aid program through Congress and that he expected the complete support of his cabinet in that effort. When confronted with reports, for example, that Treasury Secretary Humphrey was obstructing the planning of the proposed development loan fund, Eisenhower told the secretary that he was "completely dedicated and committed" to the fund and that Humphrey should iron out his differences with Secretary of State Dulles. Similarly, at a White House meeting in May at which he outlined his foreign-aid proposals for 1958, Eisenhower pressed congressional leaders not to cut mutual security and related programs from the budget.[34]

The Legislative Battle over Mutual Security: 1957

Before the president could send his mutual security requests to Congress, however, the Senate Special Committee to Study the Foreign Aid Program delivered its long-anticipated report. The committee recommended continued foreign aid to the nation's allies and to underdeveloped countries and supported a revolving loan fund, but it harshly criticized the mutual security program and expressed reservations about establishing the fund immediately. "The ambiguity concerning the purposes of foreign aid and the misconceptions of it as a single device of policy for carrying a multiplicity of programs [had] impaired its usefulness." The objectives of the various foreign-aid programs should be "separated, refined and restated . . . by the executive branch and the Congress." Legislation was needed to distinguish between the purposes and functions of the principal categories of aid. As for the loan fund, it should be established to promote economic development abroad, but it was "too important to be set up in haste," and interim measures might be necessary. More specifically, the committee recommended that the fund be administered by a government corporation and that its working capital be "built up" by Congress "over a period of years." The committee acknowledged that some local-currency loans might have to be made, but it proposed that in general the fund be administered on banking rather than foreign-policy principles, and that loans made by the fund be extended on the basis of reasonable expectation of repayment. Finally, the committee urged that the fund be used to promote private investment abroad.[35]

The Senate committee's report reminded the administration of the difficult fight it would face in Congress when it submitted its foreign-aid program for 1958. Indeed, Senator Fulbright told Undersecretary of State Herter that in order to win support for the rest of the report from the powerful Democratic chairman of the Armed Services Committee, Richard Russell of Georgia, the committee would have to strike from the report a paragraph placing military assistance and defense support in the Defense Department budget. According to Fulbright, the Georgia senator intended to do everything possible to keep the proposed loan fund a temporary measure and was prepared to vote against all economic aid.[36]

Complicating this struggle over foreign aid was a breakdown in the normally good relations between Eisenhower and the Democratic leadership in the House and Senate. The president had won reelection in 1956 by a landslide, but he had not been able to deliver Congress to the Republican party; the Democrats had retained their 50-to-46 margin in the Senate and maintained a comfortable 31-seat advantage in the House. In the previous Congress the Democratic leadership had generally given strong backing to the president's mutual security program, but in the Eighty-fifth Congress, relations between the White House and the Democrats began on much shakier grounds. The immediate issue between them was the administration's budget proposal for 1958. The president had submitted the biggest peacetime budget in the nation's history—$70 billion, or $10 billion over earlier estimates. On the one hand, Old Guard Republicans claimed that the administration was reverting to the days of New Deal spending. On the other hand, the president appeared to challenge the Democratic leadership by calling for a balanced budget and by claiming that additional cuts could be made in such "nonessential" domestic areas as federal support for home mortgages, farm surpluses, and reclamation projects. In effect, Eisenhower was telling Democrats to match his concern for fiscal prudence by cutting the fat from domestic projects. Taking up the challenge, Democrats joined Republicans in attacking the budget. Leaders of both parties claimed that spending could be cut by as much as $6.5 billion, particularly in the areas of military spending and foreign aid. This was the situation when the Senate Special Committee to Study the Foreign Aid Program presented its report.[37]

On May 21, one week after the Senate committee delivered its recommendations, President Eisenhower submitted to Congress his mutual security proposals for 1958. That evening he also outlined his program in a major television and radio broadcast. Remarking that his request for $3.87 billion was $535 million less than that estimated in his January budget message, Eisenhower said that nearly the entire reduction, $500 million, would come from savings in the military assistance program. The president advocated major changes in the operations and administration of foreign aid. Defense assistance programs should be clearly separated from programs for economic development and should be given continuing authorization under the Defense Department budget. Economic development assistance should be provided primarily in the form of loans on a continuing basis and should be closely related to technical assistance. To implement this program, Congress should establish a Development Loan Fund within the ICA capitalized at no less than $500 million for 1958 and an additional $750 million for fiscal 1959 and 1960. Finally, technical cooperation should be permanently authorized and a new "special assistance" fund of $300 million should be created for use by the president in economic and military emergencies.[38]

Already strained, relations between the administration and Capitol Hill were made even worse by submission of this foreign-aid program so late in the session.[39] The White House's decision to reduce its military assistance request also troubled legislators. Although it was part of an economy measure by Treasury Secretary Humphrey, who feared that the administration's own budget could bring on a depression, the move to cut military aid added to the already widespread belief that the program was unduly inflated and lent credibility to attacks on the cost of all foreign aid.[40] Later, in the House of Representatives, the foreign-aid bill became the scapegoat in a bitter struggle over an administration-sponsored civil rights bill designed to protect the rights of black people in federal elections and in a controversy over an order by Director of the Budget Percival F. Brundage that all government agencies restrict the next year's spending to existing levels. All this dimmed the administration's chances of getting a successful aid bill through Congress.

Hearings on the president's aid requests began before the Senate Foreign Relations Committee and the House Foreign Affairs Committee on May

22, only one day after Eisenhower had sent his special message to Congress. The Senate committee took testimony until June 3, while the House committee continued to call witnesses until June 23. In presenting the administration's case before the Senate Foreign Relations Committee, Secretary of State Dulles reiterated previous arguments in support of development aid and presented additional details of the plan for the Development Loan Fund. The fund would be specifically prohibited from making grants, but the terms of its loans would be softer than those of existing institutions. It would be allowed to participate in joint ventures with private investors, the World Bank, or the Eximbank. A large part of its financing would go to such basic public works as transportation and communication, power installations, harbors, and irrigation and drainage projects.[41]

Other administration witnesses before the Senate and House committees also spoke in support of the Development Loan Fund and advocated the separate funding of military and economic assistance programs. During the Senate hearings, Democrat Mike Mansfield of Montana warned ICA Director Hollister that he was "looking for trouble" in proposing to place defense support funds in the Defense Department budget and suggested that defense support be included in the proposed "special assistance" fund.[42] Another Democrat, Wayne Morse of Oregon, called the administration's proposal for extended presidential authorization in matters involving military and economic aid "a very dangerous" expansion of executive authority and said that he would not vote in support of such discretionary power.[43] Despite such objections, the Senate approved the administration's program, including its proposal for a Development Loan Fund. The Foreign Relations Committee cut Eisenhower's recommendations by $250 million and decided against an indefinite authorization for the technical assistance program, but it granted a two-year authorization for the military assistance and defense support programs and approved creation of the Development Loan Fund (DLF) virtually as proposed by the administration, adding to the fund only an interdepartmental (cabinet) Advisory Loan Committee. Moreover, the full Senate approved the legislation in the form passed by the committee.[44]

In the House, however, the reception given the president's foreign aid requests was quite different. Contentious executive sessions followed lengthy hearings, and when a bill was finally reported out of committee, twenty-five days after the Senate had completed action on its version of the measure, the Foreign Affairs Committee had cut the president's program by another $375 million. In its final report the committee made a strong case for the DLF, noting the widespread support it had received among those who had studied the foreign-aid program, but at one time in its deliberations it actually voted to delete the fund entirely, and in the end it cut $250 million from the fund's authorization for both 1959 and 1960.[45] Furthermore, when the bill reached the full House, it underwent additional pruning, for unlike the Senate, the House broke from its committee's recommendations in several key respects.

The atmosphere in the House was clouded by the administration's civil rights legislation. A number of Southerners vented their anger over the civil rights measure against the foreign-aid program. Other legislators, upset by the Bureau of the Budget's order that government agencies restrict next year's spending to existing levels—an action they regarded as a usurpation of congressional authority—did the same. Aware of the tide running against the foreign-aid program, House Speaker Rayburn, who in the previous year had made one of his rare speeches in order to support foreign aid, this time remained discreetly silent.[46] As a result, the House approved cuts totaling $125.5 million more than its committee had recommended. It also accepted an amendment that authorized establishment of the DLF on a one-year basis only, and it rejected all requests for long-term lending authority.[47]

The final authorization measure, worked out in conference committee and agreed to by both houses in August, more closely resembled the House bill than the Senate version. It provided for a mutual security authorization of $3.38 billion for fiscal 1958, almost $500 million less than the president had requested and over $200 million less than had been approved by the Senate, but only $80 million more than had been passed by the House. The bill split the difference between the House and Senate authorizations for the DLF, providing a two-year authorization instead of the one year agreed to by the House and the three years approved by the Senate. However, it authorized only $625 million for fiscal 1959, $125 million less than had been sought by the administration and approved by the Senate.[48]

President Eisenhower was disappointed by the cuts in his mutual security proposals and the rejection of his requests for long-term aid authorizations, but he had anticipated a difficult struggle with Congress over foreign aid. At least the House and Senate had approved his first priority, the establishment of the Development Loan Fund, and had given the fund the $500 million authorization for fiscal 1958 he had requested. In sum, the president believed that, provided no further cuts were made, the mutual security bill as approved by Congress would allow the administration to carry out most of its foreign-aid program for 1958.[49]

The Battle over Appropriations

The president realized, however, that the major struggle over foreign aid would take place during the appropriations process, particularly in the House. The chairman of the House Appropriations Committee, Clarence Cannon of Missouri, had been increasingly critical of foreign aid. Otto Passman of Louisiana, chairman of the Subcommittee on Foreign Operations, which handled the foreign-aid measure, had voted against all foreign-aid authorizations and appropriations before becoming subcommittee chairman.[50] Bryce Harlow, an administrative aid to the president, predicted in June, when the Senate Foreign Relations Committee first reported the authorization measure onto the Senate floor, that the real test would come during the appropriations process.[51] Even as Congress considered the authorization measure, therefore, the administration sought to heal the rift that had developed between it and the Democratic leadership and to win the support of the Senate and House Appropriations committees. Undersecretary of State Herter met with House Speaker Rayburn at the end of June, for example, and White House conferences with Rayburn and other legislative leaders continued on a regular basis throughout July and into August.[52] As Congress completed action on the final authorization measure, the president took the unusual step of inviting to the White House the ten members of the House and Senate who would be most directly involved in the upcoming appropriations debate. At this meeting he stated that he would sacrifice part of his own salary "to meet the pressing need of adequate funds for foreign aid." He repeated the offer the next morning at a regular meeting with Republican leaders.[53]

Despite these efforts by the White House and a threat by the president to call a special session of Congress if the Senate and House Appropriations committees made further cuts in the foreign aid bill, Congress handed the administration another major setback. In the House, the Appropriations Subcommittee on Foreign Operations slashed the authorization bill by over $842 million. Accusing the administration of "purposely losing sleep working up figures that cannot be justified and asking for more money than they need," Chairman Passman beat back every effort to increase the size of the appropriation. Eisenhower's threat of a special session produced only a backlash against the administration, and even Rayburn took no action to help pro-aid forces.[54] In the Senate, Majority Leader Lyndon Johnson was able to restore $501 million to the House-passed bill, but in conference committee the two houses split their differences. Conferees added $90 million to the House figure for military assistance, for a final appropriation of $1.34 billion for that program. They accepted the Senate's $689 million figure for new defense support funds, but approved the $300 million House figure for the DLF. Finally, they deleted a Senate amendment that would have made $20 million available for assistance to Latin America, and they placed a time limit of December 31, 1958, on the commitment of military assistance funds. (The Senate had provided that the funds be available until expended.) The final appropriation for fiscal 1958, $2.77 billion, which was agreed to by the House and Senate at the end of August, was $1 billion less than the president had requested in May.[55]

Eisenhower had anticipated such an outcome, but he could not hide his frustration and bitterness. "I am told," he wrote to a friend in August, "that the Appropriation Committees, especially the one in the House of Representatives, are determined to slash our mutual security funds and that they will probably not allow us the requested authority for development loans on a three year basis." If this were only a quarrel between Congress and the executive branch, he said, he could accept a defeat on foreign aid. But much more was involved. "Some people are still stupid enough to believe in the concept of 'Fortress America.' "[56] Nevertheless, the president abandoned his threat to call a special session of Congress, chastened perhaps by the adverse reaction it had created in both houses. Instead, in September he signed the appropriations measure, but he made known to the press his general displeasure with Congress's record for 1957, particularly that in the field of mutual security.[57]

Conclusion

There can be no denying the magnitude of the administration's defeat in Congress. As Republican Senator H. Alexander Smith of New Jersey commented during the Senate's consideration of the conference report on appropriations: "We have now witnessed the most unfortunate development, namely the unwillingness of the House to go above $2.7 billion for the final appropriation for fiscal 1958. . . . This is a devastating defeat . . . for the President."[58] Even if Congress had given Eisenhower all that he had requested, however, it would have been considerably less than many proponents of foreign aid, including Millikan and Rostow, believed was necessary for Third World economic development. In fact, both Congress and the administration were timid in their efforts in behalf of economic growth abroad. Putting aside military programs, the president's aid requests for 1958 amounted to only $104 million more than the figure for 1957. Throughout the struggle over the DLF the White House had also stressed the point that establishment of the fund was intended to save rather than add to foreign-aid expenditures.[59] While some of this emphasis on businesslike efficiency and fiscal economy was merely a political ploy designed to win support for the president's program, it also indicated that divisions remained within the administration over the extent to which public capital should be used to foster economic growth in underdeveloped countries. It suggested that the White House still intended to rely heavily on foreign trade and private investment as part of its overall foreign economic program.[60]

Nevertheless, Eisenhower's mutual security proposals for 1958 and Congress's establishment of the DLF marked a significant departure in U.S. foreign economic policy. By seeking to expand the category of development assistance within the mutual security program and place it on a long-term basis, the administration acknowledged that economic growth was the fundamental long-term problem facing the United States in the area of mutual security; such sustained growth required a commitment of public capital for an indefinite period. The White House accepted this obligation by proposing a revolving loan fund, and although Congress cut the president's proposal for the DLF and his overall foreign-aid recommendations drastically, it agreed for the moment to go along with the president.

Moreover, as in previous years, congressional opposition to the White House's aid requests hid as much as it revealed. In the first place, a sizable group of highly articulate senators and representatives from both parties continued to support the administration's aid program and, like the president, stressed the long-term interests of the United States in promoting development abroad. In the House, these legislators prevented the DLF from being scuttled in committee, and in both the House and Senate they grew progressively more effective in preventing further cuts in foreign aid. In the second place, the Senate generally responded more favorably to the White House's recommendations than did the House; for instance, it authorized most of the administration's requests for 1958, while the House generally cut or rejected them. In subsequent years, the Senate's position on foreign aid would increasingly prevail over that of the House. Finally, as Senator Wayne Morse pointed out, opponents of the president's program were not always opposed to the concept of foreign aid. Morse approved the establishment of the DLF *in principle*. He opposed giving it long-term authorization because he did not know how well it would function or how it would affect other government lending activities abroad, such as those carried out by the ICA. The Oregon senator also objected to the delegation of congressional authority to the executive branch, the ineffectiveness of earlier foreign-aid commitments, and the totalitarian or "irresponsible" nature of many of the governments the United States supported.[61]

Other opponents of the president's foreign-aid program made similar comments. They claimed that aid, as presently administered, produced a permanent state of dependency of the underdeveloped nations on the United States. They alleged a continuing failure by the White House to clarify the purposes of foreign aid, particularly in terms of making explicit the relationships between the various mutual security programs. Moreover, they maintained that current levels of funding were both sufficient to meet the administration's objectives abroad and as high as could be administered efficiently. Undoubtedly a good number of these arguments were disingenuous, but they were made often enough to suggest that they were also not entirely spurious. Indeed, even proponents of foreign aid made many of the same points.[62]

Following Congress's approval of the DLF, Undersecretary of State Herter expressed the expectation that the fund would be highly effective in stimulating foreign economic development. He found particularly attractive the fund's provision for investment guaranties, which he believed would induce private capital to finance a significant volume of development activities that the fund might otherwise have to support. But he also noted that as long as the Communist danger remained acute in Third World regions, "it would be unrealistic to plan on a complete substitution of private investment for economic assistance programs."[63]

The White House was slow to use the new fund. Not until March 1958 did the State Department announce its first loan, $75 million to India to help finance that nation's Second Five-Year Plan. But in 1958 Congress increased the fiscal 1959 appropriation for the fund by $100 million and converted the fund into a government corporation with a managing director and a board of directors. The principle of a revolving loan fund was thereby accepted, and a precedent was established for government participation in other long-term development projects, such as a new soft-loan agency operated under World Bank auspices and a regional bank for Latin America organized under U.S. auspices.[64]

7. Trade and Aid: Reciprocal Trade 1957–1958

THE SECOND SESSION of the Eighty-fifth Congress promised to be even more difficult for the Eisenhower administration than the first had been. Relations between the White House and Congress remained tense. Privately, Eisenhower scarcely concealed his contempt for Congress, but it was an election year, and political analysts expected party politics to be prominent in the legislative process. Eisenhower again asked Congress for increased foreign-aid appropriations. His aid requests were more modest than those of 1957, but he sought additional funds for development assistance, including the full $625 million for the DLF authorized the previous year. He also requested that the fund be incorporated and empowered to act as a coordinating agency with other lending institutions.

Eisenhower's major legislative priority in foreign economic policy, however, was a five-year extension of the Trade Agreements Act and additional presidential authority to reduce tariffs. The president also again tried to win congressional approval for American membership in the OTC. He believed that his trade proposals, like the mutual security program, were needed to protect and strengthen the non-Communist world against the Soviet economic challenge. No longer advocating expanded international commerce as an alternative to foreign economic aid, the White House regarded both trade and aid as essential to the economic vitality of the free world. Also, six European nations were in the process of forming a common market, and in order to bargain with this new economic community, the administration felt it had to win a long-term extension of the Trade Agreements Act and broadened presidential authority to make tariff cuts.

Congress responded to the president's requests by giving him far less than he wanted but considerably more than many Washington observers had anticipated. On the negative side, Congress slashed Eisenhower's mutual security recommendations by more than $640 million, including $250 million for the DLF. It also rejected an administration-sponsored amendment allowing aid to Soviet satellite nations, and despite Eisenhower's plea that the Trade Agreements Act not be weakened through restrictive amendments, it attached to it a number of protectionist provisions. Finally, Congress refused even to

113

consider U.S. membership in the OTC. On the positive side, the cuts in foreign aid were considerably smaller than those of the previous year. Moreover, the House and Senate added $100 million to the DLF appropriation for 1958 and approved the administration's request that the fund be incorporated with a managing director and a board of directors. In addition, they adopted a resolution introduced by Mike Monroney of Oklahoma and endorsed by the Departments of State and Treasury to have the National Advisory Council look into the possibility of establishing an International Development Association (IDA) as an affiliate of the World Bank. As for the Trade Agreements Act, Congress gave the administration most of what it requested, including a four-year extension of the reciprocal trade program and authority to reduce tariffs over this period by an additional 20 percent.

Thus, the White House had reason to be satisfied with its legislative accomplishments for 1958. The president had avoided the foreign-aid disaster of the previous year, and the House and Senate had approved a long-term extension of the Trade Agreements Act despite protectionist sentiment, which was reported by *Business Week* "to be reaching the strength of the Smoot-Hawley days."[1] In truth, the administration itself was responsible for many of its congressional achievements. It took advantage of the crisis atmosphere created by the successful Soviet launching of an earth satellite in October to emphasize the urgency of its trade-and-aid programs. In addition, Eisenhower cultivated the Democratic leadership in both the House and Senate and, following a tactic he had used before, launched a massive public relations campaign in behalf of his programs which won nationwide support from a coalition of politicians, former diplomats, business leaders, and even a few Hollywood celebrities.

Yet the administration failed more often than it succeeded with Congress, and the results it achieved actually gave proponents of liberalized trade and expanded aid very little cause for satisfaction. The House and Senate's less than total hostility to the White House's foreign economic program hardly comforted those who rightly feared that Congress would add new restrictions to the Trade Agreements Act or not ratify the OTC. Nor was much satisfaction derived from the foreign-aid cuts that Congress did make or from its unwillingness to add more than $100 million to the DLF appropriation. By continuing to follow a restrictive agricultural program, the White House also contradicted the principles of free trade. It persisted in limiting imports of farm products, subsidizing agricultural exports, and making the disposal of farm surpluses an essential part of its foreign-aid program. Finally, the administration remained opposed to the establishment of a Special United Nations Fund for Economic Development (SUNFED), despite the fact that the proposal was now supported by most of America's closest allies, and this raised doubts, even within the United States, about the White House's commitment to economic development in Third World countries.

What was remarkable about the dialogue over the nation's foreign economic policy in 1958, however, was how barren and circumscribed it remained. Impassioned arguments about short- and long-term gains from economic growth abroad became Cold War shibboleths, and the entire discussion assumed a pedestrian quality. The assumptions behind the case for expanded trade and aid blurred the administration's view of the Third World. Such basic issues as the harsh circumstances of primary producing countries in declining commodity markets or the economic consequences of their social and political systems continued to go largely unnoticed or unheeded. In their haste to industrialize, even Third World leaders often ignored the fundamental problems of their agricultural and mineral-based economies and underestimated the difficulties that would result from economic growth. Thus, criticism of the administration's foreign economic program by proponents of trade and aid often amounted to asking for more of the same.

Renewal of Reciprocal Trade

That renewal of the Trade Agreements Act in 1958 would be strongly debated in Congress became clear as early as 1956, when the House Ways and Means Committee established a subcommittee to investigate the effects of the nation's tariff laws on foreign economic policy and the domestic economy.[2] In a memorandum to the Joint Economic Committee of Congress, a copy of which he sent to Commerce Secretary Sinclair Weeks, Republican Senator Ralph Flanders of Vermont, a twenty-year veteran of the Senate and a member of the Finance Committee (which considered tariff legislation), made clear his intention to work against further extension of the reciprocal trade program. One of the first Republican leaders to back Eisenhower's candidacy for the presidency in 1952 and one of the administration's strongest supporters in Congress, Flanders was nevertheless only a moderate internationalist on most foreign-policy issues. Challenging the administration's assumption that trade by itself contributed to peace, he questioned whether the United States could "afford to let pass into foreign hands" any industry important to the American consumer or essential to the national defense.[3]

The administration did not begin to give serious consideration to renewal of the Trade Agreements Act, however, until June 1957, when the State Department called a conference to discuss the congressional status of the proposed OTC. Despite Congress's refusal even to consider American participation in the OTC, the White House remained convinced of the need for U.S. membership. Diplomats in Europe, where final talks on the formation of the Common Market were taking place, stressed the importance of the OTC in bringing about Western economic cohesion. A resolution introduced at the closing session of GATT in November urged quick ratification by all countries.

To gain congressional approval for American participation, Eisenhower turned to the Department of Commerce rather than the State Department. He hoped to gain more support for the OTC by emphasizing its advantages, along with those of GATT, in reducing trade barriers and other restrictions against U.S. exports. Furthermore, he recognized the strength of the previous year's argument in Congress that GATT was primarily an instrument of foreign policy rather than an effective body for increasing American (and world) trade.[4] Despite this change in tactics, the House and Senate again refused to act on the OTC legislation. The chairman of the House Ways and Means Committee, Jere Cooper of Tennessee, told Commerce Secretary Sinclair Weeks that he would not send a ratification bill to the House without the approval of the majority of the Republican members of the committee, which according to Weeks did not exist.[5]

As the commerce secretary indicated at a meeting called by the State Department, however, Congress's refusal to act on American membership involved more than antagonism toward the OTC. Of much greater concern to the House and Senate was renewal of the Trade Agreements Extension Act, which was due to expire the next year. Richard Simpson of Pennsylvania, a ranking Republican member of the Ways and Means Committee, told Weeks that the entire reciprocal trade program was extremely unpopular in Congress for at least two reasons. First, Congress felt that the State Department had too much influence in administering the program, and that thus the plight of some industries in the United States, when measured against international considerations, did not receive sufficient attention. Second, many congressmen objected to the fact that while the Tariff Commission had recommended protective actions for American industry on fifteen occasions, the president had approved such measures in only four instances.[6]

From his conversation with Simpson the commerce secretary concluded that only a number of concessions, made in advance to the Ways and Means Committee, could save the OTC legislation that year and the Trade Agreements Act the next year. According to Weeks, these concessions included changes that would give the Department of Commerce a larger role in the administration of the Trade Agreements Act, a promise from the president that he would strictly adhere to the Tariff Commission's recommendations, and a more precise definition of what constituted injury to American business.[7] A former finance chairman of the Republican National Committee, and a man whose economic views one historian has described as "even more conservative" than those of Treasury Secretary Humphrey,[8] Weeks had many times expressed concern about the adverse effects of foreign competition on the American economy. He had even objected to the Eximbank's financing of aircraft that foreign firms might use to compete with American airlines.[9] He was also anxious to increase the role of the Commerce Department in formulating trade policy. That goal was accomplished when the White House accepted a proposal by Clarence Randall, who had replaced Joseph Dodge as chairman of the CFEP following Dodge's return to private life in 1956, that a Trade Policy Committee be established under the direction of the Commerce Department. The committee would make general policy recommendations concerning the Trade Agreements Act and advise the president on agreements with other countries negotiated by the State Department.[10]

The commerce secretary's recommendations on tariff legislation thus aimed self-servingly at increasing the Commerce Department's authority over trade matters at the expense of the State Department. Dulles and Christian Herter, who were at the State Department meeting with Weeks, asked the commerce secretary to put his recommendations in writing for their further consideration. Later, Clarence Randall made a similar request of Weeks and confirmed to Herter that some deal with Congressman Simpson and his colleagues might be necessary to save the OTC and Trade Agreements Extension legislation from defeat.[11] A month later Weeks sent Randall a Commerce Department proposal to increase tariff rates in escape clause cases covered by the Trade Agreements Act. Existing legislation authorized the president to increase tariff rates 50 percent above 1945 levels in cases where the Tariff Commission determined that foreign imports covered by the act caused, or threatened to cause, serious injury to American industry. The Commerce Department proposed authorizing the president to raise duties by an indeterminate amount above the much higher 1934 levels (1934, of course, being the year when the Trade Agreements program began).[12]

Both President Eisenhower and Secretary of State Dulles opposed Weeks's call for unlimited presidential power over tariff rates in escape clause cases. They realized that such authority would lead to unacceptable pressure on the White House from protectionist forces. Yet the president also concluded that some concessions like those proposed by the commerce secretary were needed to save his trade program in Congress. Thus, while the White House rejected Weeks's recommendation for unrestricted presidential power in escape clause cases, over the next six months it agreed to two other changes in the reciprocal trade legislation. The first, a modification of Weeks's original proposal, gave the president authority in escape clause actions to raise tariffs by 50 percent over the 1934 rates rather than the lower 1945 levels. The second provided for an automatic escape clause proceeding in cases where the Tariff Commission, in its "peril point" investigations, found that existing tariff rates were not high enough to prevent the threat of injury to domestic producers. Under existing law there was no provision for such automatic action. By making these concessions, which were intended to speed the availability of relief and strengthen the safeguards for American industry against foreign competition, President Eisenhower and Secretary Dulles hoped to appease protectionist forces and gain congressional approval for the rest of the administration's trade program, which was then being drafted.[13]

In fact, the White House exerted considerable effort in preparing its trade recommendations for the next session of Congress even as it watched the mutilation of its foreign-aid program in the current session. Beginning in July 1957 the CFEP met regularly to formulate its proposals and to plan strategy for the session that would begin in January. At the same time, White House officials worked closely with a number of private groups, including the U.S. Council of the International Chambers of Commerce, the Committee for a National Trade Policy, and the newly formed Americans for OTC, to press for American membership in the OTC. The administration's plan was to move its bill through the House that summer and fall so that it would reach the Senate early in the next session. Thus it hoped to avoid entangling the OTC measure in the debate over extension of the Trade Agreements Act.[14]

The Renewed Controversy over Lead and Zinc Imports

The White House's well-laid plans were sidetracked, however, when Congress adjourned without taking action on the OTC legislation. More important, during the summer 1957 the administration took a position in the renewed controversy over lead and zinc imports that proved extremely embarrassing and placed the White House in the position of appearing to ignore the very legislation it wanted to extend. In 1954, following an escape clause investigation, the Tariff Commission had recommended that tariffs on lead and zinc be raised to protect the domestic mining industry. Fearing the unfavorable reaction this would cause among the nation's allies and not wishing to contravene his own liberal trade policy, the president had tried to finesse this politically sensitive issue by increasing stockpile purchases of lead and zinc and asking for voluntary restraints on their import. But he had warned that he would take "even more far-reaching measures" if the prices for the two metals did not stabilize.[15] Over the next three years the government made large purchases of domestically produced lead and zinc and bartered agricultural surpluses for foreign supplies. Although this caused substantial price increases, it also led to renewed imports. With the stockpile already too large, prices beginning to drop, and the domestic industry again threatened by foreign competition, the administration decided in June 1957 to take the additional steps Eisenhower had outlined in 1954. Thus, with the president's approval, the Department of Interior sent to Congress a proposal for a long-term program for minerals that included a recommendation for a sliding scale of excise taxes on lead and zinc imports.[16]

Although Congress might normally have backed the administration's recommendation since it protected an essential domestic industry, the proposal appeared to violate section 7 of the Trade Agreements Act, which provided that the Tariff Commission conduct an investigation in escape clause cases. On August 16 Chairman Cooper of the House Ways and Means Committee made public a letter he had sent to the president to this effect, a letter in which he also claimed to have the support of the fourteen other Democratic members of the Ways and Means Committee. In the Senate, Albert Gore of Tennessee and Paul Douglas of Illinois issued a report opposing any tariff increase as "a serious blow to our economy and an attempt to undermine our reciprocal trade program."[17] The president had told legislative leaders that he intended to stand by his tax proposal on lead and zinc, but he bowed to this congressional pressure. At a legislative leadership meeting and at a press conference the next day, he conceded that a Tariff Commission investigation was a better way of handling the matter.[18] In a letter to Cooper he warned that if Congress failed to act on his tax proposal, he would ask the Tariff Commission to investigate the lead and zinc industries under the escape clause provision of the tariff laws.[19] As the president anticipated, the Ways and Means Committee failed to report out the tax proposal, and he ordered the Tariff Commission to begin its investigation.[20]

The Administration's Trade Program

The controversy over lead and zinc imports was politically awkward for the administration, and it alienated many Democratic advocates of liberalized trade. Nevertheless, the White House continued throughout the summer of 1957 to prepare for what *Business Week* predicted would be "the roughest political fight over foreign trade in a quarter of a century."[21] The president had decided to ask Congress for a five-year extension of the Trade Agreements Act and authority to cut rates by 25 percent over five years. According to White House strategy, Commerce Secretary Weeks, who again was assigned the major responsibility for presenting the administration's trade and tariff proposals to the House and Senate, would justify the program in terms of its benefits to the American economy. Secretary Dulles would emphasize the relationship between trade and foreign policy, and Deputy Undersecretary Dillon would analyze the possible effects of the European Common Market on the United States.[22]

Eisenhower waited until a December meeting of congressional leaders at the White House to present his trade program as part of his overall foreign-policy proposals for 1958.[23] Dulles began the discussion on foreign trade with a few remarks on the international importance of world trade, the danger of the Soviet economic offensive abroad, and the need expressed by other countries for dependable access to U.S. markets, but the major spokesman for the administration was Commerce Secretary Weeks, who elaborated on the importance of foreign commerce to the domestic economy. Citing Nikita Khrushchev's boast of the previous fall that the Soviet Union was engaged in a trade war against the United States, Weeks noted that U.S. exports to countries with whom it had trade agreements had increased by the largest amounts. He then outlined the administration's proposal for a five-year extension of the Trade Agreements Act and additional presidential authority to cut tariff rates. He also mentioned other legislative items, including the need to approve American membership in the OTC and the creation of a new Trade Policy Committee.[24] Deputy Undersecretary Dillon concluded the administration's lengthy presentation with remarks on the new, single tariff of the European Common Market. He warned that it would hurt American exports because of internal reductions within the Market unless the United States was successful in bargaining for compensatory cuts as required under GATT rules.

Congressional leaders reacted to the White House presentation with caution. Citing his own devotion to the reciprocal trade program, Speaker Rayburn promised to support the administration's proposals, but he warned that this would be the toughest of any legislative session. (After the White House briefing, Rayburn said it would take "blood, sweat and tears" to get the program through Congress.) Similarly, Senate Minority Leader Everett Dirksen spoke of the difficulty of obtaining tariff relief expeditiously when needed and suggested that prompter action by the administration on relief cases would facilitate passage of the legislation.[25]

The Investigation of Foreign-Trade Policy

On December 2, the day before these congressional leaders met with the president, the Subcommittee on Foreign Trade Policy, which the House Ways and Means Committee had established in 1956, began a series of hearings that lasted through the middle of December. These hearings foreshadowed much of the debate that would begin in Congress the following February. Organized at the end of the Eighty-fourth Congress to investigate the nation's tariff laws, the subcommittee had been reestablished at the beginning of the Eighty-fifth Congress. Headed by Hale Boggs of Louisiana (and usually referred to as the Boggs Committee), it had commissioned a series of studies on foreign trade by many of the nation's leading experts. These studies were similar to those done on the mutual security program a year earlier for the special Senate committee investigating foreign aid. Unlike this other committee, however, the Boggs Committee asked the White House to participate in its investigation by preparing an analysis of the Trade Agreements Act and its relationship to overall foreign economic policy.[26]

The compendium of papers prepared for the Boggs Committee and issued in October 1957 covered most aspects of foreign trade: duty rates, the American balance of payments and its relationship to foreign trade policy, recent developments in the foreign trade policies of other countries, trade agreements legislation and administration, foreign trade policy and national security, and foreign trade policy in relation to American agriculture.[27] Perhaps the most forceful argument in behalf of liberalized trade was that presented by Professor Lincoln Gordon of Harvard University, who had served as minister to England at the beginning of the Eisenhower administration and who would become ambassador to Brazil during the Kennedy administration. Gordon remarked that since 1945 America had made considerable progress in achieving its objective of an orderly framework for private trade and investment based on international cooperation. He noted, however, that recent developments raised the possibility that some countries might again resort to a form of autarchy and organize the soft-currency countries against the dollar world. These developments included not only the protectionist tendency in the United States, as manifested by restrictive amendments to the Trade Agreements Act and failure to ratify the OTC agreement, but also a renewed world dollar shortage.[28]

Although Gordon made a strong case for a liberal trade policy, he did not elaborate on the specifics of such a program. In separate papers, however, Miriam Camps, a former chief economic officer for the Department of State, and Richard Gardner, a recognized expert on foreign trade matters, argued that the president should have new bargaining power, including the authority to reduce tariffs on an across-the-board basis. In Camps's opinion, expanded presidential authority, such as the right to restrict use of the escape clause, would reduce the uncertainty about U.S. trade policy, which was the primary concern of America's trading partners. Under such expanded authority, reciprocity would come to mean more than simply reducing tariffs.[29] According to Gardner, there was no reason why the president should be kept from reducing tariffs until he had obtained concessions from other countries, as the law then required, or from making other tariff and trade changes. At the very least, the president should have the freedom to bargain trade concessions in return for economic and political commitments quite apart from tariff and trade concerns.[30]

Just as most of the reports commissioned by the Senate special committee on foreign aid argued for expanded economic assistance to Third World nations, so most of the other studies for the Boggs Committee called for a liberalized trade policy similar to that recommended by Camps and Gardner. In fact, many of the reports were more liberal than the administration's trade program, particularly with respect to restrictive trade amendments and presidential bargaining authority.[31] But unlike the Senate study on foreign aid, the Boggs compendium contained a number of dissenting views. Opponents of liberalized trade took sharp issue with advocates on almost every point. They disputed especially the degree to which the United States was allegedly following a restrictionist trade policy, the effect of tariffs on the domestic economy, and the question of where control of tariffs should be placed. For the most part, opponents of freer trade maintained that tariffs had already been cut too much and that the tendency toward restrictionism was greater in other countries than in the United States. They also argued that irreparable harm was being done to such vital American industries as cotton manufacturing and that administration of the tariff should be made a joint responsibility of Congress and the Tariff Commission.[32]

Proponents and opponents of liberalized trade repeated most of these arguments before the Boggs Committee during its hearings in December. Most of the recommendations, which ranged from a ten-year extension of the Trade Agreements Act to none at all, also had been made earlier. Nevertheless, the hearings—and, even more important, the studies made in preparation for the hearings—defined the issues and arguments Congress would consider when it took up the administration's trade program early the next year.[33]

Foreign Trade and the Soviet Economic Offensive

At a NATO summit meeting in Paris just before Christmas, President Eisenhower promised to use the full powers of his office to gain approval of his tariff recommendations. The White House also gave preliminary approval to a series of proposals by the Department of Commerce for a nationwide campaign on behalf of its trade recommendations, including the convening of a President's Conference on World Trade and the establishment of an economic research program within the executive branch to answer congressional and public inquiries on the regional impact of foreign commerce. The president also decided to separate the trade campaign from the one in support of his mutual security program, and he named Paul Hoffman to run the campaign.[34]

Neither the president's January message to Congress on trade nor the hearings that followed the next month brought many surprises, but in an apparent last-minute change of strategy, the administration decided to emphasize the Soviet economic offensive more than it had originally planned. White House officials had watched Soviet economic activity with growing concern throughout 1957, but they became even more alarmed at the beginning of 1958 when the State Department issued a report on Soviet bloc activities in Third World regions. The report described the loans and trade agreements the Communist bloc nations had concluded with such countries as Syria, Egypt, and Afghanistan and suggested that the Soviets were making Syria and Egypt their bases for extending Communist control into the Middle East and Africa.[35] Obviously disturbed by these findings, Secretary of State Dulles asked the president to make the Soviet economic offensive the first item of business at the next cabinet meeting. At that meeting, on January 10, Dulles described at length the possibility and dangers of economic warfare with the Soviets, citing in particular Khrushchev's declaration of economic war on the West the previous fall. Dulles suggested that the administration immediately make another study of Moscow's potential for economic competition against the West and of measures to counteract the Soviet threat. The cabinet agreed and instructed Vice-President Nixon to prepare a charter for establishing a new study committee.[36] Yet at the cabinet meeting the following week, Dulles again expressed concern about the Soviet offensive and warned of the advantages Moscow would have over the United States abroad if the administration's trade program were seriously weakened by Congress.[37]

President Eisenhower therefore decided to focus on the Soviet economic offensive in his special message to Congress on trade legislation. Asking for a five-year extension of the Trade Agreements Act and for authority to cut tariffs by 25 percent over the next five years, as well as for modifications in the legislation's escape clause and peril point provisions, the president underscored the dangers the Soviet economic challenge posed to the United States. "The Soviet capacity to export is matched by its capacity and willingness to import" he warned. "This challenge in the economic field cannot be ignored without the gravest risk to our way of life." Eisenhower subordinated other issues, such as the importance of having adequate tariff authority to negotiate trade restrictions with the Common Market, to this overarching theme of the economic threat to the United States that Moscow posed in Third World countries.[38]

In lengthy hearings before the House Ways and Means Committee, administration witnesses also referred repeatedly to the Soviet challenge. The hearings, which began in February, lasted through the end of March. Commerce Secretary Weeks, Secretary of State Dulles, and Deputy Undersecretary of State Dillon all stressed the Soviet economic challenge in arguing for extension of the Trade Agreements Act. For the most part, however, opponents of the administration's trade program ignored the White House's attempt to make this linkage. One witness said it was merely "a recent addition to the arguments and slogans by which [reciprocal trade] has been put over periodically in the past." Nor did opponents of reciprocal trade have much to say about the administration's claim that a five-year tariff extension was necessary in order to negotiate successfully with the European Common Market. Instead, they relied on traditional arguments and growing protectionist sentiment in the United States to defeat the president's proposals. At the hearings their ranks were swollen by a growing number of industry, and even some labor, spokesmen and by independent oil and coal producers and representatives from other depressed mining industries. All sought relief from foreign imports through the imposition of higher duties or import quotas.[39]

Despite the White House's emphasis on the Soviet economic threat, it was clear by the end of the hearings that the administration's trade program was in deep trouble. Senate Majority Leader Johnson said as much, and in the House, opponents of the program claimed they had the votes to defeat any trade legislation. Further diminishing the White House's chances of getting the bill through Congress was the fact that by the spring of 1958 the United States had slid into a serious recession as a result of a decline in private investment and a drop in industrial production. The recession added strength to the protectionists' argument that the United States was facing unfair competition from abroad and caused a drop in the president's popularity. The president's rating in the polls plunged from 79 percent at the beginning of his second term to 49 percent in April, one of the sharpest drops ever recorded.[40]

Eisenhower's final effort to save his trade program began at a White House dinner in March, where he again emphasized the vital national interest involved in passage of his trade recommendations. Later that month he made the same argument before the National Conference on International Trade Policy in Washington. Planned and arranged by the White House, this gathering brought together business, civic, labor, and farm leaders from all sections of the country and represented the climax of months of administration activity to rally grassroots support behind the Trade Agreements Act. In a major address to the conference, the president spelled out the dangers of the Soviet economic offensive abroad and warned that non-Communist nations would "inexorably" turn to the Communist world if they could not trade with the West because of tariff barriers.[41]

The Trade Bill in the House

Considering the nation's political climate, the growing protectionist mood in Congress, and the strength of the opposition to the trade agreements program, the administration did remarkably well to win approval of most of its proposals from the Ways and Means Committee and then from the full House. In order to do so, however, it had to agree to the attachment of several restrictive amendments in committee. To help steer the bill through the House, the White House had the full support of Speaker Sam Rayburn, who the previous year had not been fully cooperative in supporting the mutual security program. At the end of April, a gloomy Rayburn, who regarded passage of the trade program as even more important than the foreign-aid legislation also being considered by Congress, told Eisenhower that Secretary Weeks did not carry "one single bit of weight" on Capitol Hill. He suggested that Douglas Dillon, who had already established a favorable reputation on Capitol Hill, be assigned more of the responsibility for pushing the reciprocal trade bill through Congress.[42]

At a meeting with Weeks on May 3, Speaker Rayburn said that passage of a five-year extension of the Trade Agreements Act might be too much to expect and that a one-year extension seemed more realistic. He added that there was sentiment to let Congress have thirty or sixty days in which to cancel any presidential decisions on escape clause recommendations. Finally, he told Weeks that he intended to take the floor himself on behalf of the trade legislation and that he was "one hundred percent" certain something needed to be done to extend the program.[43] Three days later the Ways and Means Committee, which had begun to consider the extension bill at the end of April, suspended deliberations for a week. Reports circulated in Washington that Democratic members had told President Eisenhower that changes in the trade legislation and stronger Republican support were needed to assure its passage. The president asked for this support in a speech honoring the Republican members of Congress. The next day Rayburn called for some concessions, but not "the gutting kind."[44]

On May 15 the Ways and Means Committee approved an amendment that would give Congress the power to reverse, by a two-thirds vote of each house, any decision by the president to reject a Tariff Commission recommendation in escape clause cases. The committee also agreed to give Congress the power, again by a two-thirds vote of each house, to override the president if he rejected import curbs recommended by the Tariff Commission. In addition, it increased from 120 days to 180 days the time within which the Tariff Commission had to undertake peril point investigations and it decreased from nine months to six months the duration of escape clause reviews. Finally, the committee authorized the president to cut ad valorem tariffs by only 2 percent rather than the 3 percent he had requested. But even with these provisions added to the bill, the committee reported out a measure on May 21 that was very much like the bill the president had requested, including as it did a five-year extension of the Trade Agreements Act as well as authority to reduce tariff rates 25 percent below existing levels and to lower to 50 percent of value all tariffs above that level.[45]

In the House, debate on the Ways and Means Committee's report revolved around a substitute proposal by Congressman Simpson of Pennsylvania which, if approved, would have effectively gutted the administration's trade program. The Simpson substitute extended the Trade Agreements Act for only two years and withheld the tariff-cutting authority requested by the president. The proposal also differed from the committee's bill in two other respects. It gave the Tariff Commission power to determine the tariff concessions the president could negotiate with other countries and, in effect, made the commission's recommendations for tariff increases in escape clause cases mandatory by requiring congressional approval if the president departed from the commission's recommendations.[46]

On June 10, President Eisenhower warned House Minority Leader Martin that if the Simpson "substitute should prevail, the Reciprocal Trade Program would be irreparably damaged." The same day the new chairman of the Ways and Means Committee, Wilbur Mills of Arkansas, released a letter the president had sent him at the end of May concerning two separate proposals that had circulated on Capitol Hill. These proposals would give Congress a majority-vote veto over the president's actions in escape clause cases and would extend to the Tariff Commission the final determination in such cases. The first measure "would clearly be unconstitutional," Eisenhower wrote Mills, while the second "would be a tragic blunder which could seriously jeopardize the national interest, the foreign relations, as well as the security of the United States." But the president also made clear to the Ways and Means chairman that the override amendment attached to the trade legislation by the committee was acceptable to him.[47]

The next day the House defeated the Simpson amendment by a three-to-two margin, which was considerably smaller than many congressional observers had anticipated. But after then turning down a motion by Representative Daniel Reed to recommit the bill to committee without instructions and adding an amendment providing more criteria for relief by industry under the law's national security clause, the House overwhelmingly approved the extension measure as it had come from the Ways and Means Committee.[48] A major cause for the defeat of the Simpson amendment was the fact that it took too much authority away from the president in determining tariff rates. Even congressmen who objected to the power that had accrued to the president were unwilling to return to pre–Trade Agreements Act days, when the House and Senate had had to wrestle with the difficult and often politically damaging problem of determining tariff rates. As Representative Charles Halleck of Indiana commented, the Simpson amendment was "too restrictive" and was not "geared to the necessities of this day and age." Similarly, the Reed motion to recommit the bill to committee was defeated because the protectionists failed to agree on instructions to accompany the motion, which left members with the alternative of voting for the original bill or for no trade legislation at all.[49]

Eisenhower did not like the amendments attached to the trade legislation, especially the veto power given Congress in escape clause cases, but he had agreed to go along with these concessions to the protectionists and was generally satisfied with the outcome of his tariff program in the House. With the aid of the Democratic leadership, he had gotten a satisfactory measure through committee and had helped defeat the Simpson amendment. If the Senate did as well as the House, the president told Paul Hoffman, their "hope of bettering international relations—as well as the economic situation for our friends and ourselves—[would] be vastly strengthened."[50]

The Trade Bill in the Senate

Eisenhower was aware, however, that opposition to his trade program was even stronger in the Senate than in the House. Moreover, the Senate opposition was led by his own minority leader, William Knowland of California, and included other prominent Republicans, such as Styles Bridges of New Hampshire. As early as January, Knowland had remarked that the administration's trade proposals were in for "rough going" in Congress. After the House approved the five-year extension of the Trade Agreements Act, the Senate minority leader stated that he would support efforts to cut the extension to three years. Bridges also announced that he intended to support only a three-year extension. In contrast, Majority Leader Johnson said he hoped the Senate would pass the trade legislation without major changes.[51]

The president was perplexed and annoyed by the opposition from Knowland and Bridges.[52] Denied the support of even his own party's leadership, he watched the Senate Finance Committee add a series of crippling amendments to the House-approved bill after it completed hearings on the measure in July.[53] First the Committee voted to cut the extension period from five years to three years and to trim the tariff reduction authority from 25 percent to 15 percent. It also eliminated the cumulative features of the House measure whereby any tariff-reduction authority not used in one year could be carried over to the next. It then approved an amendment by Democratic Senator

Robert Kerr of Oklahoma (an amendment proposed earlier by another conservative Democrat, Strom Thurmond of South Carolina), whereby the president would have thirty days in which to accept a Tariff Commission recommendation to raise duties or impose import quotas in escape clause cases. If he refused to accept the recommendation, it would go into effect automatically after ninety days provided the president's action was not upheld by a majority of both the House and the Senate. In other words, the Kerr-Thurmond amendment replaced the House provision for a congressional override of the president's decision to disregard Tariff Commission recommendations with one requiring affirmative action by Congress to approve such decisions.[54]

In addition to these amendments, which would sharply curtail the trade agreements program and limit the president's authority to negotiate tariff reductions, the Senate Finance Committee approved several other proposals that indicated its displeasure with existing tariff legislation and its intention to give American industry more protection from foreign imports. It added a section to the trade legislation providing that in cases of tie votes by the commission, its affirmative findings (raising tariffs or import quotas) would be considered the findings of the commission; in cases of tie votes as to the remedy for injury, the recommendation specified by the president as providing the greatest measure of relief to a domestic industry would be considered the commission's finding. The Finance Committee also broadened the House-approved national security provisions. If the president determined that imports were threatening the national security, he would be required to adjust them accordingly. Finally, the committee adopted a proposal by Ralph Flanders to establish a nine-member commission to study the objectives and operations of the reciprocal trade program and to report its findings to Congress by June 30, 1960.[55]

The Finance Committee approved its version of the trade bill by a twelve-to-two vote and sent it to the Senate on July 15. In minority statements William E. Jenner of Indiana and George Malone of Nevada, who opposed any extension of the reciprocal trade program and voted against reporting the bill to the Senate, nevertheless supported the committee's amendments as marking the "first move in 24 years to return to the U.S. constitution." At the other end of the spectrum, Paul Douglas of Illinois, who did not vote on the bill, said that its passage as reported by the committee would mean "a virtual abandonment" of reciprocal trade.[56]

President Eisenhower was greatly discouraged by the Finance Committee's emasculation of his trade legislation, particularly by its inclusion in the measure of the Kerr-Thurmond amendment. At a meeting with Committee Chairman Harry Byrd of Virginia while the amendment was still being considered, both the president and the senator had commented on the need to eliminate it from the final bill, and Byrd had assured Eisenhower that the amendment would be taken out before the measure left committee.[57] To counteract this major setback, the White House decided to concentrate its effort in getting the full senate to reject the Kerr-Thurmond amendment and to re-turn the House's language to the trade bill in the area of congressional action on presidential tariff decisions. The length of extension (five or three years) could be worked out in conference committee, where an acceptable compro-mise seemed likely. The president outlined his plan to a group of legislative leaders shortly before the Senate began its deliberations on the trade proposal.[58]

The White House strategy worked remarkably well. Occupied by other ur-gent legislative and diplomatic problems, including the mutual security ap-propriations for 1959 and disorders in Iraq and Jordan and in Lebanon, where American marines had gone ashore on July 15, Eisenhower relied heavily on the Democratic leadership to push his trade program through the Senate. Using his already well-known talents of persuasion, Majority Leader Johnson successfully sponsored an amendment to eliminate the Kerr-Thurmond amendment and that section of the bill which interpreted a tie vote of the Tariff Commission in escape clause cases as a vote for higher duties and im-port quotas.[59]

Final Passage of the Trade Bill

In conference committee Senate and House spokesmen then agreed to a compromise, proposed by Wilbur Mills, which extended the Trade Agree-ments Act for four years instead of the five years called for by the House and the three years approved by the Senate. The compromise also gave the presi-dent authority to reduce tariffs by 20 percent and allowed any unused authori-ty to accumulate over the four years of extension, with reductions to take effect no later than four years after the expiration of the bill in 1962. In addi-tion, the conferees retained the House requirement of a two-thirds vote of both the Senate and the House to override a presidential rejection of Tariff Commission recommendations. Finally, they dropped the Senate provision for a bipartisan commission to study the reciprocal trade program. That last decision caused considerable debate in the Senate, where Ralph Flanders, who had proposed the establishment of the commission, urged his fellow sena-tors to reject the conference report. But the House and the Senate agreed to accept the report after Senator Frank Carlson of Kansas assured Flanders that the Finance Committee would consider making a study along the lines Flanders proposed.[60]

President Eisenhower signed the bill on August 20, remarking that it would "further our own nation's domestic interests and [would] promote the eco-nomic strength, solidarity and security of the free and independent nations."[61] In analyzing the key votes in both houses, Secretary Weeks noted that the president had picked up considerable Republican strength in the House since the trade bill of 1955. Approximately 55 percent of the Republicans in the House voted with the administration in 1958 as opposed to only a third in

1955. In the Senate, the Republicans also performed well, with thirty-six Republicans voting to eliminate the Kerr-Thurmond amendment and only nine in opposition. But as Weeks commented, it was the administration's decision to conduct the fight for its trade bill on a bipartisan basis that accounted for final passage of the bill in the Senate. Thirty-six Democrats had joined with the Republicans in sending the measure to conference committee without the Kerr-Thurmond provision.[62]

Getting a four-year trade bill through Congress with such bipartisan support was a major presidential accomplishment, but for supporters of a more liberal trade policy, the president's achievements were less impressive. In the first place, the bill's effect was to freeze most tariff rates at existing levels for the next four years. Not until the law expired in 1962 was the United States likely to sign an extensive package of tariff reductions with the Common Market, and only then would the president's authority to cut tariffs by the full 20 percent take effect. (Cuts up to this amount could then be spread over the following four years.) For foreign businessmen, then, passage of the Trade Agreements Extension Act of 1958 brought the assurance that the American market would remain essentially the same for the next four years, not that it would be more open.[63] Furthermore, Congress had added new restrictions to the reciprocal trade program. With the White House's approval, the House and Senate had increased the penalties in escape clause cases. They had also made it easier for domestic industry to obtain relief from foreign competition under the escape clause and peril point provisions, and to do so more quickly. Finally, they had made explicit the criteria under which the national security provisions of the law could be applied against imports, and for the first time they had given to the House and the Senate the authority to override presidential actions on Tariff Commission decisions, albeit in a way that made such vetoes unlikely. It was not entirely hyperbole, therefore, when the Committee for a National Trade Policy, which had called for a ten-year extension of the Trade Agreements Act, termed the final bill "the most highly protectionist measure ever passed by Congress in all the Reciprocal Trade renewals since 1934."[64]

Other Trade Programs

Other trade policies pursued by the White House and Congress also gave free-traders cause for disappointment and concern. In a paper on agricultural trade policy prepared for the Boggs Committee, for example, D. Gale Johnson of the University of Chicago restated the need, expressed by most proponents of liberalized trade, for harmonizing the nation's agricultural policy with the principles of free trade. Johnson even challenged the widely held assumption that many segments of American agriculture would not be able to compete with cheaper foreign imports and that high price supports were necessary to assure American farmers a satisfactory income. High price supports encouraged high and uneconomic production and hence lower prices, and thus cast doubts about America's ability "to carry forward constructive international economic policies."[65] Yet these arguments failed to persuade either Congress or the administration. The White House indicated no interest in modifying its trade policy on farm imports, and the matter never came before Congress for consideration. Instead, the White House continued to subsidize the export of farm surpluses through the P.L. 480 program. As far as the administration was concerned, the damage the program caused in terms of U.S. relations with other surplus-exporting countries was tempered by the benefits it brought the Third World nations in additional food and local currencies.[66]

Congress refused for the fourth consecutive year to consider the president's request for U.S. membership in the proposed OTC. Eisenhower had renewed his appeal in behalf of membership in his budget message to Congress in January, and Sinclair Weeks had raised the issue once more during his testimony before the House Ways and Means Committee in February. But the administration did not lobby hard with Congress, perhaps concluding that the House and Senate would never approve the measure or perhaps because it simply had higher priorities. Without Eisenhower's strong backing, the OTC proposal was lost in the shuffle over extension of the reciprocal trade program.[67]

In contrast, however, Congress did take up and complete action on a bill to strengthen the Anti-Dumping Act of 1951, which had been passed to prevent the dumping of foreign goods in the United States below their cost of production. Under the revised statute approved by the House and Senate in August, the Treasury Department was given wider latitude in assessing higher punitive duties on low-priced imports that the Tariff Commission determined were threatening injury to domestic producers. The Treasury was also granted greater discretion in comparing domestic and foreign classes of goods for purposes of defining "dumping." Again the administration remained silent as Congress raised the barriers and strengthened the restrictions on foreign imports.[68]

The White House agreed to loosen ties on trade with the Soviet Union, but only reluctantly and only as a result of intense pressure at home and abroad. In June 1957 Congress routinely extended for another two years the Export Control Act of 1949, which gave the secretary of commerce licensing power over the shipment of scarce and strategic goods. In a conversation with the president of International General Electric Company, William R. Herod, Undersecretary of State Christian Herter made it clear that the administration contemplated no change in the administration of the law,[69] but in the winter of 1958 the West European governments and Japan undertook the first review of export controls since 1954. England, France, West Germany, and Japan all argued that the embargo list be limited to strictly military items since the Soviets had made technical gains despite it. American businessmen also argued for expanded East-West trade,[70] and under this pressure the White

House relented. In July the United States joined in a fifteen-nation agreement that cut in half the list of embargoed goods, a list that had last been revised in 1954. Items freed for sale to the Soviet Union included civil aircraft, most types of machine tools, ball and roller bearings, and aluminum and copper in all forms. However, the United States maintained its total embargo on trade with Communist China, North Korea, and North Vietnam—countries that were still beyond the pale of U.S. diplomacy.[71]

Conclusion

The administration's record in advancing the cause of liberalized trade was thus mixed. Certainly proponents of freer trade had ample cause for disappointment, but it is significant how little attention even they paid to the special needs of Third World countries. Arguments for applying a liberal trade policy to the Third World were couched in the most general terms and increasingly in the context of combatting the Soviet economic offensive abroad. By fostering world economic growth, trade, like aid, would promote economic and political stability abroad and thereby stop the spread of communism.[72] These arguments lacked any consideration of the peculiar situation of most underdeveloped countries—their dependence on a single commodity for export. This dependency created at least two problems for underdeveloped nations. First, they were faced with declining world commodity prices because of the elasticity of demand for their goods. Second, the reduction in trade barriers after World War II had created much growth in Northern trade, but not in Southern trade. Trade liberalization, even under GATT provisions, was much more modest for Southern export commodities—either raw or processed—than for Northern industrial products.[73] Most advocates of liberalized trade simply ignored these problems.

In 1957, however, GATT agreed to establish a panel of experts to examine current trends in international trade. In setting up the panel the trade ministers attending the meeting noted "some disturbing elements" with respect to world commerce, including the prevalence of agricultural protectionism; sharp variations in the prices of primary products, accompanied by wide fluctuations in the export earnings of primary producers; and the failure of the export trade of underdeveloped countries to keep up with growing import needs. Headed by Gottfried Haberler of Harvard University, the panel found that there had been a 5 percent average annual decline in the price of primary products since 1955 while simultaneously there had been a 6 percent increase in the price of manufactured goods. In addition, since before World War II the volume of imports in the nonindustrial countries had risen more sharply than the volume of their exports. The terms of trade in these countries, though greatly improved since the depression years of the 1930s, were at about the same level in 1958 as they had been thirty years earlier. Yet the Haberler panel concluded that the "avoidance of business cycles and the maintenance of a steady rate of domestic growth are the most important contributions which the highly industrialized countries can make to the stabilization of the markets for primary products."[74]

Often the spokesmen for developing countries themselves neglected the peculiar problems of primary product countries as they stressed the need to move out of primary production into import-substituting industries as rapidly as possible. They tended to equate economic development with industrial growth and stagnation with agricultural and raw-material dependency. Not until the first United Nations Conference on Trade and Development (UNCTAD) in 1964 did Third World leaders really begin to concentrate on the problems associated with commodity production. At UNCTAD they urged a reorientation of world trade away from the GATT principles of nondiscrimination and toward the use of trade as a device for increasing North-South income transfers—for example, through the use of international commodity agreements.[75]

The debate over trade liberalization that took place in 1957 and 1958 thus had a vacuous quality to it even among Third World leaders. In the United States it was restricted by a liberal viewpoint that generated confidence about America's ability to promote world economic growth and stop Communist expansion, but that tended to ignore many of the major obstacles to Third World economic and political development. Certainly the peculiar problems of primary product countries were not discussed at any length in the papers prepared for the Boggs Committee or in the extensive hearings on the Trade Agreements Act held before the House Ways and Means Committee and the Senate Finance Committee. This lack of awareness of the obstacles to economic and political growth in underdeveloped countries was evident as well in the continued debate over foreign aid, the other major foreign economic issue facing the Eighty-fifth Congress.

8. Trade and Aid: Mutual Security 1957–1958

THE STRUGGLE between the executive and legislative branches over mutual security legislation in 1958 paralleled the debate over foreign trade; that is, the administration received more from Congress than many had anticipated, but less than it wanted. Once again depending on the Democratic leadership and making the most of a national public relations campaign on behalf of foreign aid, the White House saved the aid program from the previous year's disastrous reductions. In addition, the Senate showed greater interest in the multilateral promotion of economic growth abroad by approving a resolution to consider the establishment of an International Development Association as an affiliate of the World Bank. Nevertheless, Congress made substantial cuts in the mutual security appropriations for 1959. An indication of the domestic constraints under which the foreign-aid program still operated was the administration's continued support of the disposal of American agricultural surpluses overseas. Moreover, by again refusing to approve the establishment of a Special United Nations Fund for Economic Development (SUNFED), and proposing instead an expanded program of technical assistance, the White House lowered U.S. prestige in many of the Third World countries whose good will the president was seeking to cultivate through his trade-and-aid policies.

The Administration's Campaign for Mutual Security

Disturbed by the growing disaffection with foreign aid it detected in and outside Congress, the White House decided in the fall of 1957 to conduct a major "educational" campaign to overcome this hostility. President Eisenhower expected the Soviet Union's October launching of the earth satellite Sputnik, as well as its political penetration of the Mideast, to help him get his program through Congress. He even anticipated that some congressional appropriations might be "unjustifiably large." But while he intended to hold federal spending for 1958 to 1957 levels, he wanted an increase in foreign aid, and he remained disturbed by the lack of public support for mutual security and similar programs.[1] In an effort to gain this backing, the president asked

133

Eric Johnston of the International Development Advisory Board, whom Christian Herter described as a "go-getter" with many personal connections, to organize a nonpartisan White House mutual security conference. The administration planned to invite civic leaders from all parts of the country to the conference, much as it was doing in organizing a meeting in support of its trade agreements legislation. White House strategists intended for the president to call the conference after being urged to do so by the Council of Churches and other civic organizations, and thus gave Johnston and Herter the responsibility for contacting these groups. In addition, Vice-President Nixon was to ask Harold Boeschenstein, already involved in promoting the trade agreements program, to select twenty influential persons in each major city to work in behalf of foreign aid.[2]

In November, in a major address before the National Foreign Trade Convention, Deputy Undersecretary of State Douglas Dillon called for the full funding of the Development Loan Fund during the next session of Congress.[3] But the administration did not outline its foreign-aid requests for 1958 until the president's meeting with cabinet members and congressional leaders in December. It was at this meeting that Secretary of State Dulles stressed the dangers of the Soviet economic offensive abroad and called for passage of the Trade Agreements Extension Act. Eisenhower, Dulles, and other cabinet officers also emphasized the Soviet challenge in urging passage of adequate foreign-aid legislation. Undersecretary Dillon outlined the White House's mutual security program for the next year. The administration would ask for $3.9 billion for 1959 as compared with its request of $4.3 billion for 1958 and the actual appropriation for 1958 of $3.4 billion. Of the $3.9 billion, $1.8 billion would go for military assistance and $0.9 billion for defense support. Because funds for special assistance were "terribly tight," with very little margin for emergencies, some additional funds would be sought for that category of aid. As for the DLF, the $625 million requested by the administration was all that remained of its earlier drive to increase economic aid. The Department of State hesitated to recommend a higher figure for 1959 because it was still not possible to show the record of lending activity upon which Congress had insisted. However, loans were being approved by a committee of three persons, including Dillon, and the committee was confident all available funds would be well placed.[4]

The December 3 meeting covered almost every aspect of the administration's foreign economic program for 1959. In a sense the White House resorted to the same "scare tactics" Harry Truman had used in 1947 when he sought congressional approval of the Truman Doctrine. But while Truman had been concerned mainly with the Soviet political and military threat to Greece and Turkey, the Eisenhower administration emphasized that the challenge from Moscow was world-wide and involved a sophisticated form of economic aggression requiring extended economic countermeasures by the United States. Congressional leaders at the meeting expressed concern about Soviet intentions but not alarm, as had been the case a decade earlier when Senator Arthur Vandenberg of Michigan told Truman to "scare the hell" out of the American people in the same way the president had just scared him.[5] Instead, the congressmen, who had grown accustomed to reports of Soviet economic activity abroad, merely asked for more information about the dimensions of the Soviet and Allied efforts in the Third World. They particularly wanted a comparison of U.S. foreign-aid efforts with those of the Soviet Union and America's allies. Senator Knowland asked for a chart showing the assistance being extended by the United States and other NATO countries to nations also receiving Soviet aid. After the meeting, the congressional leaders issued a routine statement that they had been briefed on various matters and that no commitments had been asked for or given.[6]

In his State of the Union message a few weeks later, President Eisenhower told Congress that he would seek an economic assistance program that placed greater emphasis on repayable loans through the DLF and the Eximbank and through funds generated by the overseas sale of surplus U.S. farm products. The following week he asked Eric Johnston, in a letter he made public, to organize a nonpartisan conference of business and organization leaders "on the foreign aspects of our national security."[7] As a preliminary to that meeting the president hosted a luncheon at the end of January for some of the nation's most influential business leaders, including the chairmen of Ford Motor Company, Anderson Clayton and Company, Sears Roebuck and Company, and Gillette Manufacturing Company. Eisenhower, Vice-President Nixon, Undersecretary of State Herter, Clarence Randall, and Eric Johnston all spoke at length on the need to develop public support for the nation's mutual security program. That evening Johnston stated that the White House would launch an extensive public campaign in behalf of the mutual security program, a campaign involving television and radio, newspapers, magazines, and pamphlets. It would be a crash program, "a grand effort."[8]

On February 19 the president sent Congress his special message on the mutual security program.[9] For the first time since the Korean War, the White House asked for less money for military hardware ($1.8 billion) than for its various economic programs ($2.1 billion). A week later, the administration held its long-planned and carefully orchestrated National Conference on Foreign Aspects of U.S. National Security. *Business Week* described it as the "broadest collection of leading lights in government, business, politics, and civic affairs ever assembled in one place at one time for one purpose." Twelve hundred delegates attended the conference, a one-day extravaganza of speeches, panels, and forum discussions. Besides the nation's major political figures, including former President Truman, former Secretary of State Dean Acheson, and former presidential candidates Thomas Dewey and Adlai Stevenson, such well-known figures as Archbishop Fulton J. Sheen, Washington hostess Pearl Mesta, baseball star Stan Musial, and movie actor Danny Kaye were in attendance. The delegates heard top-level Democrats and Republicans urge continuation of the foreign-aid program. Former President Truman made a moving speech in behalf of the mutual security legislation, remarking that unlike armaments, economic assistance was one of America's "best hopes" for obtaining world peace. President Eisenhower gave the keynote address. In this nationwide radio broadcast he warned that the peace of the world hinged on nonpartisan support of foreign military and economic assistance. "The urgency of the times and the opportunity before us," he emphasized, "call for greatness of spirit transcending all Party considerations."[10]

Making nonpartisanship the theme of his efforts in behalf of the mutual security program, the president worked closely with the Democratic leadership in subsequent months to get his aid program through Congress, just as he worked for passage of the Trade Agreements Extension Act. Speaker Rayburn, with whom Eisenhower conferred regularly, was more optimistic about getting a successful foreign-aid bill through the House than he was about the trade legislation. At a meeting with the president at the end of April, he informed Eisenhower that only five members of the Texas delegation in the House favored the mutual security program, but he indicated that because none of the Texas congressmen faced opposition in the upcoming Texas primary, he thought he might be able to get the president more than five votes.[11]

The Foreign-Aid Bill in Congress

Congressional hearings on the foreign-aid bill began before the House Foreign Affairs Committee on February 18. Lasting until April 1, they proved more favorable for the administration than many in Washington had anticipated. The White House argued more strongly for its mutual security requests than it had in previous years. Borrowing the strategy used by Commerce Secretary Weeks in support of the trade agreements program, Secretary of State Dulles underscored the immediate economic interests of the United States in approving the mutual security legislation. Remarking that the $3.9 billion request was a "rock-bottom" figure and that there was no "giveaway" in the program, he added that recipients spent the great bulk of foreign-aid funds (over 75 percent) in the United States and that the mutual security program accounted for the employment of an estimated 600,000 Americans. "To cut these funds would be to cut employment here at home," Dulles concluded.[12]

Business leaders with a stake in foreign trade also threw more weight behind the aid program than they had in previous years. The CED and the Business Advisory Council of the Department of Commerce, which had already appointed a committee to study Sino-Soviet economic activities abroad, were particularly active in promoting the administration's mutual security requests. Eisenhower met on a regular basis with leaders of these groups and with other prominent advocates of foreign aid such as Eugene Holman of Standard Oil of New Jersey, S. C. Allyn of the National Cash Register Company, Henry C. Alexander of J. P. Morgan and Company, R. G. Pollis of Standard Oil of California, and Philip D. Reed of General Electric.[13]

In May the House Foreign Affairs Committee reported out a bill cutting the president's foreign-aid requests by $339 million (as compared to $625 million the previous year). The committee stated that "termination or drastic curtailment of the mutual security program would inevitably mean that [the United States] would lose the cold war." Because of their strategic location or their natural resources, a number of the newly independent nations of the Third World were considered vital to U.S. interests. Communist control of these countries "would greatly strengthen the Soviet Union and its satellites." The committee thus recommended a $2.96 billion aid program. An additional $644 million, including $625 million for the DLF, had already been authorized for fiscal 1959.[14] After only three days of debate, the House approved the committee bill virtually as it had been reported. The Democrats' support for the measure was stronger than it had been in past years. In 1957, 135 Democrats had voted for the authorization bill and 78 had voted against it; in 1958 the Democratic vote was 150 in favor and only 58 opposed. More important, in 1957, 103 Democrats had joined 78 Republicans in voting to recommit the bill to committee with instructions to delete provisions for the creation of the DLF; 110 Democrats had united with 117 Republicans to defeat the move. No similar attempt to send the authorization bill back to committee was made in 1958. Clearly the president's nonpartisan approach to foreign aid seemed to be working.[15]

The administration also had considerable success with its program in the Senate, although it failed to get full restoration of the funds the House cut. Eisenhower had decided to ask the Senate to restore these funds even before the House completed final action on the authorization measure. In particular, Dillon, who had been assigned major responsibility for getting the bill through Congress, sought to persuade the Senate to authorize the full $200 million requested for the President's Contingency Fund. Because the House had approved only $100 million, Dillon calculated that it might be possible to salvage $150 million for the fund in conference committee. At a meeting with Senate leaders a few days after the House completed action on the authorization bill, Dillon stressed the importance of the fund. Eisenhower backed the undersecretary by remarking that if budget cuts had to be made, they should come from the Defense budget and not from foreign aid. Senators Alexander Wiley of Wisconsin and H. Alexander Smith of New Jersey, the ranking Republican members of the Foreign Relations Committee, assured the president the committee would agree to restore the full amount he requested. The only note of discord at this otherwise harmonious meeting came from the intractable minority leader, William Knowland, who, to Eisenhower's obvious displeasure, objected to the size of the aid program.[16]

On May 26 the Senate Foreign Relations Committee reported out a compromise bill that was less than what Wiley and Smith had promised the president but more than the House had given him. After tentatively approving full restoration of the cuts made by the House, the committee passed a bill containing new authorizations of $3.09 billion. The figure was $229 million less than what Eisenhower had asked for but $100 million more than what the House had approved and it included the full $200 million for the President's Contingency Fund, which Deputy Undersecretary Dillon had so strongly advocated. The committee bill also contained a special provision expressing the sense of Congress that the United States should join with other countries in helping India complete its Second Five-Year Plan and a provision to ensure that military assistance to Latin American countries not be used for internal security purposes. The latter provision was intended to remove the stigma of American aid being used to prop up dictatorial and unpopular regimes. Finally, in response to the uprising in Hungary the previous year and the evident hostility of Poland toward the Soviet Union, the committee approved an amendment to the Battle Act permitting economic and financial assistance to any nation except the Soviet Union, Communist China, and North Korea. The committee made this proposal, it said, to help the people of Eastern Europe achieve greater freedom by means short of war.[17]

Largely for the same reason, President Eisenhower also favored amending the mutual security program to make aid available to Eastern Europe. But once again he encountered the opposition of Senator Knowland and other conservative Republicans and Democrats, who told the president they intended to fight the Foreign Relations Committee's recommendation. Eisenhower played into their hands by agreeing to seek separate authority to extend aid to Communist satellite nations, for Knowland had made it clear that he would also oppose such separate legislation. Once the president had removed his support from the Battle Act amendment, the Senate rejected it by a 43 to 42 vote.[18]

With this exception, the full Senate passed the aid authorization bill essentially as it had come from committee. Although it added several minor amendments to the measure, none altered it in any significant way or changed the total authorization of $3.069 billion. In conference committee, the House agreed to most of the Senate's restoration of funds. The final measure, which both houses approved on June 27 and signed into law three days later, authorized the appropriation of $3.031 billion for foreign aid in fiscal 1959—$38 million less than the Senate had approved but $72 million more than had been voted by the House. In return, Senate conferees agreed to delete the Senate amendment expressing Congress's wish to help India complete its economic development program. The conferees also agreed to apportion military assistance and defense support funds in separate sections rather than to impose a ceiling on the total amount of the two items as provided in the Senate version of the bill.[19]

The Appropriations Process

The White House was fully aware, however, that the authorization measure was merely an expression of congressional sentiment, that it lacked fiscal obligation, and that the real fight over foreign aid would come during the appropriations process. The president knew he would again have to contend with the uncompromising foe of foreign aid, Otto Passman of Louisiana, who remained chairman of the subcommittee through which the appropriations bill had to pass and whom Eisenhower called a "menace to [the] nation's best interests." He also realized that the legislation would be opposed by many congressmen whose districts were suffering from high unemployment as a result of the depression gripping the nation and who were therefore anxious to make reductions in foreign programs.[20]

As the White House anticipated, the House made substantial cuts in the funds already authorized for foreign aid, although, as in the authorization measure, these cuts were not nearly as great as those made a year earlier. At the end of June, the Appropriations Committee reported out a foreign-aid appropriation of $3.08 billion, $872 million less than the president's original request (counting the $644 million approved earlier) and $598 million under the authorization measure. The cuts included $325 million from the DLF and $45 million from the President's Contingency Fund.[21]

Before the bill was sent to the full House, Eisenhower tried unsuccessfully to get the committee to reconsider its action. He made personal calls to each Republican member of the committee, and he relied on Speaker Rayburn to do the same with the Democratic members. However, although the president persuaded several Republicans to reconsider their votes, Passman held the Democrats in line.[22] When the bill reached the House floor, the president denounced the committee's action as one that seriously diminished the security of the United States. He also continued to work with the House leadership to restore some of the funds cut by the committee, particularly those for defense support, the DLF, and the contingency fund.[23] But the House approved the Appropriation Committee's recommendations without any major changes, and in the process even rejected two amendments to provide an additional $130 million in foreign aid and to recommit the bill to committee with instructions to increase by $75 million the funds for defense support.[24]

Soon after the House completed its work on the appropriations bill, a coup took place in Iraq which, from the administration's point of view, made the Senate's full restoration of the House cuts especially urgent. Directed by anti-Western elements against the friendly Iraqi government, the coup threatened to spill into neighboring Jordan and Lebanon and led the president to land marines in Beirut on July 15. According to the White House, the revolt in Iraq created the possibility that Iraq would withdraw from the Baghdad Pact, which had been formed in 1955 as a defense alliance against the Soviet

Union. Iraq's withdrawal from the pact would weaken the military position of Iran and Turkey and thus that of the entire non-Communist world. In order to compensate for this, the United States would have to grant additional military and economic assistance not only to Iran and Turkey but to such countries as Greece, Pakistan, Israel, Ethiopia, the Sudan, and Afghanistan. The administration estimated that these new requirements alone would cost about $350 million.[25] At meetings with Senate leaders following the Iraqi coup, Eisenhower underscored the importance of making adequate funds available for other regions as well. There were substantial needs in Vietnam, for example, and additional special assistance was required for all of North Africa and for Bolivia. Cuts in defense support would mean reductions in assistance to such major allies as Spain, South Vietnam, Taiwan, and South Korea.[26]

Senate leaders agreed to make a major effort in the Senate and in conference committee to restore $450–$500 million to the bill. When Lyndon Johnson reported that the Senate was likely to restore only $440 million, the president agreed that this would be adequate and that he would return to Congress later in the session with a supplementary aid request.[27] Privately he expressed his contempt of Congress in a letter to George Humphrey, who had resigned his post as treasury secretary a year earlier. Although Humphrey had differed with the president more and more over such matters as foreign aid and the budget proposals for 1958, these differences do not appear to have been the cause of his resignation. The treasury secretary had never planned to stay in government as long as he did, and as he explained to the president, the illness and retirement of one of his business partners necessitated his resignation.[28] Both he and Eisenhower continued to maintain a cordial correspondence. In his letter to Humphrey concerning Congress, the president remarked that he did not think the House and Senate would "have the wisdom—and political courage—to give us what we so desperately need in M.S.A. They would rather neglect a vital—but unpopular—program to spend billions elsewhere futilely."[29]

In the Senate the leadership delivered on its promise to Eisenhower, restoring the $440 million Johnson had predicted it would. Although this amount was subsequently cut in half in conference committee, the mutual security program as finally approved by Congress still represented a modest victory for the White House. The final appropriation of $3.3 billion included $1.5 billion for military assistance, $750 million for defense support, $400 million for the DLF, $150 million for technical cooperation, $200 million for special assistance, and $155 million for the President's Contingency Fund.[30] The House and Senate had made smaller cuts in the program than in 1957, when they had reduced the president's budget requests by $1.1 billion and the authorization measure by $600 million. Furthermore, Congress had increased the amount allotted for economic and other nonmilitary assistance programs by more than $500 million, including an additional $100 million for the DLF. How much of this was due to the White House's public and private efforts in behalf of foreign aid is difficult to determine. The administration had conducted a major national campaign in support of its program and it had worked closely with the Democratic leadership as it stressed the theme of nonpartisanship. It had also made a much more effective presentation of its foreign-aid program in 1958 than in 1957. On this basis it would seem safe to say that the administration's role was indeed decisive in increasing the size of the foreign-aid appropriation for 1959.

Yet Congress gave the president far less than he asked for, even though Eisenhower's requests, as in previous years, were modest compared to what many advocates of development assistance stated was minimally required for Third World economic growth. The president had sought an increase in total aid of less than $100 over the amount approved for 1958 and an actual decrease of $100 million in military assistance. But Congress refused to appropriate even that amount. Therefore, while a number of White House aides privately expressed satisfaction with the administration's performance on Capitol Hill, Eisenhower noted at a news conference that his greatest disappointment in foreign affairs, insofar as Congress was concerned, was the reduction it had made in his mutual security program.[31]

The Administration and the IDA

The president regarded with much more satisfaction the outcome of a resolution that Mike Monroney of Oklahoma introduced in the Senate requesting that the NAC study the possibility of establishing an International Development Association (IDA) as an affiliate of the World Bank. The idea was that the IDA would make long-term, low-interest loans that would be repayable in whole or in part in local currencies. Initially the White House opposed the idea because it threatened the DLF, but it altered its position after Monroney changed the resolution to make it clear that the IDA would supplement, not supplant, existing lending institutions. Thus the White House sought to place some foreign aid on a multilateral basis, although it limited its commitment to multilateralism, as shown by its continued opposition to a UN proposal to establish SUNFED.

As chairman of the Senate Banking and Currency Subcommittee on International Finance, Monroney had been discussing with business and government leaders in the United States and overseas for several years the idea of a multilateral, soft-lending agency affiliated with the World Bank. Having developed the concept of such a lending institution while attending an international conference in Thailand, he had returned from Thailand persuaded that the United States' foreign-aid program was not adequately responsive to the special needs of many underdeveloped countries. According to the Oklahoma senator, the response to his proposal had been overwhelmingly favorable. About the only argument he had heard against his idea was that the local currencies that would be needed by the lending agency were already committed. He argued that this could be changed either by unilateral action on the part of Washington to release the funds or by agreements reached with the nations involved.[32]

In a letter to Clarence Randall in March 1957, C. D. Jackson proposed the founding of a World Bank affiliate like the one Monroney had outlined. Again calling for a new world economic policy, Jackson pointed to the political advantages of placing soft-loan development projects on a multilateral basis through a subsidiary of the World Bank rather than continuing to rely on unilateral American aid. In the first place, many underdeveloped countries would respond more favorably to rules set forth by an international agency than to rules proposed by the United States. In the second place, while Congress might normally object to turning U.S. funds over to an international agency like the proposed SUNFED, the United States had in the World Bank "an international and multilateral organization which at the same time is very American in personality, ably run by an able American . . . and with a growing acceptance on the part of both Congress and the American people as a very businesslike outfit."[33]

Administration officials, including Undersecretary of State Herter and ICA Director Smith, also approved of the IDA concept. In the United Nations, Third World countries were again urging the United States to agree to the creation of SUNFED, and although there is no firm proof to this effect, it seems more than likely that for the reasons suggested by Jackson the White House viewed the creation of an IDA as a possible alternative to SUNFED. Furthermore, the administration and Congress were becoming increasingly concerned about the unobligated local currencies the foreign-aid programs, especially the P.L. 480 program, were generating. Eisenhower found the almost unlimited provision of these currencies to traveling congressmen and their staffs annoying. Conversely, Senator Monroney, who was convinced that the White House had impounded a large part of these funds abroad, demanded that the administration provide a full accounting of their use.[34]

At a meeting of State Department and ICA officials, therefore, the two government agencies agreed to consider seriously the establishment of a Free World Economic Development Fund, which would use local currencies on a multilateral basis. In response to a suggestion that the proposed fund be kept small, Undersecretary of State Herter argued that it should be large, in order to have greater world impact. One official at the meeting suggested that if a fund were cleared as a matter of policy, the secretary of state might launch the idea publicly with a major speech; he added that proposing such a fund would do much to persuade Congress that the administration had a long-range view of foreign aid and that large annual appropriations would soon end. ICA Director Smith emphasized the importance of making such a source of long-range credit available to underdeveloped countries.[35]

Yet, while the administration generally supported the establishment of an international soft-lending institution, certain practical considerations and differences tempered its enthusiasm for the Monroney proposal. In the first place, there were real limits to the amount of U.S.-owned local currencies that could be used for Third World purposes. By far the largest share of these local currencies were those of the less developed countries themselves. Washington could loan these currencies locally or transfer them to an international agency if the countries agreed. But funds spent within these countries' own borders would not add immediately to their real resources, as would imports of capital and other goods from abroad. The danger also existed that an excessive use of local currencies by Third World nations could have inflationary consequences. The United States did own some European currencies that it could use to export European goods to less developed areas, but a large part of these funds were already being used for government expenditures in Europe, and loan programs had been agreed to for most of the rest.[36]

Even more disturbing to the White House than these practical considerations was the fact that Senator Monroney intended the new international agency to be a substitute for the DLF. As Monroney remarked when asking the Senate to consider establishing an IDA, the formation of this international agency would eliminate the need for more unilateral lending. The IDA would require an original capital investment of $1 billion in U.S. dollars or other hard currency. Based on its contribution to the World Bank, the United States would probably put up 30 percent of this amount, or $300 million. Secretary of State Dulles was now asking for an additional $625 million for the DLF. Therefore, Monroney told the Senate, "The United States' share of the capital stock of the proposed International Development Association would be less than half of the total which Secretary Dulles is asking as additional money for more unilateral lending."[37]

The administration rejected out-of-hand any suggestion that the DLF be eliminated. Having won congressional approval for it, the president was not about to have the fund replaced by an international agency, no matter how attractive its other features might be. The concept of an IDA was an acceptable one if the practical problems concerning the use of local currencies could be worked out, but only if it was to be a modest addition to, not a substitute for, the DLF.

In three days of hearings on the Monroney proposal, the White House made its position clear. But in the month between Monroney's presentation of the proposal to the Senate and the beginning of the Banking and Currency Committee hearings, a groundswell of support for the resolution had developed, in part as a result of a press campaign that was carefully planned by the senator with the help of the *New York Times*. In the Senate, Wayne Morse had praised the resolution as opening "a new dimension in economic aid — that of multilateral aid." Mike Mansfield had expressed the hope that the Banking and Currency Committee would hold hearings on the proposal as soon as possible, "to the end that some arrangement of this sort will be put into operation." Also supporting the resolution, William E. Proxmire of Wisconsin referred to Monroney as "one of the most brilliant students of international finance in this country." Newspapers throughout the country, including the *Washington Post*, the *Christian Science Monitor*, the *St. Louis Post-Dispatch*, the *Kansas City Times*, the *Houston Chronicle*, and the *Denver Post* joined the *New York Times* in supporting a multilateral soft-lending agency affiliated with the World Bank.[38]

As for the World Bank, it took a more cautious position. In a press statement released the day before Monroney introduced his resolution in the Senate, the president of the Bank, Eugene R. Black, announced that his institution "would be willing to explore" the idea of an affiliated agency that would make mixed-currency, low-interest loans to underdeveloped nations. He added that he personally found the idea of a multilateral soft-lending agency "very interesting" and felt that it warranted further study.[39]

The administration took much the same position in its testimony before the Banking and Currency Committee, although it underscored its reservations about the specific proposal being offered by Senator Monroney. White House officials, including the new treasury secretary, Robert Anderson of Texas, agreed that the Monroney plan warranted serious consideration. Deputy Undersecretary of State Dillon assured the committee that a study of the proposal would be promptly undertaken by the administration. But Anderson noted the local-currencies problem and the other difficulties facing the establishment of an IDA. A former Navy secretary and deputy defense secretary under Eisenhower who had been recommended for the treasury post by George Humphrey, Anderson also remarked that the implications of the institution Monroney proposed were far-reaching and that "much time and effort . . . [would be required] to explore various economic, financial and legal questions." In his appearance before the committee, Dillon argued that the Monroney plan could not serve as a substitute for the DLF. He predicted that the United States' contribution to the new agency might reach $750 million annually, which he termed a "low" estimate of the underdeveloped countries' need for soft loans. Such an amount would have to be matched by other developed countries if the international agency were to maintain its multilateral character. At the moment, he concluded, he saw "no possibility" whatsoever of contributions of that magnitude being pledged by the other developed countries.[40]

The White House's attack on the Monroney resolution served its purpose well. Returning from a trip to Switzerland, Monroney learned from his staff that the administration's criticisms of his proposal, particularly of the plan to use local currencies, had given the impression that he considered the IDA a substitute for the DLF and that he was personally attacking the Republican administration. To counter this impression, he was advised to emphasize that he was merely asking for a *study* of additional steps to provide foreign aid to needy countries. In this way he could win the support of Republican internationalists who might otherwise vote against his resolution.[41] Faced with this partisan opposition, Monroney agreed to change his resolution to make it clear that he was proposing only a feasibility study and was not seeking to replace the DLF with the IDA. Monroney's staff worked out these changes in consultation with Dillon and other State Department officials, and at the end of May, the Departments of State and Treasury endorsed the Monroney resolution. A month later the Banking and Currency Committee reported favorably on the resolution, stating that "in the face of the current Soviet economic offensive, it is more than ever important that nations devoted to liberty and individual dignity work together to help developing countries."[42] On July 23, after rejecting an amendment by Homer Capehart that the proposed study include all existing international lending agencies, the Senate approved the Monroney resolution by a vote of 62 to 25.[43]

Continued Opposition to SUNFED

The White House was willing to consider establishing a multilateral soft-lending institution as an affiliate of the World Bank, but it remained strongly opposed to the establishment of a special UN economic development fund. In the previous session of the General Assembly it had warded off all efforts to form such a fund, but the following August ECOSOC voted 15 to 3 to recommend to the General Assembly the immediate establishment of SUNFED. Nevertheless, the Eisenhower administration continued to oppose the establishment of SUNFED or any other international development fund (that is, prior to its consideration of Senator Monroney's plan), claiming that without a large measure of internationally controlled disarmament, the financing of such agencies was impossible. The State Department thus instructed the U.S. delegation to the United Nations to vote against SUNFED and to make it clear that the United States would not participate in the organization of such a fund.[44]

Washington's position placed the United States in a particularly awkward position. The Soviet Union and its allies were certain to exploit this firm U.S. stand against SUNFED. Intelligence reports indicated that Moscow, in a bid for the support of the underdeveloped countries, would not only vote in favor of creating SUNFED but would also promise to contribute 100 million rubles ($25 million) to the fund. More important, as Christian Herter informed Senator Carl Hayden of Arizona, the State Department had been told that, for political reasons, England would abstain from the vote on SUNFED and was prepared to serve on the organizing committee.[45]

However, there were indications that a considerable number of governments would support the U.S. position provided Washington came up with a positive counterproposal. As an alternative to SUNFED, therefore, the White House proposed an increase in the United Nation's Technical Assistance Program from its current level of $30 million a year to an eventual annual level of $100 million. According to this proposal the United States would increase its contribution to the program from $15.5 million a year to a maximum of $33.3

million annually. The additional funds would allow the United Nations to establish a fund for engaging in numerous projects, particularly in Africa, that it had previously had to pass up or undertake on a limited and piecemeal basis. These included surveys of water, power, and mineral resources, engineering surveys, the staffing and equipping of regional technical institutes, and the formation of industrial research centers.[46] Congressman Walter Judd of Minnesota presented the American proposal to the United Nations in November. Supporters of SUNFED attempted to twist the U.S. initiative into a move aimed at establishing the fund, but the American delegation, led by Judd, rebuffed these moves. Then, on December 14, the General Assembly voted unanimously to adopt the American proposal while explicitly barring the United Nations from entering the field of capital development until such time "as resources prospectively available to the United Nations" were considered sufficient for such a purpose. The U.S. delegation made it clear that in Washington's view "sufficient resources would be in prospect only when there is dependable evidence that financial support in the neighborhood of $400 million to $500 million in generally usable currencies will be available on an annual basis." Without America's financial support, of course, this support was not likely to evolve.[47]

Not all administration officials were happy with the decision to support an expanded UN technical assistance program. One Treasury Department official expressed concern that the United States was merely preparing for the eventual formation of SUNFED.[48] U.S. leaders continued to raise objections even after the United Nations approved the proposal. For example, Ralph Roberts of the Agriculture Department complained to Assistant Secretary of Agriculture Don Paarlberg, who also objected to the proposal, that the U.S. position would only increase the pressure for a UN capital investment fund and that it was inconsistent with current recommendations for large increases in defense expenditures. Officials in the Treasury Department also expressed concern about establishing a Special Projects Fund.[49] The administration's response to these objections was best expressed by Congressman Judd, who reported to Secretary of State Dulles that the United Nations' adoption of the U.S. resolution "put SUNFED in cold storage."[50]

Yet approval of the U.S. resolution alienated many Third World countries, which voted for the proposal because it was better than none at all, but which made clear their intention to continue pushing for the establishment of SUNFED. Thus, while the General Assembly approved the U.S. proposal, it also declared that it would "continue to review, as a separate subject of its agenda, progress in the field of financing the economic development of the less developed countries, particularly progress toward the establishment of a United Nations capital development fund." The United States' position on SUNFED contrasted sharply with that of many of Washington's allies, which were willing to go along with the Third World countries in this matter, and this led Undersecretary of State Herter to express deep concern that the United States would appear isolated in world opinion.[51]

Foreign Agricultural Policy

This concern about world opinion did not extend to the administration's implementation of foreign agricultural policy, however, where domestic pressures rather than international considerations determined policy formulation. In 1956 Congress had raised the authorization for the P.L. 480 program from $1.5 billion to $3 billion and extended the program to June 30, 1957.[52] Although the Eisenhower administration had asked for this increased authorization, its position on the program was complicated. On the one hand, even the most ardent proponents of P.L. 480 (within the Department of Agriculture) regarded the program as a temporary one necessitated by the nation's excessive farm surpluses, and acknowledged that it was capable of drawing the world's hungry nations into a harmful state of dependency on American agriculture. They were also mindful of the ill will the U.S. surplus-disposal program had generated among other exporters of farm products.[53] On the other hand, even the most strident critics of P.L. 480 (those within the Department of State) came to appreciate the foreign-policy benefits of making food available to needy countries and of mobilizing local currencies and freeing hard currencies for development purposes.[54] Publicly the administration supported P.L. 480 as a temporary expedient that had useful foreign-policy benefits. But in private the Department of Agriculture attempted to prolong and expand the program as an essential part of its efforts to reduce the nation's agricultural surpluses, while the Department of State sought to restrict the program, arguing that it harmed U.S. relations with other friendly exporters of agricultural products. In this policy conflict the Agriculture Department prevailed, and the State Department was left with no alternative except to try to mitigate the program's most harmful effects on U.S. relations with other countries.

The conflict between the Departments of Agriculture and State (and other agencies opposed to expansion of the P.L. 480 program) appears to have climaxed during the summer and fall of 1957. By that time Congress was completing action on a measure to extend P.L. 480 for another year (to June 30, 1958) and to increase from $3 billion to $4 billion the authorization for foreign-currency sales. The president had requested this legislation in his annual budget message in January. Eisenhower had also asked Congress to delete P.L. 480's ban on bartering agricultural surpluses with Eastern Europe and had requested an increase from $500 million to $800 million in the authorization for foreign-relief grants.[55] Eisenhower had unsuccessfully asked for similar authority to lift the ban on bartering with Eastern Europe the year before. Although he opposed the expansion of trade with the Soviet Union, he believed that trade with the rest of Eastern Europe afforded the United States an opportunity to lessen the Soviets' influence in Europe.[56]

Except for the barter proposal and the issue of control of foreign currencies generated by the sale of farm products, the president's recommendations stirred little controversy. In the House, opposition against bartering with Eastern Europe remained strong, and a number of congressmen protested sharply against an aid agreement the State Department had signed with Poland in June. After months of delay, however, the House finally yielded to the Senate and the administration and accepted a compromise that permitted barter transactions with Eastern Europe but not with the Soviet Union, Communist China, or areas dominated by Communist China. Congress also attached to the surplus-disposal legislation an amendment introduced by Representative Harold D. Cooley, Democrat of North Carolina, providing that not more than 25 percent of the counterpart funds created as a result of the P.L. 480 program be made available to U.S. firms for use as development loans.[57]

Nothing in the Cooley amendment caused any major disagreement between the White House and Capitol Hill over the further extension of the P.L. 480 program. The NAC had recommended using local currencies for loans to private borrowers, and the Cooley amendment merely expressed Congress's wish that some of these funds go to American borrowers.[58] In fact, in contrast to most of the administration's other farm programs, P.L. 480 received strong congressional support, particularly from the farm bloc, which viewed the program as a means of protecting the prosperity of the American farmer by expanding markets for America's agricultural surpluses. Indeed, congressmen representing fruit growers and producers of other commodities not covered by price supports, whose eligibility under P.L. 480 remained uncertain, sought inclusion of these crops in the program.[59]

Within the administration, however, the P.L. 480 program continued to cause considerable disagreement. Clarence Randall expressed the view that the program conflicted with sound foreign economic policy, a position with which the Department of State fully agreed. Treasury Secretary Humphrey (who had not yet resigned from office) felt that too much emphasis was being placed on P.L. 480 as a means of getting rid of farm surpluses and that a better, cheaper method of disposing of these inventories was required. In fact, the proposal to extend the legislation for another year with additional funding had been part of a compromise between these views and that of the Department of Agriculture, which wanted an even more extensive program. It had been concluded at the meeting of the CFEP at which this agreement was reached that P.L. 480 was at best a temporary expedient and that a full study of the program should be made so that the council "[would] not again have to face such a compromise."[60]

Even after the administration agreed on its recommendations and sent its proposal to Capitol Hill, the State Department continued to object to the P.L.

480 program. In the spring of 1957 the department received a letter from the Australian government expressing dissatisfaction with the program. The Australians had voiced similar objections in the past, and other representations had been made by the Canadian government both in recent talks on a wheat agreement with the United States and in a letter from the prime minister to Eisenhower.[61] State Department officials admitted that Australia's objection to the disposal program was a matter of principle, even when its economy suffered minimal injury. But they also maintained that the Australians were justified in complaining about Washington's inadequate consultative procedures and in protesting the United States' use of special disposal programs to take advantage of favorable market opportunities to the exclusion of other suppliers. In a letter to Agriculture Secretary Benson, Undersecretary of State Herter warned that the objections that Australia and other countries had raised had become a source of considerable international friction. The time had come, he said, "for the interested United States agencies to explore the possibility of undertaking more effective remedial action."[62]

In the exchange of letters that followed between the Departments of State and Agriculture, the State Department formally outlined its position on the P.L. 480 program. It was well understood, the department stated, that the program and other similar concessional sales of agricultural goods "were developed to dispose of surpluses which could not otherwise be placed on the market, and that the benefits to foreign countries which may result from such disposal are to that extent incidental to the original purpose of the legislation." There was thus no good reason for extending P.L. 480 or for developing it "into a permanent institution of American policy."[63] In reply, at a cabinet meeting in July, Secretary Benson outlined his agricultural program for the next session of Congress. He remarked that agricultural surpluses were being drawn down quite rapidly and that he did not plan to ask Congress to extend the P.L. 480 legislation beyond fiscal 1958 or beyond the additional $1 billion authorization already requested of Congress. But when Undersecretary of State Herter tried to check on this statement with Undersecretary of Agriculture Morse, Morse told him that P.L. 480 would in all likelihood be continued, although on a smaller scale. In addition, Herter received a complaint from the U.S. ambassador in Mexico City, Francis White, that the agricultural attaché there was trying to push American farm surpluses on the Mexican government without informing him.[64]

By this time Herter had lost patience with the Agriculture Department. Although P.L. 480 had been instituted primarily as a farm surplus disposal program, not as an instrument of foreign policy, he complained to Secretary of State Dulles, "the Department of Agriculture has felt obliged to push the disposal of these surpluses and, through its Agricultural Attaches abroad as well as through representations directly to embassies in Washington, has tried to increase the disposal of these surpluses through the medium of P.L. 480."[65] It is not clear what followed between the two departments, but it soon became apparent that Secretary of Agriculture Benson had won the battle. At a meeting in November the Departments of Agriculture and State and the ICA agreed to a one-year extension of title I of the P.L. 480 program with an increased authorization of $1.5 billion and with no change in the current title II authorization of $800 million.[66] In a related matter, the Department of Agriculture also prevailed over the Bureau of the Budget (BOB), which also had wanted to cut the surplus-disposal program. The controversy with the BOB involved the question of whether surplus commodities not covered by price controls could be included in the P.L. 480 program. The BOB argued that they could not; the Agriculture Department maintained that the final determination should be left to the secretary of agriculture. Placing the dispute before the CFEP, the Agriculture Department won the council's endorsement of its position.[67]

It is not difficult to explain the administration's support for extension of the P.L. 480 legislation. In the first place, as the Agriculture Department reminded the White House, the program's popularity with Congress made any other position politically unwise.[68] In the second place, the program was highly effective in moving agricultural surpluses abroad. Figures given to the Senate Agriculture and Forestry Committee showed that in 1956 the program had accounted for 27 percent of all wheat exports, 22 percent of all cotton exports, 12 percent of all tobacco exports, 24 percent of all rice exports, and 47 percent of all vegetable oil exports.[69] Finally, the program did in fact serve U.S. foreign-policy goals by meeting the food needs of Third World countries and by releasing local and hard currencies for development purposes. For this reason a number of leading proponents of development aid, including Walt Rostow of M.I.T.'s Center for International Studies, supported the program. Even the State Department believed that the program should be abandoned only gradually and with "necessary preparatory work" in countries that had become dependent upon the program for essential economic support. "The process of weaning some countries from P.L. 480 may be painful," the department conceded, "and in a few cases may require some additional allocations of foreign aid."[70]

For these reasons the administration agreed to a one-year extension of the P.L. 480 program and an increased authorization of $1.5 billion, and Eisenhower presented these recommendations in a special message to Congress on January 18. After eight months of debate over the program, in which an effort to include P.L. 480 in general farm legislation failed, the House and Senate reached a last-minute compromise on the agricultural surplus disposal program. Instead of a one-year, $1.5 billion extension, Congress approved an eighteen-month extension and a $2.5 billion authorization.[71] Congress directed the president "to assure that barter or exchange under this act will not unduly disrupt world prices of agricultural commodities or replace cash sales for dollars."[72] This last provision was clearly a concession to State Department and other administration officials, and P.L. 480 remained fundamentally a domestic program whose foreign-policy considerations were subordinate to priorities on the home front. Nevertheless, the White House was already considering a further extension of the farm surplus disposal legislation. In January 1959, President Eisenhower would launch a "Food for Peace" program designed to help a hungry world meet the needs of its destitute people.[73]

Conclusion

By the fall of 1958, in fact, the White House was moving in several directions to broaden its program of trade and aid. The recently ended second session of the Eighty-fifth Congress had provided proponents of freer trade and greater aid ample cause for disappointment. Moreover, the president was not entirely happy with the treatment Congress had given his foreign economic programs for fiscal 1959. Still, the outcome of these programs had been better for the administration than many in Washington had anticipated at the beginning of the session, and the White House appeared firmly committed to returning to Congress in 1959 with much the same legislative requests for fiscal 1960.

Generally this proved to be the case. But in something of a policy change, the administration, which had only recently expressed skepticism about the willingness of other hard currency nations to make adequate appropriations for an international lending agency such as the IDA, and had opposed any proposal that might divert funds from the DLF, began to emphasize the need for more multilateral aid involving the use of international lending institutions and regional development schemes. This shift toward a multilateral approach in providing economic assistance came about as a result of a number of developments, the most important of which was the changing capacity of the United States and other industrial nations to meet the growth needs of Third World countries. The change in policy raised the possibility that the White House might abandon or reduce its own foreign-aid efforts. Fearing that this would happen and that funding for the DLF would be cut, a group of Senators led by J. William Fulbright of Arkansas obtained assurances from the administration that it would continue, and even expand, its unilateral efforts to promote world economic growth.

9. Multilateralism and Regionalism 1958–1959

BY 1958 THE White House was clearly committed to a foreign economic policy based on the flow of public capital abroad. Despite this, strong pressures still existed in and out of government to find new methods of substituting private investment for government aid. Passage of the Cooley amendment and of the 1958 clause in the mutual security legislation requiring a study of the relationship of private enterprise to foreign policy reflected some of these pressures, as did separate studies on the same subject undertaken by the White House and the State Department. Following the recommendations contained in these studies, the administration proposed a revision of the tax laws that would allow American businesses to form a new tax entity known as the foreign-business corporation, which would be entitled to tax deferrals on foreign earnings from underdeveloped countries until such time as these earnings were repatriated in the United States. The White House also considered other tax relief proposals, including selective tax relief to cover losses incurred by original investors in foreign-business corporations; changing the method by which foreign tax credits are computed; and permitting American firms investing in an underdeveloped country to benefit from the tax inducements offered by that country to attract new capital.

Yet the Eisenhower administration opposed more radical measures proposed in Congress and supported by large elements of the business community, including tax deferral on all reinvested earnings, regardless of region, and a 14 percent reduction in taxes on all foreign income. Part of its opposition stemmed from a concern about revenue losses and a decision by the White House to limit the promotion of private investments to investment in the world's underdeveloped regions. Even with respect to the Third World, however, the White House took few initiatives to encourage U.S. investment other than to seek tax relief and propose regional banks as a way of mobilizing private capital.

Except for these proposals, then, the administration's policy remained fundamentally one of depending on public funds to achieve foreign economic development. Indeed, at the end of 1958 the administration began to seek to expand the framework of aid-giving by placing America's foreign-aid effort within a broader multilateral context and by relying more heavily than it had on regional schemes to foster economic growth. The administration's decision to seek a greater international effort in promoting world economic development reflected new domestic and foreign-policy considerations. The White House had only recently opposed the establishment of SUNFED and had agreed to support the Monroney resolution only after the Oklahoma senator had made it clear that he did not intend the IDA to be a substitute for America's own DLF. Moreover, during the debate over the Monroney resolution, the administration had expressed doubt that other developed countries were prepared to contribute the funds needed to establish the type of multilateral soft-lending agency Monroney was proposing.

By the end of 1958, however, the White House faced growing economic problems at home and abroad, and these changed its position with regard to multilateral aid-giving. First, although conditions were improving, the United States remained in a recession that restricted its capacity to make needed dollars available abroad. At the same time, President Eisenhower feared that the recession would be followed by an inflationary spiral that would further strap the nation's ability to meet the growth needs of the underdeveloped world, although it would not do serious damage to America's own economy. Finally, the beginnings of a balance-of-payments deficit and the progress of postwar economic recovery in Europe made it seem both logical and necessary to shift some of the burden of aid-giving from the United States to the other Western industrialized nations.

There were other reasons for placing economic aid on a multilateral basis. The administration regarded the twelve months from the end of 1958 through the end of 1959 as crucial for American foreign economic policy. Walt Rostow referred to the period as "the international development year," which he described as a "make-or-break" period for the administration's programs.[1] The future of the DLF was to be decided. The problem of sustained support for India's Second Five-Year Plan had to be faced, as did a presidential offer of economic aid to the Near East. Whatever the Arabs' response to the president's offer, this aid represented a commitment to other underdeveloped areas which could be withdrawn only at great cost. Finally, the administration needed to deal with the growing uneasiness, particularly in the Senate Foreign Relations Committee, about the scale and character of the military aid program. The administration had to establish that the problems associated with foreign economic development were not a perennial U.S. responsibility necessitating large annual expenditures but were matters requiring a vast international effort under U.S. leadership. One way to do this was to place foreign aid on a multilateral basis. Another way was to encourage regional economic development. Indeed, the administration had been considering regional schemes at least since 1955, and the Mideast crisis of 1958 made clear to the White House the regional and multilateral nature of most world problems.

Of the regional proposals the administration considered, economic development of Latin America assumed the greatest significance. Largely ignored by the White House until the end of Eisenhower's first term in office, Latin America had been almost totally excluded from economic assistance under the U.S. mutual security program. A series of developments culminating with a riot during Vice-President Nixon's visit to Venezuela in 1958, however, caused the administration to review its entire Latin American policy. In 1958 the White House came out in support of a program of regional economic aid for Latin America central to which was the establishment of an Inter-American Development Bank.

For the most part Congress reacted favorably to the White House's proposals for placing the U.S. aid effort within a broader multilateral and regional context, although it failed to act on the administration's tax reform recommendations. As requested, the House and Senate increased U.S. participation in the World Bank and the International Monetary Fund (IMF), and approved legislation to establish an Inter-American Development Bank (IADB). Congress was less kind with respect to the White House's annual mutual security requests, which it once again slashed heavily. But even in the case of foreign aid, the House and Senate increased the program's emphasis on economic rather than military assistance and authorized substantial increases in the DLF for 1960 and 1961. In fact, the administration's problems with Congress in 1959 were as much with supporters of economic assistance as with its opponents. Led by J. William Fulbright of Arkansas, a group of pro-aid senators objected strenuously to the military character of the foreign-aid program and sought long-term financing of the DLF. The final aid authorization measure represented a compromise between their views and those of the president, who protested against the method of extended financing being proposed in the Senate.

The Senate bloc that had tried to grant Treasury borrowing authority to the DLF was afraid that the administration might otherwise attempt to abolish that agency or sharply curtail its funding. Although no evidence of this exists, the White House's reorientation of policy toward multilateralism and regionalism made any substantial broadening of the DLF's lending power seem anachronistic. At the very least, it behooved the administration to await the results of its shift in policy before making the type of extended commitment to the DLF being proposed in the Senate. The compromise worked out in the aid authorization measure satisfied this condition while assuring a continued, and even expanded, program of economic development supported by public capital.

Efforts to Encourage Private Investment through Tax Incentives

Despite the White House's commitment to a policy of foreign economic growth based on the flow of public capital abroad, the administration also felt obligated (and remained under great political pressure) to encourage private investment overseas. It rejected a series of proposals to foster private foreign investment, but it agreed to support the establishment of a special tax entity that would permit deferral of taxes on foreign income. This revision of the tax laws had been recommended in studies on the role of private enterprise in foreign policy.

The first of these reports was prepared by a committee of the Department of Commerce's Business Advisory Council known as the Committee on World Economic Practices. Although Vice-President Nixon had recommended formation of the committee in January in response to the expanded Soviet economic effort abroad, the group did not hold its first meeting until June. Headed by Harold Boeschenstein, the Committee on World Economic Practices was instructed by the White House "to frame a combined governmental and private enterprise program which will ensure the development of a sound expanding free world economic system, and which will effectively combat the mounting Soviet offensive." Passage of the Javits amendment to the Mutual Security Act added considerable significance to these instructions.[2]

During the next six months the Boeschenstein Committee undertook a number of tasks, such as profiling the psychological effects of Soviet bloc activities on underdeveloped countries, querying government agencies about their efforts to foster private investment abroad, and preparing a memorandum on the nation's existing aid and development efforts.[3] In drawing up its recommendations for the White House, the committee portrayed Soviet (and Chinese) economic efforts abroad in particularly bleak terms. The committee found, for example, that Moscow was continuing to expand its program of credits and grants to underdeveloped countries at a rapid rate; in 1958 alone it extended a record $1 billion in this way. Even more disturbing was the rate of growth of the Soviet economy, which was calculated to be about 7 percent a year as compared to approximately 3 percent per annum for the U.S. economy. Equally significant gains were reported for Communist China, which also was stepping up its economic activities. This meant that both Moscow and Peking would have rapidly increasing resources to apply to their aid programs. Moreover, the Soviet and Chinese economic performances foreshadowed grave propaganda consequences for the underdeveloped countries of Asia, the Middle East, Africa, and Latin America. "At present Soviet policy calls for support of the 'national bourgeoisie' in these countries," the committee concluded. Eventually, local Communist parties could be expected to make their bids for power. "In the meantime, however, much political hay can be made by supporting the present leaders in their various frictions with the industrialized West."[4]

The Boeschenstein Committee stressed "the utmost importance" of utilizing private enterprise more effectively in the less developed countries in order to combat the Soviet economic offensive. To mobilize private enterprise in the United States and among its allies and to strengthen the private sector in the Third World, the committee recommended a series of reforms, including greater use of government loans and guarantees to American businesses operating in underdeveloped countries and the establishment of local development banks and other financial institutions. But its most important recommendations were in the area of tax reform. First the committee recommended amending the tax codes to allow corporations to defer taxation of foreign income until it was brought back into the United States, and then, at the corporation's election, to subject foreign income to a tax of 7.8 percent (the current rate on intercorporate dividends) instead of the normal business rate. To permit such tax deferrals a new class of business known as the foreign-business corporation would be created. Second, the committee recommended that investment companies be permitted to pass foreign tax credits on to stockholders (through a tax-sparing clause). Next, it proposed allowing individuals to deduct losses on certain foreign business investments from their ordinary income. Finally, it recommended changing the way in which the foreign tax credit was computed in order to give businesses the advantage of the "overall limitation" rather than the current "per-country limitation." In other words, for businesses operating in more than one country, it would permit the averaging of foreign tax rates, which was not allowed under the per-country limitation. This would amount to a reversion to procedures that obtained before the tax codes were changed in 1954.[5]

Similar recommendations were contained in a State Department report, *Expanding Private Investment for Free World Economic Growth*, which was released on April 1, 1958. Authored by Ralph I. Straus of R. H. Macy's, the study was prepared in response to the Javits amendment to the Mutual Security Act. Like the Boeschenstein Report, it contained numerous recommendations for expanding private investment abroad ranging from various forms of government financial participation in private enterprise to outright government contracting for private services. At the heart of its proposals were tax incentives, particularly the creation of foreign-business corporations as recommended by the Boeschenstein Committee. The Straus Report also called for tax changes that would be applicable only to investment in underdeveloped countries, including the recommendation that a "deduction against ordinary income be allowed for capital losses sustained by individual investors and corporations (including foreign-business corporations) on their new investments in less developed countries."[6]

Although the administration gave the proposals in the Boeschenstein and Straus reports serious consideration, it opposed most of their recommendations. White House officials concluded, for example, that most of the suggestions in the Boeschenstein Report already were administration policy, were unnecessary, or were unlawful under existing statutes.[7] The only proposals the administration agreed to support or to consider further were the recommendations for changes in the tax laws, particularly the establishment of foreign-business corporations. Even in this case, however, the White House responded as much to outside political pressures as to any other considerations, and it narrowly defined the terms under which it would agree to the creation of this new tax entity.

In Congress the House Ways and Means Committee held hearings in December 1958 on private foreign investment, and there business leaders expressed overwhelming support for tax incentives for American businesses operating abroad. In January 1959, Representative Hale Boggs of Louisiana incorporated the various tax proposals into an omnibus tax bill, H. Rept. 5. As chairman of the Ways and Means Subcommittee on Foreign Trade, Boggs had become the leading congressional proponent of tax reform and was largely responsible for the December hearings on private foreign investment, at which he sharply criticized the White House for not coming up with specific tax reform recommendations.[8]

In H. Rept. 5, Boggs proposed to do what he accused the Eisenhower administration of failing to do. Otherwise known as the Foreign Investment Incentive Act, the bill contained six major changes in U.S. tax laws: (1) the establishment of foreign-business corporations; (2) a 14 percent tax reduction on foreign corporate income; (3) the reestablishment of the overall limitation on foreign tax credits; (4) the granting of tax credits in return for tax sparing by foreign countries; (5) the liberalization of restrictions on tax-free transfers of property to foreign corporations; and (6) nonrecognition of gain upon the involuntary conversion of the property of foreign subsidiaries (such as through insurance payments on destroyed property). Boggs emphasized that the provision for the establishment of foreign-business corporations was the "cornerstone" of his legislation.[9]

In December the Treasury Department had expressed opposition to the formation of foreign-business corporations. Testifying before the Ways and Means Committee, Dan Smith, a Treasury deputy in charge of tax policy, pointed out that the establishment of such corporations would mean an indefinite exemption of foreign business operations from taxation.[10] Upon receipt of the Boeschenstein Report in January and with advance knowledge of the Straus Report, however, the administration decided that, given the growing demand for incentives to encourage American business abroad, it had to make some tax reform proposals. In February, Clarence Randall organized a special committee consisting of Lewis Strauss (whom Eisenhower had named to replace retired Commerce Secretary Sinclair Weeks), Treasury Secretary Robert Anderson, and Deputy Undersecretary of State Douglas Dillon to review the tax proposals contained in the Boeschenstein Report and to offer comments on the Boggs legislation. In March the committee recommended that, subject to overriding budgetary considerations, the tax laws be amended to permit corporations to defer taxes on foreign income until it was brought back into the United States.[11]

On the basis of this recommendation the White House announced in May 1959 that it would support legislation to allow the formation of foreign-business corporations. But unlike the proposals contained in the Boggs legislation and, for that matter, in the Boeschenstein and Straus reports, the administration's recommendations would apply only to corporations that derived "substantially all of [their] income from investments in one or more of the less-developed areas of the free world." In other words, it would not include income from Europe or Canada, where almost half of the United States' total private investments overseas were located. In a letter to Wilbur Mills, chairman of the Ways and Means Committee, Treasury Secretary Anderson explained the administration's rationale for limiting the benefits of the foreign-business corporation to Third World nations in terms of fiscal necessity. But Anderson also disputed the widely held claim that private investments in industrialized nations would eventually encourage investments in underdeveloped areas as well. "Even if this should occur to some extent," he added, "it would seem to be an insufficient means of stimulating economic growth in the less developed areas [since] a relatively small amount of capital is required to put a laborer to useful work as compared with the situation in the highly industrialized countries."[12]

For much the same reasons the White House also opposed the proposal to permit a 14 percent general tax reduction on all foreign corporate income. In 1954 the administration had supported such a provision, which U.S. enterprises operating in South America had enjoyed under the Western Hemisphere Trade Corporation Act since 1942, and during the next four years Commerce Secretary Weeks (who returned to private business in 1959) had continued to advocate the reduction as essential to encouraging American investment abroad. But fiscal considerations and the desire to direct the flow of private capital toward the less developed areas of the world led the administration to oppose the recommendation when it was made again to Congress in 1959. Because of similar considerations, the administration also raised objections to the other provisions in H. Rept. 5, although it expressed willingness to consider amended versions of the tax-sparing and overall limitation proposals and the proposal not to tax proceeds from the involuntary conversion of foreign properties.[13]

The Boggs legislation failed even to be reported out of committee. In hearings on the measure in July, the Treasury Department emphasized the excessive tax losses that would result from a world-wide tax deferral program, while the Department of State stressed the need to direct private investment into the underdeveloped countries of Asia, Africa, and Latin America. Backers of the legislation disputed these arguments, but the conflict over tax deferral kept the bill in committee throughout 1959, even though Boggs agreed to drop his other major proposal for reducing the maximum corporate tax on all foreign income from 52 to 38 percent.[14] The fact was that the White House had never been enthusiastic about any of the provisions for encouraging private investment abroad. It had endorsed the creation of foreign-business corporations largely in response to growing political pressures, and although it favored increasing the flow of private capital overseas, it realized it would have to continue to rely primarily on public assistance to promote economic growth in the Third World. More important to the administration than tax reform, therefore, were its programs for broadening the framework of aid-giving.[15]

Multilateralism and Regionalism

Motivating the administration toward a multilateral program of foreign aid was the persistent depression of 1958. Unemployment, which had hovered around 4 percent since 1954, reached 7 percent by mid-1958 and remained high throughout the rest of the year. Private investment, as measured by such factors as inventory levels and purchases of producers' durable equipment, increased, but it also remained in a slump. Under these circumstances President Eisenhower believed the federal government had to limit its expenditures as much as possible. The president was also worried about the likelihood of postrecession inflation, which he believed posed the greatest potential danger to the nation. This fear increased the pressure on the administration to modify and moderate its spending plans in all areas, including foreign aid. Similarly, a balance-of-payments deficit and a subsequent loss of gold, including $2 billion in 1958 alone, were becoming matters of growing concern, although they were not yet regarded by the White House as critical. Any spending program that appeared to increase inflationary pressures in the United States would increase foreign pressures on the dollar and on U.S. gold reserves. Larger foreign outlays would also contribute directly to increasing the nation's payments deficit.[16] At the same time, White House officials realized that Western Europe was now better able, relative to the United States, to carry some of the responsibility for world economic development. Having almost fully recovered from the ravages of World War II, the West European countries were enjoying unprecedented prosperity, and the administration felt it should share with these industrial powers more of the responsibility for maintaining world economic growth.[17]

One way to do this was to increase the resources of the World Bank and the International Monetary Fund (IMF). After a slow beginning, the Bank had expanded its long-term lending program from a level of $350 million in 1950 to over $750 million by 1958. By the fall of 1958 it had invested $3.8 billion in development projects in forty-seven countries, mostly in the Third World. It had also established the IFC to make loans (without government guarantees) to private enterprise, and its president, Eugene Black, had expressed interest in the creation of an IDA as a third window of the Bank.

The IMF had gone through an even more protracted transition than the World Bank, largely due to the fundamental disequilibria that existed in the international economy and the fact that the dollar was the only fully convertible currency. Not until the Suez crisis of 1956 did the Fund, which had stopped all lending with the inauguration of the Marshall Plan in 1948, resume lending. That year it approved a stand-by credit of $738 million for England to pay for oil imported from the Western Hemisphere. By 1958 the Fund had extended short-term loans of $3 billion to thirty-five countries. Of that amount $1.8 billion had been advanced in the last two years and another $900 million had been set aside for other stand-by commitments.[18]

At the end of August, Treasury Secretary Anderson recommended to the president that the United States propose at the upcoming New Delhi meeting of the Bank and the Fund that the quotas and capital of these two institutions be increased and that the establishment of a soft-lending agency as proposed by Senator Monroney be pursued further. In his letter to the president, which the White House made public, Anderson commented that it seemed desirable that the free world cooperate in assuring the economic growth and progress of the less developed countries and that one of the best ways of achieving cooperation in this effort would be to strengthen existing financial institutions. "In the International Bank for Reconstruction and Development and the International Monetary Fund we have seasoned international instruments now engaged in this work," he told the president.[19] Eisenhower agreed with Anderson's recommendations to increase the quotas and capital of the two institutions and instructed him to make them at the meeting of the Bank and the Fund, which was scheduled to begin in October. He also asked the treasury secretary to undertake informal discussions with the other members of the Bank to determine their reaction to the establishment of an IDA. If the response was favorable, Anderson was to initiate negotiations to create the institution.[20]

The president's decision to seek expansion of the World Bank and the IMF was, however, only one aspect of what *Business Week* described as a "more vigorous and flexible foreign economic policy now being launched by the Administration."[21] The White House also began to place greater emphasis on regional efforts to promote economic growth. It had been considering such a regional approach since the administration first proposed a special Asian economic fund in 1955. In 1956 the CFEP had established a special committee to study the effects of regional economic integration on U.S. trade and other economic interests. Although the council had devoted most of its attention to plans for establishing a Common Market in Europe, it had also considered the question of economic integration in less developed areas. In September 1956 the council had given qualified approval to regional trading schemes among underdeveloped nations. The less developed countries, particularly the Latin American countries, it commented, "have been engaged in discussions among themselves and in international organizations regarding the promotion of regional trade liberalization and economic integration as a means of facilitating their economic development." According to the council, the United States was sympathetic to the formation of customs unions and free-trade areas so long as they met GATT standards or warranted the granting of a waiver by GATT, but it was unsympathetic to preferential agreements among underdeveloped countries which favored those countries' products.[22]

In 1957 Clarence Randall had formed a special interagency committee to study the specific question of regional economic integration in Southeast Asia.[23] Although in 1955 Harold Stassen had favored some kind of regional organization to dispense foreign aid, nothing had materialized from these plans, and aid continued to be granted on an individual basis. Asian leaders themselves saw disadvantages in funneling aid through a regional organization so long as it was needed exclusively for internal projects.[24] When Randall returned from a trip to Asia at the end of 1956, however, he was convinced that in addition to maintaining bilateral relations, the United States needed to promote a program of regional economic cooperation. The special assistant to the president pointed out that he did not have in mind so much the establishment of new international agencies as the effective coordination of existing regional activities. By the summer of 1958, however, the committee he had established was considering a number of proposals to bring about greater regional unity, including the formation of an Asian Chamber of Commerce and the creation of domestic Asian financial institutions.[25]

Thus, even before 1958 the administration had seriously considered regional schemes for economic development. By accentuating the regional nature of most world crises, the disorders in Iraq, Jordan, and Lebanon in the summer of 1958 increased the tendency within the White House to perceive the problem of economic development as a regional one. The crisis in the Mideast also led the president to propose to the United Nations the establishment of an Arab development institution. Eisenhower did not believe that regional development programs were appropriate everywhere, but he did think that they were useful in areas having common interests and needs, and he made it clear that the White House intended to encourage more area-wide economic schemes, such as for the Middle East. "I think that this whole proposition of dealing with areas sometimes, because the problems transcend national boundaries, must be one that we have got to look at more closely than in the past," he commented at a news conference a few days after his UN speech. "In the economic field," he concluded, "we have dealt completely on a bilateral nationalistic basis, and I think that possibly there is coming about a reason, like the Mid-East and others, where we might be better advised to attempt to use some collective organization."[26]

Latin American Development

Of the regional schemes considered by the administration, however, the one that received its highest priority was that for Latin America, not the plans for the Middle East or Southeast Asia. Despite increased Eximbank lending following the dispute in 1954 over the Bank's lending policy, the U.S. government had remained largely unresponsive to the area's economic demands. Because of the oil and other mineral resources of Latin America, private investment had been significantly higher in this region than in other underdeveloped areas. Overall, poverty was not as great there as elsewhere, and the Soviet economic challenge was not as threatening. The White House continued to believe that the most pressing needs of Latin America could be met by the private sector working in cooperation with the Eximbank and the World Bank. Hardly any public economic assistance had been extended to Latin America, even under the Mutual Security Act, although substantial military aid had been provided. This disturbed a number of congressmen who believed that U.S. money and equipment were being used merely to keep corrupt regimes in power.[27]

Beginning around 1956, however, the White House had begun to alter its policy as the National Security Council (NSC) issued a revised directive on Latin America (NSC 5163). One reason for this change was the failure of private enterprise to invest in Latin America as the administration had expected. In 1955 the CFEP had estimated that U.S. capital contributions to Central and South America would have to be stepped up by more than 50 percent between 1955 and 1958 if they were merely to maintain the same rate of growth. Thus, by 1958, contributions would have to reach $700 million a year; to give any added impetus to Latin American development, they would have to increase even more. But while reinvested earnings from private sources increased from $152 million in 1953 to an estimated $193 million by the end of 1954, direct private investments actually dropped from $93 million to $82 million during the same period. Clearly the private sector was not meeting the growth needs of Latin America; most investments went to a few countries in South America and were largely confined to the raw-materials sector of the economy.[28]

An even more important factor in convincing the administration to review its Latin American policy was its fear of Soviet economic penetration of the Western Hemisphere. Simply stated, the problem was that the Soviet Union was extending its economic offensive to Latin America in an effort to strengthen its ties with the region. This was particularly evident in the area of trade, which, while remaining modest, increased enough to cause the State Department considerable concern. Exports from Latin America to the Soviet Union and Eastern Europe had jumped from about $40 million in 1953 to almost $150 million in 1954 and $180 million in 1955, and imports had increased from just under $40 million in 1953 to $100 million in 1954 and $160 million in 1955. Given these developments, the State Department noted "an urgent need for modification and reorientation in the [nation's] existing policy toward Latin America" and thus requested the NSC review.[29]

Conducted in the spring and summer of 1956, the review hardly resulted in major improvements in existing policy, however. In fact, it contained at least one directive that, if carried out, would only exacerbate U.S.–Latin American relations. "If a Latin American state should establish with the Soviet bloc close ties of such a nature as seriously to prejudice our vital interests," the directive read, the United States should "be prepared to diminish governmental economic and financial cooperation with that country, when such action seems likely to weaken the Soviet ties." Yet the NSC did call for a more sympathetic response to Latin America's economic needs than was implicit in existing policy. It proposed, for example, that the administration expand inter-American trade by resisting efforts to limit Latin American exports to the United States. This was obviously a response to the earlier unsuccessful attempts by Congress to impose duties on lead, zinc, and tuna, much of which came from Latin America. The NSC also directed that the United States reduce existing trade barriers over the next few years. More important, it called for greater flexibility in extending credits to Latin America through the Eximbank. Under existing policy, the Eximbank could consider a loan application from a Latin American country only if funds were not available from the World Bank or from private sources. This requirement tended to restrict applications for economic development loans. In the new directive, the reference to the World Bank was deleted, although that to private sources remained.[30]

Although the recommendations contained in the NSC report were aimed at improving relations between the United States and Latin America, they failed to bring about any positive change. If anything, relations actually deteriorated during the next two years as Latin America experienced a serious recession, which it attributed in part to U.S. policy, and as the administration focused most of its attention on the Mideast crisis. President Eisenhower's decision to place quotas on imports of lead and zinc following a Tariff Commission report of serious injury to these industries stateside also hurt U.S.–Latin American ties.[31] Nor were relations helped much by the administration's continued resistance to demands for increased economic assistance for the region. At the Inter-American Conference in Buenos Aires in 1957, the United States joined with Latin American countries in recommending that a study be undertaken of the problems of financing economic development, including the formation of a regional development bank, but the U.S. delegation opposed any effort to establish a Latin American development fund or to strengthen national development corporations.[32] A few months later, Undersecretary of State Herter even advised against the adoption of a proposal by Assistant Secretary of the Interior Ross Leffler to hold a Western Hemisphere Conservation Conference. "In the current context of our relations with Latin America," Herter told Leffler, "conferences and action programs emanating from them generally look towards and constitute pressures for additional financial and technical assistance directly or indirectly from the United States Government. Budgetary and other considerations counsel against adding to such pressures at this time."[33]

In fact, the first move to increase the flow of public capital to Latin America came not from the administration but from Congress. Accusing the White

House of backing reactionary regimes in Latin America, of being subservient to American business interests in the region, of stifling social reform, and of not providing the region with adequate economic aid, a group of senators led by George Smathers of Florida amended the 1956 foreign aid bill to make available to Latin America a small amount of money for medical and other social purposes. Eventually the administration allocated $15 million for such projects. Similarly, when Congress established the DLF in 1957, it specifically included Latin America as a region to receive DLF funds.[34]

It was the riot during Vice-President Nixon's trip to Venezuela in 1958, however, that finally persuaded the Eisenhower administration to support a regional economic and development program for Latin America. The treatment accorded Nixon in Caracas had a decisive impact on administration policy. As Samuel Waugh, head of the Eximbank commented, Nixon's trip to Latin America "brought into sharp focus" the problems confronting the United States in the region. *Business Week* reported that while the previous year Washington had treated the Latin Americans' meeting in Buenos Aires to consider economic matters as just one more meeting, now "Washington ha[d] to take action."[35]

The administration chose to back a regional program for Latin America known as "Operation Pan America," central to which was the establishment of an Inter-American Development Bank (IADB). Although the newly elected president of Brazil, Juscelino Kubitschek, had suggested the concept of "Operation Pan America" to Eisenhower as early as 1956, nothing had developed from the talks between the two men. Following Nixon's return from Latin America in 1958, however, Kubitschek wrote to the president suggesting the need for a review of the United States' Latin American policy. The Brazilian president did not make specific recommendations for improving Pan-American understanding, but Eisenhower sent Assistant Secretary of State Roy Rubbotom, Jr., to Brazil to begin exploratory talks with Kubitschek. These negotiations were followed in July by a visit from Secretary of State Dulles, who proposed to the Brazilian leader the formation of a regional development bank.[36]

The establishment of a hemispheric banking institution had first been proposed by Secretary of State James Blaine at the First International Conference of American States in 1889, and for more than sixty years Latin Americans had sought such an institution. Most recently, President Perez Jiménez of Venezuela had offered to contribute $33 million if the United States would agree to participate in a regional bank or a development fund. But the United States had consistently fought the proposal, both because it generally opposed providing development aid to Latin America and because the concept of regional financial institutions conflicted with its policy of bilateral control of aid funds.[37] As part of its new regional orientation, however, the administration began to reconsider its position. Regional banks now appeared to offer an effective way of encouraging development on an area-wide basis. By making loans and technical aid available, they also provided an attractive means of mobilizing domestic and foreign capital investments in Third World countries.

Thus the administration probably would have supported a regional bank for Latin America even if Vice-President Nixon had not met with such a violent reception in South America. Certainly the president's backing for a bank in the Near East at about the same time would have made it extremely difficult for him to deny such a bank for Latin America. Still, as former Secretary of State Dean Acheson made clear before the House Banking and Currency Committee, there was no doubt that the impetus for proceeding with the bank proposal in the summer of 1958 was Nixon's hostile reception in Caracas earlier that year.[38] In proposing the IADB to President Kubitschek in July, Secretary of State Dulles had to use considerable persuasion, for the Brazilian president had initially been cool to the idea of a Latin American lending institution. Kubitschek became one of the bank's strongest proponents, however, after Dulles pointed out to him that it might limit its activities to major development projects of the kind Brazil was emphasizing.[39] Having gained the backing of the Brazilian president, the United States announced its support for a regional bank at a meeting the next month of the Inter-American Economic and Social Council.[40]

The administration's endorsement of the IADB by no means implied that the United States was about to undertake a massive program of economic assistance for Latin America. For one thing, the White House intended to keep the size of the proposed new institution small. For another, the administration was not prepared to back other economic goals being sought by Latin American leaders, such as the creation of a preferential trading area or the adoption of price stabilization measures for Latin American products.[41] Nevertheless, by backing the IADB, the United States committed itself to a program of regional economic development. In this respect the proposed institution would be a "borrowers' bank" rather than a "lenders' bank." In contrast to the World Bank, on which it was otherwise closely modeled, the IADB would be controlled by the capital-importing countries, which together would contribute more than half of its initial working capital and have more than half of its voting power. Consequently these countries would control the formulation of policy and the distribution of loan funds.[42]

The White House displayed a new interest in the economic and political problems of Latin America in other ways as well. Although the administration refused to accept price stabilization schemes for Latin American goods, the president agreed to give the matter further consideration. More important, in the fall of 1958 Eisenhower sent his brother Milton, an authority on U.S.–Latin American relations who had visited South America in 1953 at the request of the president, on a good-will trip to Central America. Early in 1959 the president also created a National Advisory Committee on Inter-American Affairs headed by Christian Herter. Later Eisenhower presented to a special committee of the Organization of American States a broad program of reforms that included proposals for increased trade; the establishment of common markets; and social development projects, involving, among other things, the construction of low-cost housing.[43]

Following the administration's announcement that it would support the establishment of a development bank for Latin America, a special committee of the Inter-American Economic and Social Council drafted a charter for the bank.[44] The major problem facing the committee was the conflict between Brazil and the United States over the size of the new institution. In the words of Treasury Secretary Anderson, the United States was determined that the bank should have "relatively modest beginnings." The administration hesitated to make the IADB too large for fear that U.S. control over bank funds would be limited and that the bank might otherwise infringe upon the Latin American lending activities of the Eximbank and the World Bank. Washington thus proposed an initial capitalization for the IADB of only $850 million, with the United States contributing $400 million. The bank's capital would consist of $700 million for ordinary loans and $150 million for soft loans. Brazil responded by urging a total capital of $5 billion. Later it modified its position by proposing an initial capitalization of $2 billion for ordinary loans and a special fund for soft loans.[45]

Under considerable pressure from the United States, which warned the drafting committee that the U.S. Congress was unlikely to approve the charter during the current session if it was not completed by the end of March, the committee finally agreed to a compromise worked out by the administration. According to this agreement, the initial capitalization of the bank was set at $1 billion, to which the United States would subscribe $450 million, $250 million of which was to be paid in installments and $200 million in callable capital. Of the $1 billion, $150 million would be set aside for a Fund for Special Operations, which would make soft loans; $100 million of the United States' subscription would be designated for this fund. The charter also specified that an additional $500 million would be added to the callable capital after all installments of initial paid-in capital had been made and provided the increase was approved by three quarters of the members represented on the board of governors. This gave the United States a veto over any increase in bank funding, but as even President Eisenhower conceded, it left Washington morally obligated to subscribe approximately $200 million more in callable capital after three to five years.[46]

Congress and the Reorientation of Administration Policy

For the most part Congress approved of the White House's efforts to promote economic growth abroad on a multilateral and regional basis. In May 1959 Eisenhower presented the draft agreement for the IADB to Congress with the recommendation of the NAC that the United States participate as a member.[47] The House and Senate received the administration's proposals warmly. In hearings before the House Banking and Currency Committee, Representative Henry S. Reuss of Wisconsin, a Democrat, remarked that the strongest criticism he could make of the legislation was that a similar bill had not been presented to Congress three or four years earlier. In the Senate, Foreign Relations Committee member Wayne Morse, an outspoken critic of the administration's mutual security recommendations, led the support for the measure, noting that the United States had too long taken Latin America for granted. In July the House and Senate passed identical bills approving U.S. membership in the IADB and adding only a minor amendment to tighten congressional control over the financing of the bank.[48]

Likewise Congress easily passed administration-sponsored legislation to increase America's subscriptions to the World Bank and the International Monetary Fund. In October the White House asked members of the Bank and Fund who were meeting in New Delhi to raise the quotas and capital of the two institutions and to consider establishing a soft-lending affiliate of the Bank. The members agreed to increase the Fund quotas of most countries by 50 percent. They also agreed to raise the total authorized capital of the Bank to $21 billion and to increase the subscription of the present members by 100 percent. This amounted to a new commitment on the part of the United States of $1.375 billion for the Fund and $3.175 billion for the Bank.[49] As a contingent liability only, the increased capital subscription for the Bank required no immediate expenditure of funds, but the revised quotas for the Fund necessitated an outlay of $344 million in gold and $1.031 billion in non-interest-bearing notes. In June, Congress passed the necessary legislation approving the World Bank increase and the new appropriation for the Fund. After a brief and partisan debate over whether the money for the Fund should be charged to the fiscal 1959 budget (which the president wanted) or to the 1960 budget (which would have left the budget unbalanced, as the Democrats wanted), the House went along with the president's request and the Senate conceded to the House's position.[50]

Congress and the Struggle over Mutual Security Legislation for 1960

Despite the reorientation of its policy toward multilateral and regional means of dealing with the problems of world economic growth, there is no evidence that the Eisenhower administration ever intended to abandon its own aid program. So long as fear of Soviet expansion dominated administration planning, the White House would emphasize the importance of expanding its own economic activities overseas. In 1958 the administration thus recommended an increase in the lending authority of the Eximbank from $5 billion to $7 billion, and Congress approved it.[51] Similarly, in testimony before the House Banking and Currency Committee in support of U.S. membership in the IADB, Deputy Undersecretary of State Dillon remarked that at some point in the future the United States might even use the DLF to augment the IADB's Fund for Special Operations.[52]

The Eximbank was a hard-lending institution, however, whose borrowing authority came directly from the Treasury Department and therefore did not require annual congressional appropriations. Its operations were also not the kind that particularly concerned most proponents of economic aid, who sought public assistance mainly through grants and soft loans. In contrast, the DLF, a soft-lending institution, was subject to the rigors and uncertainties of regular congressional authorizations and appropriations. The DLF's uncertain status concerned a number of senators because they were worried about the effects the administration's new policy (which they nevertheless generally supported) would have on the fund and because they believed that the White House had not sufficiently emphasized the kind of economic aid provided by the DLF when preparing its mutual security program. To remedy this situation they proposed a substantial increase in the size of the DLF and long-term Treasury financing of the kind enjoyed by the Eximbank.

The administration rejected these proposals, however. Notwithstanding its apparent intention to maintain and perhaps expand the size of the DLF, the White House was not prepared to make the type of commitment to the fund currently being proposed in the Senate until its new economic policy had been tested. President Eisenhower also objected in principle to Treasury borrowing as a means of avoiding the regular appropriations process. As a result, the struggle for foreign aid in 1959 pitted the administration as much against the proponents of economic aid as against its opponents. The final bill that came to the White House was a compromise between the Senate and administration versions of the mutual security legislation, although it incorporated a substantial increase in economic assistance and reflected in part the reform proposals of a group of senators led by J. William Fulbright.

Fulbright and all but one of the Democratic members of the Foreign Relations Committee (the exception being Russell Long of Louisiana), as well as Republican William Langer of North Dakota, had expressed displeasure with the existing foreign-aid program in a letter they sent to President Eisenhower at the end of August 1958, shortly after passage of the mutual security appropriations bill for 1959. Released to the press by Fulbright on September 8, the letter noted "a serious distortion" of the amounts of economic and military assistance going to Third World countries and urged the president to correct the situation.[53] Eisenhower responded that the proportion of military aid to economic aid had been reduced since he took office. Adding that enlargement of the nation's economic programs in 1959 "would of course further decrease the military proportion," he also noted that in view of "the threatening posture of the Sino-Soviet bloc" and the increasing costs of modern weapons, future reductions in military expenditures would require "a most careful weighing before they could be seriously contemplated."[54]

Eisenhower nevertheless believed that the issues raised by the senators warranted another study of the mutual security program, despite the fact that several major studies had been completed less than two years earlier. It was his intention that the new examination concentrate on the military aspects of the mutual security program, but he knew that these could not be separated from the economic questions posed in the Foreign Relations Committee's letter to him. Enclosing a copy of the senators' letter in his letter to William H. Draper, Jr., chairman of the board of the Mexican Light and Power Company and a former undersecretary of the army, the president asked Draper to head a committee of nine civilians and former military commanders to study "all relevant aspects of U.S. international security programs." "I am especially interested in your committee's critical appraisal . . . of the relative emphasis which should be given to military and economic programs, particularly in the less developed areas," the president concluded.[55]

On March 17, 1959, the Draper Committee delivered the first of three interim reports to the president. By this time Eisenhower had presented his mutual security requests for 1960 to Congress in a message that, perhaps better than any other, described his view of the Soviet design for world conquest. "[There is] loose in the world," he said, "a fanatic conspiracy [that in the past forty years has] seized control of all or part of 17 countries, with nearly one billion people, over a third of the total population of the earth." At the center of this conspiracy, the president continued, was the Soviet Union, which through ruthless means had made itself the second military and economic power in the world and which was prepared to resort to any means, including economic coercion, to intensify world unrest. Moreover, Communist China was displaying the same ruthless drive for power. "Communism masquerades as the pattern of progress, as the path to economic equality, as the way to freedom from what it calls 'Western imperialism,' as the wave of the future." It was therefore incumbent upon the free world, the president concluded, "to convince a billion people in the less developed areas that there is a way of life by which they can have bread *and* the ballot, a better livelihood *and* the right to choose the means of their livelihood, social change *and* social justice—in short, progress and liberty." To meet the threat of international communism, Eisenhower proposed a mutual security program for fiscal 1960 of $3.9 billion, or about the same as the previous year's request but $600 million more than was finally appropriated. Among his recommendations were $1.6 billion for military assistance, $835 million for defense support, and $700 million for the DLF, which were, respectively, $85 million, $85 million, and $300 million more than Congress had appropriated for fiscal 1959.[56]

Like the president, the Draper Committee emphasized the international Communist conspiracy facing the free world. Remarking that the Communist military threat was greater than ever before, the committee proposed that an additional $400 million in military assistance be made available for new commitments, primarily in the NATO area.[57] Eisenhower called the report a "top flight document" and told Draper he had already ordered the White House staff to review its recommendations. However, the president decided to defer until 1960 any decision on whether to recommend an increase in the size of the military assistance program.[58]

As Eisenhower realized, any increase in the total amount requested for the mutual security program would only diminish the bill's chances of being passed by Congress.[59] Indeed, in submitting his foreign-aid request for 1960, the president was aware that its legislative prospects were already grim. Herter told him that a poll of congressional opinion indicated that opposition to the aid program was more widespread and vigorous than at any time in the past. By now Eisenhower was accustomed to such bleak forecasts, having heard them practically every year since becoming president. As Herter pointed out, however, there were this time, in addition to those who normally opposed the program, a number of other congressmen who favored large cuts for purely political reasons having to do with the administration's domestic spending programs and its decision to undertake no new public-works projects during the next fiscal year. Moreover, 1960 was a presidential election year, and several key senators, including Fulbright and Majority Leader Johnson, had presidential ambitions that were bound to shape the fight over foreign aid. In the absence of another major effort by the White House or some world crisis, Herter predicted, the final aid appropriation for 1960 would be around $3 billion or less.[60]

Some of the difficulty the administration's program would encounter, especially during the appropriations process, became evident almost immediately after the president submitted his proposals to Capitol Hill. On March 19 the House Appropriations Committee rejected a supplemental appropriation of $225 million for the DLF. When Congress had approved the mutual security appropriation bill for 1959, giving $400 million to the DLF, Eisenhower had indicated he would return to Congress during the next session for a supplemental appropriation. In his budget message in January 1959 he thus asked for an additional $225 million for the DLF to bring the fund's capitalization to the amount originally recommended for 1959. Despite the president's insistence that the funds were needed to keep DLF loans from drying up, the Appropriations Committee rejected the supplemental request, later agreeing to restore only $150 million of the amount the president had sought.[61]

The aid authorization measure approved by the House reflected a $367 million cut in the White House's requests, or about a ten percent reduction in military aid, defense support, and special assistance. Even in the House, proponents of foreign aid made clear their displeasure with the military emphasis of the existing program. The Foreign Affairs Committee, for example, added $100 million to the president's request for the DLF. Although this was cut on the House floor, several other revisions made by the committee in an effort to place more emphasis on economic assistance were approved by the House and sent to the Senate. Among the most important of these was a provision requiring the American ambassador in a country receiving military aid to "make sure the recommendations . . . are coordinated with political and economic considerations."[62]

The most serious opposition to the administration's program, however, came in the Senate, which in the past had routinely gone along with the program before subjecting it to the appropriations process. The opposition included not only opponents of foreign aid but the same group of senators who had written to the president in August to complain of the program's military emphasis. Nothing the White House had done in the interim had changed these senators' belief that the direction and guiding principles of the program were wrong. In a speech to the Senate in April, while the aid legislation was still in House committee, Senator Fulbright proposed a series of amendments to the measure that would alter the balance between military and economic assistance, including an increase in the capitalization of the DLF to $1.5 billion a year for five years. Other amendments offered by Fulbright provided for a new Mutual Security Act policy statement stressing the common interest of the United States in strengthening the independence and well-being of other nations; a statement that military aid to underdeveloped countries should be programmed "according to the principle that economic development needs shall have first call on the resources of such countries"; presidential authority to shift up to 30 percent of military aid funds to nonmilitary uses; and specific authority for American ambassadors to coordinate military aid proposals with political and economic considerations.[63]

Of the Fulbright proposals the most important was the one to increase the capitalization of the DLF and place it on a long-term basis. A number of senators joined Fulbright in cosponsoring this measure as well as his other proposals for reforming the mutual security program. Mike Mansfield of Montana, who had his own amendments to offer, but who supported Fulbright's goal, summed up the doubts and misgivings of many senators. The uneasiness in Congress over the foreign-aid program was "not a whim out of the blue," he remarked. Nor did it represent a retreat from international responsibilities. "The uneasiness is over the way the concept of helping others and fulfilling our international responsibilities is being translated into action."[64]

The Fulbright amendments, particularly the one for long-term financing of the DLF, placed the White House in an awkward position. On the one hand, when it first proposed the establishment of the DLF in 1957, the administration itself had advocated long-term Treasury financing of the agency. On the other hand, the president was increasingly concerned about the need for budgetary restraints. Moreover, he believed that his own requests for increased funding for the DLF, along with the other measures he had taken to promote economic development on a multilateral basis and to expand the lending activities of the Eximbank, were sufficient to meet the capital needs of Third World countries. Finally, he now preferred a provision of "no year money" (whereby unexpended appropriations are automatically carried over from one year to the next) to Fulbright's proposed long-term financing through Treasury borrowing, which would by-pass the normal appropriations process. Despite the fact that his aid programs had been cut by the House and Senate Appropriations committees, Eisenhower was convinced that this was the fiscally sound procedure to follow.[65]

As a result, the White House clashed with Fulbright over the long term-financing of the DLF. In June, Leverett Saltonstall of Massachusetts, the ranking Republican member of the Senate Armed Services Committee and a close ally of the administration, wrote to the president asking for his support of the Fulbright proposal. "His purpose is, of course, the same as that which you had when you originally sought the establishment of the Development Loan Fund in 1957," Saltonstall pointed out.[66] Responding to an earlier letter from Fulbright, who had asked Eisenhower to clarify the administration's position on the DLF, the president remarked that although he shared the senator's wish to put the DLF on a long-term basis, he opposed the move to by-pass the regular appropriations procedure. He suggested instead "a long-term authorization of appropriations in reasonable amounts, together with the concurrent enactment in one appropriation bill of appropriations for each of the years for which the program is authorized." As for the size of the fund, Eisenhower remarked that doubling the $700 million figure he had proposed for fiscal 1960 would be unwise and expressed the hope that the other industrial countries would "provide a growing volume of financing for the less-developed areas."[67]

Although Fulbright had told the president that his proposal for long-term funding could not be passed without full White House support, on June 23 the Foreign Relations Committee reported out a bill containing that proposal and other Fulbright provisions for reforming the mutual security program. For the first time in the program's history, the committee actually increased the administration's aid recommendations and provided that the $1 billion authorized for the DLF in fiscal 1960 come from Treasury borrowing; to put the DLF on a long-term basis, it also authorized $1 billion per year for fiscal 1961–64. This action reflected the committee's growing concern over shortcomings in the mutual security program. In shifting somewhat the program's emphasis from military to economic assistance, the committee noted that it had merely "done to the bill what it had hoped that its previous expressions would cause the administration to do . . . [and] in the absence of administration initiative [it was] compelled to proceed unilaterally in order to present . . . a bill which is adequate to the task that confronts American foreign policy in 1959."[68]

The administration found the Foreign Relations Committee's aid recommendations unacceptable, particularly since the committee also proposed to shift $300 million in military assistance funds from non-NATO to NATO countries.[69] After some preliminary skirmishes that endangered government programs financed by Treasury borrowing outside of regular appropriations bills (the procedure Fulbright proposed for the DLF), the White House reached a compromise on the measure on the Senate floor. Faced with the prospect that the funding of at least fifteen agencies might be jeopardized, including that of the Commodity Credit Corporation, the Rural Electrification Administration, and the Eximbank, all of which were already authorized to borrow from the Treasury, both sides agreed to a proposal worked out by the new minority leader, Everett Dirksen, and Majority Leader Johnson. The compromise provided $2 billion in regular authorizations for the DLF, $750 million of which was slated for fiscal 1960 and $1.25 billion for fiscal 1961. The funds would be made available only through appropriations bills. Christian Herter, who had replaced Dulles as Secretary of State in April, following Dulles's resignation due to advanced cancer, had persuaded the president that some concessions on the Fulbright proposal should be forthcoming from the administration.[70]

The rest of the debate in Congress over the president's mutual security program was anticlimactic, although as Herter had earlier predicted, Congress made sharper reductions in the foreign aid bill than it had the year before. In the Senate, Eisenhower's military aid requests were slashed to $1.3 billion, and the president threatened to call a special session of Congress if adequate funds were not restored. (In conference committee, the figure was raised to $1.4 billion.) The House and Senate also agreed to a $700 million authorization for the DLF for 1960 and $1.1 billion for 1961.[71]

As usual, however, Congress authorized more money than it appropriated, and once again most of the cuts in appropriations were made in the House. As passed by the House, the appropriations measure included $1.3 billion for military assistance, $700 million for defense support, and $550 million for the DLF. At a press conference, Eisenhower protested that the House cuts would damage the national security and expressed the hope that the Senate would appropriate the full amount authorized. The Senate did restore some of the cuts made by the House, including $40 million for the DLF and $45 million for special assistance, but its addition of $95 million contrasted sharply with its actions in previous years. Also, like the House, the Senate rejected a request by the president to give the DLF another $500 million as a down payment for fiscal 1961.[72]

Final action on the appropriations measure was delayed until the end of the session by a dispute over civil rights legislation and by action on a public-works bill. Breaking from his bipartisan approach to foreign-aid legislation, Eisenhower attacked the Democratic leadership for holding the appropriations measure hostage to partisan politics.[73] The Senate finally sent the bill to the president on September 14, after rejecting additional cuts in the measure. As signed into law at the end of September, the appropriations bill provided $3.3 billion for mutual security for fiscal 1960, including $1.3 billion for military aid, $695 million for defense support, $550 million for the DLF, and $245 million for special assistance.[74] Eisenhower called the action by Congress deplorable and short-sighted. "In these times especially," he commented, "Americans are entitled to expect better of the Congress than this."[75]

The $704 million reduction in President Eisenhower's foreign aid requests fell between the $652 million cut in the 1958 bill and the $1.1 billion cut in the 1957 legislation. Eisenhower did not fight as hard for his foreign-aid program in 1959 as he had a year earlier; there was much less public advocacy of the mutual security program by the White House, and fewer strategy meetings and conferences with legislative leaders were held. In addition, much of the bipartisan spirit of the previous year disappeared as Democrats, stung by the administration's opposition to their domestic welfare proposals and undoubtedly having the 1960 elections in mind, led the effort to cut the president's program. As for the president, his comments on foreign aid had always been tinged with impatience and despair, but in 1959, after seven years of fighting with Congress over the mutual security program and contending with proponents and opponents of expanded economic aid, this tone was particularly noticeable.

Yet the mutual security legislation that Eisenhower signed into law contained a number of provisions that in many ways were more important than the actual appropriations approved by Congress and that continued the shift from military to economic assistance begun in 1957. Most important of these was the $1.1 billion authorization for the DLF for fiscal 1961. This authorization almost assured that the size of the fund would be increased in 1961, although probably to a figure well below $1.1 billion. In addition, in the final authorization measure, the House went along with a Senate provision placing future military assistance appropriations in the Defense Department budget. The House had not approved such a provision, and in deference to the lower chamber, Senate conferees agreed to put the plan on an experimental basis for fiscal 1961 and 1962 only. In the meantime, this action by Congress would afford an opportunity for interested persons to gauge more accurately the extent of the nation's economic—as opposed to purely military—aid programs. The accusation that the government was engaged in a vast "giveaway" would be more difficult to defend.[76]

Furthermore, the foreign-aid bill contained a number of the amendments Fulbright had authored in his effort to shift the emphasis of the legislation from military to economic assistance. As the Arkansas senator had proposed, American ambassadors were now authorized to coordinate military aid with political and economic considerations. The policy statement on foreign aid that Fulbright had prepared also was incorporated into the measure, though with one substantial change; the objective of "giving generously of our knowledge and substance" became in the final bill one of "providing assistance with due regard for our other obligations." Fulbright's proposal on programming military aid to underdeveloped countries was reflected in a provision directing administrators of military assistance to "encourage the use of foreign military forces in underdeveloped countries in the construction of public works and other activities helpful to economic development."[77]

Conclusion

In approving the 1959 mutual security legislation, the House and Senate continued to express their interest in promoting private enterprise abroad and in eliminating grant aid. They did so by passing two additional amendments. The first of these required annual studies of the role of private enterprise in foreign policy and the role of the balance of trade. One of Jacob Javits's favorite proposals, this amendment had been added by the Senate and retained by the House, as had language directing the State Department and other agencies to study methods to strengthen the economies of free nations. The second amendment, approved first by the House and then by the Senate, directed the president, in making requests for fiscal 1961 foreign aid, to submit a detailed plan for the progressive reduction of all bilateral grant assistance.[78] Despite the addition of these amendments, and despite also the sharp cuts in appropriations, the thrust of the debate over mutual security in 1959 had been not so much eliminating or reducing foreign aid as placing greater emphasis on economic rather than military assistance. On this issue, the Fulbright bloc in the Senate won a substantial victory, although the final aid legislation represented a compromise between its views on the future of the DLF and those of the White House.

As for the administration, it too enjoyed considerable success in 1959, not only in reaching a compromise with Fulbright over the DLF, but in placing its program for economic development within a multilateral and regional context. The shift toward multilateralism did not reflect any new confidence on the part of the White House as to the efficacy of a multilateral—as opposed to a bilateral—approach to world economic development. Even less was it a response to the demands of Third World nations, which generally advocated multilateral rather than bilateral assistance (with its implicit danger of big-power hegemony). Instead, the administration moved toward multilateralism because it recognized that the United States' capacity to provide economic aid relative to the other industrial powers had changed considerably. So long as the Soviet menace remained the administration's major concern, the United States would continue to emphasize the need to expand its own bilateral aid programs, but this did not lessen the obligation of the other Western powers to contribute to the common effort against international communism.

This reorientation of policy toward multilateralism and regionalism was accelerated by the nation's growing balance-of-payments problem. By the end of 1959 the problem had become so acute as to be the primary foreign economic issue facing the president in his last year in office.

10. The Balance-of-Payments Problem and Foreign Economic Policy

1959–1960

DURING EISENHOWER'S first year in office, his administration developed a foreign economic program based on the concept of "trade not aid"; lower tariffs and private investment would replace public capital in meeting the world's economic needs and assuring world economic prosperity. The program was predicated on the assumption—indeed, the reality—of a world dollar shortage resulting from the impaired output of the industrial plants of Europe and Japan following World War II. The Marshall Plan and the ensuing recuperation of the industrial powers notwithstanding, when Eisenhower became president the dollar shortage was still thought by some to be a permanent fixture of the international economy. As for the world's underdeveloped countries, the administration forecast that their needs also would be met by trade and investment, as well as by a general filtering down of the prosperity that was to come with the recovery of the world's industrial nations. To the extent that public economic assistance was provided to the Third World, therefore, it was largely military in nature or served a military purpose.

Within a few years, however, and especially during Eisenhower's second administration, the White House was forced to pay increased attention to the economic needs of these underdeveloped countries. In the process, the program of "trade not aid" was found wanting and a policy of "trade and aid" was substituted; the new emphasis clearly was on the flow of public capital abroad. Surprisingly, however, the administration's program of relying on trade and investment to bring about further economic recovery in the industrialized countries (based as it was on the assumption of an existing dollar shortage) worked even better than many had anticipated. As trade expanded and investment increased, Europe began to prosper, the dollar shortage disappeared, currency convertibility reappeared, and the role of the United States as a leader in the field of foreign economic policy seemed admirably filled.

What had been a dollar gap at the beginning of the 1950s in fact became a dollar (and gold) drain by the end of the decade. Since America's balance of trade remained favorable, one had to look to its military commitments abroad, its foreign-aid program, and its private investments overseas to ac-

176

count for this drain. During 1958, U.S. gold reserves dropped by $2 billion, the largest loss ever in a single year, and they declined by another $1 billion during the first three quarters of 1959.[1] The effects of this loss were not all negative; for instance, the conditions that produced it permitted Western Europe to make its currencies convertible at the end of 1958. Nevertheless, for a fiscally conservative administration concerned with losses of gold since at least 1955, the accelerated decline of the nation's gold reserves became an urgent matter. Indeed, no foreign economic issue received more attention from the president in his last year in office than the growing U.S. balance-of-payments deficit.

The balance-of-payments problem affected the administration's entire foreign economic program of trade and aid. On the one hand, the White House took unilateral steps to maintain the integrity of the dollar, including a trade promotion campaign and the tying of aid to the fostering of trade. On the other hand, it accelerated its efforts, begun in 1958, to place more of the burden for international economic development on a multilateral basis, and it sought to shift some of the responsibility for military defense onto its West European allies. In fact, the administration attempted to forge a new Atlantic partnership of the Western industrial powers. The White House's policies were by no means ill-conceived, nor did they represent an abandonment of its own programs for economic development abroad, as indicated by its renewed efforts in behalf of the mutual security program and its decision in 1960 to establish a special social development fund for Latin America under the jurisdiction of the IADB. Nevertheless, the efforts to form an Atlantic partnership failed, in part because French President Charles de Gaulle opposed any common Atlantic effort that included the United States and England, but also because the White House was unwilling to establish an institutional framework capable of dealing multilaterally and collectively with world economic problems.

The programs pursued by the administration did make clear, however, that the position of the United States as one center of a bipolarized world economic and political system had shifted considerably. The nation's overwhelming postwar economic supremacy had been whittled down by the military-oriented output of the Sino-Soviet bloc and even more by the production of the very countries whose postwar recovery the United States had generated. In addition, the power of the United States had been weakened by the growing economic and political unity of Western Europe and its waning dependence on Washington for economic and military assistance. Long-run developments such as the continued population growth of Asia, Africa, and Latin America and the quest of these regions for economic development and political recognition portended an even more fundamental alteration in the world power balance, a change that would affect Western Europe as well as the United States.

The Balance-of-Payments Problem

The possibility of a balance-of-payments problem was first brought to President Eisenhower's attention as early as 1955 by the then Treasury Secretary Humphrey, who presented the president with figures on the United States' declining gold reserves and increasing foreign dollar obligations. While the nation's gold holdings had dropped from a high of $24.77 billion in 1949 to $21.79 billion at the end of 1954, foreign short-term dollar claims had increased from $7.83 billion to about $13 billion during the same period. Some of these claims were necessary working balances, and other technical considerations had to be kept in mind in analyzing these figures, but it was conceivable that all these foreign accounts could be converted into gold. In that extreme case the United States would be left with a balance of $8.78 billion in gold, or $3 billion short of the legally required reserves for the Federal Reserve System. "There is nothing to worry about yet," the treasury secretary conceded, "but this illustrates definitely how the monetary reserves of other countries have been strengthened and our own weakened to a point where we need to give careful thought to making sure of continued confidence in the U.S. dollar and safeguarding our remaining reserves."[2]

Eisenhower largely ignored Humphrey's warnings about declining gold reserves relative to dollar holdings. "Frankly," he told Humphrey, "it appears from your memorandum that a lot of bad things would have to happen in a hurry to get into real trouble about the matter. . . . If people have such huge credits in this country, maybe our business is going to boom for quite a while filling their orders."[3] Over the next three years Humphrey and other financial experts made occasional reference to the balance-of-payments problem. The treasury secretary cited potential gold losses as one reason for not expanding U.S. aid commitments abroad, and in at least one cabinet meeting in 1956 he made a lengthy presentation on the gold issue.[4] The next year he sent Eisenhower a letter he had received from Russell Leffingwell, a Wall Street financier who had been warning Humphrey for some years of the increasing claims of foreigners against the nation's gold reserves and even of the possibility of a flight from the dollar. "I continually wonder if we aren't seriously overlooking the possibility of a real danger unless we change the current continuing trend from loss of position to some regular, very moderate gain or at least the maintenance of a balance by reduction of our military forces and expenses abroad," he told the president once more.[5]

The precipitous drop of $2 billion in the nation's gold holdings in 1958 produced considerable uneasiness in financial circles and widespread predictions of trouble to come, but it caused remarkably little concern within the administration. In 1958 ten West European governments took steps to make their currencies more freely convertible into dollars by making them convertible for nonresidents but not residents. Without the expansion of world trade and the flow of dollars into Europe that accompanied the U.S. payments deficit, this significant accomplishment in rebuilding a sturdy world economy most likely would not have taken place. From the White House's perspective, European convertibility was a welcome event that was even more important than the balance-of-payments problem, the full world impact of which remained undetermined. Thus it was the relative strengthening of the European economy and the rough balancing of world trade rather than any fundamental economic weakness on the part of the United States that accounted for the imbalance of payments.[6]

Nevertheless, the move toward convertibility in Europe, along with further gold losses in 1959 and general economic stagnation in the United States, led the administration to seek a multilateral approach to world economic development. In August, the White House also established a cabinet-level group headed by Treasury Secretary Anderson to formulate an overall policy for dealing with the balance-of-payments problem. To carry out the broad objectives laid down by the cabinet group, a deputies group, including representatives from most agencies involved with foreign economic matters, was constituted under Assistant Treasury Secretary Alfred H. Von Klemperer.[7]

Tying Aid to Trade

Thus, by the summer of 1959 the administration had begun to deal with the balance-of-payments problem in a concerted way, but even then it did not believe that the disequilibrium in the balance was so fundamental as to necessitate precipitous action. It rejected, for example, the notion that U.S. exporters were suffering from disadvantages so acute that they could be adjusted only by such drastic measures as devaluation of the dollar. Nor was the White House willing to risk distorting the domestic economy by raising interest rates to reduce inflation and attract foreign capital. Similarly, it refused to resort to restrictions on imports or to limit expenditures by American tourists overseas, since this would invite retaliation.[8]

Rather, the solution to the balance-of-payments problem lay in more modest measures designed to improve the nation's balance of current accounts— that is, the surplus of goods-and-services earnings over goods-and-services payments. In this respect, the administration's most pressing task was to improve the nation's trade balance (the surplus of exports over imports). In 1959, the balance of trade, which two years earlier had reached a high of $6.1 billion, fell to only $1 billion, the lowest level for the entire decade. The drop in the trade balance was actually not as drastic as it appeared, for both 1957 and 1959 were abnormal years. The huge surplus for 1957 reflected the large volume of sales abroad generated by the Suez crisis in late 1956, while the dramatic decline in 1959 was precipitated by the United States' earlier recovery from recession (relative to Europe) and its consequently greater demand for foreign imports. In 1960 the excess of exports over imports would rise above the 1956 level, and for the entire fifteen-year period from 1950 to 1964, exports would actually increase by a greater percentage than either imports or the gross national product.[9]

Yet from the perspective of 1959 the drop in the balance of trade seemed critical, and there is no doubt that had the trade balance not declined so precipitously between 1957 and 1959, it would have more than offset the drop of slightly over $3 billion in the nation's gold stocks. Furthermore, the balance of trade affected the administration's entire foreign economic program, including foreign aid. According to Don Paarlberg, who had left the Department of Agriculture to become a special assistant to the president at the White House, the trade balance had permitted the United States to contribute to economic development abroad. If the balance dropped sharply, the nation's capacity to provide economic aid would be reduced proportionately.[10]

Paarlberg attributed the decline in the trade balance to the worsening competitive situation of the United States—to differences in the price, promotion, availability, and quality of merchandise. In the minds of most other White House officials, however, an even more fundamental cause was the fact that foreign-aid funds supplied by Washington were no longer being spent in the United States. Many of Europe's industrial powers had payment surpluses not only with this country but also with the less developed countries, and it was difficult to determine what percentage of these imports was being financed directly by Washington or indirectly through a general freeing of purchasing power in the countries receiving aid. The White House believed it was considerable. The amount of untied foreign aid extended by the United States therefore affected both the nation's trade balance and its balance of payments. Conversely, any increase in development aid from the other industrial powers would alleviate these problems and, if not tied to the sale of their own merchandise, might even reverse some of the flow of capital out of the United States.[11]

To deal with the problem of U.S. foreign-aid funds spent in other countries, therefore, and possibly to encourage other industrial powers to extend their own economic assistance, the White House announced in October a new policy by which DLF loans would be used to finance goods and services from U.S. sources. As late as the previous July, the Senate had rejected Allen Ellender's amendment to the Mutual Security Act, which would have accomplished much the same purpose by requiring that not less than 75 percent of the funds authorized under the measure be for goods and services in the United States unless waived by the president. Ellender had based his proposal on the balance-of-payments argument, but opponents of the amendment successfully contended that 80 percent of mutual security funds (except for the DLF) were already spent in the United States and that even DLF dollars not tied to specific American exports eventually came back to the United States. Opponents also maintained that the proposal would be paralyzing administratively and that the purpose of the Eximbank, which required tied loans, was to promote American exports, while that of the DLF was to assist developing countries and improve their trade. Finally, they remarked that the favorable dollar balances of other countries reflected the success of the United States' previous programs for economic recovery.[12]

In fact, the Ellender amendment was unnecessary. The president already had the authority to require expenditure of aid funds on U.S. goods, and Treasury Secretary Anderson was anxious for Eisenhower to use this power in awarding DLF loans. Anderson based his position on the premise that Japan and the industrialized countries of Western Europe were economically and financially strong enough to no longer warrant DLF financing of their exports. Moreover, if other industrialized countries were required to extend their own financing, the total amount of goods for less developed countries might increase. According to Anderson, his recommendation by no means departed from the nation's commitment to multilateral trade but merely recognized that a buyer should normally expect to obtain long-term financing from a seller of goods and services, especially if the seller was in a position to provide lending facilities.[13]

Not all the members of the NAC, which acted in an advisory and coordinating capacity on foreign financial matters and would have to recommend to the president any change in the DLF's loan practices, agreed with the Treasury Department's position. The Department of State in particular opposed the tying of DLF loans to U.S. procurement because it believed the political ramifications would more than offset any improvement in the nation's balance of payments. The United States would be accused of turning back to protectionism, and other countries might retaliate. At the same time, economic development in a place like India would be slowed down while New Delhi dickered over financing. Undersecretary of State Dillon even requested that the CFEP study the problem of DLF procurement as part of an overall examination of the balance-of-payments situation.[14] But the consensus in the NAC and the DLF, whose membership for the most part overlapped, was for tying loans to American exports, and this became the administration's policy. At the end of October 1959 President Eisenhower defended the new policy at his weekly news conference. "This is not a turnaround, a reversal, or going in another direction," the president stated. "It is simply to point out that when we are making this money available, it's dollars that's being made available."[15]

Having to accept the new lending practice, Undersecretary Dillon made it clear that he intended to apply the restriction only to DLF loans and not to procurement by such other agencies as the ICA. In a letter to Senator Fulbright, Dillon explained his rationale. DLF loans largely covered capital expenditures, which he believed should be financed on a long-term basis. The West European countries that were capable of joining with the United States in providing such equipment were also capable of providing their own long-term financing. ICA funds, on the other hand, were used to procure defense support, not special assistance, and for the most part consisted of grants for industrial raw materials and consumable products. According to Dillon, therefore, the tying of ICA aid to U.S. exports was not likely to stimulate additional financing by other industrial countries, because they were "not in a position to undertake large scale additional grant programs."[16]

The Attempt to Forge an Atlantic Economic Partnership

Even so, as another part of its program for dealing with the nation's balance-of-payments problem, the White House was already negotiating with a number of West European countries in an effort to get them to provide more economic aid to Third World countries. In fact, by the fall of 1959 the United States was attempting to forge a new economic relationship with the West European powers.

The division of Western Europe into two rival trade blocs as a result of the formation of the European Economic Community (EEC, or Common Market) in 1957 and the European Free Trade Area (EFTA) in 1959 greatly troubled Washington. Because of a long-held desire to bring about a politically and economically integrated Western Europe as a barrier to the Soviet Union, the United States had strongly supported the formation of the European Common Market. Moreover, the Treaty of Rome, which established the Market, raised the possibility of eventual European political unification. Besides a common external tariff, for example, it provided for the free movement of persons, services, and capital; a common agricultural policy; and the creation of a European Social Fund and a European Investment Bank. In contrast, EFTA, which was organized by England and whose membership included six other countries, all outside the Common Market, was intended to be merely a free trade area. Thus it would create all the trade discriminations inherent in a customs union but, from Washington's point of view, none of the political advantages of an economic community. Indeed, because a rival to the Common Market was considered counterproductive to the Western harmony being promoted by the White House, EFTA was generally unwelcome in Washington, particularly in the view of Undersecretary of State Dillon, who became its most vocal opponent within the administration.[17]

Despite the formation of these rival trade groups and the differences that existed among the European powers, most of Western Europe shared America's concern about Soviet economic and political penetration abroad. Moreover, there remained a strong—albeit declining—sense of Atlantic unity in Europe and a desire to deal cooperatively with world economic questions. Article 2 of the North Atlantic Treaty, for example, provided for economic collaboration among the members of NATO, and the NATO countries in 1957 considered the possibility of using this article to coordinate aid efforts aimed at less developed countries. The United States thus hoped to get Europe to act with it in meeting the growth needs of Third World nations.[18]

Because of NATO's military orientation and its unsuitability as a forum for neutral nations or other nonmember, the idea of using NATO for economic purposes was shelved.[19] In talks with President Eisenhower in September 1959, however, Prime Minister Antonio Segni of Italy raised the possibility of NATO aid to underdeveloped areas. After Segni commented that Italy had a particular interest in providing assistance to Turkey and Iran, two countries Eisenhower planned to visit in December, Foreign Minister Giuseppe Pella remarked that the Italian government had also discussed the subject of foreign aid with French President Charles de Gaulle and with representatives of the Benelux countries, Iran, and Turkey. He spoke too about Italy's desire to develop policies within the Common Market that would enable its members to increase their aid to, and purchases from, the world's underdeveloped areas. Finally, he expressed the view that aid should be extended on a regional basis, remarking that such regional groupings would give aid recipients a greater sense of equality and participation and would induce greater responsibility in the use of the aid. Italy hoped that the proposed IDA could be linked with the implementation of this regional plan, and Pella referred to the meeting of the Common Market countries scheduled for October as a possible forum for discussion of the idea. In view of the upcoming conference, his government wanted an indication of the United States' position on Italy's ideas with respect to foreign aid.[20]

Eisenhower refused to make any firm commitment to the Italian leaders, but he took advantage of the opportunity to lay the groundwork for a future conference of the Western powers on world economic problems. He responded to Foreign Minister Pella that although all the leaders he had contacted in recent months had expressed considerable interest in aid to underdeveloped countries, a number of them had a particular group of nations in mind. For example, de Gaulle had a special interest in providing aid to the French Community, while London was interested in development within the British Commonwealth. Only the United States, Germany, Italy, and some of the smaller nations remained flexible about providing economic assistance abroad. There was thus a need to get together to consider how the burden of providing aid should be divided. When the Italians asked Eisenhower what countries he included in this last remark, he replied that he meant all of the free nations, including France and England. He had not intended to imply that just those countries that were flexible in the matter of extending aid would confer, although he conceded that France and England might not want to work on a broad international scale or assume a role with respect, for example, to Burma or some of the Mideast countries.[21]

The European powers endorsed Eisenhower's proposal for economic discussions, and the talks took place in Paris in December as part of a summit meeting of Western leaders following Eisenhower's whirlwind visit to Turkey, Pakistan, India, and Iran. Prior to the meeting the Economic Policy Committee of the Organization of European Economic Cooperation (the OEEC, which had been organized in 1948 to formulate a program of European economic recovery as part of the Marshall Plan, but which had since become a highly effective institution in the areas of intra-European trade and payments) agreed unanimously that Europe should provide increased capital to less developed areas of the world.[22] Just before the summit was to begin, Undersecretary of State Dillon reported from Paris that in his talks with European leaders he had found "full recognition" that Western Europe had to increase its level of help to the less developed nations.[23]

Yet as Treasury Secretary Anderson stated in a memorandum to the president on points to raise at the summit meeting, none of the European countries had translated these general principles into concrete actions. In fact, each of the European countries was anxious to accumulate more reserves for itself for fear its present economic strength might prove to be temporary. Each also suspected the others of being better able to shoulder the burden of economic aid, and all overemphasized the need to coordinate their own efforts with those of the United States and the World Bank. Finally, and perhaps most important, none of the European powers had established any fully satisfactory banking or budgetary arrangement for providing long-term loans adapted to the needs of the less developed countries.[24] Anderson therefore recommended to Eisenhower that in Paris he press the Western leaders for a commitment to long-term lending for the Third World. Europe's strong financial position, as well as the West's political objectives in less developed areas and the need to keep world trade in balance at a high level, all required increased European financing on both a bilateral and a multilateral basis. The United States' experience in the field of economic development had made it clear that the industrialized countries could not successfully carry out their responsibilities in financing less developed areas solely through private investment or private lending institutions. Therefore, virtually all the European countries needed to establish a public or semipublic lending institution, perhaps financing its operations through the sale of government-guaranteed securities on the local capital market.[25]

We do not know what actually took place at the summit conference, but Anderson's presummit memorandum to the president makes clear the negotiating position of the United States with respect to European aid. The United States expected Germany to make the largest contribution to Third World economic development. It was economically the strongest of the European nations and the most important exporter of heavy equipment to many less developed areas. Germany maintained that it was losing rather than gaining foreign-exchange reserves during 1959 and that this showed it was doing as much as it could in the field of foreign lending. But its total gold and dollar holdings still exceeded $4 billion (down $200 million from 1958) and it had virtually no short-term liabilities to other countries.[26]

Italy's problem was mainly psychological. Italians still considered their nation small and poor and they pointed to the development problems of southern Italy to support this view. But their official gold and dollar reserves were now the third-largest in Europe (rapidly approaching the size of England's) and showed every sign of continuing to grow. Though southern Italy's needs might make it somewhat more difficult politically for Italy to finance foreign lending, the nation had a heavy stake in the sale of equipment to less developed areas outside Italy. In addition, Italy's strong banking and capital market should make the establishment of a development lending bank a relatively easy technical matter.[27]

The British believed they were doing about all they could in the field of foreign finance, considering that their gold and dollar reserves were still low relative to their trade needs and financial responsibilities, that their prospective balance-of-payments problem was very small, and that they already had heavy development responsibilities within the Commonwealth. Their position was not unreasonable, but in view of the United States' interest in obtaining increased bilateral aid from many European countries rather than from only one or two, Anderson advised that London be encouraged to take additional steps to provide financing for development projects outside as well as inside the Commonwealth.[28]

France presented special problems, and Anderson believed it was probably not desirable to press the French immediately for help in the field of trade (except to seek their firm support for the proposed IDA). France's capacity to provide additional foreign lending was currently limited by foreign-exchange difficulties and the country's huge development responsibilities in the franc area, particularly in Africa. Moreover, Anderson reminded the president that it was of great importance to restrain President de Gaulle (whose views on Atlantic unity were already at odds with those of most other Western leaders) from pressing his previous notions about a new multilateral scheme for financing economic development, a scheme which involved Soviet participation.[29]

Despite this last note of caution in Anderson's memorandum, the Paris meeting in December proved to be highly gratifying to the United States. In a special communiqué issued after the conference, the Western leaders set the stage for new efforts to achieve U.S.–European cooperation by calling for an informal conference in Paris on January 13 of the ten European nations, the United States, and Canada.[30] News reports were already being circulated that out of the conference and a high-level OEEC meeting that was to follow, a new, twelve-nation Atlantic Council would be formed that would include the United States and Canada as full members. According to these reports, which were later confirmed, the new organization would take over the OEEC, including its staff and secretariat.[31]

Besides dealing with Western aid efforts, the new organization would act as a forum for other common economic problems, the most urgent of which remained the division of Western Europe into rival trade blocs. Prior to the Paris summit, German Chancellor Konrad Adenauer informed Undersecretary of State Dillon that British Prime Minister Harold Macmillan had told him that unless the Common Market was merged with the EFTA in a broader European free-trade area, there would be serious military and political consequences. Germany, France, and the Commission for the EEC also told the American diplomat that they were adamantly opposed to any merger, for fear it would destroy the EEC. Dillon warned that unless some initiative was taken by the United States, there was a real danger that the already serious European trade problem would develop into a bitter political dispute.[32]

The initiative taken by the United States was the winning of an agreement from the Western leaders at the Paris summit that the problem of regional trade organizations would be one of the two major topics (the other being foreign aid) discussed at the mid-January Paris conference. In their communiqué announcing the meeting, the Western leaders even emphasized the "cooperative principles" they said should be the basis for discussion of the two regional blocs. They also made it clear that they expected the two groups to operate within the framework of GATT. It thus followed that besides coordinating economic assistance to the underdeveloped countries, any new organization that might result from the Paris meeting would have as a second major purpose healing the fissures apparent in Europe and—from the White House's point of view—protecting U.S.–European trade interests in the process.[33]

At the January meeting, which was attended by the United States, Canada, and the eighteen members of the OEEC, Undersecretary of State Dillon announced that the United States was prepared "to assume full and active membership" in a reorganized OEEC designed to "facilitate cooperation between the industrialized nations of the free world" in tackling major economic problems. A preparatory committee known as the "Four Wise Men" was then formed to consider the U.S. proposal, and in April it recommended creation of the Organisation for Economic Co-operation and Development (OECD). After six months of negotiations in which the details of the new organization were worked out, twenty nations met again to sign a convention formally agreeing to the formation of the OECD.[34] In his final budget message to Congress in January 1961, President Eisenhower called for approval of U.S. membership in the body, and Congress gave it at the end of March. By this time, of course, Eisenhower was back on his farm in Gettysburg and the Democratic administration of John F. Kennedy was in the White House.[35]

In helping to organize the OECD and then seeking U.S. membership in the new organization, the president had taken an important step toward creating an Atlantic economic partnership. In his message to Congress he remarked that the organization would "extend and invigorate the practice of consultation among its members and [would] find ways to facilitate the flow of investment funds to less-developed countries."[36] Yet the administration never intended the OECD to be more than a consultative body with flexible but limited powers. Thus, as insisted upon by the administration and approved by Congress, the organization's charter provided that decisions and recommendations made by the OECD would be by unanimous vote of its members, with each member having one vote. If a member abstained from voting, a decision or recommendation would not apply to that member but would be applicable to the voting members. No decision would be binding on a member unless it complied with that country's constitutional requirements. In the case of the United States, this often meant that congressional approval was required.[37]

The reasons for putting conditions on America's membership in the OECD included, of course, the administration's concern that without them the OECD convention would never be approved by a protectionist-minded Congress, which was determined to maintain its prerogatives in the area of foreign economic policy. However, an even more fundamental consideration was involved. Despite its desire for an Atlantic partnership that would relieve the United States of some of its economic responsibilities abroad while maintaining Western unity—and, incidentally, assuring U.S. access to European markets—the White House was by no means prepared to play a more direct role in European economic and political affairs. Least of all was it ready to assume responsibility for any of the backlog of decisions dealing with trade, capital movements, and related matters which had been made by the OEEC. Largely for this reason Treasury Secretary Anderson had opposed U.S. membership in the OEEC even before Eisenhower had discussed the subject at the summit meeting in Paris. Although he failed to win the president to his position, after Paris, Eisenhower assured him that he had no intention of binding the government to European obligations and policies. As he told Anderson, "Each country would have to determine for itself its policies and intentions so that he will not be duplicating or compeating [sic]."[38]

This remained the administration's position throughout the months in which the terms of the OECD were worked out. In fact, during the negotiations, the United States made it clear that it particularly did not want the new organization to become involved in trade matters, insisting that this would merely duplicate GATT functions. Continued efforts by EFTA, led by England, to bring about a European free-trade area had failed, and the Eisenhower administration, which vigorously opposed these diplomatic maneuvers, was not prepared to countenance their continuation under OECD auspices. In other words, a direct relationship existed between the White House's interest in restructuring the OEEC to include the United States and its concern about European discrimination against American trade.

Douglas Dillon, who led the administration's efforts against EFTA and its attempt to establish a European free-trade area embracing both the members of the Common Market and the EFTA, explained the government's policy with respect to the OECD best. The American position reflected its view that the principal concerns of the OECD should be facilitating the attainment of the highest sustainable economic growth and contributing to sound economic growth in the underdeveloped world. "At the same time," he said, "we believe that the role which the new organization could play in the field of trade without duplicating the work of other organizations is limited." The establishment of a broad free-trade area, including EFTA and Common Market countries, Dillon noted, "might very well take the incentive out of a general negotiation to lower tariffs in both areas."[39]

The White House's rejection of a strong OECD and its general stand on a European free-trade zone greatly annoyed a number of the smaller nations of EFTA, which had benefited considerably from the OEEC's trade liberalization code and its other unifying ties; these countries wanted the new organization's provisions on coordinating trade policy to be binding. Similarly, the British were infuriated at Dillon for leading the opposition against their attempt to "build bridges" between EFTA and the Common Market. Clarence Randall reported that in England he had heard "the most hostile and brutal statements" made against Dillon. In addition, America's ambassador to Switzerland told Randall that the Swiss were greatly perturbed at the United States because of its opposition to EFTA and warned that something would have to be done to remove "the onus of suspicion" that Washington had engendered.[40]

Even if the United States had wanted to, it probably could not have established an organization deemed satisfactory by these countries. It is unlikely that it could have overcome France's opposition to a strengthened OECD. Although France acquiesced in the United States' initiative in forming the OECD, it would have been perfectly satisfied to have the OEEC wither away without a replacement such as the OECD; France had achieved its objective of establishing a Common Market and it would not tolerate a European free-trade arrangement. Under the leadership of de Gaulle, who had returned to power in 1958, France was already mapping out an independent foreign policy, evoking a kind of French grandeur that was clearly aimed against the United States and England.[41]

Nevertheless, by rejecting a major role for the OECD in the area of trade liberalization and by seeking in other ways to limit its authority, the White House greatly restricted the organization's capacity to provide an institutional framework for developing a coordinated foreign economic policy for the Atlantic community. Accordingly, the OECD proved to be a useful body in terms of disseminating economic information and providing a forum for discussion of common problems. In 1960, it also established a Development Assistance Committee (DAC) to promote economic development in less developed countries that were not OECD members. But the organization never had its own funds or staff of technical experts or independent status, and thus was unable to develop a unified program of Third World economic development. For the most part, each of the major industrial powers followed its own independent program, and the OECD and DAC remained unwilling to take a position in behalf of Third World countries or in support of greater Atlantic unity that might embarrass or annoy member governments.[42]

Foreign Trade and Agricultural Policy

Moreover, even as the Eisenhower administration sought to promote an Atlantic partnership to deal with the problems of Third World economic growth and to otherwise aid the United States in its balance-of-payments problems, it continued to pursue bilateral policies. This was particularly evident in its trade policies and especially in its foreign agricultural program, which actually exacerbated rather than contributed to the Atlantic harmony the president had hoped to achieve.

With respect to trade, the administration had already tied DLF loans to U.S. procurement on the assumption that this would ensure the purchase of American goods by grant recipients and cause other exporters to Third World countries to extend their own forms of assistance, perhaps on an untied basis. The administration knew, however, that the balance of trade (and payments) would be determined not only by how much untied aid the United States and other industrial powers extended but by how well they were able to penetrate one another's foreign markets. In this respect, the question for the White House was one of trade restrictions as well as trade competition. Rejecting as self-defeating the demands for protection against foreign imports, the White House sought the alternative of expanding markets for American goods by pursuing the nation's free-trade policy. Beginning in 1959 the administration launched a major export promotion drive under the direction of the Commerce Department. In a move to encourage U.S. exporters, the Eximbank liberalized its terms and expanded export credit insurance to cover the political risks of short-term export transactions.[43]

More important, the United States intensified its efforts to increase the export of American farm surpluses even as it continued to make the disposal of America's excess agricultural production an integral part of its foreign-aid program.[44] In 1958 Congress had extended the P.L. 480 program for eighteen months and had increased from $4 billion to $6.25 billion the appropriation for foreign-currency sales, but already the White House was considering a further extension of the farm surplus disposal legislation as part of a program to meet the food needs of Third World nations. In August 1958 John H. Davis, a former assistant secretary of agriculture, presented to the administration the conclusions of a study of the P.L. 480 program that he and a group of economists had been conducting for the administration for the past six months. For the most part the report was highly laudatory of the program and recommended its expansion on a long-term, five-year basis as a "Food-for-Peace Program." "P.L. 480 operations in an underdeveloped country need to become a more integral part of a United States program designed to help the country achieve economic viability and rising standards of living and to become independent of foreign aid within a reasonable time," the report thus concluded. Davis added that the study had convinced him "that the United

States has a challenging opportunity to better utilize its food fiber reserves as a positive force in world affairs. To realize this opportunity, the United States must more effectively relate P.L. 480 to agricultural and foreign policy objectives at home and to country needs and programs abroad."[45]

The reaction of the White House to the Davis Report reflected the divisiveness of the administration over the P.L. 480 program. The Department of Agriculture called the Davis proposal "a positive approach to gain foreign policy benefits rather than a negative approach." "Our food production is the greatest advantage we have over the Soviet Union," Don Paarlberg of the Agriculture Department argued.[46] In contrast, the State Department maintained that "[to] put this proposed move [for a long-term disposal program] in the light of benefitting mankind is an impossible public relations campaign. . . . If desirable for agriculture, the Davis plan would be equally applicable to the steel industry."[47] Other agencies, including the Bureau of the Budget and the CFEP, also opposed the Davis Plan, but the position of the Agriculture Department prevailed.[48] In his budget message to Congress in January, President Eisenhower asked for an increase in title I of the P.L. 480 program from $6.25 billion to $7.75 billion, and a few weeks later, in a special message to Congress prepared by the Agriculture Department, he announced the Food for Peace Program. "I am setting steps in motion," he told the House and Senate, "to explore anew with other surplus-producing nations all practical means for utilizing the various agricultural surpluses of each in the interest of reinforcing peace and the well-being of friendly peoples throughout the world—in short, using food for peace."[49]

The president talked of cooperating with other surplus-producing nations to make food available to Third World countries, but the White House's promotion of U.S. agricultural surpluses and its protection of U.S. industries continued to disturb other food-exporting nations. By 1959 much of the furor that had been caused by the P.L. 480 program had subsided. The United States had adopted tighter regulations to assure that the program did not compete with normal commercial sales by the United States and other countries. In addition, the White House was doing a better job of consulting with third-party countries to protect their interests.[50] Nevertheless, many exporting nations continued to criticize the program, particularly the barter operations and competitive dollar sales by the Commodity Credit Corporation. Moreover, despite the president's emphasis on cooperation with other exporting nations, these countries were alarmed by the Food for Peace Program, which they realized remained fundamentally a means for the United States to rid itself of some of its farm surpluses.[51]

The most difficult problems the United States faced as a result of its surplus-disposal program involved the European food-producing nations, who were determined to protect their own farmers from American exports. At the December 1958 session of GATT, the United States had proposed that the agreement sponsor a new round of tariff negotiations beginning in mid-

1960.[52] In making this proposal, the U.S. delegation pointed out that the negotiations would fit in with the need for the six members of the Common Market to adjust their existing tariff concessions before attempting (in January 1962) to establish a common external tariff. Negotiations at that time would also make possible optimum utilization of the authority to reduce tariffs granted to the president by the Trade Agreements Extension Act of 1958. The need to negotiate with the Common Market had, in fact, been one of the principal points advanced by the executive branch in arguing for a multiyear extension of the trade agreements authority.[53]

As Secretary of State Herter told Eisenhower, however, the new round of tariff negotiations was "certain to be extraordinarily technical and difficult in view of the complexities resulting from development of the common external tariff," and no problem would be more difficult than that of tariffs on agricultural imports.[54] In preparation for the GATT talks, J. H. Richter of the Agriculture Department's Foreign Agricultural Service met with Karl Brandt of the Council of Economic Advisers and Undersecretary of Agriculture True Morse. Morse stressed the need to get the Common Market, EFTA, and other regional groups to liberalize their import policies with respect to agricultural goods.[55] In a memorandum to Assistant Secretary Thomas Mann in April 1960, the Department of Agriculture presented its response to the agricultural policy proposals of the Common Market as they had developed by that time. The memorandum amounted to a repudiation of the Common Market's position. As the Agriculture Department pointed out, the draft proposals of the Common Market fixed minimum import prices and variable import fees for many commodities. They also established export subsidies for the disposal of possible surpluses and, in the words of the Agriculture Department, "a formidable apparatus of quantitative control over external trade in agricultural products." In addition, these proposals included bilateral trade preference and other quantitative restrictions, which the department termed "objectionable," "discriminatory," and "ominous." "No one would wish to rush in with proposals to tell EEC what kind of measures to adopt in place of those we find objectionable," the memorandum concluded, "but it would be desirable to re-cast the common agricultural policy in such a way as to provide gradually for market unification in the area without intensifying protection against the outside."[56]

In forwarding a copy of this memorandum to Mann, Assistant Agriculture Secretary Clarence C. Miller commented that the Department of Agriculture felt "strongly that it [was] necessary, when the agricultural proposals come in for review on some such occasion, for the United States representatives to be absolutely candid not only in expressing the basic support of the United States for the Common Market, but also our great concern that it be generally understood that this support is predicated on compliance by the countries concerned with GATT."[57] Addressing the opening meeting of GATT in September 1960, Clarence Randall stressed these very points. The United States was satisfied that the Treaty of Rome establishing the Common Market was in compliance with liberal GATT policies, but there was "a shadow in the picture." According to Randall, no matter how well the United States might resolve existing problems in other fields, "we cannot reach a satisfactory overall result unless at the same time those that relate to agriculture are dealt with in accordance with GATT principles."[58]

The Common Market was not about to open its markets to U.S. agriculture, however, and as a result, GATT failed to reach any common agreement on agricultural trade policy. The final press release on the GATT session stated only that a committee established at an earlier session of GATT to study agricultural protectionism was "now assessing the effects of national agricultural policies on world trade in agricultural products." The release also noted that the "United States, after reiterating its support for the successful integration of the member states within a liberal trade pattern, stressed the importance of a liberal common agricultural policy in harmony with the GATT objective of expanding international trade." Nevertheless, the Common Market remained unyielding in its agricultural policy. Its efforts to safeguard its agricultural interests continued to be an issue of contention with the United States even after Eisenhower left office, although the question was brought up again during the Kennedy round of trade negotiations in the early 1960s.[59]

Cutback in Military Expenditures Overseas

In the final analysis, therefore, the White House's attempt to deal with the nation's balance-of-payments problem by pursuing a modified version of its foreign economic policy of trade and aid via a closer economic partnership with the Atlantic community largely failed. In fact, the most decisive action taken by the administration to resolve the balance-of-payments problem was considerably different from what it had originally conceived. In the fall of 1960 the administration decided to cut military expenditures abroad by ordering military dependents to return home at a rate of 3 percent a month. It also added further requirements tying economic aid and defense support to U.S. procurement.

At the beginning of October, Treasury Secretary Anderson held an important conference with the president and other White House officials and cabinet officers to discuss the balance-of-payments situation, which had continued to worsen throughout 1960. Preliminary data for the third quarter of the year indicated accumulations by foreigners of $632 million in gold and another $976 million in dollars, or a combined figure, if extrapolated over three additional quarters, of $6.43 billion. The United States' current gold stocks totaled $18.69 billion, $11.91 billion of which was required as a monetary reserve to support outstanding Federal Reserve notes and Federal Reserve deposits. During recent meetings of the World Bank and the IMF a number of foreign central bankers and ministers of finance had expressed concern as to whether the United States was doing enough to maintain the integrity of the dollar in light of the nation's responsibilities as a supplier of reserve currency and obligor of a growing number of short-term loans in the hands of foreigners. The chairman of the Federal Reserve Board and other Treasury officials had held comparable talks with representatives from the European banking and financial communities. They had been told that foreign governments were becoming increasingly apprehensive about the United States' ability to carry so large a deficit in its balance of payments without precipitating a crisis or taking action that might have the same effect, such as raising the price of gold to curtail dollar and gold outflows.[60]

For a variety of reasons having to do with political damage at home and the possible disruption of the international monetary system, the White House never considered increasing the price of gold, which would have amounted to devaluing the dollar.[61] In his meeting with the president, however, Treasury Secretary Anderson urged that the United States do something additional to combat the balance-of-payments problem. As he made clear, even the policy of tying DLF loans to American purchases as a way of improving the nation's balance of trade was not working. Some of the loans made by the DLF were with international institutions that precluded tying, while other loans were being made for the purchase of local currency and to finance local institutions, such as building and loan associations, which did not result in procurement of goods from the United States. As a necessary additional step in dealing with the balance-of-payments problem, Anderson recommended a reduction in overseas military expenditures, including a cutback in the number of military dependents in Europe, the integration of America's logistics system with the systems of its NATO allies, and an increase in the defense contributions of other NATO countries. Such possibilities had been considered before, but had never received much attention. Now Anderson made a reduction in overseas military spending a matter of the highest priority.[62]

Both the Defense Department and the Department of State objected to the treasury secretary's proposals. The Defense Department maintained that Anderson's recommendations were militarily harmful and would present serious morale problems for soldiers with dependents overseas. The State Department objected to Anderson's proposals on the more political grounds of how such reductions would be received in Europe. Undersecretary of State Dillon noted that his department was now willing to pursue a more vigorous policy in phasing out American dollar contributions to the European defense community and to the redeployment of forces, but he offered 1962–63 as the earliest time frame in which a reduction in force commitments should take place. He also argued that the United States' trade balance had improved substantially and that much of the increased outflow of liquid funds during the past three months was due to the difference between short-term interest rates in the United States and those in Europe, particularly in England and

Germany. He stated that while there might be some disposition on the part of the Germans and the British to reduce their interest rates, it might become necessary for the United States to raise its rates of interest on short-term government securities in order to prevent any outflow of foreign capital.[63]

Treasury Secretary Anderson responded that the United States simply could not afford to delay a reduction in military outlays abroad until 1962–63. Instead, he stressed the need to reverse completely the trend of thinking initiated immediately after World War II, when all embassies and military personnel stationed abroad had been instructed to buy offshore as much as possible and to encourage the accumulation of dollars in foreign hands. As for Dillon's point about raising interest rates on government securities to prevent the outflow of foreign capital, Anderson replied that the adoption of such a plan would indicate that monetary policy in the United States was no longer responsive to domestic economic considerations, and that in order to protect the nation's gold, it would have to be motivated essentially by America's position with relation to other foreign central banks. This, in turn, might result in both public and congressional opposition to the whole program of mutual security and foreign assistance.[64]

President Eisenhower gave Anderson his full backing and directed most of his remarks against the position taken by the Pentagon. It had been the president's view since the establishment of NATO in 1949 that the United States would not maintain a large, permanent force in Europe at its own expense. Rather, as the countries of Western Europe developed their own armed forces, the United States would play a less preponderant military support role. The president believed that the administration "should evaluate and consider all of the concepts of the Joint Chiefs of Staff and the Service chiefs, [but] they were not national policy makers," and those who were in charge of making policy decisions "would have to accept the burden of giving such orders as [they] felt were in the national interest." Taken aback by the president's remarks, Deputy Secretary of Defense James H. Douglas, Jr., responded that the withdrawal of dependents from Europe might be accomplished without changing military concepts.[65]

With the president obviously committed to reducing U.S. military costs in Europe, the decision was made to explore a series of proposals for cutbacks, including an order prohibiting dependents from accompanying military personnel assigned abroad and a notification to NATO countries that in the future they would be expected to assume a larger share of NATO defense costs. Moreover, negotiations with Germany were to be considered with the aim of getting Germany to contribute to the maintenance of American troops in that country.[66] Even after these decisions were reached, however, the Defense and State departments continued to raise objections to any military reductions in Europe. At another meeting with the president on November 15, the two agencies presented a joint memorandum stressing the need for continued military assistance to Italy, Belgium, and the Netherlands and noting that these three countries received less than 5 percent of the military assistance budget.[67]

The president continued to receive warnings, however, about the gravity of the balance-of-payments situation and the need for immediate corrective action through a cutback in military expenditures overseas. A few days before the November 15 meeting with State and Defense Department officials, Treasury Secretary Anderson advised Eisenhower that by the end of the week the United States' supply of gold would fall below $18 billion, that $12 billion of this amount was legally required to cover the nation's currency, and that $9.5 billion in instant demands could be filed against the United States at any time. Predicting a budget deficit for fiscal 1961 (in considerable measure the result of unanticipated expenditures in defense), Director of the Budget Maurice Stans remarked that the figures projected for 1962 also were bleak, but that much could be done to improve the situation if military expenditures abroad were cut back. Indeed, Stans said that his main complaint with administration policy was that the action the White House proposed did not go far enough. The United States should cut its troop level without waiting to see what the Germans were willing to contribute, Stans argued. Anderson added that it was essential that these steps be announced before he and Undersecretary of State Dillon conferred with Chancellor Adenauer in a meeting that was to take place in just a few days.[68]

On the basis of the figures he had received from Anderson and Stans, Eisenhower decided to order a cut in the number of military dependents abroad and to ask the NATO allies, especially Germany, to share more of the burden of the common defense. He had been preaching for eight years that the United States "had been too easy with Europe," he told the State and Defense Department officials meeting with him on November 15. He was not concerned about the morale problem the Defense Department claimed would be created by a cutback in the number of dependents abroad. He did not worry much about the morale of generals, and rank-and-file morale would be "all right" if the armed services exercised proper leadership. Moreover, in a move designed to satisfy the Defense Department, but acting over the objections of Secretary of State Herter and Undersecretary of State Dillon, the president also agreed to a reduction in the number of State Department personnel assigned overseas.[69] At a press conference the next day, Eisenhower announced a reduction in the number of armed services dependents as well as "a similar reduction by all of the departments that [have] personnel stationed overseas." The cutbacks would be made at the rate of 3 percent a month down to a maximum of 200,000 persons.[70]

As for the other major parts of the administration's program to cut military expenditures abroad, the White House did get the NATO allies to purchase more of their military hardware in the United States. The secretary of defense also took actions to reduce overseas spending, including integrating more U.S. logistical operations with those of European countries. However, although Anderson and Dillon met with Chancellor Adenauer in Germany in November, they failed to reach an agreement about sharing the cost of maintaining American troops in West Germany. "From the standpoint of economics, you're right," Adenauer told them when they argued the need for Germany to contribute more to the common defense, "but you fellows are not going to be in office that long. And it could mean I'd have to impose additional taxes on my people."[71] The overall result of the president's cutback program was a gradual reduction in military expenditures overseas from $2.71 billion in 1960 to $2.541 billion in 1961 and $2.049 billion by 1964. Even so, the latter figure represented a significant drain in the American balance of payments.[72]

Conclusion

The balance-of-payments problem continued to be a major concern for the administration—indeed, its most pressing foreign economic problem—during Eisenhower's last months in the White House. Just a few days before the president's term ended, Secretary Anderson, "with the express approval of the President," wrote Douglas Dillon, whom President-elect John F. Kennedy had named as his treasury secretary, to recommend several additional steps for dealing with the balance-of-payments issue. A number of these proposals concerned tax relief for American businesses through more liberal and flexible depreciation allowances, relief that would make business more productive and hence more competitive in world markets. But Anderson also proposed changes in the tax laws which would make it easier for the government to tax the earnings of American subsidiaries operating abroad in supposed tax havens. Because of the implications of these tax havens "for the revenue, the tax system, and the balance of payments," Anderson wrote, "it would seem appropriate to modify some of the features of the present tax law."[73] Soon after taking office, President Kennedy would make the balance-of-payments problem one of his top priorities, but he would have little more success in dealing with it than Eisenhower had had before him.

11. The Final Fight over Foreign Aid 1960–1961

THE WHITE HOUSE'S preoccupation with the balance-of-payments problem did not keep it from neglecting other foreign-policy concerns associated with its program of trade and aid. Notwithstanding the outflow of gold and dollars from the United States, the administration remained convinced that America's role in defending the free world against Communist aggression and in providing capital to less developed areas could not be safely or wisely abandoned or even suddenly reduced. It concluded that the solution to the balance-of-payments problem was not to reduce foreign aid or private capital outflows, particularly to the Third World, or even suddenly or drastically to cut military operations abroad. No more in these respects than in others did the balance-of-payments problem call for a hasty or ill-conceived response. In proposing to Undersecretary of State Dillon changes in the tax laws which would eliminate tax havens, for example, Treasury Secretary Anderson remarked that he was "mindful that no barriers should be imposed upon investment abroad and further that private investment in less developed countries should be encouraged."[1] Similarly, even while it sought to get Western Europe to share more responsibility for economic development in the Third World, the United States continued to promote other forms of multilateral and bilateral aid, including the extension of its own foreign-aid program.

The Administration's Foreign-Aid Proposals for 1961

In fact, the president's impressions from his trip to the Middle East and South Asia at the end of 1959, his realization that colonial rule was coming to an end in Africa and elsewhere, the movement of Cuba toward the Communist bloc in Latin America, and a perceptible increase in East-West tensions all caused Eisenhower to take a more active role in behalf of foreign aid in 1960 than he had a year earlier. Not only did he become more involved in attempting to put his legislation through Congress, but he also proposed a broad new program of social reform for Latin America and changes in the way in which foreign aid was distributed. He displayed the same bold and assertive leadership he had shown in 1958.

197

Eisenhower was deeply moved both by the overwhelmingly friendly crowds and by the poverty and calls for greater economic assistance that greeted him during his eleven-nation trip through the Middle East and South Asia in December 1959. In each of the countries he visited, the question of American foreign assistance always came up for discussion. As Eisenhower later remarked in his memoirs, "Indeed, in one guise or other, this question was part of every business conference I held in every nation throughout the entire tour." Two matters that particularly concerned the president were (1) a bitter quarrel between India and Pakistan over the division of the Indus River and (2) the amount of aid Afghanistan was receiving from the Soviet Union; the latter issue took on special significance after Pakistani President Mohammed Ayub Khan told Eisenhower that Moscow was building important roads through Afghanistan for its own strategic purposes. In the first instance, the problem was that India and Pakistan both wanted to use the Indus River for irrigation and power purposes; in the second, Afghan leaders insisted that Moscow had given them more real aid than the United States had and that this aid was vital to the Afghan economy. In response to these problems Eisenhower told the leaders of Pakistan and India that the United States would help develop the Indus basin if the two countries would agree to a compromise program under the auspices of the World Bank. Similarly, he promised to look into the matter of U.S. aid to Afghanistan when he returned home.[2]

The president's impressions from his trip to Asia were reflected in his foreign-aid requests for 1961. Among the items he highlighted in his special mutual security message to Congress in February was the need for support of the Indus River Basin Project. As he told Congress, substantial progress had been made in resolving the problem through the World Bank, and he anticipated that a development plan would be reached in the near future. However, such a project would require aid from nations outside South Asia, including the United States. In addition to asking for support of the Indus River project, Eisenhower stated that, as in the past two years, a major share of DLF loans for fiscal 1961 would go to India and Pakistan. "We have joined with other nations in helping these countries," he said. "We envisage the total public and private effort to assist South Asia not only continuing but expanding."[3]

Also important in determining the president's aid program for 1961 was the emergence of a number of former European colonies as nations in Africa and other regions. Eisenhower was greatly impressed by France's efforts to prepare its former colonies for eventual self-rule; on the other hand, he was shocked by the total lack of preparation on the part of the Belgians in their colonies, and blamed Belgium for the riots and turbulence that soon broke out in the Belgian Congo. As he commented in February, the emergence of the new nations in Africa and elsewhere created "critical problems of essential economic development."[4] In his special message to Congress a few days later, the president asked for $20 million in special assistance for the improvement of education and training in Africa south of the Sahara. In subsequent years this amount would have to be increased "significantly," he said, as would aid from other countries, if "the pre-conditions of vigorous economic growth [were to] be established."[5]

As for the rest of the president's mutual security requests, Eisenhower asked for $4.175 billion for fiscal 1961, or $245 million more than he had requested the previous year (and almost $1 billion more than Congress had appropriated). Although the 1959 authorization legislation had provided for as much as $1.25 billion for the DLF for fiscal 1961, the president sought only $700 million. The reasons for this low request are not entirely clear, but they probably involved several considerations, including the fact that Congress had appropriated only $550 million for 1960 and was not likely to appropriate much more for 1961; that the new policy of tying DLF loans to U.S. procurement would probably restrict the scope of DLF lending; and that, in any case, the president was still attempting to place more of the burden of foreign economic aid on a multilateral basis. Nevertheless, at a legislative leadership meeting in May, the White House made clear that it still attached great importance to the DLF, albeit at a funding level below that authorized the year before.[6]

In presenting his proposals to Congress, Eisenhower repeated familiar themes about the essentiality of the mutual security program for world peace and the ever-present Communist danger. The threat came not only from the Soviet Union, whose military power "continues to grow," but also from Communist China because of its military and economic growth. The president's recommendations for South Asia and Africa (as well as a request for increased economic aid to Taiwan in response to a Taiwanese appeal) represented the administration's decision to concentrate economic aid in a few selected regions or countries where it was more urgently needed and was likely to do the most good. In this respect the president's mutual security proposals for 1961 extended the regional approach to foreign aid the White House had instituted a year earlier, although emphasis was now on individual countries, which were expected to act as catalysts for development in neighboring countries, such as India and Pakistan in South Asia and Taiwan in the Far East. No particular country was singled out in Africa, apparently because of the overall level of underdevelopment throughout the region.[7]

Establishment of the Social Development Fund for Latin America

The region that continued to concern the administration the most, however, was Latin America, for which the White House proposed at the end of 1960 the establishment of a special fund for social development. In February the president visited Brazil, Uruguay, Argentina, and Chile. Arranged in part to avoid offending Latin America after Eisenhower's visit to other parts of the world, the trip was also a response to the enthusiasm for Fidel Castro that developed following his successful revolution in Cuba in 1959. Eisenhower already suspected Castro of being a Communist, and he believed that his visit was necessary in order to strengthen the United States' own image as a friend of democracy and economic reform. As in December, masses of people turned out to greet the president, but his own personal welcome could not hide the political instability, anti-Americanism, and pro-Castro sentiment that prevailed throughout the region. Eisenhower tried to counter the deteriorating situation by warning of the dangers of "Castroism" and stressing his own support for economic and social development in the Western Hemisphere.[8]

Nevertheless, the president returned from his trip persuaded that the United States needed to do more for Latin America than it was currently doing. As his brother Milton later reported, Eisenhower had seen enough to convince him "that the choice was between rapid and peaceful actions and violent revolutions, between reform in freedom and dangerous moves toward Communist dictatorships."[9] Back home, members of the National Advisory Committee on Inter-American Affairs, which had been formed on Milton Eisenhower's recommendation a year earlier, were already putting together a proposal for a special social development fund for Latin America under IADB auspices. Despite opposition from the Treasury Department, which claimed to be reluctant to raise politically sensitive issues in Congress, but which was probably also concerned about the financial and budgetary aspects of such a fund, Eisenhower decided to support the new program.[10]

In June the president wrote President Kubitschek of Brazil to inform him that in a few days he (Eisenhower) would announce plans for "participating more effectively toward our hemispheric objectives."[11] Three days later, at a press conference, he stressed the need for the United States to do more than it had in the area of Latin American development. Without actually endorsing the establishment of a special social development fund, he made it clear that he had in mind something along these lines.[12] In July, Eisenhower submitted his request to Congress, asking for $500 million to start the fund and $100 million to aid victims of an earthquake in Chile. With Castro obviously in mind, he urged that the legislation be passed before the Organization of American States' scheduled September meeting in Bogotá, Colombia. After brief hearings, in which Secretary of State Herter argued that the administration's proposal would permit Latin American countries to help themselves through cooperative programs, but in which Senator Capehart criticized the administration for waiting so long to present its proposal and for not developing a specific plan, Congress easily approved the measure at the end of August.[13]

Congress and the Mutual Security Program for 1961

About the same time that Congress was completing action on the Latin American social development fund, it also took final action on the president's mutual security program for 1961. Eisenhower submitted his requests to the House and Senate in February, but it was seven months before he signed the program into law. The delay was due in part to the fact that late in the session the president asked for an additional appropriation for the contingency fund because conditions in the Belgian Congo had deteriorated following its independence at the end of June. Nevertheless, despite the delay and the fact that the mutual security program went through the normal process of cuts in appropriations, effective leadership by the White House and an increase in East-West tensions resulted in a final appropriations bill for 1961 that was considerably more supportive of the administration's program than that for 1960 had been.

The House Foreign Affairs Committee began its hearings on the foreign-aid program soon after the president delivered his mutual security message in February. During the month-long hearings, administration witnesses pointed out the increased contributions to the less developed countries that such allies as England, France, Germany, and Japan were now making and remarked that U.S. assistance was only a small part of the needs of the underdeveloped countries. Like the president in his message to Congress, White House officials talked of the Communist menace more in terms of a combined Sino-Soviet threat than they had in the past. James Riddleberger of the ICA testified that there would be an "important power shift in the Far East and Southeast Asia" if, as was a real possibility, Communist China continued its rapid growth over the next ten years. The West should guard against being "caught by an economic or political Pearl Harbor"— that is, a political, economic, and social offensive by the Chinese to undermine or overwhelm the arc of countries from Afghanistan to Korea. He stressed that grant aid would play an important role in developing the internal strength of these countries. Riddleberger also stated the administration's new policy of concentrating economic assistance in specific countries on a regional basis rather than spreading it "on a less catalytic scale" among all the recipient countries. One advantage of concentrated assistance, he said, was the possibility that these "islands of development" would act as models of growth for other countries and even eventually provide them with their own aid.[14]

On April 7 the committee reported out a bill that cut the administration's program by $137 million as compared to $367 million the year before. Together with the $2.72 billion authorized in 1960 for fiscal 1961, the package approved by the committee totaled $4.05 billion. In reporting the bill to the House the committee commented that despite a number of instances of waste, there was "encouraging evidence" that the program was "attaining its major objectives." It concluded that the foreign-aid program had only a "minor direct influence" on the balance-of-payments problem and recommended that expenditures under the program be predicated on the need to defend security and establish satisfactory relations abroad rather than on payments deficits or gold outflows. Finally, the committee approved an administration request for U.S. participation in the Indus River Basin Project because it "[could]mark a turning point in the history of South Asia."[15]

The House Foreign Affairs Committee's report was adopted without any major changes after only one day of perfunctory debate.[16] Moreover, after nine days of hearings, the Senate Foreign Relations Committee reported out a measure that was even kinder to the administration than the House-approved legislation had been. As sent to the floor of the Senate by the committee, the authorization legislation provided for $1.425 billion (in addition to the $2.75 billion authorized the year before) as opposed to the $1.318 billion approved by the House. In reporting the bill, the committee added several amendments regarding the DLF, the effect of which was to place more emphasis on stimulating foreign banking, agriculture, and housing. The committee felt that the DLF had concentrated too much on development projects and not enough on establishing "the kinds of economic institutions which had played such an important role in the growth of the United States."[17]

On the Senate floor some minor cuts in the authorization bill were approved and several amendments were added, the most important of which was a "freedom of navigation" resolution introduced by Democrat Paul H. Douglas of Illinois aimed at opening the Suez Canal to Israeli shipping. Except for the cuts and the Douglas amendment, however, the Senate approved the report of the Foreign Relations Committee without substantive changes. In conference committee the House went along with most of the Senate's provisions, accepting a number of proposals (mostly technical or administrative in nature or having to do with specific country programs) contained in the Senate bill but not in the House version and agreeing to an authorization figure $47.8 million higher than that approved by the House and $39.3 million lower than the Senate figure. The major cut, $25 million, was in defense support. Other mutual security programs suffered only minor reductions or none at all.[18]

President Eisenhower was delighted with the authorization measure, which he signed on May 14. "The Act embodies essentially all of the requests I have put forward as necessary for the successful continuation of the Mutual Security Program," he remarked, "and, with one regrettable exception, the Congress has resisted the addition of amendments which would adversely affect our foreign relations or impair the administration of the Program." (The exception was the "freedom of navigation" amendment, which the White House feared might harm U.S. interests in the Middle East.)[19]

It is not difficult to explain the president's success in Congress compared to the year before, when his foreign-aid program had been cut by over $450 million in the authorization process. In the first place, over half the authorizations for 1961 had been made the previous year, so there was less to cut. Even more important, however, was the fact that Congress had traditionally approved most of what the president recommended in authorization legislation, choosing to make most of its cuts during the appropriations process. That was precisely what Senator Styles Bridges said the Senate intended to do in 1960.[20] The heavy reductions in the authorization legislation the year before had merely been an exception to the general rule and had come about largely as a political backlash to congressionally unpopular spending cuts proposed by the White House.

Notwithstanding his satisfaction with the authorization measure, therefore, President Eisenhower, who well understood the authorization-appropriations cycle, expected a difficult fight over his aid program when it reached Otto Passman's appropriations subcommittee. Meeting at the White House with House Speaker Sam Rayburn, the president again asked the Speaker for cooperation and advice in dealing with Passman's "implacable resistance" to the mutual security program. As in previous years, Rayburn assured the president of his cooperation but also stressed the effectiveness of Passman's criticisms of foreign aid and reiterated the great difficulties he would have in handling the program this year. Similarly, Leverett Saltonstall told the president that twelve of the twenty-seven members of the Senate Appropriations Committee would vote in favor of every possible reduction in the program.[21] However, because of what he regarded as the deteriorating world situation, Eisenhower was determined to get a more successful bill through Congress in 1960 than he had a year earlier. As he commented to legislative leaders in February, "[he had] been breaking [his] heart over [the mutual security program] for seven years and apparently must do so once more."[22] To assist in his efforts, the president organized a grass-roots campaign similar to the one he had carried out two years earlier.

In May, after Congress approved the authorization legislation, the president delivered an address before the Committee for International Economic Growth and the Committee to Strengthen the Frontiers of Freedom, two nonpartisan organizations whose nationally known members already supported the foreign-aid program. Although preoccupied by the report of the probable loss of a U-2 spy plane during a reconnaissance mission over the Soviet Union, Eisenhower made a strong case for the mutual security program. Referring to reports that certain groups in Congress were planning to cut the program, he warned of the calamitous results such cuts would produce. "It would be, for America and all the free world, a crushing defeat in today's struggle between communistic imperialism and a freedom founded in faith and justice." It would create grave new international problems in a matter of a few months. Even though fully armed, the United States would suffer a total defeat if it "let the rest of the world be swallowed up by an atheistic imperialism."[23] The next day Eisenhower wrote to C. D. Jackson asking for his help in rallying public support for the foreign-aid program. Noting that the current situation reminded him "of a similar challenge two years ago," the president described his program as "so crucial [as to lead him], once again, to suggest a crusade for our country."[24]

Although modeled along the lines of the effort two years earlier, the White House campaign in 1960 was more subdued. C. D. Jackson directed a letter-writing campaign, for example, and conducted conversations with newspaper editors from across the country.[25] Through the Defense Department's network of connections with industry, finance, and labor, Secretary of Defense Thomas S. Gates, Jr., worked closely with the Committee to Strengthen the Frontiers of Freedom, which staged its own rallies and letter-writing campaigns and lobbied extensively in Congress in behalf of the president's aid proposals. Committee notables such as James B. Conant, Henry Luce, Averell Harriman, and Leonard Firestone lent their names to the group's work. The Army and Air Force Association, the Navy League, the U.S. Chamber of Commerce, the American Legion, and the leadership of the AFL-CIO also were enlisted in the national effort.[26] As for Eisenhower, the president made a series of speeches in which he pressed for full appropriation of the funds authorized by Congress. Reporting to the American people following the ill-fated Paris Summit Conference in May, which had been aborted because of the U-2 incident, Eisenhower stressed that the failure at Paris increased the need to fund his proposals.[27]

The White House's public-relations activities, its lobbying efforts, increased East-West tensions following the U-2 incident, and the prematurely ended Paris summit helped bring about an administration victory in Congress. Two days before the Paris conference began, Representative Passman labeled the mutual security program as being riddled with "corruption, scandal and blackmail" and predicted that his subcommittee would slash the president's requests by $1.5 billion.[28] On May 22, however, Vice-President Nixon made a personal appeal in behalf of the administration's program in separate letters to twenty Republican members of the Appropriations Committee. "Recent events [have made explicit]," he said, "the absolute need for keeping our mutual security operating at an efficient level." Three days later a group of twenty-eight House Democrats informed Eisenhower that they would oppose any "unwise cuts" in the appropriations measure.[29]

As reported out on June 13, the final House Appropriations Committee bill called for a reduction in the president's requests that was less than half what Passman had predicted. In addition, although the cuts, which totaled $791 million, were substantial and affected every category of aid (military assistance was reduced by the largest amount, $400 million, and the DLF was cut to $550 million), they were still far less than the $1.4 billion that had been cut the year before. Furthermore, the House voted to add $200 million to the Appropriations Committee's recommendation for military assistance, and it eliminated from the legislation a provision attached by the committee that would have prohibited funding of the Indus River Basin Project and the construction of buildings in connection with the president's recommended special program for tropical Africa.[30]

As in the case of the authorization legislation and previous appropriations bills, the White House did even better in the Senate than it had in the House. The Senate Appropriations Committee had been holding public and private hearings on the foreign-aid legislation intermittently since March, but it did not report a bill out of committee until August 19. This delay was primarily the fault of the president, who, citing the rapidly deteriorating crisis in the Belgian Congo, asked Congress to increase the special contingency fund to $250 million from the $175 million he had originally requested and the $150 million that had been granted in the authorization bill and approved by the House in the appropriations measure.[31] Not only did the Foreign Relations Committee recommend and the full Senate approve this figure, but they also voted to restore all of the House cuts except the $200 million reduction in military aid. In addition, they struck out of the bill almost all the House restrictions on spending for specific purposes.[32]

Indeed, the only action taken by the Senate against the wishes of the White House was approval of an amendment by Styles Bridges authorizing the president to bar foreign aid to any country that directly or indirectly furnished munitions or gave military or economic aid to the Castro regime. At a White House meeting Bridges had told the president that he might propose the amendment, not with the intention of passing it, but in order to see how the Democratic nominees for president and vice-president in the 1960 election, John Kennedy and Lyndon Johnson, would vote on it. Eisenhower had responded that he was quite willing to embarrass the Democrats, but did not want to risk embarrassing the administration. Later he had explained that if the United States did "not conduct itself in precisely the right way vis-a-vis Cuba, we could lose all of South America." Still, even the usually moderate Leverett Saltonstall regarded the Bridges proposal as a "modern interpretation of the Monroe Doctrine," and despite the administration's arguments to the contrary, the Bridges amendment was passed.[33]

Except for the anti-Castro amendment, which was not binding on the president, the Senate bill was fully in accord with the administration's program. Unfortunately for the White House, however, the Senate measure seemed to repudiate the House, which felt it had been extremely generous in its action on foreign aid, even to the point of adding more money to the bill than its Appropriations Committee had recommended. As a result, in conference committee the House took a firm stand in in support of its own measure and against the Senate's restoration of funds. Except for the $100 million in additional contingency funds approved by the Senate, the House conferees agreed to add only $31.8 million to what it had originally voted, and the Senate conferees were forced to accept the House figures.[34] In an unusual action, President Eisenhower sent letters, which he later made public, to the leadership of both the House and the Senate urging that the conference report be sent back to committee.[35] Congress rejected the president's request and approved the conference report, but before it did so, Majority Leader Johnson suggested that the White House seek additional funds in a supplemental appropriations bill that the Senate Appropriations Committee was then considering. The administration made the request, and the committee agreed to add another $190 million to the foreign-aid program. Again in conference committee, however, the House assumed a hard line and a deadlock followed. Finally, the lower chamber, acting on its own, voted to accept only a $65 million increase in defense support, and the Senate and president had no choice but to go along with the House. As a result, the final appropriation was $3.78 billion, or about $469 million less than the revised White House request. Included in the bill were $1.8 billion for military assistance, $675 million for defense support, $550 million for the DLF, $230 million for special assistance, and $250 million for the President's Contingency Fund.[36]

Eisenhower was obviously dissatisfied with the final measure, but in signing the legislation he made no public statement as had been his custom. Percentagewise, the cuts in foreign aid for fiscal 1961 (9 percent) were the smallest made in any foreign-aid request Eisenhower had submitted during his presidency.

12. Conclusion

IN A REAL SENSE, the White House's foreign-aid program for 1961 and the conflict with Congress that followed typified the administration's broader foreign economic policy and struggle with Congress over foreign economic assistance, a struggle that had lasted throughout most of Eisenhower's two terms in office. The administration's determination to wean Third World countries away from international communism and toward the West, particularly following the launching of the Soviet economic offensive in the mid-1950s, had largely determined the White House's foreign economic program. Although the House and Senate made increasingly strong objections to the size of the president's mutual security requests and cut them substantially every year, they generally went along with the White House in relying more and more on foreign aid (both bilateral and multilateral) to promote world economic growth and thereby counter the Communist menace abroad.

The House and Senate also went along with most of the administration's trade proposals, though the White House's record in this field was inconsistent. Committed to a policy of freeing the channels of world commerce and increasing the international flow of goods, the administration often assumed a position, particularly in matters of foreign agricultural policy, that seemed to contradict these principles and raised doubts at home and abroad about the extent of the nation's commitment to liberalized trade. Yet for the first time since the reciprocal trade program had been formulated more than twenty-five years earlier, the president committed the Republican party to it and laid the groundwork for the extensive talks on trade reductions that would take place after he left office. Despite growing protectionist sentiment in Congress and the addition of protectionist amendments to the nation's trade agreements program, including the tightening of the escape clause and an extension of the national security clause, Congress gave the president most of what he wanted, expanding his power to reduce tariffs by an additional 15 percent in 1955 and an additional 20 percent in 1958. In a more general sense, Congress rejected the argument made by a number of powerful interest groups, including those connected with mining, textiles, and chemicals, that the nation was no longer able to compete against foreign imports.

Trade and aid together were the major components of Eisenhower's foreign economic policy. The president was committed to a program of reducing and even eliminating foreign economic assistance when he first took office in 1953, but within two years he shifted from this policy of "trade not aid" to a program based on the concept of "trade and aid," the key feature of which was the flow of public capital abroad. This shift toward greater public assistance to less developed countries continued until 1958, when the White House placed new emphasis on multilateral and regional efforts to promote economic growth abroad. One reason for the move toward multilateralism in aid-giving was the nation's balance-of-payments deficit, which indicated for the first time since the end of World War II that the international economic scales had begun to turn against the United States. In Eisenhower's last year in office the balance-of-payments problem was the most pressing foreign economic concern, and it shaped the White House's entire trade-and-aid program. The president, however, was not very successful in resolving the problem.

Nor was the rest of Eisenhower's foreign economic policy very successful. The funds the administration asked for and received for economic development abroad always fell far short of what many Third World leaders and economic experts believed was minimally necessary to promote economic growth, especially when compared to the billions of dollars the United States had poured into Europe under the Marshall Plan in the late 1940s and early 1950s. Moreover, the debate over foreign economic policy was circumscribed and narrowly conceived throughout the entire Eisenhower administration. Concern with Communist expansion continued to be the major motivating force behind the nation's policy toward the Third World as administration officials remained persuaded that economic development would lead to the type of government the United States desired. For the most part the White House gave little thought to the interrelationship between internal social and political reform, on the one hand, and economic growth, on the other.

In responding to the growth needs of emerging and developing nations for the first time through the use of public resources, however, the Eisenhower administration was critically important. Not only did Eisenhower reorient the mutual security program away from military aid and toward economic assistance, but he was also the first president to shift the geographical direction of U.S. foreign aid toward the developing world. He also set the important precedent of directing the United States to adopt regional policies in promoting economic growth, particularly in Latin America.

Subsequent administrations merely built on the legacies that Eisenhower left them. A number of writers have stressed the transition during the Kennedy administration from a foreign-aid program directed at building up the military capabilities of America's allies on the Soviet rim to one based on "assisting the poorest people in the poorest countries by investing in 'basic human needs' projects." Walt Rostow, who became special assistant for national security affairs during the Kennedy and Johnson administrations, later claimed that after 1962 and the growing imbroglio in Southeast Asia, he had stressed inside the government the need for the United States to move toward more regional policies.[1] However, both the transition to economic assistance abroad and the emphasis on regionalism noted by Rostow began in the 1950s during the Eisenhower administration. In fact, the basis for the Alliance for Progress program of the Kennedy administration—criticized by some as being narrowly conceived, but generally regarded as representing a substantial break from past policies toward South and Central America—can be traced to the Eisenhower administration. In 1960 the White House endorsed an inter-American program of broad economic and social reform which became institutionalized in the so-called Act of Bogotá.[2]

Likewise, the Eisenhower administration deserves considerable credit for the multilateral programs of economic assistance that were begun in the 1950s, particularly IDA. In June 1960 Congress approved a bill formally authorizing the president to accept membership in the new organization, which had been agreed to following the New Delhi meeting of the World Bank and the IMF the previous year. Later, the House and Senate appropriated $73.7 million as the United States' initial payment to the new agency, which became an important source of multilateral lending.[3]

President Eisenhower was personally responsible for the new directions taken by his administration. By ignoring Eisenhower's views on executive-congressional relations, a number of recent writers have overstated the president's leadership qualities. They have also neglected to emphasize adequately the president's virulent anticommunism, which figured so prominently in White House decision making. But they have correctly asserted that Eisenhower was an activist president with a keen and cogent intellect, a president who was in complete command of his own administration. Certainly this was true in the realm of foreign economic policy, where Eisenhower's leadership was evident in the formulation of policy and in the administration's efforts to gain bipartisan and popular support for its trade-and-aid programs.

Relations between Eisenhower and his Democratic successor, John F. Kennedy, were cool but proper. The thirty-fourth president did not easily forgive Kennedy for the charges made during the 1960 campaign that Eisenhower had let the nation slide into lethargy and military unpreparedness. Nevertheless, before leaving office Eisenhower met several times with the president-elect to discuss major national issues, including the balance-of-payments problem. On one such occasion Treasury Secretary Robert Anderson made a strong case for following up on Eisenhower's order to bring home dependents of military personnel stationed abroad. He noted that this would have a strong psychological effect abroad by demonstrating to the world that the United States was determined to correct the payments problem. Anderson also remarked that the erosion of America's gold supply was continuing unabated and that immediate measures had to be taken to reverse the present trend. Kennedy's response was not recorded, but after assuming office he made the resolution of the balance-of-payments problem one of his highest priorities.[4]

In subsequent years Eisenhower and Kennedy corresponded occasionally on matters of foreign economic policy. In 1962, Kennedy solicited Eisenhower's assistance in pushing his trade bill through Congress. The bill provided for a linear reduction of tariffs (that is, a reduction by broad categories rather than on an item-by-item basis) over a five-year period. "It is quite clear that the coming of the Common Market in Europe presents to us new problems," Eisenhower responded in consenting to support the measure, "and I agree that for meeting and solving these problems, some adjustments in former practices will be necessary."[5]

Yet the former president incensed members of the Kennedy administration by attacking the poor record he claimed Kennedy had made in Congress. Following Eisenhower's assertion in 1962, for example, that his record with Congress had been better than Kennedy's, even though he had been faced with Democratic majorities for six years, Myer Feldman, a Kennedy aide, noted that the Democrats had given Eisenhower their support, while Republicans failed to support Kennedy. When Eisenhower had asked for $5 billion to continue mutual security, Feldman told Kennedy, 88 percent of the Democrats had supported him. On the other hand, 78 percent of the Republicans had opposed Kennedy's long-term foreign-aid program. Similarly, when Eisenhower had asked for an extension of the Reciprocal Trade Agreements Act in 1953, 95 percent of the Democrats had supported him, but 75 percent of the Republicans in the House had voted against Kennedy's Trade Expansion Act.[6]

In truth, the problems that Kennedy—and his successor, Lyndon Johnson—faced as president were much more difficult than those with which Eisenhower had to deal. Not only did the U.S. balance-of-payments problem increasingly threaten to undermine the Bretton Woods system and raise questions that had not been asked earlier about the flow of private investment abroad, but Kennedy and Johnson faced a more united and independent Europe. Monetary and trade problems, the distribution of foreign aid, and questions of the common defense all figured prominently in the economic relations of Europe and the United States during the 1960s and led to a good deal of divisiveness in the Atlantic community.[7]

Equally important was the fact that the Third World was becoming more assertive in its economic demands. By 1966 almost two-thirds of the members of the United Nations were Third World nations. This increase threatened to upset the balance of power in the UN because of the less developed countries' tendency to vote as a bloc on major economic and development issues.[8] The sheer number of these countries spurred them to a greater awareness of Third World interests. Consequently, the UN became more action oriented and impatient, and continued to focus increasingly on Third World development as its overriding concern. The creation of the United Nations Conference on Trade and Development (UNCTAD) in 1964 reflected the growing power of the less developed countries. They hoped to use the conference to voice their desires regarding economic cooperation. In the first session in Geneva, UNCTAD provided a forum for the viewpoint of the poor countries and stimulated the United States and various international agencies to reevaluate their efforts regarding aid to the Third World.[9]

Despite the new assertiveness of the less developed countries, however, the whole matter of economic development among them remains among the most pressing and discussed of the world's problems, and the question of its relationship to the establishment of some form of stable, representative, and responsible government continues to elicit a wide range of opinion. But for the Eisenhower administration, which devised its foreign economic program largely as an emergency response to a perceived Communist conspiracy abroad and at a time when relatively little was known about the process of economic and political development, these were issues whose complexity was scarcely grasped, much less acted upon.[10] Speaking at Rice University in October 1960, for example, just three months before he left office, the president commented on the continued need to promote world economic growth and development. "Free nations, when they unite effectively," he claimed, "can defeat specific efforts at economic penetration and political subversion in newly developed areas." In closing he remarked that he "count[ed] the nation's foreign aid program as being one of the most important, necessary and successful ventures for sustaining world peace and stability that our nation has ever undertaken."[11] Events of the 1960s and 1970s would prove the president wrong and would show how complicated the process of economic growth and political development really is. But given the political climate of the 1950s and the assumptions on which the White House based its foreign economic policy, it is hardly surprising that the administration strove to achieve the type of world order the president outlined in his speech at Rice. It is also not surprising that he failed.

Notes

CHAPTER 1

1. Independent Commission on International Development Issues, *North-South: A Program for Survival* (Cambridge, Mass., 1980); Council on Environmental Quality and Department of State, *The Global 2000 Report to the President: Entering the Twenty-first Century*, 2 vols. (Washington, D.C., 1980).

2. Thomas G. Paterson, *Soviet-American Confrontation: Postwar Reconstruction and the Origins of the Cold War* (Baltimore, 1973), pp. 1–29; Richard N. Gardner, *Sterling-Dollar Diplomacy: The Origins and the Prospects of Our International Economic Order*, 2d ed. (New York, 1969), pp. 1–23. Unless otherwise noted, this section on the quest for a new economic order is based on Gardner's *Sterling-Dollar Diplomacy*, pp. xviii–xcv.

3. U.S. Department of State, *A Constitution for World Trade*, Commercial Policy Series, no. 108 (Washington, D.C., 1947); see also idem, *The Charter for World Prosperity—The How and Why of the ITO*, Commercial Policy Series, no. 115 (Washington, D.C., 1948).

4. U.S. Department of State, *Analysis of General Agreement on Tariffs and Trade Signed at Geneva, October 30, 1947*, Commercial Policy Series, no. 109 (Washington, D.C., 1947), pp. 195–206.

5. Alfred E. Eckes, Jr., *A Search for Solvency: Bretton Woods and the International Monetary System, 1941–1971* (Austin, Tex., 1975), pp. 107–64.

6. Ibid., pp. 211–29.

7. "The Administration's Reciprocal Trade Program under Fire," *Congressional Digest* 30 (April 1951): 99–111.

8. John H. Williams, "End of the Marshall Plan," *Foreign Affairs* 30 (July 1952): 593–611; see also Harry Bayard Price, *The Marshall Plan and Its Meaning* (Ithaca, N.Y., 1955), pp. 156–57.

9. "Recent History of Economic Assistance," n.d., Dodge Series, Subject Subseries, Box 2, U.S. Council on Foreign Economic Policy, Office of the Chairman, Records, Dwight D. Eisenhower Library, Abilene, Kans. (hereafter cited as CFEP, Office of the Chairman, Records).

10. U.S. Department of State, *Analysis of Protocol of Accession and Schedules to the General Agreement on Tariffs and Trade Negotiated at Annecy, France, April–August 1949*, Commercial Policy Series, no. 120 (Washington, D.C., 1949), pp. 1–4.

11. Eckes, Jr., *A Search for Solvency*, p. 229.

12. See, for example, *Export-Import Bank of Washington: Fourteenth Semiannual Report to Congress for the Period January–June, 1952* (Washington, D.C., 1952), pp. 1–26.

13. *Report to the President on Foreign Economic Policies* (Washington, D.C., 1950), p. 19.

14. *Partners in Progress: A Report to the President by the International Development Advisory Board* (Washington, D.C., 1951), pp. 1–15.

15. *Report to the President on Foreign Economic Policies*, esp. pp. 1–18.

16. *Partners in Progress*, pp. 18–26, 43–51, and 78–86; see also "Report on the Proposal for

an International Finance Corporation," April 1952, Box 57, Records of the Department of the Treasury, RG 56, National Archives, Washington, D.C.

17. See, for example, U.S. Department of State, "Special Report on American Opinion Prepared by the Division of Public Studies, January 15, 1951," and "Conclusions and Recommendations Approved by the National Advisory Council, July 27, 1951," *Foreign Relations of the United States, 1951, National Security Affairs: Foreign Economic Policy* (Washington, D.C., 1979), pp. 270–76 and 345–46.

18. See, for example, Fred I. Greenstein, "Eisenhower as an Activist President: A Look at New Evidence," *Political Science Quarterly* 94 (Winter 1979–80): 575–96; Richard H. Immerman, "Eisenhower and Dulles: Who Made the Decisions?" *Political Psychology* 1 (Autumn 1970): 13–19; Gary W. Reichard, "Eisenhower as President: The Changing View," *South Atlantic Quarterly* 77 (Summer 1978): 266–81; Vincent De Santis, "Eisenhower Revisionism," *Review of Politics* 38 (April 1978): 180–207; Barton J. Bernstein, "Foreign Policy in the Eisenhower Administration," *Foreign Service Journal* 50 (May 1973): 17–20, 29–30, 38.

19. Emmet John Hughes, *The Ordeal of Power: A Political Memoir of the Eisenhower Years* (New York, 1963), pp. 123–29.

20. Richard H. Rovere, "Eisenhower Revisited—A Political Genius? A Brilliant Man?" *New York Times Magazine*, February 7, 1971, p. 14; Blanche Wiesen Cook, *Dwight D. Eisenhower: Antimilitarist in the White House*, Forums in History (St. Charles, Mo., 1974); Bernstein, "Foreign Policy in the Eisenhower Administration," pp. 17–20, 29–30, and 38; Arthur Larson, *Eisenhower: The President Nobody Knew* (New York, 1968), pp. 68–80; Townsend Hoopes, *The Devil and John Foster Dulles* (Boston, 1973); Herbert Finer, *Dulles over Suez: The Theory and Practice of His Diplomacy* (Chicago, 1964); Joyce and Gabriel Kolko, *The Limits of Power: The World and United States Foreign Policy, 1945–1954* (New York, 1972), pp. 677–78; W. W. Rostow, *The United States in the World Arena: An Essay in Recent History*, pbk. ed. (New York, 1969), pp. 384–97; Hans Morgenthau, "John Foster Dulles," in *An Uncertain Tradition: American Secretaries of State in the Twentieth Century*, ed. Norman Graebner (New York, 1961), pp. 261–70.

21. In the most detailed study so far made of Eisenhower's foreign policy, however, Peter Lyon, who in many ways is sympathetic to the president, has rejected this emphasis on Eisenhower's pacific inclinations. Among other things, Lyon has noted that Eisenhower used covert operations to overthrow legally established governments in Iran and Guatemala, involved the United States deeply in Vietnam, allowed Chiang Kai-shek to harass Communist China, and sent marines to occupy Lebanon. "In no way can the Cold Warrior [Eisenhower] be divorced from his Cold War policies," Lyon has therefore concluded. Peter Lyon, *Eisenhower: Portrait of the Hero* (Boston, 1974), esp. pp. 853–56. More recently, in an article on Eisenhower's strategy for nuclear disarmament, Thomas F. Soapes has remarked that the president's "conventional Cold War attitude placed a major obstacle in his path" toward bringing about a reduction in nuclear armaments and relieving East-West tensions. It was an obstacle he did not overcome. Thomas F. Soapes, "A Cold Warrior Seeks Peace: Eisenhower's Strategy for Nuclear Disarmament," *Diplomatic History* 4 (Winter 1980): 57–58.

CHAPTER 2

1. Dwight D. Eisenhower, *Crusade in Europe* (New York, 1948), pp. 476–77.

2. Elmo Richardson, *The Presidency of Dwight D. Eisenhower* (Lawrence, Kans., 1979), pp. 14–15; Herbert S. Parmet, *Eisenhower and the American Crusades* (New York, 1972), pp. 46–47, 68–69.

3. Charles C. Alexander, *Holding the Line: The Eisenhower Era, 1952–1961* (Bloomington, Ind., 1975), pp. 1–6.

4. Eisenhower to Dulles, June 20, 1952, Box 6, Stephen Benedict Papers, Dwight D. Eisenhower Library, Abilene, Kans.

5. Peter Lyon, *Eisenhower: Portrait of the Hero* (Boston, 1974), pp. 499–52; Parmet, *Eisenhower and the American Crusades*, pp. 123–25.

6. Eisenhower to Gruenther, May 4, 1953, Box 2, DDE Diary Series, Dwight D. Eisenhower Papers, Dwight D. Eisenhower Library, Abilene, Kans. (hereafter cited as Eisenhower Papers); Memorandum for Dodge prepared by Paul T. Carroll, July 7, 1953, Box 1, Legislative Meeting Series, ibid.; Legislative Leadership Meeting, July 20, 1953, Box 2, DDE Diary Series, ibid.; Presidential News Conference, July 22, 1953, *Public Papers of the Presidents of the United States: Dwight D. Eisenhower, 1953* (Washington, D.C., 1960), p. 507.

7. Eisenhower to Gruenther, May 4, 1953, Box 2, DDE Diary Series, Eisenhower Papers; Memorandum for Dodge prepared by Paul T. Carroll, July 7, 1953, Box 1, Legislative Meeting Series, ibid.; Legislative Leadership Meeting, July 20, 1953, Box 2, DDE Diary Series, ibid.; Presidential News Conference, July 22, 1953, *Public Papers of the Presidents: Eisenhower, 1953*, p. 507. See also Minutes of Cabinet Meeting, March 6, 1953, Box 1, Cabinet Series, Eisenhower Papers; Memorandum of Secretary Dulles Presenting the Comments of Assistant Secretary Merchant on William Draper's Letter of June 5, July 13, 1953, Box 14, Administration Series, ibid.; Supplementary Notes on Legislative Leadership Meeting, December 18, 1953, Box 1, Legislative Meeting Series, ibid.

8. Parmet, *Eisenhower and the American Crusades*, p. 113.

9. Alexander, *Holding the Line*, pp. 29–30; Richardson, *The Presidency of Dwight D. Eisenhower*, pp. 42–44.

10. See, for example, Radio Address to the American People on the National Security and Its Costs, May 19, 1953, *Public Papers of the Presidents: Eisenhower, 1953*, pp. 306–17; Address at the Annual Convention of the National Junior Chamber of Commerce, Minneapolis, Minn., June 10, 1953, ibid., pp. 384–92.

11. For a statement of administration policy as interpreted by the Commerce Department, see "The Commerce Department's International Function," attached to Samuel W. Anderson to Arthur Flemming, January 28, 1953, Box 26, Sinclair Weeks Papers, Dartmouth College Library, Hanover, N.H. (hereafter cited as Weeks Papers). See also Memorandum for the President from Sinclair Weeks, February 25, 1953, attached to Weeks to Nelson Rockefeller, February 25, 1953, Box 32, ibid.; Memorandum to the Secretary of Commerce from Gabriel Hauge, March 5, 1953, OF-116-P, Eisenhower Papers.

12. Inaugural Address, January 20, 1953, *Public Papers of the Presidents: Eisenhower, 1953*, p. 4; see also "Proposal for Inaugural Speech," January 12, 1953, Box 1, Cabinet Series, Eisenhower Papers.

13. Annual Message to Congress on the State of the Union, February 2, 1953, *Public Papers of the Presidents: Eisenhower, 1953*, pp. 15–16.

14. Solicitor to Secretary of Agriculture, February 16, 1953, Box 2320, Records of the Department of Agriculture, RG 16, National Archives, Washington, D.C.

15. Diary Entry, July 2, 1953, Box 5, DDE Diary Series, Eisenhower Papers.

16. Ibid.

17. Public Advisory Board for Mutual Security, *A Trade and Tariff Policy in the National Interest* (Washington, D.C., 1953), pp. 1–6. For similar views see also C. D. Jackson to Gabriel Hauge, February 6, 1953, Box 48, C. D. Jackson Papers, Dwight D. Eisenhower Library, Abilene, Kans. (hereafter cited as Jackson Papers); *Business Week*, February 7, 1953, p. 100; ibid., March 7, 1953, p. 122; ibid., March 21, 1953, pp. 160–62.

18. Minutes of Cabinet Meeting, February 20, 1953, Box 1, Cabinet Series, Eisenhower Papers; Lewis Douglas to Eisenhower, July 14, 1953, OF-116-U, ibid.; *Business Week*, January 3, 1953, pp. 68–69; ibid., March 7, 1953, p. 126.

19. Diary Entry, January 6, 1953, Box 5, DDE Diary Series, Eisenhower Papers; Eisenhower to Humphrey, June 24, 1953, Box 2, ibid. See also *Business Week*, March 14, 1953, pp. 159–60; Memorandum of Conversation at the White House between the President, Dr. G. S. Hauge, and L. W. Douglas, June 30, 1953, and Lewis Douglas to Eisenhower, July 14, 1953, OF-116-U, ibid.

20. See, for example, George W. Malone to Eisenhower, February 25, 1953, Box 2320, Records of the Department of Agriculture, RG 16; Supplementary Notes on Legislative Leadership Meeting, March 30, 1953, Box 1, Legislative Meeting Series, Eisenhower Papers.

21. Commenting on the pressure groups that were attempting to influence trade and tariff policy and on proposals for a system of regulatory commissions combining legislative, executive, and judicial functions as a means of avoiding these pressures on the legislative process, Eisenhower thus remarked: "In the degree that we depend more and more upon the Regulatory Commission, we are departing from the system laid down in our Constitution, a system that groups all functions into three categories and keeps these mutually independent of each other. Since America has always believed that this functional dispersion of power is equally important with the geographical dispersion [of power] it follows that in the degree that we depend upon the Regulatory Commission, we are threatening the individual liberties and the entire system of free government that they established" (Diary Entry, February 9, 1953, Box 5, DDE Diary Series, Eisenhower Papers).

22. Supplementary Notes on Legislative Leadership Meeting, March 30, 1953, Box 1, Legislative Meeting Series, ibid.; Eisenhower to Dulles, January 15, 1953, Box 2, DDE Diary Series, ibid.

23. Memorandum for Mr. Dodge from Sherman Adams, March 31, 1953, Box 1, Legislative Meeting Series, ibid.; Minutes of Cabinet Meeting, April 3 and July 17, 1953, Box 2, Cabinet Series, ibid.; Special Message to Congress Recommending the Renewal of the Reciprocal Trade Agreements Act, April 7, 1953, *Public Papers of the Presidents: Eisenhower, 1953*, pp. 163–65; U.S. Congress, House, Committee on Ways and Means, *Trade Agreements Extension Act of 1953*, 83d Cong., 1st sess., 1953, H. Rept. 521, pp. 3–5; U.S. Congress, Senate, Committee on Finance, *Trade Agreements Extension Act of 1953*, 83d Cong., 1st sess., 1953, S. Rept. 472, pp. 2–7; *Congressional Quarterly Almanac* 9 (1953): 210, 252.

24. Memorandum of Gabriel Hauge for Nelson Rockefeller, March 13, 1953, OF-116-M, Eisenhower Papers; Minutes of Cabinet Meeting, March 13, 1953, Box 1, Cabinet Series, ibid.; Memorandum to C. D. Jackson from Eisenhower, March 20, 1953, Box 43, Jackson Papers.

25. Special Message to the Congress on the Organization of Executive Branch for the Conduct of Foreign Affairs, June 1, 1953, *Public Papers of the Presidents: Eisenhower, 1953*, pp. 342–48.

26. Memorandum of Gabriel Hauge to Sherman Adams, April 25, 1953, Box 1, Gabriel Hauge Papers, Dwight D. Eisenhower Library, Abilene, Kans. (hereafter cited as Hauge Papers); Memorandum for Dr. Hauge from Gerald D. Morgan, April 25, 1953, OF-116-M, Eisenhower Papers.

27. Letter to the President of the Senate and the Speaker of the House of Representatives Recommending Establishment of a Commission on Foreign Economic Policy, May 2, 1953, *Public Papers of the Presidents: Eisenhower, 1953*, pp. 252–54.

28. Raymond A. Bauer, Ithiel De Sola Pool, and Lewis Anthony Dexter, *American Business and Public Policy: The Politics of Foreign Trade* (Chicago, 1972), p. 34.

29. Clarence B. Randall, *A Creed for Free Enterprise* (Boston, 1952), p. 157; see also idem, *A Foreign Economic Policy for the United States* (Chicago, 1954), esp. pp. 25–54.

30. Minutes of Cabinet Meeting, July 31, 1953, Box 2, Cabinet Series, Eisenhower Papers.

31. Gordon to Hauge, December 10, 1953, Box 56, U.S. President's Commission on Foreign Economic Policy, Records, Dwight D. Eisenhower Library, Abilene, Kans. (hereafter cited as Randall Commission Records); see also *Business Week*, September 19, 1953, pp. 166–68.

32. *Staff Papers Presented to the Commission on Foreign Economic Policy* (Washington, D.C., 1954); Clarence Randall to Commission Members, October 1, 1953, Box 13, Randall Commission Records.

33. Randall to Commission Members, October 1, 1953, Box 13, Randall Commission Records.

34. Bauer et al., *American Business and Public Policy*, p. 42.

35. The testimony before the commission can be found in Randall Commission Records, Box 13.

36. Bauer et al. *American Business and Public Policy*, pp. 44–45; *Business Week*, November 21, 1953, p. 164.

37. See, for example, Randall Commission paper "Public Lending," November 25, 1953, and "Summary of Executive Session of Commission on Public Investment," December 1, 1953, Box 59, Randall Commission Records; see also Memorandum of William Adams Brown, Jr., to John H. Whitney, December 17, 1953, Box 13, ibid.

38. Commission on Foreign Economic Policy, *Report to the President and the Congress* (Washington, D.C., 1954), pp. 77–89; see also *Business Week*, January 30, 1954, pp. 118–20.

39. Commission on Foreign Economic Policy, *Report to the President and the Congress*, pp. 1–26.

40. Ibid., pp. 43–62. See also "Statement Submitted to Mr. Whitney on Labor Adjustment and Increased Imports," Box 59, Randall Commission Records; Memorandum of R. F. Mikesell, January 14, 1954, ibid.; Raymond F. Mikesell to John Hay Whitney, December 30, 1953, ibid.

41. Commission on Foreign Economic Policy, *Report to the President and the Congress*, pp. 28–38.

42. Ibid., pp. 65–68.

43. Ibid., pp. 72–75.

44. Eugene Staley to Joseph S. Davis, November 19, 1953, Box 56, Randall Commission Records.

45. Klaus Knorr and Gardner Patterson, *A Critique of the Randall Commission Report* (Princeton, N.J.: International Finance Section and Center of International Studies, Princeton University, 1954), esp. pp. 62–65.

46. Ibid.

47. Memorandum for Mr. Rabb prepared by Gabriel Hauge, February 4, 1954, Box 3, Cabinet Series, Eisenhower Papers; Memorandum to the President from James P. Mitchell, February 9, 1954, OF-116-M, ibid.; "Preliminary Department of Defense Views on the Randall Commission Report," attached to C. E. Wilson to Gabriel Hauge, ibid.; Memorandum of Robert M. Macy to Clarence B. Randall on "Summary of Agency Reaction to Commission Recommendations and Suggestions for Resolution of Disagreements," February 16, 1954, ibid.; Sinclair Weeks to Clarence Randall, March 12, 1954, and Weeks to Eisenhower, March 15, 1954, Box 31, Weeks Papers.

48. Eisenhower to Winthrop W. Aldrich, February 24, 1954, OF-116-M, Eisenhower Papers. See also "Resume of Presentation to the Cabinet by Clarence B. Randall concerning Report of the Commission on Foreign Economic Policy," February 26, 1954, attached to Maxwell M. Rabb to John Foster Dulles, March 2, 1954, Box 2, Cabinet Series, ibid.; Gabriel Hauge to Governor Adams January 14, 1954, attached to Adams to Hauge, January 15, 1954, OF-116-M, ibid.

49. Memorandum of Alfred C. Neal for Gabriel Hauge and Robert M. Macy, January 28, 1954, enclosing Memorandum of Alfred C. Neal to Clarence B. Randall, January 28, 1954, OF-116-M, ibid.

50. Bauer et al., *American Business and Public Policy*, pp. 44–45.

51. Supplementary Notes, Legislative Leadership Meeting, March 29, 1954, Box 1, Legislative Meeting Series, Eisenhower Papers; see also Minutes of Cabinet Meeting, March 19, 1954, Box 2, Cabinet Series, ibid.

52. Special Message to Congress on Foreign Economic Policy, March 30, 1954, *Public Papers of the Presidents of the United States: Dwight D. Eisenhower, 1954* (Washington, D.C., 1960), pp. 352–64.

53. Remarks at the Forty-second Annual Meeting of the U.S. Chamber of Commerce, April 26, 1954, ibid., pp. 423–57.

54. Bauer et al., *American Business and Public Policy*, pp. 50–54.

55. Eisenhower to Daniel A. Reed, May 6, 1954, and Eisenhower to Charles H. Percy, May 19, 1954, Box 4, DDE Diary Series, Eisenhower Papers; *Business Week*, May 29, 1954, p. 40.

56. *Business Week*, April 24, 1954, pp. 39–40; Bauer et al., *American Business and Public Policy*, pp. 54–58.

57. Commission on Foreign Economic Policy, *Report to the President and the Congress*, p. 32.

58. Solicitor to Secretary of Agriculture, February 16, 1953, Box 2320, Records of the Department of Agriculture, RG 16; Ezra Taft Benson to the President, April 8, 1953, Box 2321, ibid.; U.S. Department of Agriculture, "Special Regulations on United States Imports of Agricultural Products," in U.S. Congress, House, Committee on Ways and Means, Subcommittee on Foreign Trade Policy, *Foreign Trade Policy: Compendium of Papers on United States Foreign Trade Policy*, 85th Cong., 2d sess., 1958, pp. 679–705; D. Gale Johnson, "Agricultural Price Policy and International Trade," ibid., pp. 713–14.

59. John C. Lynn to Ezra Taft Benson, March 27, 1953, Box 2320, Records of the Department of Agriculture, RG 16; see also Loring C. Macy to Samuel W. Anderson, September 11, 1953, Box 56, Randall Commission Records.

60. Trudy Huskamp Peterson, *Agricultural Exports, Farm Income, and the Eisenhower Administration* (Lincoln, Nebr., 1979), pp. 13–15.

61. Lynn to Benson, March 27, 1953, Box 2320, Records of the Department of Agriculture, RG 16.

62. "Policy Statement, Foreign Agricultural Trade and Technical Assistance," May 1953, Box 1, Hauge Papers. See also Benson to the President, April 8, 1953, and June 10, 1953, and Benson to Mike K. Swanton, April 23, 1953, Box 2321, Records of the Department of Agriculture, RG 16; Eisenhower to Edgar B. Broussard, April 8, 1953, Box 5, Administration Series, Eisenhower Papers.

63. Johnson, "Agricultural Price Policy and International Trade," p. 715; Lawrence Witt, "Trade and Agriculture Policy," *Annals of the American Academy of Political and Social Science* 331 (September 1960): 1–7. See also "Policy Statement, Foreign Agricultural Trade and Technical Assistance," May 1953, Box 1, Hauge Papers.

64. Robert G. Stanley, *Food for Peace: Hope and Reality of U.S. Food Aid* (New York, 1973), pp. 59–62.

65. Peter A. Toma, *The Politics of Food for Peace: Executive-Legislative Interaction* (Tucson, Ariz., 1967), p. 40.

66. Karl Fox to Don Paarlberg, June 5, 1953, Box 2320, Records of the Department of Agriculture, RG 16; Ezra Taft Benson to Gerald L. Dearing, September 4, 1953, ibid.

67. *Congressional Quarterly Almanac* 10 (1954): 121.

68. Annual Budget Message to the Congress: Fiscal Year 1955, January 21, 1954, *Public Papers of the Presidents: Eisenhower, 1954*, pp. 139–42.

69. *Congressional Quarterly Almanac* 10 (1954): 121–24; Statement by the President upon Signing the Agricultural Trade Development and Assistance Act of 1954, July 10, 1954, *Public Papers of the Presidents: Eisenhower, 1954*, p. 626.

70. Toma, *The Politics of Food for Peace*, pp. 41–42.

71. See, for example, Minutes of Cabinet Meeting, April 22, 1954, Box 5, Cabinet Series, Eisenhower Papers; Special Message to Congress on the Mutual Security Program, June 23, 1954, *Public Papers of the Presidents: Eisenhower, 1954*, pp. 590–93. On the mutual security program see also Memorandum for the President from Joseph Dodge, April 3, 1953, Box 13, Administration Series, Eisenhower Papers; U.S. Congress, Senate, Committee on Appropriations, *Mutual Security Appropriations Bill, 1954*, 83d Cong., 1st sess., 1953, S. Rept. 645, pp. 1–10; U.S. Congress, Senate, Committee on Foreign Relations, *The Mutual Security Act of 1954*, 83d Cong., 2d sess., 1954, S. Rept. 1799, pp. 1 57. On criticism of the military orientation of foreign aid from a former administration adviser and speechwriter, see C. D. Jackson to Secretary of State, April 9, 1954, Box 2, Dodge Series, Subject Subseries, CFEP, Office of the Chairman,

Records. On Eisenhower's indifferent reaction see Eisenhower to C. D. Jackson, April 14, 1954, Box 4, DDE Diary Series, Eisenhower Papers.

72.   It is significant to note in this respect that a year later Eisenhower's administrative assistant, Gabriel Hauge, told Treasury Secretary Humphrey that the president had "only a rather vague knowledge" of the new loan policy of the Eximbank and suggested to Humphrey that he talk to Eisenhower about the bank's loan policy. Hauge to Humphrey, April 15, 1954, Box 5, George M. Humphrey Papers, Western Reserve Historical Society, Cleveland, Ohio (hereafter cited as Humphrey Papers).

73.   On this point see especially Marquis Childs, *Eisenhower, Captive Hero: A Cabinet Study of the General and the President* (New York, 1958), pp. 166–68; see also Emmet John Hughes, *The Ordeal of Power: A Political Memoir of the Eisenhower Years* (New York, 1963), pp. 72–74.

74.   Humphrey to Sherman Adams, March 18, 1953, and enclosures, OF-116-P, Eisenhower Papers.

75.   Humphrey to Stassen, September 23, 1953, and February 17, 1954, Box 4, Humphrey Papers; see also *Business Week*, March 6, 1954, pp. 142–44.

76.   On Dulles's disinterest in economic affairs, see *Business Week*, February 14, 1953, p. 134.

77.   Ibid., March 6, 1954, pp. 142–44.

78.   Special Message to Congress Transmitting Reorganization Plan 5 of 1953 concerning the Export-Import Bank of Washington, April 30, 1953, *Public Papers of the Presidents: Eisenhower, 1953*, pp. 222–25.

79.   *Business Week*, August 15, 1953, pp. 136–37; ibid., September 26, 1953, p. 164.

80.   Robert Bendiner, "The Apostasy of Homer Capehart," *The Reporter*, May 12, 1953, pp. 30–32.

81.   Copy of letter from the Secretary of the Treasury, [October 1954], Box 2, DDE Diary Series, Eisenhower Papers.

82.   U.S. Congress, Senate, Committee on Banking and Currency, *Hearings: Study of Export-Import Bank and World Bank*, 83d Cong., 2d sess., 1954, esp. pp. 1–76; see also *Business Week*, October 31, 1953, p. 142.

83.   Milton Eisenhower, *The Wine is Bitter: The United States and Latin America* (New York, 1963), p. 187; Minutes of Cabinet Meeting, July 3, 1953, Box 2, Cabinet Series, Eisenhower Papers.

84.   M. Eisenhower, *The Wine is Bitter*, p. 199. See also Memorandum for the President from the Department of State, October 13, 1953, Box 2, International Series, Eisenhower Papers; Milton Eisenhower, "United States–Latin American Relations: Report to the President," *Department of State Bulletin* 29 (November 23, 1953): 695–717; Homer E. Capehart to Edgar B. Brossard, January 20, 1954, OF-116-5, Eisenhower Papers.

85.   Minutes of Cabinet Meeting, February 5 and 26, 1954, Box 3, Cabinet Series, Eisenhower Papers; *New York Times*, March 5, 1954; *Business Week*, March 6, 1954, pp. 142–44; Telephone Call of Eisenhower to George Humphrey, February 15, 1954, Box 4, DDE Diary Series, Eisenhower Papers.

86.   *New York Times*, June 11, 1954; U.S. Congress, House, Committee on Banking and Currency, *Export-Import Bank Act Amendments of 1954*, 83d Cong., 2d sess., 1954, H. Rept. 2270, pp. 1–2; U.S. Congress, Senate, Committee on Banking and Currency, *Export-Import Bank Act Amendments of 1954*, 83d Cong., 2d sess., 1954, S. Rept. 1624, pp. 1–4.

CHAPTER 3

1.   Memorandum for Governor Adams, November 18, 1954, OF-116-M, Eisenhower Papers. See also Maxwell M. Rabb to Cabinet, December 8, 1954, Box 4, Cabinet Series, ibid.; Memorandum on Procedure for Supporting the President's Foreign Economic Policy, prepared by Samuel W. Anderson, December 14, 1954, Box 31, Weeks Papers.

2.   Special Message to Congress on the Foreign Economic Policy of the United States, Jan-

uary 10, 1955, *Public Papers of the Presidents of the United States: Dwight D. Eisenhower, 1955* (Washington, D.C., 1959), pp. 32–40.

3. Hawthorne Arey to C. Dillon Glendinning, November 2, 1954, OF-15, Eisenhower Papers; A. N. Overby to Gabriel Hauge, November 5, 1954, ibid. See also Charles G. Quinlan to Hawthorne Arey, November 16, 1954, Box 4, File 651, Records of the Export-Import Bank, RG 275, National Archives, Washington, D.C.; Henry C. Wallich to Clarence Randall, April 22, 1955, attached to M. Quill to Gabriel Hauge, April 29, 1955, OF-15, Eisenhower Papers; *Business Week*, October 9, 1954, pp. 16–62.

4. Statement of Policy, Approved and Issued by the President, on Foreign Trade as Related to Agriculture, September 9, 1954, *Public Papers of the Presidents of the United States: Dwight D. Eisenhower, 1954* (Washington, D.C., 1960), pp. 841–43; Ezra Benson to Eisenhower, October 26, 1954, Box 6, Administration Series, Eisenhower Papers.

5. Eisenhower to Francis, September 9, 1954, *Public Papers of the Presidents: Eisenhower, 1954*, pp. 843–44.

6. See Executive Order of November 6, 1954, Box 32, Weeks Papers.

7. Minutes of Cabinet Meeting, July 6, 1954; Eisenhower to Nelson Rockefeller and Rowland Hughes, July 22, 1954; and Memorandum of Sherman Adams to the Cabinet, July 15, 1954, attached to Art Kimball to Maxwell Rabb, July 16, 1954, Box 3, Cabinet Series, Eisenhower Papers.

8. Marshall M. Smith to Assistant Secretary Anderson, August 23, 1954, attached to Smith to Gabriel Hauge, September 8, 1954, OF-116-P, Eisenhower Papers; Loring K. Macy to Samuel Anderson, October 11, 1954, File 059.4, Records of the Department of Commerce, Department of Commerce Building, Washington, D.C. (hereafter cited as DOC Records).

9. Ezra Taft Benson to the President, July 2, 1954; Henry Cabot Lodge to Benson, July 12, 1954; and Benson to Lodge, July 28, 1954, Box 2501, Records of the Department of Agriculture, RG 16, National Archives, Washington, D.C.; see also Clayton E. Whipple to Earl L. Butz, September 10, 1954, ibid.

10. Eisenhower to Nelson Rockefeller and Rowland Hughes, July 22, 1954, attached to Art Kimball to Maxwell Rabb, July 16, 1954, Box 3, Cabinet Series, Eisenhower Papers. Even Humphrey recognized the need for some kind of coordinating agency, however; see Humphrey to Joseph Dodge, October 14, 1954, Box 4, Humphrey Papers.

11. Eisenhower to Rowland Hughes, July 12, 1954, Dodge Series, Correspondence Subseries, Box 1, CFEP, Office of the Chairman, Records; see also Memorandum of Sherman Adams to Cabinet, July 15, 1954, attached to Art Kimball to Maxwell Rabb, July 16, 1954, Box 3, Cabinet Series, Eisenhower Papers.

12. Sherman Adams, *First-hand Report: The Story of the Eisenhower Administration* (New York, 1961), pp. 45–46; Emmet John Hughes, *The Ordeal of Power: A Political Memoir of the Eisenhower Years* (New York, 1963), pp. 50 and 60; see also Telephone Call of Eisenhower to Dodge, July 17, 1954, Box 4, DDE Diary Series, Eisenhower Papers.

13. Copies of the draft and a semifinal report are attached to Eisenhower to Dodge, November 18, 1954, OF-116-AA, Eisenhower Papers. For the final report see Dodge to Sinclair Weeks, December 15, 1954, and attachment, Box 31, Weeks Papers.

14. Memorandum for Governor Adams from Hauge, December 1, 1954, Box 1, Hauge Papers; see also Hauge to Dodge, August 11, 1954, OF-116-EE, Eisenhower Papers.

15. Eisenhower to Dodge, December 1, 1954, OF-116-EE, Eisenhower Papers; Memorandum for the President from Gabriel Hauge, December 22, 1954, Box 1, Hauge Papers; *Business Week*, December 18, 1954, p. 28.

16. Special Message to Congress on the Foreign Economic Policy of the United States, January 10, 1955, *Public Papers of the Presidents: Eisenhower, 1955*, pp. 32–40.

17. See Chalmers M. Roberts, "Tariff Dilemma: President Seeks Happy Solution," *Washington Post and Times Herald*, July 20, 1954; see also Alfred E. Eckes, Jr., *The United States and the Global Struggle for Minerals* (Austin, Tex., 1979), p. 213.

18. U.S. Congress, Senate, Committee on Armed Services, Preparedness Subcommittee No. 6, *Hearings: Essentiality to the National Defense of the Domestic Horological Industry*, 83d Cong., 2d sess., 1954, pp. 32–55 and 163–83; Memorandum for the Director of Defense Mobilization, June 4, 1954, Box 4, DDE Diary Series, Eisenhower Papers; see also Eckes, Jr., *The United States and the Global Struggle for Minerals*, pp. 210–12.

19. Eckes, Jr., *The United States and the Global Struggle for Minerals*, pp. 210–12.

20. *Congressional Quarterly Almanac* 10 (1954): 270.

21. Quoted in Memorandum for the Secretary of State, August 12, 1954, Box 4, DDE Diary Series, Eisenhower Papers; Memorandum for the Secretary of State, August 16, 1954, ibid.; see also Harry Pollock to Sinclair Weeks, July 15, 1954, and Weeks to Pollock, July 24, 1954, Box 40, Weeks Papers.

22. Eisenhower to William E. Robinson, August 4, 1954, Box 4, DDE Diary Series, Eisenhower Papers. See also Eisenhower to E. E. Hazlett, July 20, 1954, Box 3, ibid.; Eisenhower to Bernard Baruch, July 30, 1954, Box 5, Administration Series, ibid.

23. Comparison of Alternate Plans for Relief of Domestic Lead-Zinc Mining Industry [1954], Box 40, Weeks Papers.

24. Eisenhower to Bullis, August 26, 1954, Box 1, Harry Bullis Papers, Dwight D. Eisenhower Library, Abilene, Kans. (hereafter cited as Bullis Papers); Presidential News Conference, July 28, 1954, *Public Papers of the Presidents: Eisenhower, 1954*, pp. 659–60; Adams, *First-hand Report*, p. 381.

25. *Business Week*, September 18, 1954, p. 200.

26. Ibid., November 27, 1954, p. 176.

27. Ibid., July 31, 1954, pp. 30 and 91, and August 7, 1954, p. 120; see also Harry A. Bullis to Eisenhower, July 29, 1954, Box 1, Bullis Papers.

28. Memorandum for the Secretary of State from Eisenhower, June 1, 1954, Box 1, Hauge Papers; Minutes of Cabinet Meeting, August 18, 1954, Box 3, Cabinet Series, Eisenhower Papers; *Business Week*, June 19, 1954, pp. 146, 148; Adams, *First-hand Report*, p. 338.

29. U.S. Department of State, *General Agreement on Tariffs and Trade: Analysis of Protocol (Including Schedules) for Accession of Japan; Analysis of Renegotiations of Certain Tariff Concessions, Negotiated at Geneva, Switzerland, February–June, 1955*, Commercial Policy Series, no. 150 (Washington, D.C., 1955).

30. "Agreement Reached on Japan's Participation in GATT: U.S. Renegotiates Agreements with Benelux Countries and Canada," *Department of State Bulletin* 32 (June 27, 1955): 1051–54; *New York Times*, November 4, 1955.

31. "Contracting Parties to GATT Conclude Ninth Session," *Department of State Bulletin* 32 (March 21, 1955): 496.

32. U.S. Department of State, "Statement by James C. Bonbright," *Bulletin* 33 (November 21, 1955): 860–61; *New York Times*, October 28, 1955.

33. *New York Times*, October 29 and November 21, 1955.

34. Ibid., November 7, 1955.

35. "Review of Tenth Session of Contracting Parties to GATT," *Department of State Bulletin* 33 (December 19, 1955): 1067.

36. Special Message to Congress on the Foreign Economic Policy of the United States, January 10, 1955, *Public Papers of the Presidents: Eisenhower, 1955*, pp. 33–40. See also Memorandum for the President from Gabriel Hauge, February 7, 1955, Box 1, Hauge Papers; Eisenhower to Joseph Martin, February 17, 1955, Box 31, Weeks Papers.

37. Legislative Conference of January 18, 1955, Box 1, Legislative Meeting Series, Eisenhower Papers. For the administration's early discussion of the trade bill with congressional leaders, see also Bipartisan Leadership Meeting, December 14, 1954, ibid.

38. *Congressional Quarterly Almanac* 11 (1955): 289–93. The administration had anticipated such an attack on trade concessions with Japan even before it had opened tariff negotiations with the Tokyo government. See Minutes of Cabinet Meeting, August 18, 1954, Box 3, Cabinet Series, Eisenhower Papers; Legislative Leadership Meeting, February 8, 1955, Box 1, Legislative

Meeting Series, ibid.; *Journal of Commerce*, January 18, 1955; see also U.S. Congress, House, Committee on Ways and Means, *Hearings: Trade Agreements Extension*, 84th Cong., 1st sess., 1955, pp. 149–53 and 2101–9.

39. U.S. Congress, House, Committee on Ways and Means, *Trade Agreements Extension Act of 1955*, 84th Cong., 1st sess., 1955, H. Rept. 50, pp. 1–10; *Congressional Quarterly Almanac* 11 (1955): 293–94.

40. Legislative Leadership Meeting, February 8 and March 2, 1955, Box 1, Legislative Meeting Series, Eisenhower Papers.

41. U.S. Congress, Senate, Committee on Finance, *Trade Agreements Extension Act of 1955*, 84th Cong., 1st sess., 1955, S. Rept. 232, pp. 2–6; U.S. Congress, Senate, Committee on Finance, *Hearings: Trade Agreements Extension*, 84th Cong., 1st sess., 1955; *Congressional Quarterly Almanac* 11 (1955): 296.

42. *Congressional Quarterly Almanac* 11 (1955): 297–98.

43. Ibid., pp. 298–99; U.S. Congress, Committee on Conference, *Conference Report*, 84th Cong., 1st sess., 1955, H. Rept. 745, pp. 1–7.

44. Statement by the President upon Signing the Trade Agreements Extension Act, June 21, 1955, *Public Papers of the Presidents: Eisenhower, 1955*, p. 615.

45. *Congressional Quarterly Almanac* 11 (1955): 297–98; *Business Week*, May 14, 1955, p. 32; see also *New York Times*, April 26, 1955.

46. Macy to Smith, March 11, 1955, File 450, I-5/55, DOC Records.

47. For the Department of Agriculture's position on the GATT prior to the negotiations, see Clayton E. Whipple to John H. Davis, July 20, 1954, Box 2501, Records of the Department of Agriculture, RG 16; see also James C. Foster to Samuel W. Anderson, August 3, 1954, File 450, 10–12/53, DOC Records.

48. Special Message to Congress on U.S. Membership in the Proposed Organization for Trade Cooperation, April 4, 1955, *Public Papers of the Presidents: Eisenhower, 1955*, pp. 393–98.

49. Ibid.

50. Legislative Leadership Meeting, February 8, 1955; and Memorandum for Director Hughes, March 29, 1955, Box 1, Legislative Meeting Series, Eisenhower Papers; see also *Business Week*, March 26, 1955, p. 146.

51. Benson to Eisenhower, July 11, 1955, Box 6, Administration Series, Eisenhower Papers; Telegram from Ambassador Aldrich to Secretary of State, March 24, 1955, Box 2, ibid. See also Earl L. Butz to Gabriel Hauge, May 6, 1955, Box 2669, Records of the Department of Agriculture, RG 16; John C. Lynn to Gabriel Hauge, June 24, 1955, ibid.; Minutes of Cabinet Meeting, May 13, 1955, Box 5, Cabinet Series, Eisenhower Papers.

52. Commission on Foreign Economic Policy, *Report to the President and the Congress* (Washington, D.C., 1954), p. 45; *Business Week*, September 3, 1955, p. 112.

53. Minutes of Cabinet Meeting, August 18, 1954, Box 3, Cabinet Series, Eisenhower Papers; "Executive Order Prescribing Uniform Procedures for Determination under the Buy-American Act," December 20, 1954, Box 4, ibid.

54. Comment by Joseph M. Dodge after the Discussions at the Senior Officers' Meeting, Paris, September, 1955, Dodge Series, Correspondence Subseries, Box 5, CFEP, Office of the Chairman, Records; *Business Week*, September 3, 1955, p. 112.

55. *Business Week*, September 3, 1955, 112.

56. Minutes of Cabinet Meeting, May 13, 1955, Box 5, Cabinet Series, Eisenhower Papers; Ezra Taft Benson to Eisenhower, July 11, 1955, Box 6, Administration Series, ibid.

57. Special Message to Congress on the Foreign Economic Policy of the United States, January 10, 1953, *Public Papers of the Presidents: Eisenhower, 1955*, p. 36.

58. Marshall M. Smith to Assistant Secretary Anderson, August 23, 1954, attached to Smith to Gabriel Hauge, September 8, 1954, OF-116-P, Eisenhower Papers; see also Memorandum for Mrs. Whitman from Gabriel Hauge, November 10, 1954, Box 1, Hauge Papers.

59. *Journal of Commerce*, January 17, 1955; Transcript of Oral Interview with Eugene Black,

May 13, 1975, Dwight D. Eisenhower Library, Abilene, Kans. (hereafter cited as Black, Oral Interview).

60. For the Treasury Department's opposition to extending these provisions on a world-wide basis, see M. B. Folsom to Gabriel Hauge, June 3, 1955, Box 161, Records of the Treasury Department, RG 56.

61. Special Message to Congress on the Foreign Economic Policy of the United States, January 10, 1955, *Public Papers of the Presidents: Eisenhower, 1955*, p. 36; Memorandum for Mr. Kevin McCann from Gabriel Hauge, April 27, 1955, Box 1, Hauge Papers.

62. B. E. Matecki, *Establishment of the International Finance Corporation and United States Policy: A Case Study in International Organization* (New York, 1957), pp. 30–74; see also U.S. Congress, Senate, Committee on Banking and Currency, *Hearings: International Finance Corporation*, 84th Cong., 1st sess., 1955, pp. 22–23.

63. Matecki, *Establishment of the International Finance Corporation*, pp. 75–91. See also Memorandum for Mrs. Whitman from Gabriel Hauge, November 10, 1954, Box 1, Hauge Papers; Black, Oral Interview, pp. 19–21.

64. Matecki, *Establishment of the International Finance Corporation*, p. 135.

65. Ibid., pp. 133–39; Black, Oral Interview, pp. 19–21.

66. Matecki, *Establishment of the International Finance Corporation*, pp. 139–49.

67. Memorandum for the President from Peter Carroll, September, 1954, Box 24, Administration Series, Eisenhower Papers; Senate, Committee on Banking and Currency, *Hearings: International Finance Corporation*, pp. 27–30.

68. Special Message to Congress on U.S. Participation in the International Finance Corporation, May 2, 1955, *Public Papers of the Presidents: Eisenhower, 1955*, pp. 449–52. See also *New York Times*, June 7, 11, and July 12, 1955; *Washington Star*, May 1, 1955.

69. *Congressional Record*, June 21, 1955, pp. 8812–14; *Congressional Quarterly Almanac* 11 (1955): 288.

70. Sherman Adams, *First Hand Report: The Story of the Eisenhower Administration* (New York, 1961), pp. 109–11; Emmet John Hughes, *The Ordeal of Power: A Political Memoir of the Eisenhower Years* (New York, 1963), pp. 106–7.

71. Jackson to Eisenhower, August 13, 1954, Box 41, Jackson Papers.

72. Eisenhower to Jackson, August 16, 1954, ibid.

73. Jackson to Dodge, November 24, 1954, and attachment, "Proposal for a New United States Foreign Economic Policy," Dodge Series, Correspondence Subseries, Box 2, CFEP, Office of the Chairman, Records. On the preparation of this report see also W. W. Rostow, *The Diffusion of Power: An Essay in Recent History* (New York, 1972), p. 89.

74. Rostow, *The Diffusion of Power*, p. xvii.

75. Jackson to Dodge, November 24, 1954, and attachment, "Proposal for a New United States Foreign Economic Policy," Dodge Series, Correspondence Subseries, Box 2, CFEP, Office of the Chairman, Records; see also Walt Rostow to C. D. Jackson, July 12, 1954, Box 41, Jackson Papers.

76. Jackson to Dodge, November 24, 1954, Dodge Series, Correspondence Subseries, Box 2, CFEP, Office of the Chairman, Records. See also Jackson to Dodge, December 18, 1954, Box 38, Jackson Papers; Jackson to Henry Luce, December 20, 1954, Box 56, ibid.

77. Jackson to Dulles, August 19 and 26, 1954, Box 40, Jackson Papers.

78. Jackson to Herbert Hoover, November 4, 1954, Box 56, ibid.

79. Log of Jackson, August 7, 1954, Box 56, ibid.; Jackson to Dulles, August 19, 1954, Box 40, ibid.

80. Dulles to Jackson, August 24, 1954, Box 4, ibid.; see also Bipartisan Leadership Meeting, December 14, 1954, Box 1, Legislative Meeting Series, Eisenhower Papers.

81. Memorandum for the President from Peter Carroll, August 27, 1954, Box 24, Administration Series, Eisenhower Papers; see also C. D. Jackson to Dulles, August 19, 1954, Box 40, Jackson Papers.

82. Oral Interview with John B. Hollister, Dwight D. Eisenhower Library, Abilene, Kans. Hollister remarked that the administration "wanted to get away from the fact that Stassen had run with the ball a number of times slightly opposite to what the Secretary of State wanted him to do, or what George Humphrey, or any of them. He was not cooperative. He had great ideas of grandeur and he wanted to run his own show" (p. 25).

83. See, for example, Memorandum for the President from Dulles, December 4, 1954, and Eisenhower to Dulles, December 7, 1954, Dodge Series, Correspondence Subseries, Box 1, CFEP, Office of the Chairman, Records: "Organizational Advantages in Transferring FOA to State," January 12, 1955, ibid., Box 2; Memorandum for the President from Joseph M. Dodge, March 31, 1955, ibid.; C. D. Jackson to Henry Luce, December 20, 1954, Box 56, Jackson Papers. Ironically, Secretary Dulles, who, Sherman Adams claims, was driven to "distraction" by Stassen's diplomatic missions, was one of the cabinet officers willing to have the FOA remain an independent operation. As far as he was concerned the FOA-State relationship had worked out satisfactorily. See Memorandum of Conversation with John Foster Dulles, Rowland Hughes, and Nelson Rockefeller, February 14, 1955, Dodge Series, Correspondence Subseries, Box 2, CFEP, Office of the Chairman, Records; see also Adams, *First-hand Report*, pp. 90–91.

84. Memorandum for the Honorable Joseph M. Dodge from Dwight D. Eisenhower, January 26, 1955, Dodge Series, Correspondence Subseries, Box 1, CFEP, Office of the Chairman, Records.

85. Dulles had insisted upon such a relationship. Memorandum of Conversation with John Foster Dulles, Rowland Hughes, and Nelson Rockefeller, February 14, 1955, ibid., Box 2. See also Memorandum to the President from Harold Stassen, April 7, 1955, ibid., Box 3; Eisenhower to Dulles, April 15, 1955, *Public Papers of the Presidents: Eisenhower, 1955*, pp. 399–403.

86. *Washington Post*, May 2, 1955; *Business Week*, May 7, 1955, p. 38. On state-owned industries see *New York Times*, February 18, 1955.

87. Stassen to George Humphrey, March 31, 1955, and Humphrey to Stassen, March 31, 1955, Box 4, Humphrey Papers; see also *Washington Post*, May 2, 1955.

88. U.S. Department of State, "Special Report on American Opinion Prepared by the Division of Public Studies, January 15, 1951," *Foreign Relations of the United States, 1951, National Security Affairs: Foreign Economic Policy* (Washington, D.C., 1979), p. 272.

89. *New York Times*, October 8 and 9, 1954; *Business Week*, October 16, 1954, pp. 25–56; Matecki, *Establishment of the International Finance Corporation*, pp. 132–33.

90. Memorandum for the President from John Foster Dulles, October 28, 1954, Box 38, Administration File, Eisenhower Papers; *Business Week*, November 20, 1954, p. 196; ibid., December 11, 1954, pp. 37–38; see also Memorandum for the President from Joseph M. Dodge, December 15, 1954, Dodge Series, Correspondence Subseries, Box 1, CFEP, Office of the Chairman, Records.

91. Presidential News Conference, December 8, 1954, *Public Papers of the Presidents: Eisenhower, 1954*, p. 1088.

92. Bipartisan Leadership Meeting, December 14, 1954, Box 1, Legislative Meeting Series, Eisenhower Papers; Marquis Childs, "Humphrey Vetoes Large Asian Aid," *Washington Post and Times Herald*, December 24, 1954.

93. Presidential News Conference, March 2, 1955, *Public Papers of the Presidents: Eisenhower, 1955*, pp. 303–4; *New York Times*, January 19 and February 16, 1955; *Business Week*, January 29, 1955, p. 118.

94. Memorandum for Mr. Hensel, February 8, 1955; Memorandum for Mr. Nolting et al., February 8, 1955; and "Programming $205 Million A. E. P. Fund in FY 1956 Budget," February 22, 1955, Dodge Series, Subject Subseries, Box 2, CFEP, Office of the Chairman, Records.

95. Memorandum to the President from Harold Stassen, March 14, 1955, Box 31, Administration Series, Eisenhower Papers; see also "Governor Stassen's Trip to Seven Free Asian Countries," March 21, 1955, Dodge Series, Subject Subseries, Box 5, CFEP, Office of the Chairman, Records.

96. Special Message to Congress on the Mutual Security Program, April 20, 1955, *Public Papers of the Presidents: Eisenhower, 1955*, pp. 404–14; see also Minutes of Cabinet Meeting, July 23, 1954, Box 3, Cabinet Series, Eisenhower Papers.

97. This is not to suggest that the former Republican chairmen of the House Foreign Affairs Committee and Senate Foreign Relations Committee, Representative Robert Chiperfield of Illinois and Senator Alexander Wiley of Wisconsin, did not generally support the administration. As Gary Reichard has commented, they demonstrated relatively strong support for the president's foreign-policy views. But as Reichard also notes, "In the lower house, Republicans on the most important foreign policy–related committees were not so solidly behind the President" (Gary W. Reichard, *The Reaffirmation of Republicanism: Eisenhower and the Eighty-third Congress* [Knoxville, Tenn., 1975], pp. 46–47 and 92–93). Moreover, Democrats were in a better position to lend bipartisan support to Republican internationalists in Congress. See also *Congressional Quarterly Almanac* 11 (1955): 301–9; U.S. Congress, House, Committee on Foreign Affairs, *Mutual Security Act of 1955*, 84th Cong., 1st sess., 1955, H. Rept. 912, pp. 1–43.

98. *Congressional Quarterly Almanac* 11 (1955): 235–39; see also U.S. Congress, Senate, Committee on Appropriations, *Mutual Security Appropriations Bill, 1956*, 84th Cong., 1st sess., 1955, S. Rept. 1033, pp. 1–13.

99. Memorandum for the President from Joseph Dodge April 28, 1955, and attachment, Dodge Series, Correspondence Subseries, Box 1, CFEP, Office of the Chairman, Records.

100. "Annex E: A U.S. International Development Authority," n.d., Dodge Series, Subject Subseries, Box 5, ibid.; see also Joseph Dodge to Arnold G. Stifel, February 14, 1955, Dodge Series, Correspondence Subseries, Box 4, ibid.

101. *Congressional Quarterly Almanac* 11 (1955): 235–39.

102. David A. Baldwin, *Economic Development and American Foreign Policy, 1943–62* (Chicago, 1966), pp. 125–28 and 168–71.

103. *Congressional Quarterly Almanac* 10 (1954): 275–81.

104. "Foreign Development Loans vs. Grants," n.d.; "Foreign Development Loan Corporation," March 1955; Joseph M. Dodge to George M. Humphrey, February 21, 1955; and Memorandum of Conversation with Mr. Stassen, Dodge Series, Subject Subseries, Box 3, CFEP, Office of the Chairman, Records; see also Legislative Leadership Meeting, June 28, 1955, Legislative Meeting Series, Eisenhower Papers.

CHAPTER 4

1. "History of Congressional Action on Executive Branch Requests: Mutual Security," n.d., Box 29, Administration Series, Eisenhower Papers.

2. U.S. Congress, Senate, Committee on Foreign Relations, *The Mutual Security Act of 1954*, 83d Cong., 2d sess., 1954, S. Rept. 1799, p. 8.

3. Alvin Z. Rubinstein, *The Soviets in International Organizations: Changing Policy toward Developing Countries, 1953–1963* (Princeton, N.J., 1964), pp. 11–13; Joseph S. Berliner, *Soviet Economic Aid: The New Aid and Trade Policy in the Underdeveloped Countries* (New York, 1958), pp. 3–18; Leo Tansky, *U.S. and U.S.S.R. Aid to Developing Countries: A Comparative Study of India, Turkey, and the U.A.R.* (New York, 1967), pp. 7–9; U.S. Department of State, *The Sino-Soviet Economic Offensive in the Less Developed Countries*, Europe and British Commonwealth Series, no. 51 (Washington, D.C., 1958), p. 31.

4. Rubinstein, *The Soviets in International Organizations*, pp. 32–36; U.S. Congress, Joint Economic Committee, *Dimensions of Soviet Economic Power: Studies Prepared for Joint Economic Committee*, 87th Cong., 2d sess., 1962, p. 461; Robert Loring Allen, *Soviet Economic Warfare* (Washington, D.C., 1960), pp. 8–23.

5. John Lewis Gaddis, *Russia, the Soviet Union, and the United States: An Interpretive History* (New York, 1978), pp. 213–18.

6. Radio and Television Address to the American People on the Geneva Conference, July 25,

1955, *Public Papers of the Presidents of the United States: Dwight D. Eisenhower, 1955* (Washington, D.C., 1959), pp. 726–31.

7. "The Question of U.S. Foreign Economic Policy," *Congressional Digest* 33 (August–September 1954): 199–200; U.S. Congress, House, Committee on Foreign Affairs, *The Mutual Security Act of 1956*, 84th Cong., 2d sess., 1956, H. Rept. 2213, p. 31; U.S. Congress, Senate, Committee on Government Operations, *East-West Trade*, 84th Cong., 2d sess., 1956, S. Rept. 2621, pp. 3–8; Sinclair Weeks to Secretary of Defense, December 12, 1955, Box 29, Weeks Papers.

8. *Congressional Quarterly Almanac* 12 (1956): 733; see also Trudy Huskamp Peterson, *Agricultural Exports, Farm Income, and the Eisenhower Administration* (Lincoln, Nebr.), pp. 120–26.

9. Morse to Herbert Hoover, Jr., August 4, 1955, Box 2669, Records of the Department of Agriculture, RG 16, National Archives, Washington, D.C.

10. Presidential News Conference, January 19, 1955, *Public Papers of the Presidents: Eisenhower, 1955*, pp. 196–97.

11. "East-West Trade: Threat or Promise?" n.d., Dodge Series, Box 1, CFEP, Office of the Chairman, Records.

12. Statement of Dodge at the Bilderberg Conference, September 23, 1955, ibid.

13. Emmet John Hughes, *The Ordeal of Power: A Political Memoir of the Eisenhower Years* (New York, 1963), p. 76; Presidential News Conference, May 18, 1955, *Public Papers of the Presidents: Eisenhower, 1955*, pp. 516–17.

14. Statement on East-West Contacts Delivered at the Geneva Conference, July 22, 1955, *Public Papers of the Presidents: Eisenhower, 1955*, p. 717.

15. *Business Week*, November 12, 1955, pp. 32–33.

16. Memorandum to Colonel Cullen from Joseph M. Dodge, January 26, 1956, and Dodge to Admiral W. S. DeLany, February 13, 1956, Dodge Series, Correspondence Subseries, Box 1, CFEP, Office of the Chairman, Records.

17. Joint Statement Following Discussions with Prime Minister Eden, February 1, 1956, *Public Papers of the Presidents of the United States: Dwight D. Eisenhower, 1956* (Washington, D.C., 1958), p. 217; Dodge to Admiral W. S. DeLany, February 13 and March 2, 1956, Dodge Series, Correspondence Subseries, Box 1, CFEP, Office of the Chairman, Records.

18. Memorandum to Herbert V. Prochnow from Joseph Dodge, with photocopies sent to General Goodpaster and Gabriel Hauge, February 29, 1956, Dodge Series, Correspondence Subseries, Box 1, CFEP, Office of the Chairman, Records; see also *Congressional Quarterly Almanac* 12 (1956): 733.

19. *Congressional Quarterly Almanac* 12 (1956): 733–34.

20. Presidential News Conference, March 7, 1956, *Public Papers of the Presidents: Eisenhower, 1956*, pp. 296–97.

21. *Congressional Quarterly Almanac* 12 (1956): 734–35; Senate, Committee on Government Operations, *East-West Trade*, pp. 29–49.

22. Memorandum to Herbert V. Prochnow from Joseph Dodge, with photocopies sent to General Goodpaster and Gabriel Hauge, February 29, 1956, Dodge Series, Correspondence Subseries, Box 1, CFEP, Office of the Chairman, Records.

23. Conversation with Bernard Baruch, March 28, 1956, and Diary Entry, March 30, 1956, Box 8, DDE Diary Series, Eisenhower Papers.

24. The issue was relaxing trade controls with China. See Memorandum for Colonel Andrew Goodpaster, April 4, 1956, Dodge Series, Correspondence Subseries, Box 1, CFEP, Office of the Chairman, Records.

25. *Business Week*, April 14, 1956, p. 160; ibid., May 19, 1956, p. 166.

26. Senate, Committee on Government Operations, *East-West Trade*, esp. pp. 46–50.

27. Sinclair Weeks to Sherman Adams, July 24, 1956, Box 30, Weeks Papers.

28. Berliner, *Soviet Economic Aid*, pp. 30–35; Rubinstein, *The Soviets in International Organizations*, pp. 32–33; Tansky, *U.S. and U.S.S.R. Aid to Developing Countries*, pp. 106–10; Joint Economic Committee, *Dimensions of Soviet Economic Power*, p. 468.

29. Tansky, *U.S. and U.S.S.R. Aid to Developing Countries*, p. 31; Berliner, *Soviet Economic Aid*, pp. 57–59; Joint Economic Committee, *Dimensions of Soviet Economic Power*, pp. 443–56; Allen, *Soviet Economic Warfare*, pp. 110–28; Economic Intelligence Committee, "Biweekly Report: Sino-Soviet Bloc Economic Activities in Underdeveloped Areas," no. 2, March 5, 1956, Box 13, Administration Series, Eisenhower Papers; Council for Economic and Industry Research, Inc., "Foreign Assistance Activities of the Communist Bloc and Their Implications for the United States," in U.S. Congress, Senate, Special Committee to Study the Foreign Aid Program, *Foreign Aid Programs: Compilation of Studies and Surveys*, 85th Cong., 1st sess., 1957, pp. 637–38.

30. Council for Economic and Industry Research, Inc., "Foreign Assistance Activities of the Communist Bloc," pp. 641–43 and 667–74; Allen, *Soviet Economic Warfare*, pp. 12–13 and 18–19; Economic Intelligence Committee, "Biweekly Report: Sino-Soviet Bloc Economic Activities in Underdeveloped Areas," no. 2, March 5, 1956, Box 13, Administration Series, Eisenhower Papers.

31. Council for Economic and Industry Research, Inc., "Foreign Assistance Activities of the Communist Bloc," pp. 641–43.

32. Ibid., pp. 675–77; Rubinstein, *The Soviets in International Organizations*, pp. 22–23, 40, 47–48, and 189–90; Berliner, *Soviet Economic Aid*, pp. 140–64; Raymond F. Mikesell and Jack N. Behrman, *Financing Free World Trade with the Sino-Soviet Bloc* (Princeton, N.J., 1958), pp. 20–25; see also Joseph M. Dodge to Herbert Hoover, Jr., March 26, 1956, Dodge Series, Correspondence Subseries, Box 1, CFEP, Office of the Chairman, Records.

33. Council for Economic and Industry Research, Inc., "Foreign Assistance Activities of the Communist Bloc," pp. 675–77.

34. Ibid.

35. Bipartisan Legislative Meeting, December 14, 1954, and May 3, 1955, Box 1, Legislative Meeting Series, Eisenhower Papers.

36. Legislative Leadership Meeting, June 28, 1955, ibid.; see also U.S. Congress, Senate, Committee on Foreign Relations, *Hearings: Mutual Security Act of 1956*, 84th Cong., 2d sess., 1956, pp. 25–27.

37. Jackson to Rockefeller, November 10, 1955, and Rockefeller to Jackson, November 21, 1955, Box 75, Jackson Papers. Rockefeller said he would forward Jackson's letter to the president. See also Jackson to John Foster Dulles, January 12, 1956, attached to Dulles to Jackson, January 31, 1956, Box 40, ibid. In November, Walt Rostow wrote to Jackson to warn him of the dangers the Soviet economic offensive raised in the Middle East and Southeast Asia. If Egypt moved toward the Soviet Union, he feared, Western ties to Jordan, Syria, and Saudi Arabia would be threatened. India's link to the West would be endangered by a Soviet loan in support of its Second Five-Year Plan, and this would have profound consequences for Burma and Indonesia. See Rostow to Jackson, November 18, 1955, Box 75, ibid.

38. Eisenhower to Douglas, March 29, 1955, Box 10, DDE Diary Series, Eisenhower Papers.

39. Eisenhower to Douglas, January 20, 1956, attached to Ann Whitman to Joseph M. Dodge, January 21, 1956, Dodge Series, Correspondence Subseries, Box 1, CFEP, Office of the Chairman, Records. At a news conference, Eisenhower said he had first become concerned about the Soviet economic offensive in October 1955. See Presidential News Conference, March 14, 1956, *Public Papers of the Presidents: Eisenhower, 1956*, p. 301; see also Bipartisan Legislative Leaders Meeting, December 13, 1956, Box 1, Legislative Meeting Series, Eisenhower Papers; *Business Week*, December 24, 1955.

40. Dodge to Herbert Hoover, Jr., April 25, 1956; Draft of Speech to Advertising Panel, April 3, 1956; Memorandum to Secretary Hoover from Dodge, January 13, 1956; and Dodge to Gordon Gray, May 8, 1956, Dodge Series, Correspondence Subseries, Box 1, CFEP, Office of the Chairman, Records.

41. Memorandum to Robert Amory, Jr., from Joseph Dodge; Dodge to Herbert Hoover, Jr., February 18, 1956; Dodge to Admiral Arthur W. Radford, February 27, 1956; and Dodge to John Foster Dulles, January 23, 1956, ibid.

42. Memorandum for the President from Joseph Dodge, March 17, 1956, Box 13, Administration Series, Eisenhower Papers. See also "An Organizational Approach to Problems Resulting from Soviet Bloc Economic Penetration Programs," prepared by Joseph Dodge, and Memorandum for Gabriel Hauge from Dodge, March 30, 1956, Dodge Series, Correspondence Subseries, Box 1, CFEP, Office of the Chairman, Records.

43. Special Message to Congress on the Mutual Security Program, March 19, 1956, *Public Papers of the Presidents: Eisenhower, 1956*, pp. 314–24.

44. Ibid.

45. Ibid.; Presidential News Conference, March 7, 1956, ibid., pp. 292–93.

46. Cabinet Paper, "Mutual Security Program for Fiscal Year, 1956," April 21, 1956, Box 5, Cabinet Series, Eisenhower Papers.

47. Dodge to Herbert Hoover, Jr., April 25, 1956, Dodge Series, Correspondence Subseries, Box 1, CFEP, Office of the Chairman, Records; *Business Week*, January 28, 1956, pp. 70–71.

48. U.S. Congress, House, Committee on Foreign Affairs, *Hearings: Mutual Security Act of 1956*, 84th Cong., 2d sess., 1956, pp. 7–12, 34–35, 39–40, and 64–67; Senate, Committee on Foreign Relations, *Hearings: Mutual Security Act of 1956*. Only a few weeks earlier, however, Hollister had commented that "there would be nothing more stupid than to try to meet the new Russian change of front and pace by spending enormous sums of money in the Near and Far East" (Hollister to Dodge, February 2, 1956, Dodge Series, Correspondence Subseries, Box 5, CFEP, Office of the Chairman, Records).

49. See, for example, Legislative Leadership Meeting, May 1 and June 2, 1956, Box 2, Legislative Meeting Series, Eisenhower Papers; L. A. Minnich, Jr., to Percival F. Brundage, June 5, 1956, Box 9, DDE Diary Series, ibid.

50. *Congressional Quarterly Almanac* 12 (1956): 418 and 427–28. The authorization bill had left the question of continuing aid to Yugoslavia to the president. The House Appropriations Committee had attached to the appropriations bill the rider prohibiting aid.

51. *Congressional Record*, June 8, 1956, pp. 9886–87; U.S. Congress, House, Committee on Foreign Affairs, *Mutual Security Act of 1956: Minority View*, 84th Cong., 2d sess., 1956, H. Rept. 2213, pt. 2, pp. 1–5. On Republican opposition to foreign aid, see Gary W. Reichard, *The Reaffirmation of Republicanism: Eisenhower and the Eighty-third Congress* (Knoxville, Tenn., 1975), p. 70.

52. *Congressional Quarterly Almanac* 9 (1953): 156; ibid. 10 (1954): 168 and 276; ibid. 11 (1955): 235–39 and 307.

53. Legislative Leadership Meeting, June 14, 1955, Box 1, Legislative Meeting Series, Eisenhower Papers.

54. See, for example, the remarks of Paul Hoffman attached to John Davenport to C. D. Jackson, March 21, 1956, Box 49, Jackson Papers; see also Walt Rostow to C. D. Jackson, November 18, 1955 and February 29, 1956, Boxes 75 and 91, ibid.

55. Legislative Leadership Meeting, June 14, 1955, Box 1, Legislative Meeting Series, Eisenhower Papers.

56. Legislative Leadership Meeting, June 14 and 28, 1955, ibid.

57. L. A. Minnich, Jr., to Percival F. Brundage, June 5, 1956, Box 9, DDE Diary Series, Eisenhower Papers; Legislative Leadership Meeting, June 5, 1956, and Minutes of Legislative Meeting, July 10, 1956, Box 2, Legislative Meeting Series, ibid.

58. *Congressional Record*, June 6 and 8, 1956, pp. 9665–71 and 9870–74; *Congressional Quarterly Almanac* 12 (1956): 418–19.

59. Ibid.

60. Ibid.

61. *Congressional Record*, June 8, 1956, pp. 9887–89.

62. Ibid., June 27, 1956, p. 11108.

63. *Congressional Quarterly Almanac* 12 (1956): 418–19; U.S. Congress, Senate, Committee on Foreign Relations, *The Mutual Security Act of 1956*, 84th Cong., 2d sess., 1956, S. Rept. 2273, pp. 7–8.

64.   Senate, Special Committee to Study the Foreign Aid Program, *Foreign Aid Programs*, pp. iii–iv; *Congressional Quarterly Almanac* 12 (1956): 641.

65.   Phone Calls of April 17 and 20, 1956, Box 8, DDE Diary Series, Eisenhower Papers.

66.   Phone Calls of April 23, 1956, ibid.; Legislative Leadership Meeting, May 1, 1956, Box 2, Legislative Meeting Series, ibid.; L. A. Minnich, Jr., to Percival F. Brundage, May 1, 1956, Box 9, DDE Diary Series, ibid.

67.   U.S. Congress, Senate, Committee on Foreign Relations, *Arranging for Exhaustive Studies to Be Made Regarding Foreign Assistance by the United States*, 84th Cong., 2d sess., 1956, S. Rept. 2278, pp. 1–3.

68.   Memorandum to Mr. Randall prepared by C. Edward Galbreath, July 12, 1956, Dodge Series, Correspondence Subseries, Box 5, CFEP, Office of the Chairman, Records.

69.   Presidential Committee to Review Foreign Assistance Programs, August 14, 1956, and John McCloy to Eisenhower, August 20, 1956, ibid.; *Business Week*, September 15, 1956, p. 204.

70.   Report of Roderic L. O'Connor, for use by the Fairless Committee, September 21, 1956, Dodge Series, Correspondence Subseries, Box 5, CFEP, Office of the Chairman, Records.

71.   Presidential News Conference, September 5, 1956, *Public Papers of the Presidents: Eisenhower, 1956*, pp. 738–39.

CHAPTER 5

1.   U.S. Congress, Joint Economic Committee, *Hearings: Foreign Economic Policy*, 84th Cong., 1st sess., 1955, esp. pp. 3–7; U.S. Congress, Joint Economic Committee, *Foreign Economic Policy*, 84th Cong., 2d sess., 1956, S. Rept. 1312, p. 24.

2.   Annual Message to Congress on the State of the Union, January 5, 1956, *Public Papers of the Presidents of the United States: Dwight D. Eisenhower, 1956* (Washington, D.C., 1958), pp. 7–8; Annual Budget Message to Congress for Fiscal Year 1957, January 16, 1956, ibid., p. 110; see also Minutes of Cabinet Meeting, December 3, 1955, Box 6, Cabinet Series, Eisenhower Papers.

3.   U.S. Congress, House, Committee on Ways and Means, *Hearings: Organization for Trade Cooperation*, 84th Cong., 2d sess., 1956, pp. 5–11, 88–92, 153–60, 286–91, 311–16, and 914–18; see also "Controversy over the Proposed O.T.C.," *Congressional Digest* 35 (May 1956): 139–60.

4.   See, for example, House, Committee on Ways and Means, *Hearings: Organization for Trade Cooperation*, pp. 311–16, 340–47, and 689–95.

5.   Legislative Leadership Meeting, May 8, 1956, Box 2, Legislative Meeting Series, Eisenhower Papers.

6.   Diary Entry, May 18, 1956, Box 8, DDE Diary Series, ibid.; see also Phone Calls of May 17, 1956, ibid.

7.   *Congressional Quarterly Almanac* 12 (1956): 485.

8.   Eisenhower to Watson, November 11, 1956, *Public Papers of the Presidents: Eisenhower, 1956*, p. 310; see also *Business Week*, June 23, 1956, p. 188.

9.   On these points see C. D. Jackson, Telephone Calls, May 14, 1956, Box 56, Jackson Papers; Legislative Leadership Meetings, April 17 and May 15, 1956, Box 2, Legislative Meeting Series, Eisenhower Papers.

10.   Memorandum for the Cabinet, January 24, 1956, Box 45, Weeks Papers.

11.   A summary of the contents of this report is in a memorandum signed by Joseph Dodge, November 23, 1955, Dodge Series, Correspondence Subseries, Box 1, CFEP, Office of the Chairman, Records; see also Trudy Huskamp Peterson, *Agricultural Exports, Farm Income, and the Eisenhower Administration* (Lincoln, Nebr., 1979), pp. 70–73.

12.   Dodge to Hollister, December 20, 1955, Dodge Series, Correspondence Subseries, Box 1, CFEP, Office of the Chairman, Records; see also Cabinet Paper, August 11, 1955, Box 5, Cabinet Series, Eisenhower Papers; Memorandum for Mr. Joseph Rand from John H. Stambaugh, January 5, 1956, Box 1, Joseph Rand Papers, Dwight D. Eisenhower Library, Abilene, Kans. (hereafter cited as Rand Papers); Peterson, *Agricultural Exports, Farm Income, and the Eisenhower Administration*, pp. 73–76.

13. Special Message to Congress on Agriculture, January 9, 1956, *Public Papers of the Presidents: Eisenhower, 1956*, pp. 38, 40, and 48–50.

14. *Congressional Quarterly Almanac* 12 (1956): 489–92; Joseph Dodge to George M. Humphrey, and Humphrey to Dodge, June 8, 1956, Dodge Series, Correspondence Subseries, Boxes 1 and 4, CFEP, Office of the Chairman, Records; Memorandum for Clarence Randall from Joseph Rand, July 26, 1956, Chronological File 5–9/56, Rand Papers. On agricultural trade with the Soviet Union see Dodge to Herbert Hoover, Jr., December 19, 1955, Dodge Series, Correspondence Subseries, Box 1, CFEP, Office of the Chairman, Records; Memorandum for Hoover, March 12, 1956, Dodge Series, Chronological Subseries, Box 1, ibid.; Sinclair Weeks to Clarence B. Randall, August 3, 1956, Box 3, Weeks Papers.

15. CFEP Staff Study on International Commodity Agreements, September 13, 1955, attached to Paul H. Cullen to Don Paarlberg, September 10, 1955, Box 2669, Records of the Department of Agriculture, RG 16, National Archives, Washington, D.C. See also Robert D. Krumme, "International Commodity Agreements: Purpose, Policy, and Procedure," *George Washington Law Review*, April 1963, pp. 784–811; Commission on Foreign Economic Policy, *Report to the President and the Congress* (Washington, D.C., 1954), pp. 28–32.

16. CFEP Staff Study on International Commodity Agreements, September 13, 1955, attached to Paul H. Cullen to Don Paarlberg, September 10, 1955, Box 2669, Records of the Department of Agriculture, RG 16.

17. Ibid.; see also CFEP Meeting, October 11, 1955, ibid.

18. CFEP Staff Study on International Commodity Agreements, September 13, 1955, attached to Paul H. Cullen to Don Paarlberg, September 10, 1955, ibid.; see also CFEP Meeting, October 11, 1955, ibid.

19. Memorandum for Herbert Hoover, Jr., May 9, 1956, Dodge Series, Chronological Subseries, Box 1, CFEP, Office of the Chairman, Records.

20. For the ratification of the agreement see *Department of State Bulletin* 36 (January 7, 1957): 41–42.

21. Memorandum for Herbert Hoover, Jr., May 9, 1956, Dodge Series, Chronological Subseries, Box 1, CFEP, Office of the Chairman, Records.

22. L. T. Higby, "The 1956 International Wheat Agreement," *Department of State Bulletin 36 (February 25, 1957): 318*–25. See also U.S. Congress, Senate, Committee on Foreign Relations, *Hearings: International Wheat Agreement of 1956*, 84th Cong., 2d sess., 1956, p. 119; *Congressional Quarterly Almanac* 12 (1956): 605–6.

23. See "Bearing of U.S. Antitrust Laws on Foreign Commerce," prepared by Henry Chalmers, May 9, 1955, Box 12, Rand Papers.

24. Among the companies against which the Justice Department brought indictments were National Lead, Dupont, and Bendix. See letters exchanged in 1944 between such administration leaders as President Franklin Roosevelt, Secretary of the Navy James Forrestal, Secretary of the Army Robert Patterson, Assistant Attorney General Wendell Berge, Special Assistant to the Secretary of War Julius N. Amberg, and White House Assistant D. J. Brady in OF 277, Franklin D. Roosevelt Papers, Franklin D. Roosevelt Library, Hyde Park, New York. Under administration prodding Secretary of State Cordell Hull established an interdepartmental committee on cartels. The minutes of this committee's meetings can be found in Records of the Federal Trade Commission, RG 122, "The Prewitt Papers," National Archives, Washington, D.C.

25. Federal Trade Commission, *Report on the Copper Industry* (Washington, D.C., 1947); idem, *Report on the Sulfur Industry and International Cartels* (Washington, D.C., 1947); idem, *Report on the International Electric Equipment Industry* (Washington, D.C., 1948); idem, *Report on International Steel Cartels* (Washington, D.C., 1948); idem, *Report on Fertilizer Industry* (Washington, D.C., 1950); idem, *Report on International Cartels in the Alkali Industry* (Washington, D.C., 1950); U.S. Congress, Senate, Select Committee on Small Business, *The International Petroleum Cartel: Staff Report to the Federal Trade Commission*, 82d Cong., 2d sess., 1952, Committee Print no. 6.

26. U.S. Congress, Senate, Committee on the Judiciary, *Hearings: Foreign Trade and the*

Antitrust Laws, 88th Cong., 2d sess., 1964, pp. 1–44 and 123–37; idem, *Hearings: International Aspects of Antitrust*, 90th Cong,., 1st sess., 1967, pp. 1–72, 293, and 459–63; see also Mira Wilkins, *The Maturing of Multinational Enterprise: American Business Abroad from 1914 to 1970* (Cambridge, Mass., 1974), pp. 292–300.

27. For the legal aspects of foreign antitrust see Wilbur Lindsay Fugate, *Foreign Commerce and the Antitrust Laws* (Boston, 1973), and Kingman Brewster, Jr., *Antitrust and American Business Abroad* (New York, 1958). Sec also *Report of the Attorney General's National Committee to Study the Antitrust Laws* (Washington, D.C., 1955), pp. 70–91; Wilkins, *The Maturing of Multinational Enterprise*, pp. 272–300.

28. *Public Papers of the Presidents of the United States: Harry S. Truman, 1948* (Washington, D.C., 1964), pp. 233–34.

29. *Report of the Attorney General's National Committee to Study the Antitrust Laws*, p. 93; U.S. Congress, Senate, Committee on the Judiciary, *Hearings: A Study of the Antitrust Laws*, 84th Cong., 1st sess., 1955, pp. 1594 and 1840.

30. U.S. Congress, Senate, Committee on Banking and Currency, *The Defense Production Act of 1950*, 81st Cong., 2d sess., 1950, S. Rept. 2250, pp. 1–8 and 11–12.

31. "Report of the Attorney General to the National Security Council Relative to the Grand Jury Investigation of the International Oil Cartel—January 1953," in U.S. Congress, Senate, Committee on Foreign Relations, *The International Petroleum Cartel, The Iranian Consortium, and U.S. National Security*, 93d Cong., 2d sess., 1974, Committee Print, pp. 29–33; Truman to Attorney General James McGranery, January 12, 1953, ibid., p. 33.

32. Commission on Foreign Economic Policy, *Report to the President and the Congress* (Washington, D.C., 1954), pp. 17–18.

33. *Report of the Attorney General's National Committee to Study the Antitrust Laws*, pp. 65–114; U.S. Congress, House, Committee on the Judiciary, *Hearings: Current Antitrust Problems*, 84th Cong., 1st sess., 1955, pp. 5–40, 78–93, and 185–90.

34. House, Committee on the Judiciary, *Hearings: Current Antitrust Problems*, esp. pp. 5 and 78; Senate, Committee on the Judiciary, *Hearings: A Study of the Antitrust Laws*, pt. 4 (devoted exclusively to foreign trade); *Congressional Quarterly Almanac* 11 (1955): 546–49 and 552–54.

35. Memorandum for Mr. Randall by Joseph Rand, April 6, 1960, Policy Papers Series, Box 4, CFEP, Office of the Chairman, Records; Memorandum for Governor Sherman Adams, November 18, 1954, and Eisenhower to Dodge, December 1, 1954, OF 116-M and OF 116-E, Eisenhower Papers.

36. See the following memoranda prepared by Henry Chalmers of the Department of Commerce: "Bearing of U.S. Antitrust Laws on Foreign Commerce," May 9, 1955; "Bearing of U.S. Antitrust Laws on Foreign Investment," May 6, 1955; and "Bearing of Antitrust on Foreign Distributorships and Foreign Investment," n.d., Box 12, Rand Papers. In addition, see "Suggested Specific Types of Current Problems on Impact of Antitrust on U.S. Foreign Activities," May 24, 1955, ibid.

37. Dodge to George Humphrey, December 3, 1955, Dodge Series, Correspondence Subseries, Box 1, CFEP, Office of the Chairman, Records; Henry Chalmers to Joseph Randall August 10, 1955, and attachments, Box 12, Rand Papers; Joseph Dodge to Stanley N. Barnes, January 23, 1956, Dodge Series, Correspondence Subseries, Box 1, CFEP, Office of the Chairman, Records.

38. On these points see, for example, Memorandum from Robert M. Macy to Dr. Reid, December 23, 1955; and Monroe Leigh to Joseph Rand, August 15, 1955, Box 12, Rand Papers.

39. Memorandum from Robert Macy to Dr. Reid, November 23, 1955, ibid.

40. "Bearing of Antitrust on Foreign Distributorships and Private Investment," attached to Henry Chalmers to Joseph Rand, ibid.; Memorandum for Mr. Randall by Joseph Rand, April 6, 1960, Policy Papers Series, Box 4, CFEP, Office of the Chairman, Records.

41. *Public Papers of the Presidents of the United States: Dwight D. Eisenhower, 1954* (Washington, D.C., 1960), p. 216; *Report of the Attorney General's National Committee to Study the*

Antitrust Laws, p. iv. See also Emmet John Hughes, *The Ordeal of Power: A Political Memoir of the Eisenhower Years* (New York, 1973), p. 67.

42. Telephone Conversation, August 7, 1954, Box 4, DDE Diary Series, Eisenhower Papers.

43. Walter B. Smith to Attorney General Herbert Brownell, April 27, 1953, Case 60-57-140, Records of the Department of Justice, Department of Justice, Washington, D.C., (hereafter cited as DOJ, 60-57-140); U.S. Congress, Senate, Committee on Foreign Relations, *Multinational Corporations and U.S. Foreign Policy*, 94th Cong., 1st sess., 1975, Committee Print, p. 63.

44. Senate, Committee on Foreign Relations, *Multinational Oil Corporations and U.S. Foreign Policy*, pp. 65–66; Senate, Committee on Foreign Relations, *The Internationl Petroleum Cartel*, p. 51.

45. J. S. Leach to Walter Bedell Smith, February 16, 1954, DOJ, 60-57-140. See also Orville Harden to John Foster Dulles, December 4, 1953, in Senate, Committee on Foreign Relations, *The International Petroleum Cartel*, p. 58.

46. Memorandum from assistant Attorney General Barnes to the Attorney General, December 10, 1953; Herbert Phleger to Herbert Brownell, Jr., January 8, 1954; John Foster Dulles, Memorandum, January 8, 1954; Stanley N. Barnes, "For the Files," January 13, 1954; Attorney General to National Security Council, January 15, 1954; Attorney General to the President, January 21, 1954; and Memorandum for the Attorney General from Stanley N. Barnes, April 29, 1954, in Senate, Committee on Foreign Relations, *The International Petroleum Cartel*, pp. 59–63, 69, 75–76, and 87–89; Benjamin Schwadran, *The Middle East: Oil and the Great Powers* (New York, 1973), pp. 144–45. See also Herbert Hoover, Jr., to Attorney General Brownell, September 14, 1954; Brownell to the President, September 15, 1954; and Kenneth R. Harkins to W. B. Watson Snyder, September 20, 1954, DOJ, 60-57-140.

47. W. B. Watson Snyder to Stanley N. Barnes, September 18, 1954, DOJ, 60-57-140. See also "Objectives of the Government in the Oil Cartel Suit," November 1, 1954, ibid.; Memo to Stanley N. Barnes, Assistant Attorney General, from Kenneth R. Harkins, September 15, 1954, in Senate, Committee on Foreign Relations, *The International Petroleum Cartel*, p. 91.

48. Burton I. Kaufman, *The Oil Cartel Case: A Documentary Study of Antitrust Activity in the Cold War Era* (Westport, Conn., 1978), pp. 80–103.

49. On these points see also David Haberman to Alan A. Dobey, May 9, 1966, DOJ, 60-57-140.

50. U.S. Congress, Senate, Committee on the Judiciary, *Petroleum, the Antitrust Laws, and Government Policies*, 85th Cong., 1st sess., 1957, S. Rept. 1147, pp. 51–63 and 96–155.

51. Ibid., pp. 19–22, 25–26, and 51–55; Robert Engler, *The Politics of Oil: A Study of Private Power and Democratic Institutions* (New York, 1961), pp. 305–7.

52. U.S. Congress, Senate, Committees on the Judiciary and on Interior and Insular Affairs, *Joint Hearings: Emergency Oil Lift Program and Related Problems*, 85th Cong., 1st sess., 1957, p. 95; Senate, Committee on the Judiciary, *Petroleum, the Antitrust Laws, and Government Policies*, pp. 1–8, 55–62, and 82–84.

53. Senate, Committee on the Judiciary, *Petroleum, the Antitrust Laws, and Government Policies*, pp. 85–156.

54. Ibid., p. 1–8.

55. United Nations, Statistical Office, *World Energy Supplies, 1951–1954* (New York, 1956), p. 82; idem, *World Energy Supplies, 1955–1958* (New York, 1960), p. 90.

56. "Report of the Presidential Advisory Commission on Energy Supplies and Resources Policy," February 26, 1955, OF-134-H, Eisenhower Papers.

57. Roland W. Doty, Jr., "The Oil Import Problem during the Truman and Eisenhower Administrations" (M.A. thesis, Kansas State University, 1970), pp. 36–37; Joseph O'Mahoney to Gordon Gray, April 18, 1957; Memorandum for Dr. Hauge from Samuel Waugh, April 8, 1955; and H. S. to Dr. Hauge, March 25, 1955, OF-149-B-2, Eisenhower Papers.

58. U.S. Congress, House, Committee on Ways and Means, *Hearings: Trade Agreements Extension*, 84th Cong., 1st sess., 1955, p. 130. As early as January, 1955, before the Cabinet Committee on Energy Supplies and Resources had delivered its report to the president recom-

mending quotas on imported oil, Attorney General Brownell had warned that "in the interest of the antitrust laws" any discussion by government officials with the oil companies had to be limited merely to pointing out the consequences of failure to limit imports voluntarily (Minutes of Cabinet Meeting, January 21, 1955, Box 4, Cabinet Series, Eisenhower Papers). On this same point see also Memorandum of Conference with the President, September 12, 1956, Box 10, DDE Diary Series, ibid.

59.   United Nations, Statistical Office, *World Energy Supplies, 1955–1958*, p. 90; Memorandum for the President from Leo A. Hoegh, November 20, 1958, Box 7, Rand Papers; Memorandum for the Director, Office of Defense Mobilization, April 25, 1957; Robert Murphy to Percival Brundage, n.d.; and Eisenhower to John Foster Dulles, June 26, 1957, OF-134-F-8, Eisenhower Papers.

60.   Senate, Committee on the Judiciary, *Petroleum, the Antitrust Laws, and Government Policies*, pp. 3–4.

61.   Doty, Jr., "The Oil Import Problem," pp. 56–60.

62.   Dillon Anderson to Eisenhower, July 24, 1957, and Eisenhower to Anderson, July 30, 1957, Papers Accompanying Dillon Anderson, Oral Interview, Dwight D. Eisenhower Library, Abilene, Kans.

63.   See Wilton B. Persons to Robert Wood, February 11, 1957, OF 149-B-2, Eisenhower Papers and Sinclair Weeks to Robert F. Downer, August 6, 1957, Box 45, Weeks Papers.

64.   United Nations, Economic and Social Council, *Report of the Ad Hoc Committee on Restrictive Business Practices* (E/2380 E/AC 37/3), March 30, 1953; (E/2380/Corr. 1, E/AC 37/3/Cor. 1), May 18, 1953.

65.   Senate, Committee on the Judiciary, *Hearings: A Study of the Antitrust Laws*, pp. 1555–84.

66.   Ibid., pp. 1839–48.

67.   Ibid., pp. 1580–82.

68.   Ibid., pp. 1592–99.

69.   Ibid., pp. 1600–1602 and 1620–21.

70.   Ibid., pp. 1599.

71.   Raymond Vernon, "Trade Policy in Crisis," *Essays in International Finance* (Princeton University, International Finance Section), no. 29 (March 1958), pp. 1–13.

72.   Ibid., pp. 12–14.

CHAPTER 6

1.   H. Field Haviland, Jr., "Foreign Aid and the Policy Process: 1957," *American Political Science Review* 52 (September 1958): 689.

2.   U.S. Congress, Senate, Special Committee to Study the Foreign Aid Program, *Foreign Aid Program: Compilation of Studies and Surveys*, 85th Cong., 1st sess., 1957, S. Rept. 52, pp. iii–iv; see also, Roderic L. O'Connor to Mr. Hoover, August 17, 1956, Dodge Series, Correspondence Subseries, Box 5, CFEP, Office of the Chairman, Records.

3.   Brookings Institution, "Administrative Aspects of United States Foreign Assistance Programs," in Senate, Special Committee to Study the Foreign Aid Program, *Foreign Aid Program*, pp. 407–558; Koreger and Associates, "Personnel for the Mutual Security Program," ibid., pp. 75–148; Jerome Jacobson Associates, "The Use of Private Contractors in Foreign Aid Programs," ibid., pp. 247–356; National Planning Associates, "Agricultural Surplus Disposal and Foreign Aid," ibid., pp. 357–406; Council for Economic and Industry Research, "Foreign Assistance Activities of the Communist Bloc and Their Implications for the United States," ibid., pp. 619–766; Stuart Rice Associates, "Foreign Aid Activities of Other Free Nations," ibid., pp. 1057–1161; Center for International Studies, Massachusetts Institute of Technology, "The Objectives of United States Economic Assistance Programs," ibid., pp. ix–73; Research Center in Economic Development and Cultural Exchange, The University of Chicago, "The Role of Foreign Aid in the Development of Other Countries," ibid., pp. 149–246.

4. Center for International Studies, Massachusetts Institute of Technology, "The Objective of United States Economic Assistance Programs," pp. ix–73; Max F. Millikan and W. W. Rostow, *A Proposal: Key to an Effective Foreign Policy* (New York, 1957). See also testimony of Walt Rostow before the Subcommittee on Foreign Economic Policy, U.S. Congress, Joint Economic Committee, *Hearings: World Economic Growth*, 84th Cong., 2d sess., 1956, pp. 126–27; testimony of Max Millikan, U.S. Congress, Senate, Special Committee to Study the Foreign Aid Program, *Hearings: Foreign Aid Program*, 85th Cong., 1st sess., 1957, pp. 2–26.

5. Center for International Studies, Massachusetts Institute of Technology, "The Objectives of United States Economic Assistance Programs," pp. 1–15.

6. Ibid., pp. 16–25.

7. Ibid., pp. 29–36 and 68–69.

8. Ibid., pp. 19–25; see also Robert A. Packenham, *Liberal America and the Third World: Political Development Ideas in Foreign Aid and Social Science* (Princeton, N.J., 1973), pp. 56–57.

9. Ibid.

10. See, for example, Brookings Institution, "Administrative Aspects of United States Foreign Assistance Programs," pp. 527–58; Council for Economic and Industry Research, "Foreign Assistance Activities of the Communist Bloc," pp. 630–31 and 685–86; Research Center on Economic Development and Cultural Exchange, The University of Chicago, "The Role of Foreign Aid in the Development of Other Countries," pp. 155–57.

11. U.S. Congress, House, Committee on Foreign Affairs, *Report on Foreign Policy and Mutual Security*, 85th Cong., 1st sess., 1957, H. Rept. 551, pp. 1–83r.

12. International Development Advisory Board, *A New Emphasis on Economic Development Abroad* (Washington, D.C., 1957), pp. 18–19.

13. *Report to the President by the President's Citizen Advisers on the Mutual Security Program, March 1, 1957* (Washington, D.C., 1957), pp. 8–9.

14. Eugene Black to Clarence Randall, March 11, 1957, Randall Series, Box 5, CFEP, Office of the Chairman, Records.

15. *Report to the President by the President's Citizens Advisers on the Mutual Security Program*, pp. 2 and 13.

16. George Humphrey to Eisenhower, May 7, 1956, Box 23, Administration Series, Eisenhower Papers; see also Humphrey to Lodge, December 20, 1956, Dodge Series, Correspondence Subseries, Box 5, CFEP, Office of the Chairman, Records.

17. Memorandum for Mrs. Whitman by Joseph N. Greene, December 19, 1956, containing Lodge's testimony of November 30, 1956, before the Fairless Committee, and Paul Hoffman to Eisenhower, December 17, 1956, Box 21, Administration Series, Eisenhower Papers.

18. Humphrey to Lodge, December 20, 1956, Dodge Series, Correspondence Subseries, Box 5, CFEP, Office of the Chairman, Records.

19. Memorandum for the President from John Foster Dulles, January 10, 1957, Box 21, Administration Series, Eisenhower Papers.

20. On December 1, 1956, Eisenhower had told Dulles that the United States needed a long-range plan for the Middle East. He had asked Dulles: "What do we do if we are going to exclude Russia?" (Phone Calls, December 1, 1956, Box 11, DDE Diary Series, ibid.).

21. Special Message to Congress on the Situation in the Middle East, January 5, 1957, *Public Papers of the Presidents of the United States: Dwight D. Eisenhower, 1957* (Washington, D.C., 1958), pp. 12–13; Annual Budget Message to the Congress for Fiscal Year 1958, January 16, 1957, ibid., p. 48; Second Inaugural Address, January 21, 1957, ibid., pp. 63–64.

22. Memorandum for Colonel Cullen prepared by G. A. W., February 7, 1957, Box 1, Rand Papers.

23. Humphrey to Clarence Randall, March 20, 1957, Box 4, Humphrey Papers.

24. The position of the various agencies on the Fairless Committee can be found in Randall Series, Box 5, CFEP, Office of the Chairman, Records, but see especially "Summary Report and Staff Recommendations [March, 1957]." See also Memorandum for the Honorable Clarence B.

Randall from Robert Cutler, March 11, 1957; Supplement to Cutler's March 11 Memorandum for Mr. Randall, March 12, 1957; and Memorandum for Governor Adams from Clarence Randall, March 14, 1957, ibid.; John W. McDonald to Sinclair Weeks, March 14, 1957, and enclosure, Box 44, Weeks Papers; *Business Week*, March 9, 1957, p. 196.

25. Christian Herter to Clarence Randall, March 16, 1957, enclosing "Comments on the Report of the International Development Advisory Board," n.d., Box 1, Christian A. Herter Papers, Dwight D. Eisenhower Library, Abilene, Kans. (hereafter cited as Herter Papers).

26. Ibid.

27. Earl Butz to Clarence B. Randall, March 18, 1957, Box 80, Records of the department of Agriculture, RG 16, National Archives, Washington, D.C.; John W. McDonald to Sinclair Weeks, March 19, 1957, and enclosure, Box 31, Weeks Papers.

28. Memorandum of Conference with the President prepared by General A. J. Goodpaster, March 27, 1957, Box 1, Herter Papers. On the attitude of Congress toward foreign aid see also *Business Week*, February 16, 1957, p. 155.

29. Memorandum for Governor Adams from Clarence B. Randall, March 19, 1957, enclosing the president's handwritten memorandum on Fairless Report, n.d., Randall Series, Box 5, CFEP, Office of the Chairman, Records; Memorandum of Conference with the President, March 27, 1957, prepared by A. J. Goodpaster, March 27, 1957, Box 1, Herter Papers; Memorandum for the Secretary by Christian Herter, April 1, 1957, Box 9, ibid. See also Eisenhower to Carl D. Marsh, February 6, 1957, and Eisenhower to James P. Mitchell, March 11, 1957, Box 12, DDE Diary Series, Eisenhower Papers.

30. Eisenhower to Humphrey, March 27, 1957, Box 13, DDE Diary Series, ibid. See also Humphrey to Hoffman, March 26, 1957, OF 116-B, and Eisenhower to Hoffman, March 8, 1957, Box 13, DDE Diary Series, ibid.

31. Senate, Special Committee to Study the Foreign Aid Program, *Hearings: Foreign Aid Program*, pp. 394–407.

32. At the beginning of February, Jackson attended a meeting organized by Clarence Randall to discuss Jackson's new world economic plan. Those at the meeting included Secretary of State Dulles, Treasury Secretary Humphrey, ICA Director Hollister, White House Assistants Robert Cutler and Gabriel Hauge, Chairman of the Council of Economic Advisers Raymond J. Saulnier, Undersecretary of Agriculture True D. Morse, and Karl Harr representing the Department of Defense. According to Jackson the meeting produced nothing constructive. He described Humphrey and Hollister as having "closed minds" to any program of development aid and characterized Dulles's response as one of "groping hopelessness." "From the start, it was a session in which I could not win," Jackson told Henry Luce. "If I talked about opportunity and theory, someone would demand nuts and bolts. If I started on a nut and bolt, before any plan could emerge it was under quick attack and the thread was lost" (Memorandum to Mr. Luce from C. D. Jackson, February 7, 1957, Box 91, Jackson Papers). Yet that very day the Department of State's Policy Planning Staff recommended creation of a Development Loan Fund. See also Jackson to Dulles December 27, 1956, and Dulles to Jackson, January 10, 1957; Box 40, ibid.; "Notes for College of Cardinals on World Economic Policy" by C. D. Jackson, February 12, 1957, and Jackson to Clarence Randall, March 4, 1957, Box 91, ibid.; Randall to Jackson, March 14, 1957, Box 74, ibid.

33. Christian Herter to Paul Hoffman, March 28, 1957, Box 1, Herter Papers; Memorandum for Governor Adams from Eisenhower, April 12, 1957, enclosing C. D. Jackson to Eisenhower, April 11, 1957, Box 13, DDE Diary Series, Eisenhower Papers; Eisenhower to C. D. Jackson, April 18, 1957, Box 41, Jackson Papers; Jackson to Herter, April 19, 1957, Box 91, ibid.; C. D. Jackson to Eisenhower, April 29, 1957, Box 41, ibid.; Eisenhower to C. D. Jackson, April 30, 1957, Box 13, DDE Diary Series, Eisenhower Papers.

34. Memorandum of Conversation with the President, May 7, 1957, Box 9, Herter Papers; Eisenhower to Humphrey, May 7, 1957, Box 13, DDE Diary Series, Eisenhower Papers; Legislative Bipartisan Meeting, May 9, 1957, Box 2, Legislative Meeting Series, ibid.

35. U.S. Congress, Senate, Special Committee to Study the Foreign Aid Program, *Foreign*

Aid: Report of the Special Committee to Study the Foreign Aid Program, 85th Cong., 1st sess., 1957, S. Rept. 300, pp. 4–10, 15–16, and 30–32; see also *Business Week*, May 18, 1957, p. 149.

36. Memorandum of Conversation with Senator Fulbright, May 16, 1957, Box 9, Herter Papers.

37. Elmo Richardson, *The Presidency of Dwight D. Eisenhower* (Lawrence, Kans., 1979), pp. 127–28; Charles C. Alexander, *Holding the Line: The Eisenhower Era, 1952–1961* (Bloomington, Ind., 1975), pp. 191–93.

38. Special Message to the Congress on the Mutual Security Program, May 21, 1957, *Public Papers of the Presidents: Eisenhower, 1957*, pp. 372–85; Radio and Television Address to the American People on the Need for Mutual Security—Waging the Peace, May 21, 1957, ibid., pp. 385–96.

39. As early as April 2, Senator Mike Mansfield of Montana told Christian Herter that a delay of three weeks would be "most unfortunate since Congress wished to adjourn early this year" (Memorandum of Conversation with Senator Mike Mansfield by Christian Herter, April 2, 1957, Box 9, Herter Papers). House Speaker Rayburn told Herter much the same thing; see Telephone Conversation between Undersecretary Herter and Speaker Rayburn, April 3, 1957, Box 1, ibid.

40. In March, when the budget cut was first proposed, President Eisenhower had complained that he was "highly disappointed that the administration did not see the savings before the budget was put in" (Memorandum of Conference with the President prepared by General A. J. Goodpaster, March 27, 1957, Box 1, ibid.). According to House Democratic leader John McCormack, Humphrey's call for budget cuts in Eisenhower's proposed $71.8 billion budget for 1959 had set Humphrey apart from the president and had laid Eisenhower's foreign-aid program open to severe slashes by Congress. *Journal of Commerce*, February 18, 1957.

41. U.S. Congress, House, Committee on Foreign Affairs, *Hearings: Mutual Security Act of 1957*, 85th Cong., 1st sess., 1957, pp. 1–15.

42. But Mansfield also believed that military-end items and economic support for the military should be clearly distinguished from economic development. Memorandum of Conversation with Senator Mike Mansfield, April 2, 1957, Box 9, Herter Papers.

43. U.S. Congress, Senate, Committee on Foreign Relations, *The Mutual Security Act of 1957*, 85th Cong., 1st sess., 1957, S. Rept. 417, pt. 2, "Minority Views of Senator Wayne Morse," pp. 2–3 and 12.

44. Ibid., pp. 1–28; Unsigned Memorandum for Eisenhower Summarizing Telephone Conversation of Senator Knowland with Bryce Harlow, June 8, 1957, Box 14, DDE Diary Series, Eisenhower Papers; *Congressional Quarterly Almanac* 13 (1957): 606–7.

45. U.S. Congress, House, Committee on Foreign Affairs, *Mutual Security Act of 1957*, 85th Cong., 1st sess., 1957, H. Rept. 776, pp. 1–22.

46. *Washington Post*, July 12, 1957; Telephone Conversation of Herter with Speaker Rayburn, July 12, 1957, Box 10, Herter Papers.

47. *Congressional Quarterly Almanac* 13 (1957): 608–9.

48. Ibid., pp. 609–10.

49. Presidential News Conference, August 14, 1957, *Public Papers of the Presidents: Eisenhower, 1957*, pp. 604–9; Statement by the President on Senate Restoration of Mutual Security Funds, August 27, 1957, ibid., pp. 634–35.

50. Haviland, Jr., "Foreign Aid and the Policy Process: 1957," pp. 709–10.

51. Report to President of Telephone Conversation between Bryce Harlow and William Knowland, June 8, 1957, Box 14, DDE Diary Series, Eisenhower Papers.

52. Memorandum of Telephone Conversation with Speaker Rayburn, June 28, 1957, and Telephone Conversation of Christian Herter with Bryce Harlow, July 5, 1957, Box 10, Herter Papers; Herter to Representative J. Vaughan Gary, July 16, 1957, and enclosure, "Congressional Control of the Fund," Box 2, ibid.; Telephone Conversation of Eisenhower with Secretary of State Dulles, August 19, 1957, Box 15, DDE Diary Series, Eisenhower Papers; Summary Notes on Legislative Leadership Meeting, August 20, 1957, Box 2, Legislative Meeting Series, ibid.

53. Presidential Meeting with Congressional Leaders on Mutual Security, August 14, 1957, Box 15, DDE Diary Series, Eisenhower Papers; see also Telephone Conversation of Eisenhower with Secretary of State Dulles, August 7, 1957, ibid.

54. *Congressional Quarterly Almanac* 13 (1957): 611; Haviland, Jr., "Foreign Aid and the Policy Process: 1957," pp. 710–12.

55. U.S. Congress, Senate, Committee on Appropriations, *Mutual Security Appropriations Bill*, 85th Cong., 1st sess., 1957, S. Rept. 1117, pp. 3–9; Haviland, Jr., "Foreign Aid and the Policy Process: 1957," pp. 712–14; *Congressional Quarterly Almanac* 13 (1957): 612. See also Legislative Leadership Meeting, August 13, 1957, Box 2, Legislative Meeting Series, Eisenhower Papers; Memorandum of Appointment with Lyndon Johnson, August 26, 1957, Box 15, DDE Diary Series, ibid.

56. Eisenhower to Robert W. Woodruff, August 6, 1957, Box 15, DDE Diary Series, Eisenhower Papers.

57. Presidential News Conference, September 3, 1957, *Public Papers of the Presidents: Eisenhower, 1957*, pp. 641–42; see also Telephone Conversation of Eisenhower with Secretary of State Dulles, August 19, 1957, Box 15, DDE Diary Series, Eisenhower Papers.

58. *Congressional Quarterly Almanac* 13 (1957): 612.

59. See, for example, Eisenhower to Humphrey, May 7, 1957, Box 13, DDE Diary Series, Eisenhower Papers; Telephone Call of Eisenhower to Humphrey, August 20, 1957, Box 15, ibid.

60. On these matters see, for example, Telephone Call of Herter to John B. Hollister, June 27, 1957, Box 10, Herter Papers.

61. Senate, Committee on Foreign Relations, *The Mutual Security Act of 1957*, pp. 7–8; see also *Congressional Record*, June 13, 1957, pp. 8963–75.

62. *Congressional Record*, June 13, 1957, pp. 8975–82, 8997–98, and 9006–15; ibid., June 14, 1957, pp. 9117–29; see also "Congress Reappraises U.S. Foreign Aid," *Congressional Digest* 36 (August-September 1957): 200, 202, 204, 206, 208, and 210.

63. Herter to Westmore Willcox, August 22, 1957, Box 2, Herter Papers. See also Herter's Memorandum to John B. Hollister, June 19, 1957; and Herter to Westmore Willcox, June 19, 1957, ibid.; Herter to Morris D. Pendleton, June 21, 1957, Box 1, ibid.

64. *Congressional Quarterly Almanac* 14 (1958): 184.

CHAPTER 7

1. *Business Week*, November 16, 1957, pp. 142–44.

2. U.S. Congress, House, Committee on Ways and Means, Subcommittee on Foreign Trade Policy, *Foreign Trade Policy: Compendium of Papers on United States Foreign Trade Policy*, 85th Cong., 2d sess., 1958, pp. 1–3.

3. Flanders to Weeks, November 14, 1956, Box 56, Weeks Papers; see also Gary W. Reichard, *The Reaffirmation of Republicanism: Eisenhower and the Eighty-third Congress* (Knoxville, Tenn., 1975), p. 201.

4. Sinclair Weeks to Sherman Adams, February 13 and 15, 1957, Box 45, Weeks Papers.

5. Memorandum of Conference in the Secretary's Office with respect to OTC, June 4, 1957, Box 2, Herter Papers.

6. Ibid.

7. Ibid.

8. Elmo Richardson, *The Presidency of Dwight D. Eisenhower* (Lawrence, Kans., 1979), p. 33.

9. Weeks to Director, Bureau of the Budget, May 27, 1957, Box 32, Weeks Papers.

10. John Stambaugh to Clarence Randall, February 20, 1957, and Memorandum of Joseph Rand for Colonel Cullen, October 24, 1957, Box 1, Rand Papers; State Department Circular No. 476, November 25, 1957, Box 29, Weeks Papers. See also Henry Kearns to Sinclair Weeks, September 26, 1957, and Sinclair Weeks to Joseph Martin, December 3, 1957, ibid.; Clarence Randall to Sinclair Weeks, August 7, 1957, Box 47, ibid.

11. Memorandum of Conference in the Secretary's Office with respect to OTC, June 4, 1957, Box 2, Herter Papers.

12. Memorandum, "Proposed Changes in the Escape Clause Provision," July 5, 1957, attached to Weeks to Randall, July 8, 1957, Box 3, Weeks Papers.

13. "Analysis of Administration's Proposal on Foreign Trade Legislation in 1958," Box 51, ibid. See also Sinclair Weeks to Puel H. Smith, January 27, 1958, 450 1–6/58, Records of the Department of Commerce, U.S. Department of Commerce, Washington, D.C.

14. *Business Week*, July 6, 1955, p. 120. See also George H. Becker to Sinclair Weeks, November 7, 1957, Box 57, Weeks Papers; *Business Week*, November 16, 1957, pp. 142 and 144.

15. Memorandum Regarding Lead and Zinc, n.d., attached to Christian Herter to Redington Fiske, August 14, 1957, Box 2, Herter Papers.

16. Ibid.

17. *Congressional Quarterly Almanac* 13 (1957): 654; see also U.S. Congress, Senate, Committee on Finance, *Hearings: Import Tax on Lead and Zinc*, 85th Cong., 1st sess., 1957, pp. 4–27 and 35–72.

18. Summary Notes on Legislative Leadership Meeting, August 20, 1957, Box 2, Legislative Meeting Series, Eisenhower Papers; Presidential News Conference, August 21, 1957, *Public Papers of the Presidents of the United States: Dwight D. Eisenhower, 1957* (Washington, D.C., 1958), pp. 619–20.

19. Letter to Jere Cooper, Chairman, House Ways and Means Committee, on Duties on Lead and Zinc, August 23, 1957, *Public Papers of the Presidents: Eisenhower, 1957*, pp. 629–30.

20. Alfred E. Eckes, Jr., *The United States and the Global Struggle for Minerals* (Austin, Tex., 1979), pp. 222–24.

21. *Business Week*, November 16, 1957, pp. 142 and 144; November 30, 1957, p. 160.

22. Henry Kearns to Secretary Weeks, November 25, 1957, Box 26, Weeks Papers.

23. Clarence Randall and Sherman Adams had wanted the president to announce his trade program as early as the end of October. Telephone Call of Sherman Adams to Christian Herter, October 23, 1957, Box 11, Herter Papers.

24. Legislative Bipartisan Meeting, December 3, 1957, Box 2, Legislative Meeting Series, Eisenhower Papers.

25. Ibid.

26. "Proposed Executive Branch Response to Request from Honorable Hale Boggs . . . ," November 25, 1957, attached to Gabriel Hauge to Guilford Jameson, November 27, 1957, OF-8-Q, Eisenhower Papers.

27. House, Committee on Ways and Means, Subcommittee on Foreign Trade Policy, *Foreign Trade Policy*, pp. 5–15, 211–29, 303–60, 443–90, and 643–760.

28. Lincoln Gordon, "Economic Aid and Trade Policy as an Instrument of National Strategy," ibid., pp. 171–77 and 182.

29. Miriam Camps, "Implications for United States Trade Policy of the European Common Market and Free Trade Area," ibid., pp. 451–53.

30. Richard N. Gardner, "Proposals for Reform of the Trade Agreements Act," ibid., pp. 496–505.

31. See, for example, Charles P. Kindleberger, "Imports, the Tariff, and the Need for Adjustment," ibid., pp. 73–87; W. S. Woytinsky, "World Commerce and United States Foreign Trade Policy," ibid., pp. 121–70; Raymond R. Mikesell, "Quantitative Import Restrictions and United States Foreign Trade Policy," ibid., pp. 457–76.

32. See, for example, Lewis E. Lloyd, "Tariffs and United States Foreign Trade Policy," ibid., pp. 109–20; Oscar R. Strackbein, "Analysis of Executive Domination over Tariff and Trade Administration," ibid., pp. 559–78; Russell B. Brown, "United States Imports of Petroleum and the Domestic Industry," ibid., pp. 1059–71.

33. U.S. Congress, House, Committee on Ways and Means, *Hearings: Foreign Trade Policy*, 85th Cong., 1st sess., 1957, pp. 3–12.

34. *Business Week*, December 21, 1957, p. 97; Memorandum for the File, "Organizing Public

Opinion in Favor of the Mutual Security Program and the Reciprocal Trade Agreements Act," November 23, 1957, Box 3, Herter Papers; Memorandum of Henry Kearns to Secretary Weeks, December 13, 1957, Box 57, Weeks Papers.

35. A copy of the intelligence report, entitled "The Sino-Soviet Economic Offensive in the Less Developed Countries of the Free World" and prepared by the State Department's Office of Intelligence Research and Analysis, is in Box 8, Rand Papers. Although the report is dated March 12, 1958, its contents were leaked out in January; see *Business Week*, January 11, 1958, p. 103.

36. Memorandum for the President, January 9, 1958, Box 5, Cabinet Series, Eisenhower Papers; Minutes of Cabinet Meeting, January 10, 1958, Box 10, ibid.; The Cabinet, Record of Action, January 14, 1958, ibid.

37. Minutes of Cabinet Meeting, January 17, 1958, ibid.

38. Special Message to Congress on the Reciprocal Trade Agreements Program, January 30, 1958, *Public Papers of the Presidents of the United States: Dwight D. Eisenhower, 1958* (Washington, D.C., 1959), pp. 132–35.

39. U.S. Congress, House, Committee on Ways and Means, *Hearings: Renewal of Trade Agreements Act*, 85th Cong., 2d sess., 1958, pp. 13–69, 267–69, 381–87, 758–73, and 2643–51; see also *Business Week*, March 8, 1958, pp. 85–86.

40. *Congressional Quarterly Almanac* 14 (1958): 169–70. Charles C. Alexander, *Holding the Line: The Eisenhower Era, 1952–1961* (Bloomington, Ind., 1975), p. 242.

41. Address at the National Conference on International Trade Policy, March 27, 1957, *Public Papers of the Presidents: Eisenhower, 1958*, pp. 243–50. See also Henry Kearns to Secretary Weeks, March 8, 1958, Box 57, Weeks Papers; Memorandum for the President prepared by Douglas Dillon, March 10, 1958, Box 12, Administration Series, Eisenhower Papers.

42. Staff Notes, April 22, 1958, Box 19, DDE Diary Series, Eisenhower Papers. On Dillon see also *Business Week*, December 7, 1957, pp. 131–32.

43. Memorandum of Conversation with Speaker Rayburn This Date, May 3, 1958, Box 56, Weeks Papers.

44. Address at Republican National Committee Dinner in Honor of the Republican Members of Congress, May 6, 1958, *Public Papers of the Presidents: Eisenhower, 1958*, pp. 381–82; *Congressional Quarterly Almanac* 14 (1958): 169–70.

45. U.S. Congress, House, Committee on Ways and Means, *Trade Agreements Extension Act of 1958*, 85th Cong., 2d sess., 1958, H. Rept. 1761, p. 1–23.

46. *Congressional Quarterly Almanac* 14 (1958): 170–71.

47. Ibid., p. 170; Letter to the Chairman, House Committee on Ways and Means, on the Escape Clause Provisions of the Trade Agreements Bill, June 10, 1958, *Public Papers of the Presidents: Eisenhower, 1958*, pp. 461–63.

48. *Congressional Quarterly Almanac* 14 (1958): 170–71.

49. Ibid.

50. Eisenhower to Hoffman, June 23, 1958, Box 21, Administration Series, Eisenhower Papers.

51. *Congressional Quarterly Almanac* 14 (1958): 171.

52. Eisenhower to Hoffman, June 23, 1958, Box 21, Administration Series, Eisenhower Papers.

53. Administration testimony before the Finance Committee closely resembled the earlier testimony before the House Ways and Means Committee, with great emphasis being placed on the need to combat the Soviet economic offensive. See, for example, U.S. Congress, Senate, Committee on Finance, *Hearings: Trade Agreements Act Extension*, 85th Cong., 2d sess., 1958, pp. 7–13, 36–40, and 75–87.

54. U.S. Congress, Senate, Committee on Finance, *Trade Agreements Extension Act of 1958*, 85th Cong., 2d sess., 1958, S. Rept. 1838, pp. 1–15.

55. Ibid. On Flanders's doubts about the reciprocal trade legislation see also his Memorandum to Sinclair Weeks, Box 56, Weeks Papers.

56. Senate, Committee on Finance, *Trade Agreements Extension Act of 1958*, pp. 1–35.

57. Memorandum for the Record, July 8, 1958, Box 21, DDE Diary Series, Eisenhower Papers.

58. L. A. Minnich, Jr., to Maurice Stans, July 16, 1958, ibid.

59. *Congressional Quarterly Almanac* 14 (1958): 172–73.

60. Ibid.

61. Statement by the President upon Signing the Trade Agreements Extension Act, August 20, 1958, *Public Papers of the Presidents: Eisenhower, 1958*, p. 632.

62. Weeks to Eisenhower, July 23, 1958, Box 32, Weeks Papers.

63. For discussion of this point even as the administration transmitted the bill to Congress, see Weeks to Rayburn, January 30, 1958, Box 29, Weeks Papers; see also "Analysis of Administration's Proposals on Foreign Trade Legislation—1958," January 8, 1958, Box 57, ibid.

64. *Congressional Quarterly Almanac* 14 (1958): 175.

65. D. Gale Johnson, "Agricultural Price Policy and International Trade," in House, Committee on Ways and Means, Subcommittee on Foreign Trade Policy, *Foreign Trade Policy*, pp. 707–26.

66. See, for example, "Foreign Economic Policy and the Trade Agreements Program," n.d., attached to Gabriel Hauge to Guilford Jameson, November 27, 1957, OF-8-Q, Eisenhower Papers; Don Paarlberg to Martin Sorkin and Secretary Benson, March 31, 1958, Box 265, Records of the Department of Agriculture, RG 16, National Archives, Washington, D.C. See also Department of Agriculture to Council on Foreign Economic Policy, October 11, 1957, Box 80, ibid.; Trudy Huskamp Peterson, *Agricultural Exports, Farm Income, and the Eisenhower Administration* (Lincoln, Nebr., 1980), pp. 83–87.

67. Annual Budget Message to Congress—Fiscal Year 1959, January 13, 1958, *Public Papers of the Presidents: Eisenhower, 1958*, p. 38; Senate, Committee on Finance, *Hearings: Trade Agreements Act Extension*, pp. 152–53.

68. *Congressional Quarterly Almanac* 14 (1958): 59.

69. Memorandum of Conversation between Herod and Herter, December 4, 1957, Box 3, Herter Papers.

70. Raymond F. Mikesell and Jack N. Behrman, *Financing Free World Trade with the Sino-Soviet Bloc* (Princeton, N.J., 1958), esp. pp. 100–01; *Business Week*, March 8, 1958, pp. 101–2; March 22, 1958, p. 160; April 5, 1958, pp. 98–99, 102, and 104; June 4, 1958, pp. 32–33.

71. Herter to Herod, May 15, 1958, Box 4, Herter Papers.

72. See, for example, "Foreign Economic Policy and the Trade Agreements Program," n.d., attached to Gabriel Hauge to Guilford Jameson, November 27, 1957, OF-8-Q, Eisenhower Papers.

73. On this point see, for example, John Pincus, *Trade, Aid, and Development: The Rich and Poor Nations* (New York, 1967), pp. 64–65. See also Tibor Mende, *From Aid to Re-colonization: Lessons in a Failure* (New York, 1973), esp. pp. 78–79; Harry G. Johnson, *Economic Policy toward Less Developed Countries* (Washington, D.C., 1967), pp. 11–16.

74. General Agreement on Tariffs and Trade, *Trends in International Trade: A Report by a Panel of Experts* (Geneva, 1958), foreword and pp. 3–12.

75. Pincus, *Trade, Aid, and Development*, pp. 81–82; see also Independent Commission on International Development Issues, *North-South: A Programme for Survival* (Cambridge, Mass., 1980), pp. 38–39.

CHAPTER 8

1. Memorandum for the Director of the Bureau of the Budget from Eisenhower, August 30, 1957, Box 9, Administration Series, Eisenhower Papers; Eisenhower to Frank Altschul, October 25, 1957, Box 16, DDE Diary Series, ibid. See also Memorandum of Appointment, August 26, 1957, Box 15, ibid.; Eisenhower to Cochran Supplee, September 7, 1957, ibid.

2. Memorandum of Telephone Conversation between the Vice President and the Undersecretary, October 30, 1957, Box 11, Herter Papers; Memorandum for the Files, n.d., Box 3, ibid.

3. "International Trade and Development—The Year Ahead," *Report of the Forty-fourth National Foreign Trade Convention, 1957* (New York, 1958), pp. 25–26.

4. Legislative Bipartisan Meeting, December 3, 1957, Box 2, Legislative Meeting Series, Eisenhower Papers.

5. Stephen E. Ambrose, *Rise to Globalism: American Foreign Policy since 1938* (London, 1971), p. 151; John Lewis Gaddis, *The United States and the Origins of the Cold War, 1941–1947* (New York, 1972), pp. 348–49.

6. Legislative Bipartisan Meeting, December 3, 1957, Box 2, Legislative Meeting Series, Eisenhower Papers.

7. Annual Message to Congress on the State of the Union, January 9, 1958, *Public Papers of the Presidents of the United States: Dwight D. Eisenhower, 1958* (Washington, D.C., 1959), pp. 5–7 and 9–10; Letter to Eric A. Johnston on the Need for Public Information as to the Foreign Aspects of National Security, January 11, 1958, ibid., pp. 16–17; see also Digest of 1959, Budget, n.d., Box 10, Cabinet Series, Eisenhower Papers.

8. Memorandum for the Record, January 30, 1958, Box 18, DDE Diary Series, ibid.

9. Special Message to Congress on the Mutual Security Program, February 19, 1958, *Public Papers of the Presidents: Eisenhower, 1958*, pp. 160–68.

10. Keynote Address at the National Conference on the Foreign Aspects of U.S. National Security, February 25, 1958, ibid., pp. 176–85; *Business Week*, March 1, 1958, p. 29.

11. Staff Notes, April 22, 1959, Box 19, DDE Diary Series, Eisenhower Papers; see also Legislative Leadership Meeting, Supplementary Notes, May 13, 1958, Box 2, Legislative Meeting Series, ibid.

12. U.S. Congress, House, Committee on Foreign Affairs, *Hearings: Mutual Security Act of 1958*, 85th Cong., 2d sess., 1958, pp. 179–86.

13. Richard Nixon to Sinclair Weeks, [March, 1958], Box 25, Weeks Papers; *Business Week*, March 22, 1958, p. 120; Eisenhower to S. D. Bechtel, March 21, 1958, Box 19, DDE Diary Series, Eisenhower Papers.

14. U.S. Congress, House, Committee on Foreign Affairs, *Mutual Security Act of 1958*, 85th Cong., 2d sess., 1958, H. Rept. 1696, pp. 1–50.

15. *Congressional Quarterly Almanac* 14 (1958): 185–86 and 380; Legislative Leadership Meeting, Supplementary Notes, May 19, 1958, Box 2, Legislative Meeting Series, Eisenhower Papers.

16. Legislative Leadership Meeting, Supplementary Notes, May 19, 1958, Box 2, Legislative Meeting Series, Eisenhower Papers.

17. U.S. Congress, Senate, Committee on Foreign Relations, *The Mutual Security Act of 1958*, 85th Cong., 2d sess., 1958, S. Rept. 1627, pp. 1–3, 6–7, 30–31, and 37–38. On India see also Memorandum for Mr. Macomber and Mr. Roundtree from Christian Herter, October 31, 1957, Box 3, Herter Papers.

18. L. A. Minnich, Jr., to Maurice H. Stans, June 5, 1959, Box 20, DDE Diary Series, Eisenhower Papers; *Congressional Quarterly Almanac* 14 (1958): 186–88.

19. *Congressional Quarterly Almanac* 14 (1958): 187–88.

20. Eisenhower to Paul Hoffman, June 23, 1958, Box 21, Administration Series, Eisenhower Papers; *Business Week*, May 17, 1958, p. 131.

21. "Analysis of Reductions in Mutual Security Appropriations," Box 22, DDE Diary Series, Eisenhower Papers.

22. Memorandum for Miss Whitman signed Jack Z. Anderson, June 26, 1958, and attachment, Box 20, ibid.; Telephone Call of Dulles to Eisenhower, July 1, 1958, Box 21, ibid.

23. L. A. Minnich, Jr., to Maurice Stans, July 1, 1958, Box 21, ibid.; Report of the President's Breakfast with Clarence Cannon, July 21, 1958, ibid.

24. *Congressional Quarterly Almanac* 14 (1958): 188–90.

25. L. A. Minnich, Jr., to Maurice Stans, July 16, 1958, Box 21, DDE Diary Series, Eisenhower Papers; Legislative Leadership Meeting, Supplementary Notes, July 16, 1958, Box 2, Legislative Meeting Series, ibid.

26. L. A. Minnich, Jr., to Maurice Stans, July 16, 1958, Box 21, DDE Diary Series, ibid.; Legislative Leadership Meeting, Supplementary Notes, July 16, 1958, Box 2, Legislative Meeting Series, ibid.; Telephone Call of Eisenhower to Dulles, July 16, 1958, Box 21, DDE Diary Series, ibid.; "Need for Restoration of Mutual Security Program Cuts," July 18, 1958, Box 2, Legislative Meeting Series, ibid. See also Minutes of Cabinet Meeting, July 25, 1958, Box 11, Cabinet Series, ibid.; L. A. Minnich, Jr., to Maurice Stans, July 29, 1958, Box 21, DDE Diary Series, ibid.

27. Eisenhower to Johnson, August 4, 1958, Box 21, DDE Diary Series, ibid.

28. *New York Times*, May 30, 1957.

29. Eisenhower to Humphrey, July 22, 1958, Box 23, Administration Series, Eisenhower Papers.

30. "Analysis of Reductions in Mutual Security Appropriations," Box 22, DDE Diary Series, ibid.; see also Memorandum for Ann Whitman, August 15, 1958, and Memorandum by Jack Z. Anderson, August 19, 1958, ibid.

31. Presidential News Conference, August 27, 1958, *Public Papers of the Presidents: Eisenhower, 1958*, pp. 640–41.

32. James A. Robinson, *The Monroney Resolution: Congressional Initiative in Foreign Policy Making* (New York, 1959), pp. 1–2; James H. Weaver, *The International Development Association: A New Approach in Foreign Aid* (New York, 1965), pp. 37–41; U.S. Congress, Senate, Committee on Banking and Currency, *Hearings: International Development Association*, 85th Cong., 2d sess., 1958, pp. 1–56.

33. Jackson to Randall, March 4, 1957, Box 91, Jackson Papers.

34. Minutes of Cabinet Meeting, January 17, 1958, Box 10, Cabinet Series, Eisenhower Papers; Memorandum of Conversation, January 25, 1958, Box 9, Herter Papers.

35. Memorandum of Conversation, January 25, 1958, Box 9, Herter Papers.

36. Senate, Committee on Banking and Currency, *Hearings: International Development Association*, pp. 58–60 and 123–24.

37. *Congressional Record*, February 24, 1958, pp. 2261–67.

38. These and other statements of support for the Monroney Resolution can be found in Senate, Banking and Currency Committee, *Hearings: International Development Association*, pp. 16–49.

39. Weaver, *The International Development Association*, pp. 56–60.

40. Senate, Committee on Banking and Currency, *Hearings: International Development Association*, pp. 99–219, 140–41, 153–71, and 178–82.

41. Robinson, *The Monroney Resolution*, pp. 10–11.

42. Senate, Committee on Banking and Currency, *Hearings: International Development Association*, pp. 1–6 and 10–11; Robinson, *The Monroney Resolution*, pp. 11–13.

43. *Congressional Quarterly Almanac* 14 (1958): 257.

44. Herter to Carl Hayden, October 25, 1957, Box 3, Herter Papers.

45. Ibid.

46. "Proposed United States Counter-Proposal to 'SUNFED' at Twelfth United Nations General Assembly," attached to ibid.

47. Francis O. Wilcox to Don Pearlberg, January 7, 1958, Box 265, Records of the Department of Agriculture, RG 16, National Archives, Washington, D.C.

48. Telephone Call of Herter to Mr. Wilcox, and Telephone Call to Herter from Vice-President Nixon, December 13, 1957, Box 11, Herter Papers.

49. Ralph S. Roberts to Don Paarlberg, January 13, 1958, Box 265, Records of the Department of Agriculture, RG 16.

50. Quoted in Francis O. Wilcox to Don Paarlberg, January 7, 1958, ibid.

51. Ibid.; David A. Baldwin, *Economic Development and American Foreign Policy, 1943–62* (Chicago, 1966), pp. 209–11.

52. *Congressional Quarterly Almanac* 12 (1956): 489–92.

53. See, for example, Minutes of Cabinet Meeting, June 17, 1957, Box 9, Cabinet Series, Eisenhower Papers; "A Review of Foreign Economic Aid and Assistance Programs of the United

States, 1945–1956, as They Affect U.S. Agriculture," April 10, 1957, Box 80, Records of the Department of Agriculture, RG 16.

54. See, for example, State Department Memorandum attached to Christian Herter to Clarence Randall, May 15, 1957, Box 1, Herter Papers.

55. Annual Budget Message to Congress for Fiscal Year 1958, January 16, 1957, *Public Papers of the Presidents of the United States: Dwight D. Eisenhower, 1957* (Washington, D.C., 1958), p. 55.

56. Special Message to Congress on Agriculture, January 9, 1956, *Public Papers of the Presidents of the United States: Dwight D. Eisenhower, 1956* (Washington, D.C., 1958), pp. 49–50.

57. *Congressional Quarterly Almanac* 13 (1957): 641–44.

58. Memorandum on the Use of P.L. 480 Foreign Currencies for Loans to Private Enterprise in General and U.S. Business in Particular, August 31, 1957, Box 7, Rand Papers; Trudy Huskamp Peterson, *Agricultural Exports, Farm Income, and the Eisenhower Administration* (Lincoln, Nebr.), p. 66.

59. See, for example, U.S. Congress, Senate, Commitee on Agriculture and Forestry, *Hearings: Extension of Public Law 480*, 85th Cong., 1st sess., 1957, esp. pp. 34–35; Ezra Taft Benson, *Cross Fire: The Eight Years with Eisenhower* (New York, 1962), p. 358; *Congressional Quarterly Almanac* 13 (1957): 641–44.

60. Memorandum of Clarence Randall for CFEP, November 13, 1956, Box 5, Council on Foreign Economic Policy, Policy Papers Series, Dwight D. Eisenhower Papers, Abilene, Kans. (hereafter cited as CFEP, Policy Papers Series); see also Randall to Thorsten V. Kalijarvi, November 27, 1956, ibid.

61. Staff Notes, September 13, 1957, Box 11, DDE Diary Series, Eisenhower Papers; Department of State Memorandum, n.d., attached to Christian Herter to Ezra T. Benson, May 4, 1957, Box 1, Herter Papers.

62. Staff Notes, September 13, 1957, Box 11, DDE Diary Series, Eisenhower Papers; Department of State Memorandum, n.d., attached to Christian Herter to Ezra T. Benson, May 4, 1957, Box 1, Herter Papers. See also Herter to John E. Hollister, May 4, 1957, ibid.; U.S. Congress, Senate, Committee on Agriculture and Forestry, *Hearings: Policies and Operations under Public Law 480*, 85th Cong., 1st sess., 1957, pp. 87–96.

63. The memorandum is attached to Herter to Clarence Randall, May 15, 1957, Box 1, Herter Papers.

64. Memorandum for the Secretary from Christian Herter, July 23, 1957, Box 2, ibid.

65. Ibid.

66. Memorandum of Raymond A. Jones to Don Paarlberg, November 7, 1957, Box 80, Records of the Department of Agriculture, RG 16.

67. Department of Agriculture to CFEP, October 11, 1957, ibid.

68. Ibid.

69. U.S. Congress, Senate, Committee on Agriculture and Forestry, *Hearings: Public Law 480 Extension*, 85th Cong., 2d sess., 1958, pp. 8–34; see also Senate, Committee on Agriculture and Forestry, *Hearings: Policies and Operations under Public Law 480*, pp. 26–33.

70. Senate, Committee on Agriculture and Forestry, *Hearings: Policies and Operations under Public Law 480*, pp. 87–97; "The Agenda for Economic Foreign Policy: 1958," by Walt Rostow, Box 75, Jackson Papers.

71. Special Message to the Congress on Agriculture, January 16, 1958, *Public Papers of the Presidents: Eisenhower, 1958*, p. 106; *Congressional Quarterly Almanac* 14 (1958): 277. In fact, the major issue between the White House and Congress involved not the size of the P.L. 480 program but a controversial barter provision inserted by the House which would have required the secretary of agriculture to barter $500 million in surplus goods. The administration opposed these barter transactions because they were resulting in the shipment of surplus goods into countries that normally bought agricultural exports for dollars. The House inserted the barter provision into the P.L. 480 program after the administration issued new, tougher regulations for the barter program. After a bitter legislative battle, during which the P.L. 480 program actually ran

out of funds, a compromise was worked out on the barter provision which satisfied both Congress and the administration. The compromise omitted reference to a $500 million barter program but directed the secretary of agriculture to barter goods "whenever he determines that such action is in the best interests of the United States and to the maximum extent possible" (ibid. 14 [1959]: 278–80). See also Peterson, *Agricultural Exports*, pp. 77–79; "Future Barter Policy," attached to Walter C. Berger to Hubert Humphrey, October, 1957, Box 80, and Marvin L. McLain to Thomas L. Hughes, May 16, 1957, Box 80, Records of the Department of Agriculture, RG 16; Senate, Committee on Agriculture and Forestry, *Hearings: Public Law 480 Extension*; U.S. Congress, Senate, Committee on Agriculture and Forestry, *Extension and Amendment of Public Law 480*, 85th Cong., 2d sess., 1958, S. Rep. 1357, esp. pp. 6–7; U.S. Congress, Senate, Committee on Agriculture and Forestry, *Extension of Public Law 480*, 85th Cong., 2d sess., 1958, S. Rept. 1323, pp. 1–12.

72. *Congressional Quarterly Almanac* 14 (1958): 280.

73. Don Paarlberg to Martin Sorkin and Secretary Benson, March 31, 1958, Box 265, Records of the Department of Agriculture, RG 16; Memorandum for Mr. Randall, July 1, 1958, Box 1, Rand Papers.

CHAPTER 9

1. Agenda for Economic Foreign Policy, 1958–59, proposed by W. W. Rostow, Box 75, Jackson Papers; see also Rostow to C. D. Jackson, July 30, 1958, ibid.

2. Memorandum of Clarence B. Randall to Council on Foreign Economic Policy, July 2, 1958, and attachments, Randall Series, Box 3, CFEP, Office of the Chairman, Records.

3. See, for example, ibid.; Report of Subcommittee on Trade and Commodities, July 9, 1958, and Staff Memorandum of Subcommittee on Psychological Aspects, July 11, 1958, ibid. For some of the deliberations of the committee see Memorandum to the Members, Drafting Committee, from John J. Corson, Committee on World Economic Development, September 10, 1958, Box 25, Weeks Papers.

4. Staff Memorandum of Subcommittee on Psychological Aspects, July 11, 1958, Randall Series, Box 3, CFEP, Office of the Chairman, Records; Committee on World Economic Practices, Working Paper on Tentative Conclusions and Points for Further Study: Tab B, n.d., Box 25, Weeks Papers; *Report of the Committee on World Economic Practices* (Washington, D.C., 1959), pp. 1–3 and 4–8.

5. *Report of the Committee on World Economic Practices*, pp. 4 and 15.

6. Ralph I. Straus, *Expanding Private Investment for Free World Economic Growth* (Washington, D.C., 1959).

7. Clarence Randall to Robert Anderson, Lewis L. Strauss, C. Douglas Dillon, and Leonard J. Saccio, March 19, 1959; Memorandum to Mr. Randall from Paul H. Cullen, attached to Clarence Randall to Robert B. Anderson, March 31, 1959; and Memorandum for Clarence Randall from Attorney General William P. Rogers, March 4, 1959, Randall Series, Box 3, CFEP, Office of the Chairman, Records.

8. U.S. Congress, House, Committee on Ways and Means, *Hearings: Private Foreign Investment*, 85th Cong., 2d sess., 1958, pp. 34–35 and 58.

9. *Congressional Quarterly Almanac* 16 (1960): 336.

10. House, Committee on Ways and Means, *Hearings: Private Foreign Investment*, pp. 44–54.

11. Clarence Randall to Robert Anderson, Douglas Dillon, and Lewis Strauss, January 23, 1959, and Randall to Eisenhower, January 23, 1959, Randall Series, Box 3, CFEP, Office of the Chairman, Records; Memorandum for Mr. Randall by Paul H. Cullen, March 2, 1959, Box 1, Rand Papers.

12. Anderson to Mills, May 6, 1959, Randall Series, Box 3, CFEP, Office of the Chairman, Records.

13. Ibid. See also Memorandum for Mr. Randall by Paul H. Cullen, March 2, 1959, Box 1, Rand Papers; *Business Week*, April 4, 1959, p. 36.

14. U.S. Congress, House, Committee on Ways and Means, *Hearings: Foreign Investment Incentive Act*, 86th Cong., 1st sess., 1959, pp. 60–82, 97–104, and 210–18. *Congressional Quarterly Almanac* 16 (1960): 336–37.

15. Thus, during the hearings on private foreign investment conducted by the House Ways and Means Committee, Undersecretary of State Dillon first pointed out the desirability of promoting private investment, but made it clear that the private sector could not substitute for the mutual security program. House, Committee on Ways and Means, *Hearings: Private Foreign Investment*, pp. 8–9.

16. Harold G. Vatter, *The U.S. Economy in the 1950's: A Study of the Contours of Economic Change during a Crucial Decade in American Economic History* (New York, 1963), pp. 115–17; Charles C. Alexander, *Holding the Line: The Eisenhower Era, 1952–1961* (Bloomington, Ind., 1975), p. 242; *Business Week*, August 23, 1958, pp. 71–72.

17. *Business Week*, July 11, 1959, p. 105; August 30, 1958, pp. 14–15.

18. Robert Anderson to Eisenhower, August 18, 1958, attached to Eisenhower to Anderson, August 20, 1958, OF-8-Q-6, Eisenhower Papers; Alfred E. Eckes, Jr., *A Search for Solvency: Bretton Woods and the International Monetary System, 1941–1947* (Austin, Tex., 1975), pp. 233–35.

19. Anderson to Eisenhower, August 18, 1958, attached to Eisenhower to Anderson, August 26, 1958, OF-8-Q-6, Eisenhower Papers.

20. Eisenhower to Anderson, August 26, 1958, ibid.

21. *Business Week*, August 30, 1958, p. 80.

22. "Relevant U.S. Policies and the Need for Their Review re Regional Economic Integration," September 1956, Box 7, CFEP, Policy Papers Series; see also Memorandum for Mr. Randall from Paul H. Cullen, July 26, 1956, ibid.

23. Clarence C. Randall to John J. McCloy, July 16, 1957, ibid.; see also Comment on the Draft Statement and Working Papers, n.d., Box 20, Weeks Papers.

24. Joseph Rand to Paul Cullen, March 22, 1955, Box 7, CFEP, Policy Papers Series.

25. Clarence Randall to James Smith, Jr., and Dempster McIntosh, January 8, 1959, and Memorandum to Mr. Randall from Paul Cullen, May 23 and December 16, 1958, ibid.

26. Address to the Third Special Emergency Session of the General Assembly of the United Nations, August 13, 1958, *Public Papers of the Presidents of the United States: Dwight D. Eisenhower, 1958* (Washington, D.C., 1959), pp. 611–12; Presidential News Conference, August 20, 1958, ibid., p. 624.

27. See, for example, unsigned memorandum "Latin America," March 29, 1957, Dodge Series, Correspondence Subseries, Box 3, CFEP, Office of the Chairman, Records; "U.S. Capital Contributions to Latin American Growth: Highlights," Box 2, ibid.; "Latin America: United States Military Assistance and Economic Development," March 7, 1956, Box 8, ibid.; Memorandum for Mr. James Webb from Kenneth R. Iverson, December 29, 1958, Box 29, James E. Webb Papers, Harry S. Truman Library, Independence, Mo. (hereafter cited as Webb Papers).

28. "U.S. Capital Contributions to Latin American Growth: Highlights," Dodge Series, Correspondence Subseries, Box 2, CFEP, Office of the Chairman, Records.

29. Thorsten V. Kalijarvi to Clarence Randall, August 28, 1956, Randall Series, Box 1, ibid.

30. "Economic Courses of Action from Proposed NSC Policy in Latin America" (NSC 5613), attached to Memorandum for Clarence B. Randall from James C. Lay, August 20, 1956, ibid.

31. The State Department had preferred quotas rather than an increase in duties since the former were less permanent than tariffs and could be transferred into multilateral arrangements, which it was seeking. See Sinclair Weeks to Eisenhower, September 9, 1958, and enclosure, Box 39, Weeks Papers. Nevertheless, both quotas and higher tariffs were strongly opposed by advocates of freer trade, who considered the imposition of duties a further retreat from the principles

advocated by the White House. See, for example, Philip Courtney to Sinclair Weeks, September 26, 1958, enclosing Statement by the U.S. Council of the International Chamber of Commerce on Quotas on the Importation of Lead and Zinc, Box 40, ibid. See also Lamar Fleming to Eisenhower, November 19, 1958, and Eisenhower to Fleming, December 5, 1958, OF-116-J, Eisenhower Papers; Christian Herter to Claudius Pendall, October 18, 1958, Box 5, Herter Papers.

32. CFEP Subcommittee on Buenos Aires Conference Memorandum, June 10, 1957; R. R. Rubottom to Clarence Randall, July 24, 1957; and Memorandum for Randall from Cutler, Box 7, CFEP, Policy Papers Series.

33. Herter to Leffler, December 5, 1957, Box 3, Herter Papers.

34. R. Harrison Wagner, *United States Policy toward Latin America: A Study in Domestic and International Politics* (Stanford, Calif., 1970), p. 43.

35. Samuel Waugh to Family, May 26, 1958, Box 1, Samuel Waugh Papers, Dwight D. Eisenhower Library, Abilene, Kans. (hereafter cited as Waugh Papers); *Business Week*, May 24, 1958, pp. 43–44 and 46. For Nixon's belief that the riot was Communist inspired and that the United States needed to broaden its contact in Latin America beyond the traditional elite to include university leaders, communications people, and group leaders, among others, see Minutes of Cabinet Meeting, May 16, 1958, Box 9, Cabinet Series, Eisenhower Papers; see also Samuel L. Bailey, *The United States and the Development of South America, 1945–1975* (New York, 1976), pp. 76–77.

36. Kubitschek to Eisenhower, May 28, 1958, and Eisenhower to Kubitschek, June 5, 1958, Box 4, International Series, Eisenhower Papers; see also Milton S. Eisenhower, *The Wine is Bitter: The United States and Latin America* (New York, 1963), p. 202.

37. Sidney Dell, *The Inter-American Development Bank: A Study in Development Financing* (New York, 1972), pp. 1–12.

38. U.S. Congress, House, Committee on Banking and Currency, *Hearings: Inter-American Development Bank Act*, 86th Cong., 1st sess., 1959, p. 54.

39. Minutes of Cabinet Meeting, August 8, 1958, Box 12, Cabinet Series, Eisenhower Papers; Kubitschek to Eisenhower, September 9, 1958, Box 4, International Series, ibid.

40. Bailey, *The United States and the Development of South America*, pp. 76–77.

41. *Business Week*, November 22, 1958, p. 114.

42. Dell, *The Inter-American Development Bank*, pp. 37–116.

43. M. Eisenhower, *The Wine is Bitter*, pp. 230–31.

44. Dell, *The Inter-American Development Bank*, p. 15.

45. Memorandum for Mrs. Whitman by Don Paarlberg, March 15, 1959, and attachment, Box 25, DDE Diary Series, Eisenhower Papers.

46. Ibid.

47. U.S. Congress, House, *Message from the President of the United States Relative to a Special Report of the National Advisory Council on the Proposed Inter-American Development Bank*, 86th Cong., 1st sess., 1959, H. Doc. 133, pp. 1–19.

48. House, Committee on Banking and Currency, *Hearings: Inter-American Development Bank Act*, p. 22; U.S. Congress, Senate, Committee on Foreign Relations, *Hearings: Inter-American Development Bank Act*, 86th Cong., 1st sess., 1959, pp. 26–27; *Congressional Quarterly Almanac* 15 (1959): 217.

49. U.S. Congress, House, Committee on Banking and Currency, *Hearings: Bretton Woods Agreement Act*, 86th Cong., 1st sess., 1959, pp. 1–16.

50. *Congressional Quarterly Almanac* 15 (1959): 195–96.

51. U.S. Congress, House, Committee on Banking and Currency, *Hearings: Increased Export-Import Bank Lending Authority*, 85th Cong., 2d sess., 1958, pp. 1–9.

52. House, Committee on Banking and Currency, *Hearings: Inter-American Development Bank Act*, pp. 34–35. See also Douglas Dillon to William H. Draper, Jr., February 12, 1959, Box 29, Webb Papers; Eisenhower to Robert P. Mullen, June 8, 1959, Box 27, DDE Diary Series, Eisenhower Papers.

53. The letter, dated August 25, 1958, was signed J. William Fulbright, Theodore Francis Green, John J. Sparkman, Hubert Humphrey, Mike Mansfield, Wayne Morse, John F. Kennedy, and William Langer, Jr. It is attached to Eisenhower to Draper, November 24, 1958, Box 29, Webb Papers.

54. *Congressional Quarterly Almanac* 14 (1958): 188.

55. Eisenhower to Draper, November 24, 1958, and attachment, Box 29, Webb Papers. See also Memorandum for Mr. Dillon from Christian Herter, November 12, 1958, Box 11, Herter Papers; Memorandum for the Record by Robert C. Merriam, November 24, 1958, Box 23, DDE Diary Series, Eisenhower Papers.

56. Special Message to Congress on the Mutual Security Program, March 13, 1959, *Public Papers of the Presidents of the United States: Dwight D. Eisenhower, 1959* (Washington, D.C., 1960), pp. 258–72.

57. See "Economic Development Aid," April 27, 1959, Box 29, Webb Papers; "Preliminary Conclusions of the President's Committee to Study the United States Military Assistance Program," March 17, 1959, Box 14, Administration Series, Eisenhower Papers.

58. Eisenhower to William H. Draper, Jr., March 18, 1959, attached to Draper to James E. Webb, March 21, 1959, Box 29, Webb Papers.

59. Memorandum of Conversation with the President, April 6, 1959, Box 7, Herter Papers.

60. Memorandum for the President from Herter, March 19, 1959, Box 25, DDE Diary Series, Eisenhower Papers; see also *Business Week*, March 28, 1959, p. 162.

61. *Congressional Quarterly Almanac* 15 (1959): 179; Annual Budget Message to Congress: Fiscal Year 1960, January 19, 1959, *Public Papers of the Presidents: Eisenhower, 1959*, p. 44; see also Statement by the President on the House Appropriations Committee's Rejection of the Development Loan Fund, March 20, 1959, ibid., pp. 290–91.

62. U.S. Congress, House, Committee on Foreign Affairs, *Mutual Security Act of 1959*, 86th Cong., 1st sess., 1959, H. Rep. 440, pp. 4–23 and 74.

63. *Congressional Quarterly Almanac* 15 (1959): 182–83.

64. Ibid., p. 184.

65. Memorandum of Conference with the President prepared by A. J. Goodpaster, May 22, 1959, Box 26, DDE Diary Series, Eisenhower Papers.

66. Saltonstall to Eisenhower, June 2, 1959, ibid.; see also Homer E. Capehart to Eisenhower, May 28, 1959, attached to Eisenhower to Capehart, June 4, 1959, ibid.

67. Eisenhower to Fulbright, June 4, 1959, ibid.; see also Fulbright to Eisenhower, May 25, 1959, ibid.

68. U.S. Congress, Senate, Committee on Foreign Relations, *The Mutual Security Act of 1959*, 86th Cong., 1st sess., 1959, S. Rept. 412, pp. 1–5 and 15–17.

69. Memorandum of Conference with the President by A. J. Goodpaster, June 17, 1979, Box 7, Herter Papers.

70. Memorandum for Dillon from Max V. Krebs, June 29, 1959, Box 7, Herter Papers; *Congressional Quarterly Almanac* 15 (1959): 187–88.

71. *Congressional Quarterly Almanac* 15 (1959): 188–89; Presidential News Conference, July 8, 1959, *Public Papers of the Presidents: Eisenhower, 1959*, pp. 513–14.

72. *Congressional Quarterly Almanac* 15 (1959): 191–94.

73. Legislative Meeting, September 8, 1959, Box 3, Legislative Meeting Series, Eisenhower Papers.

74. *Congressional Quarterly Almanac* 15 (1959): 194.

75. Statement by the President Following the Adjournment of the First Session of the Eighty-sixth Congress, September 20, 1959, *Public Papers of the Presidents: Eisenhower, 1959*, p. 225.

76. For a summary of the authorization legislation see *Congressional Quarterly Almanac* 15 (1959): 178–79.

77. Ibid.

78. Ibid.

CHAPTER 10

1. See Table 1, United States Balance of Payments, 1951–1959, attached to Memorandum to Council on Foreign Economic Policy prepared by Paul H. Cullen, November 10, 1955, OF-116-EE, Eisenhower Papers; see also Howard S. Piquet, *The U.S. Balance of Payments and International Monetary Reserves* (Washington, D.C., 1966), pp. 1–4.

2. Humphrey to Eisenhower, April 15, 1955, attached to Eisenhower to Humphrey, April 26, 1955, Box 22, Administration Series, Eisenhower Papers.

3. Eisenhower to Humphrey, April 26, 1955, ibid.; see also Telephone Call of Eisenhower to Humphrey, July 7, 1955, Box 5, DDE Diary Series, ibid.

4. Memorandum for Governor Adams prepared by Maxwell M. Rabb, n.d., Box 7, Cabinet Series, ibid.

5. Humphrey to Eisenhower, May 14, 1957, enclosing Leffingwell to H. C. A., February 18, 1957, Box 23, Administration Series, ibid.; see also Leffingwell to Humphrey, June 21, 1955, attached to Humphrey to Eisenhower, April 15, 1955, Box 22, ibid.

6. See the lengthy (forty-three-page) memorandum "Foreign Financial Issues Facing the United States," [1960], Box 2, ibid.; see also *Business Week*, September 26, 1959, p. 184.

7. Cabinet Paper, August 7, 1959, Box 1, Cabinet Series, Eisenhower Papers.

8. "Foreign Financial Issues Facing the United States," [1960], Box 2, Administration Series, ibid. See also Memorandum to Council on Foreign Economic Policy prepared by Paul H. Cullen, November 10, 1959, OF-116-EE, ibid.; *Business Week*, November 21, 1959, pp. 28–29.

9. Piquet, *The U.S. Balance of Payments*, pp. 13–15.

10. Paper on Foreign Economic Policy Issues prepared by Don Paarlberg, n.d., attached to Memorandum to Council on Foreign Economic Policy, November 10, 1959, OF-116-EE, Eisenhower Papers.

11. Ibid.; *Business Week*, October 31, 1959, p. 140.

12. Memorandum for Mr. Randall from Joseph Rand, July 10, 1959, Box 1, Rand Papers; *Congressional Quarterly Almanac* 15 (1959): 190.

13. Memorandum for the President prepared by Robert Anderson, December 3, 1959, Box 3, Administration Series, Eisenhower Papers.

14. *Business Week*, September 26, 1959.

15. Presidential News Conference, October 22, 1959, *Public Papers of the Presidents of the United States: Dwight D. Eisenhower, 1959* (Washington, D.C., 1960), p. 737.

16. Dillon to Fulbright, November 14, 1959, attached to Bradley Fisk to W. Ray Bell, May 11, 1960, 466.01, 1959, DOC Records.

17. Max Beloff, *The United States and the Unity of Europe* (Washington, D.C., 1963), esp. pp. 78–92; Randall Hinshaw, *The European Community and American Trade: A Study in Atlantic Economics and Politics* (New York, 1964), pp. 6–14 and 20–37; J. Robert Schaetzel, *The Unhinged Alliance: America and the European Community* (New York, 1975), pp. 36–40; Telegram for the President from the Acting Secretary, December 16, 1959, Box 12, Administration Series, Eisenhower Papers.

18. Milton J. Esman and Daniel S. Cheever, *The Common Aid Effort: The Development Assistance Activities of the Organization for Economic Co-operation and Development* (Columbus, Ohio, 1967), pp. 37–39 and 44–45; Telegram for the President from the Acting Secretary of State, December 16, 1959, Box 12, Administration Series, Eisenhower Papers.

19. Esman and Cheever, *The Common Aid Effort*, pp. 45–46.

20. Memorandum of Conversation: Segni Visit, September 30, 1959, Box 8, Herter Papers.

21. Ibid.

22. Memorandum for the President from the Secretary of the Treasury, December 2, 1959, Box 3, Administration Series, Eisenhower Papers.

23. Telegram for the President from the Acting Secretary of State, December 16, 1959, Box 12, ibid.

24. Memorandum for the President from the Secretary of the Treasury, December 2, 1959, Box 3, ibid.

25. Ibid.

26. Ibid.

27. Ibid.

28. Ibid.

29. Ibid.

30. Joint Statement concerning the Economic Agreements Reached at the Western Summit Conference, December 21, 1959, *Public Papers of the Presidents: Eisenhower, 1959*, p. 335.

31. *Business Week*, December 26, 1959, p. 65.

32. Telegram for the President from the Acting Secretary of State, December 16, 1959, Box 12, Administration Series, Eisenhower Papers.

33. Esman and Cheever, *The Common Aid Effort*, pp. 46–47; see also *Business Week*, January 2, 1960, p. 96.

34. Esman and Cheever, *The Common Aid Effort*, pp. 51–57.

35. Annual Budget Message to Congress: Fiscal Year 1962, January 16, 1961, *Public Papers of the Presidents of the United States: Dwight D. Eisenhower, 1960–1961* (Washington, D.C., 1961), p. 414; *Congressional Quarterly Almanac* 17 (1961): 332–34.

36. Annual Budget Message to Congress: Fiscal Year 1962, January 16, 1961, *Public Papers of the Presidents: Eisenhower, 1960–1961*, p. 414.

37. *Congressional Quarterly Almanac* 17 (1961): 332; Esman and Cheever, *The Common Aid Effort*, pp. 59–76.

38. Telephone Call of Eisenhower to Anderson, December 29, 1959, and Memorandum of Conference with the President prepared by A. J. Goodpaster, December 30, 1959, Box 29, DDE Diary Series, Eisenhower Papers; see also Esman and Cheever, *The Common Aid Effort*, pp. 48–49.

39. Dillon to C. D. Jackson, July 1, 1960, Box 38, Jackson Papers. See also Beloff, *The United States and the Unity of Europe*, p. 98; *Business Week*, January 23, 1960, p. 99.

40. Economic Notes prepared by Clarence B. Randall, September 14, 1960, and unsigned Memorandum for Mr. Randall, September 22, 1960, Box 2, Rand Papers. See also Hinshaw, *The European Community and American Trade*, pp. 21–29 and 37–47; Esman and Cheever, *The Common Aid Effort*, pp. 48–49 and 51.

41. Esman and Cheever, *The Common Aid Effort*, pp. 49–50.

42. Ibid., esp. pp. 341–44. See also Schaetzel, *The Unhinged Alliance*, p. 118; Richard N. Cooper, *The Economics of Interdependence: Economic Policy in the Atlantic Community* (New York, 1968), esp. pp. 193–202.

43. Cabinet Paper, August 7, 1959, Box 1, Cabinet Series, Eisenhower Papers. See also Memorandum for Mr. Randall prepared by C. Edward Galbreath, November 10, 1960, Box 2, Rand Papers; *Business Week*, September 26, 1959, p. 143; ibid., March 26, 1960, p. 134.

44. On this point see E. T. Benson to D. W. Brooks, July 22, 1960, Box 222, Records of the Department of Agriculture, RG 16, National Archives, Washington, D.C.

45. Davis to Dillon, August 5, 1958, and enclosure, Box 265, ibid.

46. Memorandum prepared by Joseph Rand, July 2, 1958, Chronological File 6–12/58, Rand Papers. As Trudy Peterson points out, however, even the Agriculture Department had at first expressed some doubts about the Davis Report. Secretary of Agriculture Benson warned, for example, that if the administration adopted the Food-for-Peace idea, "it might be accused of embracing a proposal favored by Senator [Hubert] Humphrey and others from the opposition camp." He was also concerned about the client relationship the program might create. But he soon changed his mind and advocated a version of the Davis plan. For Benson's comments and the reaction of the Agriculture Department to the Food-for-Peace concept, see Trudy Huskamp Peterson, *Agricultural Exports, Farm Income, and the Eisenhower Administration* (Lincoln, Nebr., 1980), pp. 88–89.

47. Memorandum prepared by Joseph Rand, July 2, 1958, Chronological File 6–12/58, Rand Papers; see also Memorandum for Mr. Randall from Joseph Rand, July 1, 1958, Box 2, Rand Papers.

48. Peterson, *Agricultural Exports*, pp. 88–89.

49. Annual Budget Message to Congress: Fiscal Year 1960, January 19, 1960, and Special Message to Congress on Agriculture, January 29, 1959, *Public Papers of the Presidents: Eisenhower, 1960–1961*, pp. 89–91 and 149–51; Peterson, *Agricultural Exports*, p. 89. According to Don Paarlberg, no one in the administration expected the proposal to result in the disposal of more surplus products. Its principal purpose was political (Memorandum for C. Edward Galbreath, August 5, 1960, Box 2, Rand Papers). While this may have been true, it does not negate the fact that one of the main purposes of the P.L. 480 program had always been and remained, even under its "Food-for-Peace" label, the disposal of America's farm surpluses.

50. See summaries of the Tokyo talks of the GATT held at the end of October and beginning of November, 1959, attached to Memorandum for Mr. Randall prepared by C. Edward Galbreath, November 6, 1959, Box 5, Rand Papers; see also Memorandum of Robert B. Schwanger to Martin Sorkin, December 23, 1959, Box 226, Records of the Department of Agriculture, RG 16.

51. Memorandum for Mr. Randall From C. Edward Galbreath, June 13, 1960, Box 2, Rand Papers; see also Peterson, *Agricultural Exports*, p. 90.

52. At a ministerial meeting of GATT in Tokyo the next year, Undersecretary of State Dillon urged the prompt removal of discriminatory restrictions against imports from dollar areas. He said that if "forward steps" were not taken, the trend toward greater freedom of trade might be reversed and there might be a resurgence of protectionism and restrictionism. However, during the plenary discussion of the waiver for U.S. agricultural import restrictions, Australia and a number of other GATT members expressed strong disappointment at the lack of progress by the United States in relaxing its waiver on agricultural imports. See summaries of the Tokyo talks of GATT held at the end of October and the beginning of November 1959, attached to Memorandum for Mr. Randall prepared by C. Edward Galbreath, November 6, 1959, Box 5, Rand Papers.

53. Memorandum for the President from Christian Herter, December 29, 1958, Box 6, Herter Papers.

54. Ibid.

55. J. H. Richter to Administrator, Deputy Administrator, FAS, March 21, 1960, Box 226, Records of the Department of Agriculture, RG 16. See also "A Proposal Regarding Agricultural Problems of U.S. Policy toward the Economy of the Free World," attached to R. B. Schwenger to Martin Sorkin, March 8, 1960, ibid.; Peterson, *Agricultural Exports*, pp. 114–15.

56. Clarence L. Miller to Thomas Mann, Box 222, Records of the Department of Agriculture, RG 16; see also "United States Delegation . . . Position Paper, Consultations on Agricultural Policies," April 22, 1960, Box 226, ibid.

57. Clarence L. Miller to Thomas Mann, Box 222, ibid.; "United States Delegation . . . Position Paper, Consultations on Agricultural Policies," April 22, 1960, Box 226, ibid.; Peterson, *Agricultural Exports*, pp. 115–16.

58. Statement of Mr. Randall, September 1, 1960, *Department of State Bulletin* 43 (September 19, 1960): 453–55; see also C. Edward Galbreath to Victor K. Scavullo, September 19, 1960, Box 2, Rand Papers.

59. Press Release, November 21, 1959, *Department of State Bulletin* 43 (December 12, 1960): 894–97; see also J. H. Richter to Max Myers, June 24, 1960, Box 226, Records of the Department of Agriculture, RG 16. In November, Assistant Secretary of Agriculture Clarence Miller wrote Undersecretary of State Dillon to express his appreciation for Dillon's efforts to move European countries with no balance-of-payments problems toward a more liberalized agricultural trade policy. But he also noted the "slowness" with which liberalization was taking place. "Nowhere is the situation more striking than in Germany," he remarked, "with its far-flung system of bilateral trade agreements and other discriminatory practices, involving farm products." He urged Dillon to press the issue of agricultural trade liberalization in his forthcoming talks with German leaders. Miller to Dillon, November 10, 1960, Box 222, Records of the Department of Agriculture, RG 16. Along these same lines see E. T. Benson to Senator Milton Young, December 23, 1960, ibid.

60. Memorandum for Record prepared by Wilton B. Persons, October 4, 1960, Box 6, Herter Papers.

61. Even the eclectic Yale University economist Robert Triffin, who strongly attacked the dependence of the international monetary system on the dollar and advocated increasing world liquidity by revamping the IMF into a central bank for central banks and allowing it to create loans and deposits, spoke out strongly against an increase in gold prices or the abandonment of free convertibility of the dollar into gold. Such actions, he said, "would be . . . sheer folly and a wanton crime against the people of this country, and against the friendly nations who have long accepted our financial leadership and placed their trust in the U.S. dollar and the integrity and intelligence of our monetary management" (Robert Triffin, *Gold and the Dollar Crisis: The Future of Convertibility* [New Haven, Conn., 1960], p. 232). See also Martin Mayer, *The Fate of the Dollar* (New York, 1980), pp. 53–63.

62. Memorandum for the Record prepared by Wilton B. Persons, October 4, 1960, Box 6, Herter Papers.

63. Ibid.

64. Ibid.

65. Ibid.

66. Ibid.

67. Memorandum of Conference with the President prepared by John S. D. Eisenhower, November 15, 1960, Box 35, DDE Diary Series, Eisenhower Papers.

68. Memorandum of Conference with the President prepared by A. J. Goodpaster, Box 6, Herter Papers. See also Minutes of Cabinet Meeting, October 7, 1960, Box 16, Cabinet Series, Eisenhower Papers; Memorandum of Telephone Conversation with the President, November 15, 1960, Box 10, Herter Papers.

69. Memorandum of Conference with the President prepared by John S. D. Eisenhower, November 15, 1960, Box 35, DDE Diary Series, Eisenhower Papers.

70. Presidential News Conference, November 16, 1960, *Public Papers of the Presidents: Eisenhower, 1960–1961*, pp. 861–62; see also Directive by the President concerning Steps to be Taken with Respect to the U.S. Balance of Payments, November 16, 1960, Box 2, Rand Papers.

71. Quoted in Mayer, *The Fate of the Dollar*, pp. 80–81.

72. Piquet, *The U.S. Balance of Payments*, pp. 33–38.

73. Anderson to Dillon, January 11, 1961, Box 2, Administration Series, Eisenhower Papers; Diary Entry, November 10, 1961, Box 35, DDE Diary Series, ibid.

CHAPTER 11

1. Anderson to Dillon, January 11, 1961, Box 2, Administration Series, Eisenhower Papers.

2. Dwight D. Eisenhower, *Waging Peace: The White House Years, 1955–1961* (New York, 1965), pp. 499–504.

3. Special Message to Congress on the Mutual Security Program, February 16, 1960, *Public Papers of the Presidents of the United States: Dwight D. Eisenhower, 1960–1961* (Washington, D.C., 1961), pp. 186–87.

4. Legislative Leadership Meeting, February 16, 1960, Box 3, Legislative Meeting Series, Eisenhower Papers.

5. Special Message to Congress on the Mutual Security Program, February 16, 1960, *Public Papers of the Presidents: Eisenhower, 1960–1961*, pp. 184–85; see also Outline of Proposed Message [early 1960], Box 30, DDE Diary Series, Eisenhower Papers. To deal with the problems of Africa, Eisenhower thought greater use should be made of the United Nations. As he remarked to Secretary of State Herter, the nations of Africa were "not naturally friendly," and if you "went along with Ghana for a bilateral [aid agreement], you ran into [the] jealousy of Sekou Toure." "While trying to help one," he concluded, "we incurred the enmity of all." Herter said he agreed fully with the president. Telephone Conversation of Secretary Herter with President Eisenhower, February 11, 1960, Box 10, Herter Papers.

6. Legislative Leadership Meeting, June 2, 1960, Box 3, Legislative Meeting Series, Eisenhower Papers.

7. Special Message to Congress on the Mutual Security Program, February 16, 1960, *Public Papers of the Presidents: Eisenhower, 1960–1961*, pp. 177–87. See also Legislative Leadership Meeting, February 16, 1960, Box 3, Legislative Meeting Series, Eisenhower Papers; Robert E. Merriam to James E. Webb, March 12, 1960, Box 29, Webb Papers.

8. D. Eisenhower, *Waging Peace*, pp. 520–33.

9. Milton S. Eisenhower, *The Wine is Bitter: The United States and Latin America* (New York, 1963), p. 248.

10. Ibid., p. 329; "Aid to Latin America," July 19, 1960, OF-116-J, Eisenhower Papers.

11. Eisenhower to Kubitschek, June 8, 1960, Box 4, International Series, Eisenhower Papers.

12. Presidential News Conference, July 11, 1960, *Public Papers of the Presidents: Eisenhower, 1960–1961*, pp. 57–71.

13. M. Eisenhower, *The Wine is Bitter*, pp. 249–50; *Congressional Quarterly Almanac* 16 (1960): 216–17; see also "Aid to Latin America," July 19, 1960, OF-116-J, Eisenhower Papers.

14. U.S. Congress, House, Committee on Foreign Affairs, *Hearings: Mutual Security Act of 1960*, 86th Cong., 2d sess., 1960, pp. 1 7 and 199–210.

15. U.S. Congress, House, Committee on Foreign Affairs, Mutual Security Act of 1960, 86th Cong., 2d sess., 1960, H. Rept. 1464, pp. 6–12.

16. *Congressional Quarterly Almanac* 16 (1960): 172–74.

17. U.S. Congress, Senate, Committee on Foreign Relations, *The Mutual Security Act of 1960*, 86th Cong., 2d sess., 1960, S. Rept. 1286, pp. 1–11.

18. *Congressional Quarterly Almanac* 16 (1960): 174–78.

19. Statement by the President upon Signing the Mutual Security Act of 1960, May 16, 1960, *Public Papers of the Presidents: Eisenhower, 1960–1961*, p. 421.

20. Legislative Leadership Meeting, May 10, 1960, Box 3, Legislative Meeting Series, Eisenhower Papers.

21. Ibid.; Memorandum for the Record, May 10, 1960, Box 32, DDE Diary Series, ibid.

22. Legislative Leadership Meeting, February 16, 1960, Box 3, Legislative Meeting Series, ibid.

23. D. Eisenhower, *Waging Peace*, pp. 547–48; Address at a Dinner Sponsored by the Committee for International Economic Growth and the Committee to Strengthen the Frontiers of Freedom, May 2, 1960, *Public Papers of the Presidents: Eisenhower, 1960–1961*, pp. 378–84.

24. Eisenhower to Jackson, May 14, 1960, attached to Bryce Harlow to Jackson, May 16, 1960, attached to C. D. Jackson to Bryce Harlow, May 18, 1960, Box 41, Jackson Papers.

25. Jackson to Bryce Harlow, May 18, 1960, ibid.

26. Charles C. Alexander, *Holding the Line: The Eisenhower Era, 1952–1961* (Bloomington, Ind., 1975), pp. 254–55.

27. Radio and Television Report to the American People on the Events in Paris, May 25, 1960, *Public Papers of the Presidents: Eisenhower, 1960–1961*, p. 445.

28. *New York Times*, May 15, 1960.

29. Ibid., May 16, 1960; *Congressional Quarterly Almanac* 16 (1960): 179; see also Legislative Leadership Meeting, Box 3, Legislative Meeting Series, Eisenhower Papers.

30. *Congressional Quarterly Almanac* 16 (1960): 179–82.

31. Special Message to Congress upon Its Reconvening, August 8, 1960, *Public Papers of the Presidents: Eisenhower, 1960–1961*, p. 615.

32. *Congressional Quarterly Almanac* 16 (1960): 182–84.

33. Legislative Leadership Meetings, June 28 and August 16, 1960, Box 3, Legislative Meeting Series, Eisenhower Papers.

34. *Congressional Quarterly Almanac* 16 (1960): 184.

35. Statement of the President concerning Mutual Security Appropriations, August 26, 1960, *Public Papers of the Presidents: Eisenhower, 1960–1961*, pp. 659–60.

36. *Congressional Quarterly Almanac* 16 (1960): 184; see also Richard N. Gardner, *New Directions in U.S. Foreign Policy* (New York, 1959), pp. 45 and 52–55.

CHAPTER 12

1. W. W. Rostow, *The Diffusion of Power: An Essay in Recent History* (New York, 1972), pp. 283 and 583–84; see also Robert A. Pastor, *Congress and the Policies of U.S. Foreign Economic Policy, 1929–1976* (Berkeley, Calif., 1980), pp. 256–57.

2. For two harsh and, in my view, unfair indictments of Eisenhower's Latin American policy, see Samuel L. Bailey, *The United States and the Development of South America, 1945–1975* (New York, 1976), p. 90, and F. Parkinson, *Latin America, the Cold War, and the World Powers, 1945–1973* (Beverly Hills, Calif., 1974), p. 52; see also Jerome Levinson and Juan de Onis, *The Alliance That Lost Its Way: A Critical Report on the Alliance for Progress* (Chicago, 1970), p. 36. For a more balanced view consult R. Harrison Wagner, *United States Policy toward Latin America: A Study in Domestic and International Politics* (Stanford, Calif., 1970). Commenting on the 1950s and early 1960s, Wagner notes that the United States "judged the relevance of any proposed form of inter-American cooperation in the light of its central concern, namely, preventing any event that might invite a challenge to United States military power in the Western Hemisphere. And it . . . attempted to accomplish this objective with the smallest possible drain on its political and economic resources" (ibid., p. 43).

3. *Congressional Quarterly Almanac* 16 (1960): 216–18.

4. Memorandum on Conference between President Eisenhower and President-elect Kennedy and Their Chief Advisers, January 19, 1961, Box 29A, President's Office, Files, Special Correspondence, John F. Kennedy Papers, John F. Kennedy Library, Boston, Mass.

5. Eisenhower to Kennedy, January 15, 1962, ibid.; see also Kennedy to Eisenhower, July 16, 1961, ibid.

6. Memorandum for the President prepared by Myer Feldman, October 10, 1962, ibid.

7. "The United States has long promoted a stronger, more independent and more united Europe, in close alliance with us," UN Ambassador Adlai Stevenson thus remarked in 1964. "Unfortunately, present trends seem to be toward stronger, more independent but less united European states in looser alliance with us." See Adlai E. Stevenson, *The Papers of Adlai E. Stevenson*, ed. Walter Johnson, 8 vols. (Boston, 1972–79), 6:632; see also Henry A. Kissinger, *The Troubled Partnership: A Re-appraisal of the Atlantic Alliance* (New York, 1965).

8. Walter M. Kotschnig, "The United Nations as an Instrument of Economic and Social Development," in *The Global Partnership*, ed. Richard N. Gardner and Max F. Millikan (New York, 1968), p. 21.

9. *Proceedings of the United Nations Conference on Trade and Development, Geneva, 23 March–16 June 1964*, 7 vols. (New York, 1964).

10. On this point see especially Independent Commission on International Development Issues, *North-South: A Programme for Survival* (Cambridge, Mass., 1980). Interestingly, the report has received considerable attention in Europe but not much in the United States. For a historical survey of U.S. views on political development abroad, see also Robert A. Packenham, *Liberal America and the Third World: Political Development Ideas in Foreign Aid and Social Science* (Princeton, N.J., 1973), esp. pp. 313–60.

11. Address in Houston before the Faculty and Students of Rice University, October 24, 1960, *Public Papers of the Presidents: Eisenhower, 1960–1961*, p. 800.

Selected Bibliography

This study is based primarily on the Presidential Papers of Dwight D. Eisenhower at the Dwight D. Eisenhower Library in Abilene, Kansas. The most important of the Eisenhower Papers are in the Ann Whitman Files, which are subdivided into several series. Of the series, the most germane to this work were the Cabinet Series, the DDE Diary Series, the Legislative Meeting Series, and the Administration Series.

Second in importance have been the Records of the Chairman, U.S. Council on Foreign Economic Policy, which are subdivided into the Joseph M. Dodge and Clarence B. Randall series. They are supplemented by the separate Records of the U.S. Council on Foreign Economic Policy. In this collection the Policy Papers series was especially useful.

Numerous other collections of private papers, mainly at the Eisenhower Library, also have been used extensively, as have the records of various government agencies. Finally, the Presidential Papers of Franklin D. Roosevelt, Harry S. Truman, and John F. Kennedy have provided useful information on a number of matters related to this study.

Also essential to this study have been various congressional and other government publications, particularly the hearings and reports accompanying the annual mutual security authorization bills and the extension of the Trade Agreements Act in 1955 and 1958. The *Public Papers of the Presidents of the United States: Dwight D. Eisenhower* has been an indispensable source for Eisenhower's public statements and news conferences.

To fill in gaps various magazines and newspapers were consulted, most notably *Business Week*, *Journal of Commerce*, and the *New York Times*. Indispensable for tracing the history of major legislation through Congress was the *Congressional Quarterly Almanac*, which also contained useful background information not easily obtained elsewhere.

PRIMARY SOURCES

Manuscript Collections

Dwight D. Eisenhower Library, Abilene, Kans.
Dillon Anderson Oral Interview
Eugene Black Oral Interview
Harry A. Bullis Papers

Joseph M. Dodge Papers
John Foster Dulles Papers
Dwight D. Eisenhower Papers
Milton S. Eisenhower Papers
Gabriel Hauge Papers
Christian A. Herter Papers
John B. Hollister Oral Interview
C. D. Jackson Papers
Joseph Rand Papers
U.S. Council on Foreign Economic Policy, Records
U.S. Council on Foreign Economic Policy, Office of the Chairman, Records
U.S. President's Citizen Advisors on the Mutual Security Program Records
U.S. President's Commission on Foreign Economic Policy, Records
Samuel C. Waugh Papers
      John F. Kennedy Library, Boston, Mass.
John F. Kennedy Papers
      Franklin D. Roosevelt Library, Hyde Park, N.Y.
Franklin D. Roosevelt Papers
      Harry S. Truman Library, Independence, Mo.
Harry S. Truman Papers
James E. Webb Papers
      Western Reserve Historical Society, Cleveland, Ohio
George M. Humphrey Papers
      Dartmouth College Library, Hanover, N.H.
Sherman Adams Papers
Sinclair Weeks Papers
      National Archives, Washington, D.C.
Records of the Department of Agriculture, RG 16
Records of the Export-Import Bank, RG 275
Records of the Federal Trade Commission, RG 122
Records of the Department of the Treasury, RG 56
      U.S. Department of Commerce, Washington, D.C.
Records of the Department of Commerce
      U.S. Department of Justice, Washington, D.C.
Records of the Department of Justice, Oil Cartel Case, 60-57-140

Government Publications

Commission on Foreign Economic Policy. *Report to the President and the Congress.* Washington, D.C., 1954.

———. *Staff Papers Presented to the Commission on Foreign Economic Policy.* Washington, D.C., 1954.

Council on Environmental Quality and Department of State. *The Global 2000 Report to the President: Entering the Twenty-first Century.* 2 vols. Washington, D.C., 1980.

Federal Trade Commission. *Report on the Copper Industry.* Washington, D.C., 1947.

———. *Report on Fertilizer Industry.* Washington, D.C., 1950.

———. *Report on International Cartels in the Alkali Industry.* Washington, D.C., 1950.

————. *Report on the International Electric Equipment Industry*. Washington, D.C., 1948.

————. *Report on International Steel Cartels*. Washington, D.C., 1948.

————. *Report on the Sulfur Industry and International Cartels*. Washington, D.C., 1947.

International Development Advisory Board. *A New Emphasis on Economic Development Abroad*. Washington, D.C., 1957.

————. *Partners in Progress: A Report to the President by the International Development Advisory Board*. Washington, D.C., 1951.

The Organization and Administration of the Military Assistance Program. Washington, D.C., 1959.

Public Advisory Board for Mutual Security. *A Trade and Tariff Policy in the National Interest*. Washington, D.C., 1953.

Public Papers of the Presidents of the United States: Dwight D. Eisenhower. Washington, D.C., 1958–61.

Report of the Attorney General's National Committee to Study the Antitrust Laws. Washington, D.C., 1955.

Report of the Committee on World Economic Practices. Washington, D.C., 1959.

Report to the President by the President's Citizen Advisers on the Mutual Security Program, March 1, 1957. Washington, D.C., 1957.

Straus, Ralph I. *Expanding Private Investment for Free World Economic Growth*. Washington, D.C., 1959.

U.S. Congress, Committee on Conference. *Conference Report: Extension and Amendment of Public Law 480*. 85th Cong., 2d sess., 1958, H. Rept. 2694.

————, ————. *Conference Report: Mutual Security Act of 1959*. 85th Cong., 2d sess., 1958, H. Rept. 2704.

————, ————. *Conference Report: Mutual Security Act of 1960*. 86th Cong., 2d sess., 1960, H. Rept. 1593.

U.S. Congress, House. *Message from the President of the United States Relative to a Special Report of the National Advisory Council on the Proposed Inter-American Development Bank*. 86th Cong., 1st sess., 1959, H. Doc. 133.

————, ————. *Special Report of the National Advisory Council on the Proposed International Development Association*. 86th Cong., 2nd sess., 1960, H. Doc. 345.

————, ————. Committee on Agriculture. *Extension of Public Law 480*. 85th Cong., 1st sess., 1957, H. Rept. 432.

————, ————, ————. *Hearings: Extend Public Law 480*. 85th Cong., 2d sess., 1958.

————, ————, Committee on Appropriations. *Hearings: Mutual Security Appropriations for 1960*. 86th Cong., 2d sess., 1960.

————, ————, ————. *Mutual Security and Related Agencies Appropriation Bill, 1961*. 86th Cong., 2d sess., 1960, H. Rept. 1798.

————, ————, ————. *Mutual Security Appropriation Bill, 1958*. 85th Cong., 1st sess., 1957, H. Rept. 1172.

————, ————, Committee on Banking and Currency. *Bretton Woods Agreement Act*. 86th Cong., 1st sess., 1959, H. Rept. 225.

————, ————, ————. *Export-Import Bank Act Amendments of 1954*. 83d Cong., 2d sess., 1954, H. Rept. 2270.

————, ————, ————. *Extension of Export Control Act of 1949*. 86th Cong., 2d sess., 1960, H. Rept. 1415.

————, ————, ————. *Hearings: Increased Export-Import Bank Lending Authority.* 85th Cong., 2d sess., 1958.

————, ————, ————. *Hearings: Independent Management, Export-Import Bank.* 83d Cong., 2d sess., 1954.

————, ————, ————. *Hearings: Inter-American Development Bank Act.* 86th Cong., 1st sess., 1959.

————, ————, ————. *Hearings: International Development Association Act.* 86th Cong., 2d sess., 1960.

————, ————, ————. *International Development Association.* 86th Cong., 2d sess., 1960, H. Rept. 1766.

————, ————, Committee on Foreign Affairs. *Hearings: Mutual Security Act of 1954.* 83d Cong., 2d sess., 1954.

————, ————, ————. *Hearings: Mutual Security Act of 1957.* 85th Cong., 1st sess., 1957.

————, ————, ————. *Hearings: Mutual Security Act of 1958.* 85th Cong., 2d sess., 1958.

————, ————, ————. *Hearings: Mutual Security Act of 1959.* 86th Cong., 1st sess., 1959.

————, ————, ————. *Hearings: Mutual Security Act of 1960.* 86th Cong., 2d sess., 1960.

————, ————, ————. *Mutual Security Act of 1954.* 83d Cong., 2d sess., 1954, H. Rept. 1925.

————, ————, ————. *Mutual Security Act of 1955.* 84th Cong., 1st sess., 1955, H. Rept. 912.

————, ————, ————. *Mutual Security Act of 1956: Minority View.* 84th Cong., 2d sess., 1956, H. Rept. 2213.

————, ————, ————. *Mutual Security Act of 1957.* 85th Cong., 1st sess., 1957, H. Rept. 776.

————, ————, ————. *Mutual Security Act of 1958.* 85th Cong., 2d sess., 1958, H. Rept. 1696.

————, ————, ————. *Mutual Security Act of 1959.* 86th Cong., 1st sess., 1959, H. Rept. 440.

————, ————, ————. *Mutual Security Act of 1960.* 86th Cong., 2d sess., 1960, H. Rept. 1464.

————, ————, ————. *Report of the Special Study Mission to Asia, Western Pacific, Middle East, Southern Europe, and North Africa.* 86th Cong., 2d sess., 1960, H. Rept. 1386.

————, ————, ————. *Report on Foreign Policy and Mutual Security.* 85th Cong., 1st sess., 1957, H. Rept. 551.

————, ————, ————. *Report on United States Relations with Latin America.* 86th Cong., 1st sess., 1959, H. Rept. 354.

————, ————, Committee on Government Operations. *Hearings: Operations of the Development Loan Fund.* 86th Cong., 2d sess., 1960.

————, ————, ————. *Operations of the Development Loan Fund.* 86th Cong., 2d sess., 1960, H. Rept. 1526.

————, ————, Committee on the Judiciary. *Hearings: Current Antitrust Problems.* 84th Cong., 1st sess., 1955.

———, ———, Committee on Ways and Means. *Hearings: Foreign Investment Incentive Act.* 86th Cong., 1st sess., 1959.

———, ———, ———. *Hearings: Foreign Trade Policy.* 85th Cong., 1st sess., 1957.

———, ———, ———. *Hearings: Organization for Trade Cooperation.* 84th Cong., 2d sess., 1956.

———, ———, ———. *Hearings: Private Foreign Investment.* 85th Cong., 2d sess., 1958.

———, ———, ———. *Hearings: Renewal of Trade Agreements Act.* 85th Cong., 2d sess., 1958.

———, ———, ———. *Hearings: Trade Agreements Extension.* 84th Cong., 1st sess., 1955.

———, ———, ———. *Overall Limitation on Foreign Tax Credit.* 86th Cong., 2d sess., 1960, H. Rept. 1358.

———, ———, ———. *Trade Agreements Extension Act of 1953.* 83d Cong., 1st sess., 1953, H. Rept. 521.

———, ———, ———. *Trade Agreements Extension Act of 1955.* 84th Cong., 1st sess., 1955, H. Rept. 50.

———, ———, ———. *Trade Agreements Extension Act of 1958.* 85th Cong., 2d sess., 1958, H. Rept. 1761.

———, ———, ———. Subcommittee on Foreign Trade Policy. *Foreign Trade Policy: Compendium of Papers on United States Foreign Trade Policy.* 85th Cong., 2d sess., 1958.

———, Joint Economic Committee. *Dimensions of Soviet Economic Power: Studies Prepared for Economic Committee.* 87th Cong., 2d sess., 1962, joint committee print.

———, ———. *Economic Policies and Programs in South America.* 87th Cong., 2d sess., 1962, joint committee print.

———, ———. *Economic Policies toward Less Developed Countries.* 87th Cong., 1st sess., 1961, joint committee print.

———, ———. *Foreign Economic Policy.* 84th Cong., 2d sess., 1956, S. Rept. 1312.

———, ———. *Hearings: Foreign Economic Policy.* 84th Cong., 1st sess., 1955.

———, ———. *Hearings: World Economic Growth.* 84th Cong., 2d sess., 1956.

U.S. Congress, Senate. *A Review of United States Government Operations in Latin America.* 86th Cong., 1st sess., 1959, S. Doc. 13.

———, ———, Committee on Agriculture and Forestry. *Extension and Amendment of Public Law 480.* 85th Cong., 2d sess., 1958, S. Rept. 1357.

———, ———, ———. *Extension of Public Law 480.* 85th Cong., 1st sess., 1957, S. Rept. 188.

———, ———, ———. *Extension of Public Law 480.* 85th Cong., 2d sess., 1958, S. Rept. 1323.

———, ———, ———. *Hearings: Extension of Public Law 480.* 85th Cong., 1st sess., 1957.

———, ———, ———. *Hearings: Policies and Operations under Public Law 480.* 85th Cong., 1st sess., 1957.

———, ———, ———. *Hearings: Public Law 480 Extension.* 85th Cong., 2d sess., 1958.

————, ————, Committee on Appropriations. *Mutual Security Appropriations Bill, 1954.* 83d Cong., 1st sess., 1953, S. Rept. 645.

————, ————, ————. *Mutual Security Appropriations Bill, 1956.* 84th Cong., 1st sess., 1955, S. Rept. 1033.

————, ————, ————. *Mutual Security Appropriations Bill, 1958.* 85th Cong., 1st sess., 1957, S. Rept. 1117.

————, ————, Committee on Armed Services, Preparedness Subcommittee No. 6. *Hearings: Essentiality to the National Defense of the Domestic Horological Industry.* 83d Cong., 2d sess., 1954.

————, ————, Committee on Banking and Currency. *The Defense Production Act of 1950.* 81st Cong., 2d sess., 1950, S. Rept. 2250.

————, ————, ————. *Export-Import Bank Act Amendments of 1954.* 83d Cong., 2d sess., 1954, S. Rept. 1624.

————, ————, ————. *Hearings: International Development Association.* 85th Cong., 2d sess., 1958.

————, ————, ————. *Hearings: International Finance Corporation.* 84th Cong., 1st sess., 1955.

————, ————, ————. *Hearings: Study of Export-Import Bank and World Bank.* 83d Cong., 2d sess., 1954.

————, ————, ————. *Hearings: U.S. Private Foreign Investment.* 86th Cong., 1st sess., 1959.

————, ————, Committee on Government Operations. *East-West Trade.* 84th Cong., 2d sess., 1956, S. Rept. 2621.

————, ————, Committee on Finance. *Hearings: Foreign Investment Incentive Tax Act of 1960.* 86th Cong., 2d sess., 1960.

————, ————, ————. *Hearings: Import Tax on Lead and Zinc.* 85th Cong., 1st sess., 1957.

————, ————, ————. *Hearings: Trade Agreements Act Extension.* 85th Cong., 2d sess., 1958.

————, ————, ————. *Hearings: Trade Agreements Extension.* 84th Cong., 1st sess., 1955.

————, ————, ————. *Trade Agreements Extension Act of 1953.* 83d Cong., 1st sess., 1953, S. Rept. 472.

————, ————, ————. *Trade Agreements Extension Act of 1955.* 84th Cong., 1st sess., 1955, S. Rept. 232.

————, ————, ————. *Trade Agreements Extension Act of 1958.* 85th Cong., 2d sess., 1958, S. Rept. 1838.

————, ————, Committee on Foreign Relations. *Arranging for Exhaustive Studies to Be Made Regarding Foreign Assistance by the United States.* 84th Cong., 2d sess., 1956, S. Rept. 2278.

————, ————, ————. *Hearings: Inter-American Development Bank Act.* 86th Cong., 1st sess., 1959.

————, ————, ————. *Hearings: International Wheat Agreement of 1956.* 84th Cong., 2d sess., 1956.

————, ————, ————. *Hearings: Mutual Security Act of 1954.* 83rd Cong., 2d sess., 1954.

————, ————, ————. *Hearings: Mutual Security Act of 1955.* 84th Cong., 1st sess., 1955.

————, ————, ————. *Hearings: Mutual Security Act of 1956.* 84th Cong., 2d sess., 1956.

————, ————, ————. *Hearings: Mutual Security Act of 1957.* 85th Cong., 1st sess., 1957.

————, ————, ————. *Hearings: Mutual Security Act of 1958.* 85th Cong., 2d sess., 1958.

————, ————, ————. *Hearings: Mutual Security Act of 1959.* 86th Cong., 1st sess., 1959.

————, ————, ————. *Hearings: Mutual Security Act of 1960.* 86th Cong., 2d sess., 1960.

————, ————, ————. *Hearings: Organization for Economic Cooperation and Development.* 87th Cong., 1st sess., 1961.

————, ————, ————. *Hearings: Review of Foreign Policy, 1958.* 85th Cong., 2d sess., 1958.

————, ————, ————. *The International Petroleum Cartel, the Iranian Consortium, and U.S. National Security.* 93d Cong., 2d sess., 1974, committee print.

————, ————, ————. *Multinational Corporations and U.S. Foreign Policy.* 94th Cong., 1st sess., 1975, committee print.

————, ————, ————. *The Mutual Security Act of 1954.* 83d Cong., 2d sess., 1954, S. Rept. 1799.

————, ————, ————. *The Mutual Security Act of 1955.* 84th Cong., 1st sess., 1955, S. Rept. 383.

————, ————, ————. *The Mutual Security Act of 1956.* 84th Cong., 2d sess., 1956, S. Rept. 2273.

————, ————, ————. *The Mutual Security Act of 1957.* 85th Cong., 1st sess., 1957, S. Rept. 417.

————, ————, ————. *The Mutual Security Act of 1958.* 85th Cong., 2d sess., 1958, S. Rept. 1627.

————, ————, ————. *The Mutual Security Act of 1959.* 86th Cong., 1st sess., 1959, S. Rept. 412.

————, ————, ————. *The Mutual Security Act of 1960.* 86th Cong., 2d sess., 1960, S. Rept. 1286.

————, ————, ————. *Study of Foreign Aid Program.* 85th Cong., 1st sess., 1957, S. Rept. 2.

————, ————, ————. *United States-Latin American Relations: Compilation of Studies.* 86th Cong., 2d sess., 1960, S. Doc. 125.

————, ————, Committee on the Judiciary. *Antitrust and Monopoly.* 85th Cong., 1st sess., 1957, S. Rept. 128.

————, ————, ————. *Hearings: Foreign Trade and the Antitrust Laws.* 88th Cong., 2d sess., 1964.

————, ————, ————. *Hearings: International Aspects of Antitrust.* 90th Cong., 1st sess., 1967.

————, ————, ————. *Hearings: A Study of the Antitrust Laws.* 84th Cong., 1st sess., 1955.

————, ————, ————. *Petroleum, the Antitrust Laws, and Government Policies.* 85th Cong., 1st sess., 1957, S. Rept. 1147.

————, ————, ————. *Trading with the Enemy Act.* 85th Cong., 1st sess., 1957, S. Rept. 120.

————, ————, Committee on the Judiciary and on Interior. *Joint Hearings: Emergency Oil Lift Program and Related Problems.* 85th Cong., 1st sess., 1957.

————, ————, Committee on Rules and Administration. *Study of the Trading with the Enemy and War Claims Act.* 85th Cong., 1st sess., 1957, S. Rept. 24.

————, ————, Select Committee on Small Business. *The International Petroleum Cartel: Staff Report to the Federal Trade Commission.* 82d Cong., 2d sess., 1952, Committee Print no. 6.

————, ————, Special Committee to Study the Foreign Aid Program. *Foreign Aid Program: Compilation of Studies and Surveys.* 85th Cong., 1st sess., 1957, S. Rept. 52.

————, ————, ————. *Foreign Aid: Report of the Special Committee to Study the Foreign Aid Program,* 85th Cong., 1st sess., 1957, S. Rept. 300.

————, ————, ————. *Hearings: Foreign Aid Program.* 85th Cong., 1st sess., 1957.

U.S. Department of State. *Analysis of General Agreement on Tariffs and Trade Signed at Geneva, October 30, 1947,* Commercial Policy Series, no. 109. Washington, D.C., 1947.

————. *Analysis of Protocol of Accession and Schedules to the General Agreement on Tariffs and Trade Negotiated at Annecy, France, April–August 1949,* Commercial Policy Series, no. 120. Washington, D.C., 1949.

————. *Analysis of Torquay Protocol of Accession, Schedules, and Related Documents: General Agreement on Tariffs and Trade Negotiated at Torquay, England, September 1950–April 1951,* Commercial Policy Series, no. 135. Washington, D.C., 1951.

————. *Department of State Bulletin.*

————. *A Constitution for World Trade,* Commercial Policy Series, no. 108. Washington, D.C., 1947.

————. *A Review of Foreign Economic Policy,* Economic Cooperation Series, no. 50. Washington, D.C., 1959.

————. *The Sino-Soviet Economic Offensive in the Less Developed Countries,* Europe and British Commonwealth Series, no. 51. Washington, D.C., 1958.

Books and Articles

Adams, Sherman. *First Hand Report: The Story of the Eisenhower Administration.* New York, 1961.

Bendliner, Robert. "The Apostasy of Homer Capehart." *Reporter,* May 12, 1953, pp. 30–32.

Benson, Ezra Taft. *Cross Fire: The Eight Years with Eisenhower.* New York, 1962.

Eisenhower, Dwight D. *Crusade in Europe.* New York, 1948.

————. *The White House Years: Mandate for Change, 1953–1956.* Garden City, N.Y., 1963.

————. *The White House Years: Waging Peace, 1956–1961.* Garden City, N.Y., 1965.

Eisenhower, Milton. *The Wine Is Bitter: The United States and Latin America.* New York, 1963.

Hughes, Emmet John. *The Ordeal of Power: A Political Memoir of the Eisenhower Years.* New York, 1963.

Knorr, Klaus, and Patterson, Gardner. *A Critique of the Randall Commission Report*. Princeton, N.J.: Princeton University, International Finance Section and Center for International Studies, 1954.

Lodge, Henry Cabot. *As It Was: An Inside View of Politics and Power in the '50s and '60s*. New York, 1976.

Millikan, Max F., and Rostow, W. W. *A Proposal: Key to an Effective Foreign Policy*. New York, 1957.

Stevenson, Adlai E. *The Papers of Adlai E. Stevenson*. Edited by Walter Johnson. 8 vols. Boston, 1972–79.

Other Primary Sources

Business Week

Congressional Digest

Congressional Quarterly Almanac

General Agreement on Tariffs and Trade. *Trends in International Trade: A Report by a Panel of Experts*. Geneva, 1958.

Journal of Commerce

New York Times

Proceedings of the United Nations Conference on Trade and Development, Geneva, 23 March–16 June, 1964. 7 vols. New York.

United Nations, Statistical Office. *World Energy Supplies, 1951–1954*. New York, 1956.

————, ————. *World Energy Supplies, 1955–1958*. New York, 1960.

SECONDARY SOURCES

Books

Alexander, Charles C. *Holding the Line: The Eisenhower Era, 1952–1961*. Bloomington, Ind., 1975.

Allen, Robert Loring. *Soviet Economic Warfare*. Washington, D.C., 1960.

Ambrose, Stephen E. *Rise to Globalism: American Foreign Policy since 1938*. London, 1971.

Bailey, Samuel L. *The United States and the Development of South America, 1945–1975*. New York, 1976.

Baldwin, David A. *Economic Development and American Foreign Policy, 1943–62*. Chicago, 1966.

————, ed. *Foreign Aid and American Foreign Policy: A Documentary Analysis*. New York, 1966.

Barnet, Richard J. *Intervention and Revolution: The United States in the Third World*. New York, 1968.

Bauer, Raymond; De Sola Pool, Ithiel; and Dexter, Lewis Anthony. *American Business and Public Policy: The Politics of Foreign Trade*. Chicago, 1972.

Beloff, Max. *The United States and the Unity of Europe*. Washington, D.C., 1963.

Bergsten, C. Fred. *The Dilemmas of the Dollar: The Economics and Politics of United States Monetary Policy*. New York, 1975.

Berliner, Joseph S. *Soviet Economic Aid: The New Aid and Trade Policy in the Underdeveloped Countries*. New York, 1958.

Blair, John M. *The Control of Oil.* New York, 1976.

Block, Fred L. *The Origins of International Economic Disorder: A Study of United States International Monetary Policy from World War II to the Present.* Berkeley, Calif., 1977.

Bohi, Douglas R., and Russell, Milton. *Limiting Oil Imports: An Economic History and Analysis.* Baltimore, 1978.

Brewster, Kingman, Jr. *Antitrust and American Business Abroad.* New York, 1958.

Camps, Miriam. *Britain and the European Community, 1955–1963.* Princeton, N.J., 1962.

Childs, Marquis. *Eisenhower, Captive Hero: A Cabinet Study of the General and the President.* New York, 1958.

Clark, Paul G. *American Aid for Development.* New York, 1972.

Cleveland, Harold van B. *The Atlantic Idea and Its European Rivals.* New York, 1966.

Cooper, Richard N. *The Economics of Interdependence: Economic Policy in the Atlantic Community.* New York, 1968.

Coppock, Joseph D. *International Economic Instability: The Experience after World War II.* New York, 1962.

Corbet, Hugh, and Robertson, David, eds. *Europe's Free Trade Area Experiment: EFTA and Economic Integration.* New York, 1970.

Curzon, Gerard, and Curzon, Victoria, eds. *The Multinational Enterprise in a Hostile World: Proceedings of a Conference Held in Geneva.* New York, 1977.

Dell, Sidney. *The Inter-American Development Bank: A Study in Development Financing.* New York, 1972.

DeWitt, R. Peter, Jr. *The Inter-American Development Bank and Political Influence: With Special Reference to Costa Rica.* New York, 1977.

Diebold, William, Jr. *The United States and the Industrial World: American Foreign Economic Policy in the 1970s.* New York, 1972.

Divine, Robert A. *Blowing on the Wind: The Nuclear Test Ban Debate, 1954–1960.* New York, 1978.

Eckes, Alfred E., Jr. *A Search for Solvency: Bretton Woods and the International Monetary System, 1941–1971.* Austin, Tex., 1975.

————. *The United States and the Global Struggle for Minerals.* Austin, Tex., 1979.

Ellis, Howard S., ed. *Economic Development for Latin America: Proceedings of a Conference Held by the International Economic Association.* London, 1961.

Engler, Robert. *The Brotherhood of Oil: Energy Policy and the Public Interest.* Chicago, 1977.

————. *The Politics of Oil: A Study of Private Power and Democratic Institutions.* New York, 1961.

Esman, Milton J., and Cheever, Daniel S. *The Common Aid Effort: The Development Assistance Activities of the Organization for Economic Co-operation and Development.* Columbus, Ohio, 1967.

Finer, Herbert. *Dulles over Suez: The Theory and Practice of His Diplomacy.* Chicago, 1964.

Fugate, Wilbur Lindsay. *Foreign Commerce and the Antitrust Laws.* Boston, 1973.

Gaddis, John Lewis. *Russia, the Soviet Union, and the United States: An Interpretive History*. New York, 1978.

————. *The United States and the Origins of the Cold War, 1941–1947*. New York, 1972.

Gardner, Richard N. *In Pursuit of World Order: U.S. Foreign Policy and International Organizations*. New York, 1965.

————. *New Directions in U.S. Foreign Policy*. New York, 1959.

————. *Sterling-Dollar Diplomacy: The Origins and the Prospects of Our International Economic Order*. 2d ed. New York, 1969.

Gordon, Lincoln. *A New Deal for Latin America: The Alliance for Progress*. Cambridge, Mass., 1963.

Hanson, Simon G. *Five Years of the Alliance for Progress: An Appraisal*. Washington, D.C., 1967.

Hayter, Teresa. *Aid as Imperialism*. Harmondsworth, England, 1971.

Higgins, Benjamin. *United Nations and U.S. Foreign Economic Policy*. Homewood, Ill., 1962.

Hinshaw, Randall. *The European Community and American Trade: A Study in Atlantic Economics and Policy*. New York, 1964.

Hoopes, Townsend. *The Devil and John Foster Dulles*. Boston, 1973.

Hudson, Michael. *Super Imperialism: The Economic Strategy of American Empire*. New York, 1969.

Johnson, Harry G. *Economic Policies toward Less Developed Countries*. Washington, D.C., 1967.

Jones, Hywel G. *An Introduction to Modern Theories of Economic Growth*. London, 1975.

Kaplan, Jacob J. *The Challenge of Foreign Aid: Policies, Problems, Possibilities*. New York, 1967.

Kaufman, Burton I. *The Oil Cartel Case: A Documentary Study of Antitrust Activity in the Cold War Era*. Westport, Conn., 1978.

Kissinger, Henry A. *The Troubled Partnership: A Re-appraisal of the Atlantic Alliance*. New York, 1965.

Kolko, Gabriel. *The Roots of American Foreign Policy*. Boston, 1969.

Kolko, Joyce, and Kolko, Gabriel. *The Limits of Power: The World and United States Foreign Policy, 1945–1954*. New York, 1972.

Krause, Lawrence B. *European Economic Integration and the United States*. Washington, D.C., 1968.

Larson, Arthur. *Eisenhower: The President Nobody Knew*. New York, 1968.

Levinson, Jerome, and de Onis, Juan. *The Alliance That Lost Its Way: A Critical Report on the Alliance for Progress*. Chicago, 1970.

Lyon, Peter. *Eisenhower: Portrait of the Hero*. Boston, 1974.

McClellan, Grant S., ed. *U.S. Foreign Aid*. New York, 1957.

MacDougall, Donald. *The World Dollar Problem: A Study in International Economics*. London, 1957.

Magdoff, Harry. *The Age of Imperialism: The Economics of U.S. Foreign Policy*. New York, 1969.

Matecki, B. E. *Establishment of the International Finance Corporation and United States Policy: A Case Study in International Organization*. New York, 1957.

Mayer, Martin. *The Fate of the Dollar*. New York, 1980.

Mende, Tibor. *From Aid to Re-colonization: Lessons of a Failure*. New York, 1973.

Mikesell, Raymond F., and Behrman, Jack N. *Financing Free World Trade with the Sino-Soviet Bloc*. Princeton, N.J., 1958.

Montgomery, John D. *The Politics of Foreign Aid: American Experience in Southeast Asia*. New York, 1962.

Moore, Barrington, Jr. *Reflections on the Causes of Human Misery and upon Certain Proposals to Eliminate Them*. Boston, 1970.

Moran, Theodore H. *Multinational Corporations and the Politics of Dependence: Copper in Chile*. Princeton, N.J., 1974.

Morawetz, David. *Twenty-Five Years of Economic Development*. Baltimore, 1977.

Nurkse, Ragnar. *Problems of Capital Formation in Underdeveloped Countries*. New York, 1953.

O'Leary, Michael Kent. *The Politics of American Foreign Aid*. New York, 1967.

Packenham, Robert A. *Liberal America and the Third World: Political Development Ideas in Foreign Aid and Social Science*. Princeton, N.J., 1973.

Parkinson, F. *Latin America, the Cold War, and the World Powers, 1945–1973*. Beverly Hills, Calif., 1974.

Parmet, Herbert S. *Eisenhower and the American Crusades*. New York, 1972.

Paterson, Thomas G. *Soviet-American Confrontation: Postwar Reconstruction and the Origins of the Cold War*. Baltimore, 1973.

Payer, Cheryl. *The Debt Trap: The IMF and the Third World*. Harmondsworth, England, 1974.

Perloff, Harvey S. *Alliance for Progress: A Social Invention in the Making*. Baltimore, 1969.

Peterson, Trudy Huskamp. *Agricultural Exports, Farm Income, and the Eisenhower Administration*. Lincoln, Nebr., 1979.

Pincus, John. *Trade, Aid, and Development: The Rich and Poor Nations*. New York, 1967.

Piquet, Howard S. *The U.S. Balance of Payments and International Monetary Reserves*. Washington, D.C., 1966.

Price, Harry Bayard. *The Marshall Plan and Its Meaning*. Ithaca, N.Y., 1955.

Ranis, Gustav, ed. *The United States and the Developing Economies*. New York, 1973.

Reichard, Gary W. *The Reaffirmation of Republicanism: Eisenhower and the Eighty-third Congress*. Knoxville, Tenn., 1975.

Richardson, Elmo. *The Presidency of Dwight D. Eisenhower*. Lawrence, Kans., 1979.

Robinson, James A. *The Monroney Resolution: Congressional Initiative in Foreign Policy Making*. New York, 1959.

Roosa, Robert V. *The Dollar and World Liquidity*. New York, 1967.

Rostow, W. W. *The Diffusion of Power: An Essay in Recent History*. New York, 1972.

_____. *The United States in the World Arena: An Essay in Recent History*. Paperback edition. New York, 1969.

Rubinstein, Alvin Z. *The Soviets in International Organizations: Changing Policy toward Developing Countries, 1953–1963.* Princeton, N.J., 1964.

Sampson, Anthony. *The Seven Sisters: The Great Oil Companies and the World They Made.* New York, 1975.

Schaetzel, Robert. *The Unhinged Alliance: America and the European Community.* New York, 1975.

Schwadran, Benjamin. *The Middle East and the Great Powers.* New York, 1973.

Solberg, Carl. *Oil Power: The Rise and Imminent Fall of an American Empire.* New York, 1976.

Stanley, Robert G. *Food for Peace: Hope and Reality of U.S. Food Aid.* New York, 1973.

Steel, Ronald. *The End of Alliance: America and the Future of Europe.* New York, 1964.

Tansky, Leo. *U.S. and U.S.S.R. Aid to Developing Countries: A Comparative Study of India, Turkey, and the U.A.R.* New York, 1967.

Tax Institute Inc. *Tax Policy on United States Investment in Latin America: Symposium Conducted by the Tax Institute Incorporated.* Princeton, N.J., 1963.

Thorp, Willard L. *The Reality of Foreign Aid.* New York, 1971.

Tinbergen, Jan. *Shaping the World Economy: Suggestions for an International Economic Policy.* New York, 1962.

Toma, Peter A. *The Politics of Food for Peace: Executive-Legislative Interaction.* Tucson, Ariz., 1967.

Triffin, Robert. *Gold and the Dollar Crisis: The Future of Convertibility.* New Haven, Conn., 1960.

Tucker, Robert W. *The Radical Left and American Foreign Policy.* Baltimore, 1971.

Vatter, Harold G. *The U.S. Economy in the 1950's: A Study of the Contours of Economic Change during a Crucial Decade in American Economic History.* New York, 1963.

Vernon, Raymond. *Sovereignty at Bay: The Multinational Spread of U.S. Enterprises.* New York, 1971.

———, ed. *The Oil Crisis.* New York, 1976.

Wagner, R. Harrison. *United States Policy toward Latin America: A Study in Domestic and International Politics.* Stanford, Calif., 1970.

Ward, Barbara. *The Rich Nations and the Poor Nations.* New York, 1962.

Weaver, James H. *The International Development Association: A New Approach in Foreign Aid.* New York, 1965.

Weil, Gordon, and Davidson, Ian. *The Gold War: The Story of the World's Monetary Crisis.* New York, 1970.

Whitman, Marina von Neumann. *Government Risk-Sharing in Foreign Investment.* Princeton, N.J., 1965.

Wilkins, Mira. *The Maturing of Multinational Enterprise: American Business Abroad from 1914 to 1970.* Cambridge, Mass., 1974.

Wolf, Charles C., Jr. *Foreign Aid: Theory and Practice in Southern Asia.* Princeton, N.J., 1960.

———. *United States Policy and the Third World: Problems and Analysis.* Boston, 1967.

Articles and Essays

Behrman, Jack N. "Promoting Free World Economic Development through Direct Investment." *American Economic Review* 50 (May 1960): 271–81.

Bernstein, Barton J. "Foreign Policy in the Eisenhower Administration." *Foreign Service Journal* 50 (May 1973): 17–20, 29–30, 38.

Cook, Blanche Wiesen. *Dwight D. Eisenhower: Antimilitarist in the White House.* Forums in History. St. Charles, Missouri, 1974.

De Santis, Vincent. "Eisenhower Revisionism." *Review of Politics* 38 (April 1978): 181–207.

Dibacco, Thomas V. "American Business and Foreign Aid: The Eisenhower Years." *Business History Review* 41 (Spring 1967): 21–35.

Greenstein, Fred I. "Eisenhower as an Activist President: A Look at New Evidence." *Political Science Quarterly* 94 (Winter 1979–80): 575–99.

Hardin, Charles M. "Congressional Farm Politics and Economic Foreign Policy." *Annals of the American Academy of Political and Social Science* 331 (September 1960): 98–102.

Haviland, H. Field, Jr. "Foreign Aid and the Policy Process: 1957." *American Political Science Review* 52 (September 1958): 589–724.

Hirschman, Albert O., and Bird, Richard M., "Foreign Aid—A Critique and a Proposal." *Essays in International Finance* 69 (July 1968).

Immerman, Richard H. "Eisenhower and Dulles: Who Made the Decisions?" *Political Psychology* 1 (Autumn 1979): 3–20.

Katz, Samuel I. "Sterling Speculation and European Convertibility: 1955–1958." *Essays in International Finance* 37 (October 1961).

Kindleberger, Charles P. "The Politics of International Money and World Language." *Essays in International Finance* 61 (August 1967).

Klopstock, Fred H. "The Euro-Dollar Market: Some Unresolved Issues." *Essays in International Finance* 65 (March 1968).

Kotschnig, Walter M. "The United Nations as an Instrument of Economic and Social Development." In *The Global Partnership*, edited by Richard N. Gardner and Max F. Millikan. New York, 1968.

Krumme, Robert D. "International Commodity Agreements: Purpose, Policy, and Procedure." *George Washington Law Review*, April 1963, pp. 784–811.

MacDougall, Donald. "The Dollar Problem: A Reappraisal." *Essays in International Finance* 35 (November 1960).

Maier, Charles S. "Revisionism and the Interpretation of Cold War Origins." *Perspectives in American History* 4 (1970): 313–47.

Martin, Edwin M. "New Trends in United States Economic Foreign Policy." *Annals of the American Academy of Political and Social Science* 330 (July 1960): 67–76.

Meek, Paul. "The Revival of International Capital Markets." *American Economic Review* 50 (May 1960): 282–93.

Mikesell, Raymond F. "America's Economic Responsibilities as a Great Power." *American Economic Review* 50 (May 1960): 258–70.

Morgenthau, Hans. "John Foster Dulles." In *An Uncertain Tradition: American Secretaries of State in the Twentieth Century*, edited by Norman Graebner. New York, 1961.

Reichard, Gary W. "Eisenhower as President: The Changing View." *South Atlantic Quarterly* 77 (Summer 1978): 266–81.

Rovere, Richard H. "Eisenhower Revisited—A Political Genius? A Brilliant Man?" *New York Times Magazine*, February 7, 1971, p. 14.

Soapes, Thomas F. "A Cold Warrior Seeks Peace: Eisenhower's Strategy for Nuclear Disarmament." *Diplomatic History* 4 (Winter 1980): 57–71.

Swoboda, Alexander K. "The Euro-Dollar Market: An Interpretation." *Essays in International Finance* 64 (February 1968).

Tew, Brian. "The International Monetary Fund: Its Present Role and Future Prospects." *Essays in International Finance* 36 (March 1961).

Triffin, Robert. "The Balance of Payments and the Foreign Investment Position of the United States." *Essays in International Finance* 55 (September 1956).

Vernon, Raymond. "Trade Policy in Crisis." *Essays in International Finance* 29 (March 1958).

Wang, N. T. "New Proposals for the International Finance of Development." *Essays in International Finance* 59 (April 1967).

Witt, Lawrence. "Trade and Agriculture Policy." *Annals of the American Academy of Political and Social Science* 331 (September 1960): 1–7.

Unpublished Work

Doty, Roland W., Jr. "The Oil Import Problem during the Truman and Eisenhower Administrations." M.A. thesis, Kansas State University, 1970.

Index

AAA. *See* U.S. Foreign agricultural policy
Acheson, Dean, 135, 165
Adams, Sherman, 36–37
Adenauer, Konrad: on maintenance of U.S. troops in West Germany, 196; opposes merger of the EEC and EFTA, 185–86
Afghanistan, 198
AFL-CIO, 75
Agriculture Department, 35, 78–79, 191
Aldrich, Winthrop, 45
Alexander, Henry C., 136
Alliance for Progress, 209
Allyn, S. C., 136
American Bar Association, 92
American Farm Bureau Federation, 27–28
Americans for OTC, 118
Anderson, Dillon, 90
Anderson, Robert: background of, 144; on the balance-of-payments problem, 193–97, 209–10; on the benefits of foreign-business corporations, 158; on European foreign aid, 184; on funding for the IADB, 166; on funding for the IMF and IBRD, 160; on the IDA concept, 144; meets with Chancellor Konrad Adenauer, 196; on tying DLF loans to procurement of U.S. goods, 181
Anti-Dumping Act, 130
Antitrust laws, 81; congressional hearings on, 82–83; and the courts, 80, 82; the Eisenhower administration's pol-

icy on, 8, 80–85; and oil import restrictions, 89; and the oil industry, 9, 85–91; and the Randall Commission, 21, 82; and the Truman administration, 81–82. *See also* Restrictive business practices
Asia: and regional-development scheme, 161; U.S. economic aid program for, 53–56, 68–69
Atlantic community, 210
Atlantic partnership, 177, 182–88

Bailey, Cleveland M., 75
Balance-of-payments problem, 11, 153, 159, 176–80, 182, 192–96; effects of, on U.S. foreign economic program, 159, 177
Balance of trade, 176–77, 189
Baruch, Bernard, 63
Battle Act, 60–63
Benson, Ezra Taft, 27, 36, 45, 61, 79
Benton amendment, 81
Bicycle case, 45
Black, Eugene, 20, 47, 99, 144, 149
Blaine, James, 164
Boeschenstein, Harold, 104, 134, 155. *See also* Boeschenstein Report
Boeschenstein Report, 155–57
Boggs, Hale, 120, 157
Boggs Committee. *See* Reciprocal trade, special House committee on
Bonbright, James, 40
Brandt, Karl, 191
Brandt, Willy, 1
Bretton Woods. *See* IBRD; IMF
Bridges, Styles, 202; on extension of for-

The Johns Hopkins University Press

This book was composed in Times Roman text and Times Roman Bold display type by Oberlin Printing Company from a design by Lisa S. Mirski. It was printed on 50-lb. Sebago Eggshell Cream Offset paper and bound in Roxite A by The Maple Press Company.